Patterns of Exploitation

Patterns of Exploitation

Understanding Migrant Worker Rights in Advanced Democracies

ANNA K. BOUCHER

OXFORD
UNIVERSITY PRESS

Oxford University Press is a department of the University of Oxford. It furthers the University's objective of excellence in research, scholarship, and education by publishing worldwide. Oxford is a registered trade mark of Oxford University Press in the UK and certain other countries.

Published in the United States of America by Oxford University Press
198 Madison Avenue, New York, NY 10016, United States of America.

© Oxford University Press 2023

All rights reserved. No part of this publication may be reproduced, stored in a retrieval system, or transmitted, in any form or by any means, without the prior permission in writing of Oxford University Press, or as expressly permitted by law, by license, or under terms agreed with the appropriate reproduction rights organization. Inquiries concerning reproduction outside the scope of the above should be sent to the Rights Department, Oxford University Press, at the address above.

You must not circulate this work in any other form
and you must impose this same condition on any acquirer.

Library of Congress Cataloging-in-Publication Data
Names: Boucher, Anna, author.
Title: Patterns of exploitation : understanding migrant worker rights in advanced democracies / Anna Boucher.
Description: New York, NY : Oxford University Press, [2023] | Includes bibliographical references and index.
Identifiers: LCCN 2022029944 (print) | LCCN 2022029945 (ebook) | ISBN 9780197599112 (hardback) | ISBN 9780197599136 (epub) | ISBN 9780197599143
Subjects: LCSH: Migrant labor. | Migrant labor—Legal status, laws, etc. | Migrant labor—Abuse of. | Exploitation.
Classification: LCC HD5855 .B68 2023 (print) | LCC HD5855 (ebook) | DDC 331.5/44—dc23/eng/20220909
LC record available at https://lccn.loc.gov/2022029944
LC ebook record available at https://lccn.loc.gov/2022029945

DOI: 10.1093/oso/9780197599112.001.0001

Contents

List of Illustrations   vii
Acknowledgments   xi

Introduction: A Comparative Method to Understand Migrant Worker Rights   1

1. What is Exploitation?   16
2. "A Member of the Family"? Gender, Domestic Work, and Violations   44
3. Ethnicity, Race, Country of Origin, and the Challenges of Antidiscrimination Claims for Migrant Workers   68
4. A Fatal Fall: Workplace Death, Injury, and Employment Sector   95
5. Labor Rights or Immigration Enforcement? Conflict in Protecting Undocumented Migrant Workers   126
6. Regulation and Migrant Vulnerability: The Role of Visas in Workplace Violations   151
7. Decertification, Blacklisting, and Circular Migration: The Challenges of Trade Union Representation for Migrant Workers   170
8. Strategic or General Enforcement of Migrant Workplace Rights   194

Conclusion: Understanding the Patterns of Migrant Worker Exploitation   221

Interview Schedule   237
Notes   241
References   251
Index   287

List of Illustrations

Figures

1.1	Number of migrants bringing successful violation claims, including intersecting claims, as a proportion of all successful MWRD claimants	35
8.1	Comparison of success rates in enforcement- and non-enforcement-led actions	217

Tables

1.1	Number of successful claims of violations, by violation category and jurisdiction (reported as a percentage of country cases and overall)	35
1.2	Intersections of successful violation claims, reported as N claimants and as percentage of migrants bringing that claim type	36
1.3	Most common violation type claims in Australia, arranged by N claims	38
1.4	Most common violation type claims in Canada, arranged by N claims	39
1.5	Most common violation type claims in California, arranged by N claims	40
1.6	Claims in England arranged according to number of claims by violation type and success ratio	42
2.1	Gender representation in claims across the population, by jurisdiction and migrant sex	58
2.2	Gender disaggregated immigrant entrants and representation in the MWRD, adjusted percentages	59
2.3	Migrants bringing successful underpayment claims, as a percentage of the gender/jurisdiction MWRD population	60
2.4	Successful sex discrimination claims, by jurisdiction and migrant sex	61
2.5	Migrants bringing successful sexual orientation discrimination claims, as a percentage of the gender/jurisdiction MWRD population	61
2.6	Migrants bringing successful sexual violence claims, as a percentage of the gender/jurisdiction MWRD population	62

viii LIST OF ILLUSTRATIONS

2.7	Migrants bringing successful trafficking claims, as a percentage of the gender/jurisdiction MWRD population	63
2.8	MWRD claimants, by gender and region of origin, compared with overall immigration flows	65
3.1	Percentage of claimants in MWRD by country of origin compared with immigration flow intake (Australia, 1996–2016)	82
3.2	Percentage of claimants in MWRD by country of origin compared with immigration flows (Alberta, Ontario, and British Columbia, 1996–2016)	84
3.3	Percentage of claimants in MWRD by country of origin compared with immigration flows (United Kingdom, 1996–2016)	86
3.4	Percentage of claimants in MWRD by country of origin compared with immigration flows (California, 1996–2016)	88
3.5	Events of racial discrimination in Australia (total and successful) as number	89
3.6	Events of racial discrimination in Canada (total and successful) as number	90
3.7	Events of racial discrimination in the United Kingdom (total and successful) as number	91
3.8	Events of racial discrimination in California (total and successful) as number	92
3.9	Events with the same outcomes out of cases bringing concurrent discrimination claims, where racial discrimination and another discrimination claim were brought	92
3.10	Frequency of coethnic exploitation across the MWRD (N of coethnic exploitation)	93
4.1	Work, health, and safety laws across the jurisdictions	107
4.2	Distribution of occupations of migrants in MWRD compared to in foreign-born population	117
4.3	Number of successful injury claims, by sector and jurisdiction (N migrants)	119
4.4	Traumatic fatalities and injuries of domestic population	120
4.5	Comparison of success rates of different injury types and death, by ISCO grouping	121
5.1	Undocumented migrants, in MWRD and as total population	145
5.2	Violation type, claims brought, and claims substantiated, by jurisdiction and undocumented or visaed migration status	147

6.1	Distribution of visa types, by migrants in the MWRD (M) and total migrant flows (P) 2006–2016	167
7.1	Percentage of union density and foreign-born population, by occupation and jurisdiction	189
7.2	Union interventions, by migrants represented	191
8.1	Structure of enforcement bodies, in all six labor law jurisdictions	199
8.2	Differential allocation of resources to labor and immigration enforcement across the six jurisdictions	212
8.3	Number of migrants per case, enforcement actions vs. other actions	215
8.4	Distribution of alleged violations in enforcement actions, by jurisdiction	216
8.5	Number of cases where penalties were ordered, by jurisdiction	218
C.1	Binary regression analysis of variables' effect on likelihood of bringing a claim of that violation type	223
C.2	Foreign-born workers as a proportion of the total employed population (%)	232

Acknowledgments

Patterns of Exploitation is my most ambitious intellectual endeavor to date, and I am grateful to all the people and institutions that assisted me on the journey of researching and writing this book. A project that covers 1,917 migrants across 907 court cases in six labor law jurisdictions as well as interviews with fifty-three barristers and solicitors is conceptually and empirically large. I could not have accomplished it without funding from the Australian Research Council (DE170100801) and a University of Sydney SOAR Fellowship. I also received a Laffan Fellowship for Disability in 2015, which was crucial in developing the pilot of the Migrant Worker Rights Database and ironing out problems in the original conceptualization, which was smaller in scope.

The book covers four countries and six labor law jurisdictions, and there are people to thank in each. In Australia, at the University of Sydney, thanks to Lisa Adkins, Minglu Chen, Karen Chilcott, Luara Ferracioli, Graeme Gill, Ben Goldsmith, Elizabeth Hill, Chris Hilliard, Shae McCrystal, Megan MacKenzie, Allan McConnell, Adam Morton, Nicola Piper, Rodney Tiffen, Gaby Ramia, Aim Sinpeng, Simon Rice, Suneha Seetahul, Rita Shackel, Laura Shepherd, Josh Stenberg, Chao Sun, Ariadne Vromen, Christopher F. Wright, Michael Vaughan, and Kim Weatherall. Law librarians Grant Wheeler, Patrick O'Mara, and Catie Croaker were particularly useful with comparative legal research assistance. Thanks to Henry Sherrell at the Grattan Institute (now the Minister for Immigration's Office) for his insights on migration policy, Jo Howe at Adelaide University for her expertise on immigration and employment law, and Joellen Riley Munton and Laurie Berg at UTS for their considerable expertise in labor and immigration law respectively. The journalist Peter Mares and Louise Peters and Catherine Duff, Lyn Barnett, Rachelle Loosen, and Ying Zheng of the Fair Work Ombudsman also provided me with help and opportunities to present my research. Also, deepest thanks to Jonathon Collerson for excellent copyediting, good humor, and attention to detail. The University of Sydney SSHARC Centre arranged an Ultimate Book Review for the full manuscript in November 2021 run by Chris Hillard and with commentary from Chris F. Wright, Joellen Riley Munton, Judy Fudge, and Jeannette Money. Their comments substantially improved the work, and I am very grateful for that opportunity to present, discuss, and refine the manuscript.

During the period of writing this book, I was inspired by the cases in the database to become a practicing lawyer, alongside my academic career (I already held a law degree). During long service leave, I completed a Diploma of Legal Practice and undertook a clinical placement at Clayton Utz Law Firm in Sydney. I am thankful to the Pro Bono team's Hai-Van Nguyen, David Hillard, and Jess Morath for hosting me and involving me in some of their cases. Their applied legal knowledge and deep understanding of the practicalities of litigation furthered the arguments in this book.

In the United States, thanks to Justin Gest of George Mason University and to Sameer Ashar, Scott Cummings, Ingrid Eagly, Blake Emerson, Tobias Higbie, Hiroshi Motomura, Victor Narro, Ben Nyblade, and Roger Waldinger at UCLA, where I had a visiting position in law in 2019. At Berkeley Law, thanks to David Oppenheimer for giving me the opportunity to present my research to colleagues and students and to Kim Voss and Catherine Albiston for their brilliant insights. At Cornell University, thanks to Lance Compa. Kate Hooper from the Migration Policy Institute and Daniel Costa from the Economic Policy Institute also provided opportunities to present my work in Washington.

In the United Kingdom, Lizzie Barmes of Queen Mary University of London assisted with a visiting position at Queen Mary Law School, and Kate Malleson allowed me to use her lovely office near the Inns of Court. Thanks also for advice from Amy Ludlow and Jeremias Prassl of Oxford University. I was lucky to be able to present at Bristol University and thank Tonia Novitz and Bridget Anderson for their comments on my work and Simon Tormey for assisting in organizing these events.

In Canada, Mireille Paquet of Concordia University invited me to the symposium The New Politics of Immigration and the End of Settler States, where this book was presented. Thanks to Cathy Alzner for assisting me in a visiting research position at the University of Toronto Faculty of Law and to Audrey Macklin, Randall Hansen, Judy Fudge, William Maas, Leah Voska, Fay Faraday, and Steven Bittle for their advice on various aspects of this book. Within Immigration, Refugees and Citizenship Canada's Knowledge Management Unit, Eleanor Berry and Jodi Peterson were very helpful, as was the Statistical Reporting Group.

Several national and international agencies have provided their insights to this project. Thanks is owed particularly to Johnathon Chaloff and Yves Breems of the Organisation for Economic Cooperation and Development (OECD). I was able to present this research to the OECD's Migration Section, the Australian Department of Home Affairs, the Australian federal Attorney General's Department, the Australian Fair Work Ombudsman, the Australian federal Senate's Economic Reference Committee, and the British Department of Business, Energy and Industrial Strategy. Non-governmental agencies that I have presented this research to and from which I received valuable feedback are the Economic Policy Institute (Washington, D.C.), the Migration Policy Institute (Washington, D.C.), the Human Rights Law Centre (Sydney), and the Community Legal Centres NSW Legal Professional Development Summit (Sydney) (with Umeya Chadhuri).

I have been provided with numerous opportunities to present this research in seminars and conferences in the disciplines of government, international relations, sociology, criminology, gender studies, and cultural studies, and at the School of Law and the Migrant @ Work Research Group at the University of Sydney, the Australian Political Studies Association Conference, the Australian Labour Law Association Conference, the American Political Science Association General Meeting, and the Symposium on Transnational People Movement and Social Rights (Sydney).

This project would not be possible without the legal, statistical, and social science support and expertise of the following research assistants: Tatiana Altman, Angus Brown, Umeya Chauduri, Tess Deegan, DeCarol Davis, Nina Dillion Britton, Eda Gunyadin, Nela Salamon, Robert Seals, and Tom Wynter. In several instances, they took time out of their careers in law and judges associateships to work on the project, and I am deeply grateful.

Some people have helped but asked for anonymity due to the high stature of their public positions. You know who you are: thank you for contributing your deep intellectual knowledge and lived legal and policy experience to this book. This includes, but is not limited to, the fifty-three interview subjects listed in the appendix, some of whom are deidentified as requested.

Deepest thanks, naturally, to the Commissioning Political Science Editor at Oxford University Press, New York, Angela Chnapko and to Alexcee Bechthold as Project Editor for the book's production.

To the 1,917 migrants represented in this book, you have experienced an array of quite shocking, sometimes fatal, workplace violations. Your stories have moved and inspired me and highlighted the importance, but also the limitations, of the protection of migrant rights by and through the legal systems. Some of the legal appeals depicted in this book remind me of a Pina Bausch dance choreography—with the legal applicants tumbling, then rising again, despite considerable challenges. This bravery is remarkable to observe, even if in a somewhat detached, legal form.

Finally, my husband, Kåre Martens, has been, as always, a calm and patient Nordic presence in my life. My little boy, Jasper Martens, was an excellent traveling companion during fieldwork in 2019 and tolerated any failings in single mothering I may have exhibited while Kåre remained at home. Somehow, Jasper and I ended up in some rather strange accommodations—including living with an eccentric puppeteer in Toronto—yet all venues were, at the very least, entertaining and friendly. To all the caregivers who looked after Jasper while I was working, interviewing, and juggling motherhood and academia, I could not have done it without you.

Sections of the introduction were first published in A. Boucher, "Access to Justice for Migrant Workers," in Edward Shizha and Edward Makwarimba, eds., *Intersectionality, Transnationality and Immigrant Lives: Critical Issues and Approaches to International Migration* (New York: Oxford University Press, forthcoming).

Some aspects of Chapter 1 were first published in A. Boucher, "What Is Exploitation and Workplace Abuse? A Classification Schema to Understand Exploitative Workplace Behavior towards Migrant Workers," *New Political Economy* (2022), https://doi.org/10.1080/13563467.2021.1994541.

Permission to republish has been provided in both instances.

Introduction

A Comparative Method to Understand Migrant Worker Rights

Migrants live and work in our midst, whether they have been resident in their host society for many years or for only several months. They are sometimes present on a tourist visa or are living without papers. They may have entered on work-related visas, with their spouses, as international students, or as asylum seekers and refugees. To say that some migrants work and that some have their workplace rights violated is a truism. Scandals involving wage theft, trafficking of migrants, their sexual abuse or racial vilification in the workplace, among other possible violations, are now well known and documented in the global media and in government reports (for a recent overview: Farbenblum and Berg 2021). This book adds to a growing body of evidence that demonstrates that migrant workplace rights are being violated in the contemporary period. Moreover, it attempts to explain the patterns of such violations in terms of the characteristics of those who do experience them, through a mixed quantitative and qualitative evidence base. And it also seeks to understand how countries vary in the ways they regulate the workplace treatment and protection of migrants. A "migrant worker" in this book includes anyone on a short-term visa or with under ten years' residency in a host society who also works, whether lawfully or unlawfully. Therefore, this book does not consider long-term migrants, of over ten years' residency, or the second generation of migrants, who were born in host societies. These might be more appropriately described as workers of migrant background or simply as domestic workers.

Why focus on the rights of migrant workers specifically when the rights of many groups of workers are threatened by global market forces, deregulation, and, most recently, the COVID-19 pandemic? There are several reasons for this. First, there is at least some qualitative evidence that migrant workers experience among the most egregious of workplace violations by virtue of their often precarious visa status (e.g., International Labor Organisation

[ILO] et al. 2021). In Chapter 6, we investigate the extent to which visa status matters for driving exploitation, but certainly there is at least cursory evidence that visa design does limit temporary migrant workers' rights in some important ways, most notably in their limited capacity to leave an exploitative employer while also avoiding deportation. The situation may be less egregious for permanent migrants or those not tied to a sponsor. Second, if we accept this to be true, then migrant workers can be viewed as a canary in the coal mine of workplace rights. If migrants' rights are seen as being undermined with unique patterning, then we might assume that such rights will also eventually be violated for domestic workers. Violations against migrants stand as a warning for potential future developments of labor and industrial laws for other workers. Third, as we see in Chapter 4, migrants may be more likely than domestic workers to be employed in certain economic sectors. These may have low-paid jobs, or poor conditions, or be involved in work with higher rates of industrial accidents and deaths. Further, precarious economic conditions correlate with poorer health outcomes (Shenker et al. 2014). In this sense, delving into migrant worker rights in detail is important for the broader normative defense of work as a place of basic dignity, respect, and well-being and for understanding how such conditions are more likely to be undermined in some sectors than in others.

Intellectually, migrant workers present several puzzles. There is the practical question of whether and how labor rights can be secured for people with restricted immigration rights or no voting rights. If we accept that citizenship status confers greater social protections through the power of the ballot box, then focusing on migrants who generally lack citizenship status allows us to investigate the pincer interaction of labor, immigration, and citizenship policies and laws. Second, migrant workers may fall into lapsed or undocumented status. There is a compelling philosophical and theoretical question of whether those who have entered a country illegally or remain illegally should have recourse to the legal system and, if so, in which ways (Ferracioli 2021, Chapter 8). Does the initially unlawful act vitiate the full protections of the law outside of the immigration law area once a person has entered illegally? We consider this question in Chapter 5 on undocumented migration. Third, the patterns of workplace violations experienced by migrant workers are hard to study given their vulnerability. Therefore, developing new methods to study migrant workers and workplace violations presents a hard case for labor studies more broadly and for other types of vulnerable workers (Boucher 2021b). Fourth, we can ask if courts are actually protective of migrant worker rights or not? In contrast to some work by migration scholars that contends that the courts are often a venue to shield or enforce the human rights of migrants against executive or legislative excesses (e.g., Hollifield 1992, 2004; Tichenor 2002), this book demonstrates, more consistently with recent research on freedom of speech and minority rights (Bleich 2017), that courts are not uniformly protective of migrants. In fact, in some instances, the judicial system reinforces rather than protects against exploitative workplace practices, and its decisions can lead to a worsening of conditions for migrant workers. This outcome may be attributable less to the conservative posturing of judges themselves and more to the laws they must implement, which at times include unavoidable loopholes that benefit employers and disadvantage migrant workers. The nuances of this dynamic between courts and lawmakers are considered throughout the book, with the U.S. Supreme Court case of *Hoffman Plastics* in (Chapter 5) providing a particular instructive example.

This book addresses these empirical and theoretical challenges in two main ways. First, it presents and analyzes a rich data source, the Migrant Worker Rights Database (MWRD), which codes 907 court cases brought in the labor law jurisdictions of Australia, England, the State of California, and the Canadian provinces of Alberta, British Columbia, and Ontario over a twenty-year period from 1996 through to 2016. This database, which is set out in more detail in Chapter 1, codes not only the litigants in the cases and the types of workplace violations raised but also key attributes of the migrants involved, including their gender, nationality, visa status, sector of work, type of violation experienced, and whether they are involved in a class action or individual form of litigation. In total, seventy-nine variables were coded for each and every case and for the 1,912 migrants represented in these cases, amounting to 151,048 observations. The data are analyzed according to a five-type classification schema of exploitation, presented in Chapter 1, that differentiates between (1) criminal infringements against the body and mind, (2) economic violations against wage and hour entitlements, (3) safety violations, (4) leave and other workplace entitlement violations, and (5) discrimination-based claims.

Second, this book presents qualitative evidence from fifty-three semi-structured elite interviews with leading legal counsel (lawyers and barristers), government officials, and the heads of non-governmental organizations involved in the representation of migrant workers in each of these jurisdictions. Where informants were knowledgeable on the topic, the interviews focused on seven key court cases that are analyzed in detail in Chapters 2 through 8. Drawing on the tradition of New Legal Realism, salient legal narratives are used to set out key features and themes (see Barmes 2015b; Motomura 2014).

Through this combined evidence base, we find that variation in the types of rights violation claims brought by migrant workers across the six labor law jurisdictions is centrally explained by differences in the industrial relations systems in those contexts. In reaching this finding, the book challenges immigration and employment studies scholarship that argues that exploitation is centrally driven by migrant attributes, such as ethnicity or language capacity (Deegan 2008; Evans 2008, cited in Healy 2008, 4; Hall and Partners 2016, 243). Regarding language barriers, migrants from lower-income countries where English is not the lingua franca are assumed, under this scholarship, to be less likely to seek enforcement of their rights and more likely to experience violations (Vosko, Tucker, and Casey 2019, 235). But, this book finds that aside from Spanish-speaking migrants in the United States, country of origin does not emerge as a central explanation for legal claim-making; at least note in the litigated cases. Nor is the existence of an employer of the same nationality a central driver of claim-making, despite frequent assertions of the role played by co-ethnic exploitation in shaping migrants' workplace violations (e.g., Campbell, Boese, and Tham 2016, 293; see also Li 2015; Migrant Worker Taskforce 2019, 39; Underhill et al. 2019; WEstJustice 2016, 77; McGregor 2007). The gender of the migrant is important in some instances but not others, while economic sector of employment,[1] which is often identified as a central explanatory variable for workplace exploitation (Underhill and Rimmer 2015; Weil 2020), is not statistically significant across all occupational categories, other than a few instances. And while temporary work visa holders do bring far more legal claims than those on other visas (see the discussion in Chapter 6), visa type is not a central explanation for differences in the types of violation claims brought by migrants. In fact, the most significant factors that drive variation in the types of violations are the country in which the violation occurred and the involvement of enforcement bodies in the litigation. This underscores an argument that runs through this book: that institutional context matters for the quality of litigation brought by migrant workers and the types of claims brought within these jurisdictions.

Before turning to the qualitative cases, it is important to set out the case selection rationale for this book, with regard to both the countries and subnational regions selected and the period covered. The advantages of the empirical focus of the MWRD over alternative approaches to measuring workplace violations are also touched on, before we move to a discussion of some of its potential limitations. In the final section of this introduction, we provide an overview of the seven court cases featured in this book and how they relate to the central arguments.

Why focus on Australia, England, the State of California, and three Canadian provinces?

This book focuses on four immigration countries and six labor law jurisdictions within these countries: Australia, England, the State of California, and the three Canadian provinces of Alberta, British Columbia, and Ontario. This selection is driven by a most-similar rationale, where key features of these contexts, such as economic, political, and social features, can be controlled for and the small number of differences are inferred to be explanatory (Mill 1874; Przeworski and Teune 1970, 32). These jurisdictions share many characteristics. Aside from the United States, these countries are all classified as "neoliberal regime types" within immigration regime typologies, marked by large immigration flows, high naturalization rates, a focus on economic migration, and an increasingly temporary economic composition in their visa mix (Boucher and Gest 2018, 141–143). While the U.S. immigration regime has been classified otherwise, the large scale of undocumented migration does tilt that country toward a short-term work visa focus in its immigration selection that renders it similar to the other countries considered (143–144). Further, all of these countries share either a history of colonialization (Australia, Canada, the United States) or are themselves colonizers (United Kingdom). As migration scholars have documented, this shared history of colonialism and the displacement of indigenous populations across these countries may underpin inequalities present in other areas of contemporary policymaking, in particular immigration regulation (e.g. Abu-Laban 2020). Politically, these countries are generally identified as being more right-of-center than other developed countries over the period of analysis (Armingeon, Engler, and Leemann 2021), although this has shifted over time and the election of the British Labour Party in 1997–2010 did reflect a more left-wing placement.[2] Although more conservative, right-wing executive governments may often be correlated with greater restrictions on industrial rights for workers (Hall and Soskice 2001), this book shows that there is considerable variation within these most-similar cases and even within sub-national units, such as the provinces of Canada.

The median political score for these countries is lower (i.e., more conservative) than the Organisation for Economic Cooperation and Development (OECD) average over the period of analysis (1996–2016).[3] In light of this shared economic and political history, these four countries are generally clustered as liberal market economies (LMEs) within the varieties of capitalism typology of capitalist systems (Hall and Soskice 2001).

Labor law, which is the central legal concern in a study of workplace exploitation, is not a federal area of policymaking in all of the countries under examination. In the United States and Canada, the constitutional design of their federalist structures renders labor law a provincial or state-based issue. In light of internal variation in the regulation of labor law in these countries, we focus on sub-national regions—in the United States, the State of California, and in Canada, the three provinces of Alberta, British Columbia, and Ontario. California is selected because it has the largest number of undocumented workers, the largest number of migrant workers, and the largest total volume of migrants (either authorized or not) of any U.S. state (Costa 2018, 4). Further, the State of California is often viewed as having more liberal (protective) labor laws than other U.S. states aside from New York (e.g., Shin and Koenig 2018),[4] rendering it a good baseline for analysis; if Californian labor laws are not protective of migrant workers, then we expect other U.S. states to fall even further below this standard. Within Canada, the three chosen provinces vary in their labor and workplace health and safety laws, as well as minimum pay standards (Burkett et al. 2013; Haddow and Klassen 2006). Together, these provinces represent 79% of immigration flows into Canada (see online Methods Annex at annaboucher.org for Chapter 6). Variation across these three provinces is explored throughout the book but particularly in Chapter 8 on enforcement, where differences across the provinces are revealed, and in the conclusion, where the key findings regarding industrial variation and its relevance to patterns of workplace violations are presented.

Finally, these four countries have industrial relations systems that are often identified, as noted, as most-similar in the scholarship, although the United States is generally viewed as the most neoliberal of the four (see, e.g., Colvin and Darbishire 2013; Hall and Soskice 2001). Yet, despite broad similarities across these systems, there may be more specific dimensions of how governments set their industrial and employment laws that could explain the differing patterns of migrant worker exploitation that the database reveals. We set out these differences, jurisdiction by jurisdiction, in Chapter 1 and weave this analysis throughout subsequent chapters. In the conclusion, we employ binary logistic regressions to test the relative weight of the various factors in informing the patterns of exploitation identifiable in the database. This combination permits us to control for potential individual-level explanations—such as the ethnicity, gender, or visa type of migrant workers—and explore the patterning and nature of exploitative practices from different angles.

In terms of the temporal selection for the database, the years from 1996 through to 2016 were chosen as pivotal in the immigration and employment policy areas in these countries. Over this period, several of the countries, including Australia and Canada, and to a lesser extent the United Kingdom, have seen a shift toward selecting more economically focused and temporary migrant workers (Boucher 2016, 69–93; on the United Kingdom, see Boucher and Gest 2018, 73). It is precisely this kind of migrant worker we would anticipate as most likely to experience workplace violations, as they have higher rates of employment than those on humanitarian or family-based visas (e.g., Cobb-Clark and Khoo 2006; Green and Green 1995).

Empirical focus of the MWRD and alternative measures of exploitation

The MWRD assesses all available court cases brought by migrant workers that are litigated, published, and finalized in the six labor law jurisdictions. As such, it excludes cases that are settled, unpublished, or subject to a non-disclosure agreement, such as sexual harassment cases, where the respondent employer may settle only if the matter is kept confidential to avoid bad publicity (Prasad 2018). Further, women experience far higher rates of sexual violence and sexual harassment in the workplace than men do, and there are often also high levels of shame around these kinds of offenses, meaning that often informal strategies rather than formal legal avenues are used to address them (Barmes 2015a, 17, citing Handy 2006 and Blackstone, Uggen, and McLaughlin 2009). As such, the database likely heavily underrepresents cases related to workplace sexual violence, particularly of women. The database also excludes cases that lapse or that are never brought due to obstacles in access to justice that we outline in more detail below. It also does not include cases raised in courts or tribunals where decisions are never published, such as the Labor Commissioner's Office of California or the Australian Human

Rights Commission. As such, there is a risk that the database contains nonrandom bias: the cases that are included or excluded are somehow not representative in their omission.

Despite this fact, there are also methodological challenges for alternative approaches, most prominently surveys of migrant workers. As Lizzie Barmes (2015a, 12) argues, "[i]t is extraordinarily challenging to devise reliable ways of investigating the incidence of, and circumstances surrounding, bad behavior at work." Surveys of migrant workers have been conducted in Australia (Berg and Farbenblum 2018; Hall and Partners 2016; National Union of Workers [NUW] 2019), the United Kingdom (Kalayaan 2014), and the United States (Bernhardt et al. 2009) and generally find higher rates of workplace violations among migrant workers than among domestic populations. These surveys capture a higher number of complainants than legal cases due to the access to justice reasons that we outline below. However, there are several potential limitations of survey-based approaches. First, these studies often do not use a representative sample of workers benchmarked against population statistics (e.g., Farbenblum and Blum 2018, 13), meaning that some survey respondents will be overrepresented in the findings and others will be underrepresented. Second, complaints about violations are not the same as actual violations. Workers may misunderstand the law in host societies and make spurious complaints. Or they may not be aware that a violation has occurred and not report it in the instrument. There is necessarily a subjective element to survey-based measures of workplace violations (Barmes 2015a, 16), and there is no established methodology for how survey responses can be independently verified (Hall and Partners 2016, 115–116). In contrast, court cases are objectively determined by judges, tribunal members, and, in some cases, juries, and, as such, complaints that have no basis under legal minima will not be decided in favor of the complainant, nor will they be awarded penalties, damages, or remedies. Reflecting upon this, while most migrant litigants in the MWRD are successful, not all are, especially in some jurisdictions, most notably the United Kingdom, where success rates for migrants are comparatively low. We return to success rates throughout the book, but especially in Chapter 1; their varying levels provide a powerful critique of relying only on survey methods to explore this topic.

A second option to study this topic quantitatively would be to look at complaints data or issuances of tickets or fines by enforcement bodies for employment breaches against migrant workers e.g. (Tucker et al. 2019). However, such data do not exist uniformly across the labor law jurisdictions and are also driven, as we discuss in Chapter 8, by differences in funding of enforcement. Furthermore, these approaches generally focus on underpayment rather than the far broader array of workplace violations that are considered in this book. Scholars have also coded employment and immigration laws to measure rights protection for migrant workers (Ruhs 2013) or used such methods to focus on immigration laws (e.g., Beine et al. 2016) and the relationship between immigration laws and international law (e.g., Gest, Kysel, and Wong 2019). However, such approaches cannot address the gap between laws and their enforcement, which is the focus of the ensuing chapters of this book. What happens on the ground may differ substantially from legal norms, and it is precisely this dissonance that motivates us.

An exhaustive database of available court and tribunal cases, which the MWRD presents, has the advantage of systematically examining the functioning of legal systems in their actual operation (Barmes 2015b, 108). It opens the black box of legal enforcement through a study of court and tribunal decisions. While such an approach has been applied in other areas of employment law (Barmes 2015a) and through a selective sample of tribunal cases brought by EU migrant workers in the United Kingdom (Barnard and Ludlow 2015), its comprehensive application to a full data set across country and time is unique to this book. Court and tribunal decisions, as Barnard and Ludlow note, provide a "rich source of contextual data" (20) when studying a population like migrants that is difficult to contact because it is highly mobile.

Access to justice limitations of the MWRD

Despite its strengths as a measure of workplace violations against migrant workers, there are potential limitations with the MWRD. Issues of selection bias emerge due to access to justice limitations migrant workers face in bringing litigation in the first place. As such, the cases presented in the database likely do not capture the full array of violations. It is also possible that some species of cases may be underrepresented as they are more often than others to be settled; for instance, sexual harassment cases may be more often subject to non-disclosure agreements, which are by their very nature confidential. Where visa status was not clear on the face of the judgment, the case was excluded from the database (Howe 2017, 7). In this way, undocumented litigants may be underrepresented in the database as they are less likely to want to reveal their lapsed or illegal visa status. Further, the database lacks a comprehensive evidence base for benchmarking the violations it documents against the broader domestic population's experience of workplace violations. Where possible, we address this limitation through reference to national statistics, although these are not always available.

There are also limitations on access to litigation opportunities that will constrain the overall quantum of cases contained in the database. In some contexts, compulsory arbitration might affect the capacity to bring litigation (Vosko and Thomas 2014). In unionized workplaces in the Province of Ontario, for instance, cases cannot proceed without workers first undertaking arbitration. It is difficult to ascertain what percentage of actual violations usually result in litigation. A British study of legal actions of workers broadly defined (not limited to migrant workers) found that 21% of serious workplace claims resulted in formal legal proceedings (Genn 1999, 150–153). With regard to migrant workers we can assume this percentage would be even lower due to access to justice issues (Barnard 2014).

Individual complaints-driven legal processes, rather than enforcement processes led by government, can reduce access to justice for migrant workers, given the lower tendency of individuals to complain than governments. Complaints-driven systems appear to lead to less enforcement and therefore fewer cases (Vosko, Tucker, and Casey 2019; Fudge 2018b, 429). We explore this issue further in Chapter 8, on enforcement. It may also relate to whether the workplace is actually being inspected and/or has sufficient workplace blitzes, whereby inspection bodies attend workplaces unannounced to check on compliance with workplace conditions (Vosko, Tucker, and Casey 2019, 253). This trend has been documented in the case of enforcement of labor laws but also workplace health, safety, and housing protections in Canada (e.g., Colindres, Cohen, and Caxai 2021, 3). Even where government-funded enforcement mechanisms do exist, such as the Fair Work Ombudsman in Australia (which has carriage of complaints over workplace wage infringements), surveyed migrants have reported that bringing a recovery action is often too onerous or challenging (Farbenblum and Berg 2017, 323).

In other contexts, migrant workers are entirely denied judicial rights of review so they will not appear in the database. Migrants who are subject to short-term visas, such as those in rotational agricultural work, may be unable to bring complaints as they have left the country and no longer have legal standing (Thomas 2016; see also Vosko, Tucker, and Casey 2019, 232). In the United States, H2A visa holders (temporary agricultural workers) are denied the right to sue their employers in federal courts, as they are often offshore before a claim can be brought (Bada and Gleeson 2019, 90; see also Chapter 6 below).

Undocumented visa status can heavily reduce the likelihood that a migrant worker makes a complaint. As Judy Fudge (2016c) notes, "[u]ndocumented workers who are at risk of labor exploitation will be unwilling to come forward to report violations of labor standards if they fear that they will be penalized for 'illegal working.'" In the United States, the rendering illegal of employment by an undocumented worker, following the Immigration Reform and Control Act (1986) (IRCA) and its interpretation through the *Hoffman Plastics* case,[5] had a negative effect upon claim-making by migrant workers. Ho and Chang (2005, 478–479) argue that the IRCA provisions, as interpreted through the lens of *Hoffman Plastics*, had the effect that "undocumented workers are reluctant to enforce their rights to begin with, given the risks not only of retaliatory discharge but also of retaliatory reporting to the Department of Homeland Security." These risks include immigration sanctions for lacking visa status or deportation.

In several jurisdictions, undocumented workers have no rights to bring some species of employment law claims, such as for back pay in the United States. The remedies that follow actions brought by undocumented workers, or the absence of remedies for classic employment law actions such as reinstatement or monetary compensation, can powerfully influence whether migrants are incentivized to bring actions or not. Visa status can also affect claim-making in a more subtle way: the migrant may feel they are unlikely to have a temporary visa renewed if they bring an employment claim against their sponsoring employer.

Regarding selection bias, we can posit that some cases may be more likely than others to come forward for litigation. Complex aspects of employment law, such as time limitations for bringing an unfair or unlawful dismissal case, may limit litigation opportunities for some migrant workers (e.g., WEstJustice 2016, 204). For instance, in Australia, the twenty-one-day rule in bringing unfair dismissal claims can create limits for migrants who are reaching the end of temporary visa periods (Howe 2017, 11–12; Fair Work Act (2009) (Australia), s394(2)(a)).

This also relates to whether migrants can access legal representation and in which areas of law. The literature has long established that socioeconomic factors such as low income or rental accommodation rather than house ownership influence the propensity to bringing litigation (Genn and Paterson 2001, cited in Barmes 2015a, 31). Higher-income litigants are more likely to appeal court cases than lower-income litigants (Galanter 1974; Songer, Smith, and Sheehan 1989). Lawyers may take on some cases and not others for funding reasons. It may be difficult for migrants to bring cases at all if proper and affordable legal representation is lacking (Barnard and Ludlow 2015, 23). In most of the jurisdictions considered in this book, legal aid is not available for employment-based claims, or its provision is seriously limited, whereas it may exist for criminal proceedings (e.g., Barmes 2015a, 27–28).

Evidentiary burdens can also limit access to justice for migrant workers. The threshold for various remedies can differ; for instance, criminal actions require a higher standard of proof, and sometimes greater evidence, than civil actions. Evidentiary aspects can make claim-bringing by migrant workers challenging. Gathering proof of employment records is challenging and can create obstacles to bringing a case in the first place. This may include the absence of a written contractual agreement to demonstrate that there was an employment relationship in place (Fels 2019).

Finally, the filing fees in court systems can be a significant obstacle to migrants bringing cases. Even if these fees are not high for everyday litigants, they may be prohibitive for underpaid migrant workers. Increases to the fees required to bring claims in the Employment Tribunal of England have been criticized on this basis (Fudge 2018a, 567; Barmes 2015a, 27–28). As the Australian community legal clinic WEstJustice (2016, 87) argued in its report on migrant workers, many clients struggle to pay for food and basic housing, let alone filing fees. On this basis, government reviews into underpayment such as the Migrant Worker Taskforce in Australia have recommended that small claims processes be established for migrant workers to recover unpaid wages more expeditiously and cheaply (Fels 2019, recommendation 19; Chaudhuri, Boucher, and Sydney Policy Lab 2021, 21).

On the issue of economic sector of employment, Alex Reilly and collaborators (2018, 5) argue that migrants may be more likely to be employed in low-skilled jobs where they are viewed as "replaceable and expendable." These attributes have several dimensions that potentially affect access to justice: (1) a view of migrants as vulnerable and therefore exploitable, (2) a propensity for migrants to be hired in sectors where honoring of employment conditions is already low and breaches of law are normalized, and (3) the higher likelihood of labor hire arrangements that also block legal claims. The legal clinic WEstJustice (2016, 77) in Australia found that such workers were less likely to approach its clinic than other migrants.

On the basis of these access to justice concerns, there are several potential challenges to the scale and representativeness of the database. Regarding scale, this alone is not a problem because the data in the book are not presented as exhaustive of the potential full population of violations. Instead, they are presented as exemplars and percentages. There is no clear way to ameliorate concerns over database representativeness. Available survey data are, as noted, limited, more open to subjectivity of the survey respondents than other coding methods, and, in any case, not consistently administered or benchmarked across countries we cannot therefore compare the database with survey data. As such, it is best to view the MWRD as a conservative evidence base of migrant worker exploitation patterns; what it represents, insofar as it captures litigated cases, will be a small fraction of the types of cases that are complained about. Despite this limitation, the MWRD does provide an indisputably objective evidence base of workplace violations: the determinations of independent judges, tribunal members, and, in some rare cases, juries on an array of purported workplace violations. This quantitative analysis is coupled with seven qualitative case studies that structure the ensuing chapters of the book.

Qualitative case studies and book structure

This book argues that there are a variety of vulnerabilities that could shape the violation patterns experienced by migrant workers. These include the gender and ethnicity of the migrant worker and their concentration in dangerous, dirty, or demeaning work. Whether the migrant is on a visa and whether their visa is temporary will also be important. Finally, the extent of representation of the migrant, either through trade unions and other worker organizations or through government enforcement bodies, might be crucial.

Seven case studies are presented to address the major themes in Chapters 2 through 8. To explore the role of gender and ethnicity in Chapter 2, we analyze two conjoined cases where it was alleged—although not substantiated—that young women in the United Kingdom were trafficked into domestic work and denied minimum wage payments as they were considered a "member of the family" under British employment law: *Nambalat v. Taher and Anor*: (2012) and *Nambalat v. Taher and Anor: Udin v. Pasha & Ors.* (2012). In Chapter 3, we consider the case of *Hounga v. Allen* (2014), which found that the dismissal of a domestic worker was racially motivated. In Chapter 4, on the topic of unsafe work practices and the role of economic sector, we consider the Canadian case of *R v. Metron Construction* (2013), which involved the industrial manslaughter of migrant workers. The visa status of migrants is considered in Chapters 5 and 6. In Chapter 5, we explore the seminal U.S. case *Hoffman Plastic Compounds Inc. v. NLRB* (2002) and the effects of undocumented visa status upon limiting the capacity to pursue workplace claims. In Chapter 6, we look at whether temporary work visas worsen workplace conditions for migrants and how these differ from permanent visas through an Australian case: *Minister for Immigration and Border Protection v. Choong Enterprises Pty. Ltd.* (2015). Chapter 7 canvasses some of the key challenges to migrant workers in mobilizing collectively through trade unions or worker centers through the analysis of a decade-long series of litigation in Canada known as *Floralia Growers*, which involved Mexican agricultural workers having their right to collective action curtailed on a farm in British Columbia. Finally, in Chapter 8, we explore the scope and limits of government enforcement of workplace rights through the Australian case of *Fair Work Ombudsman v. Bento Kings Meadows* (2013), where the Australian enforcement body, the Fair Work Ombudsman, represented fifty workers, mostly migrants, who had been seriously underpaid.

These seven cases were chosen because of their salience, the egregious and varied forms of workplace violations that they document, how they allow us to explore some of the key themes that each vulnerability presents, and because in several cases (*Udin, Hounga, Metron, Hoffman, Floralia*) they involve highly contested litigation that underwent several stages of appeal. The cumulative litigation in these cases allows us to consider varying judicial perspectives on the issues raised in each case as they advanced through the judicial hierarchies. Furthermore, several of the cases dealt with undocumented visa status and how this in turn challenges or complicates the enforcement of workplace rights for migrant workers (*Hounga, Hoffman*).

Each case also exemplifies a possible explanatory factor, whether the attributes of the migrant themselves (their gender, country of origin), the economic sector in which they work, their visa status (the role of regulation), the extent of collective representation (the role of trade unions), or the existence of government enforcement. As noted, these various individual-level, meso, and macro factors have all been presented in the immigration, sociolegal, and industrial relations scholarship as central drivers of exploitation experienced by migrant workers. But the central finding of this book, defended in detail in the conclusion, is that country-level factors are the most crucial in explaining differences across the cases. In particular, the nature of the single industrial relations and enforcement systems of each country is the single most significant driver of differences across the four countries. To maximize the policy relevance of this book, each chapter also ends with some core policy recommendations to government. While general in nature, these are also focused on the labor law jurisdiction that is the focus of that particular chapter. The qualitative analysis in this book states the law as of 2021. The Database captures cases from 2006 through to 2016 and the Codebook (annaboucher.org) collates the legal principles (statute and case law) from 2019 for the establishment of the indicator violations. This marks the time point when the coding for the project began. The online Methods Annex (annaboucher.org) sets out further methodological decisions underpinning the database and its analysis.

1
What is Exploitation?

A multitude of exploitative practices can harm migrant workers in contemporary workplaces. How do we best conceptualize these violations? What theoretical accounts of exploitation can assist us? And what does the MWRD reveal about the patterns of exploitation present in the 907 court and tribunal cases it contains? This chapter focuses on labor and other laws as sources of evolving standards of exploitative behavior in the workplace. Labor law emerged over time and was designed to protect against what was deemed to be unacceptable labor exploitation. As such, it presents key categories that can be used to build a schematic account of exploitation. The historical presentation of exploitation identifies five main components: (1) criminal infringements against the body and mind, (2) economic violations against wage and hour entitlements, (3) safety violations, (4) leave and other workplace entitlement violations, aside from overtime, and (5) discrimination. This classification schema is cumulative. Rather than build on a regular linear continuum, there are more or less serious violations within each component. We also defend in this chapter the use of law, especially labor law, as an empirical baseline for developing a working definition of exploitation rather than alternative, more normative concepts. The classification schema presented here is practical and applied rather than aspirational in nature. Further, given that labor laws are embedded within broader industrial relations and employment systems, the key differences in such systems across the six labor law jurisdictions are also presented in this chapter.

To conclude the chapter, we present key findings from the MWRD, clustered around these five major classes of violation types. Importantly we reveal both the rates of claims—or violations—and rates of successful claims under each of these five classes, and we demonstrate variation across both violations and jurisdictions. We also consider the leading types of violations in each jurisdiction, of which underpayment is the most common but certainly not the only one.

Patterns of Exploitation. Anna K. Boucher, Oxford University Press. © Oxford University Press 2023.
DOI: 10.1093/oso/9780197599112.003.0002

Defining "exploitation" in migrant worker cases

Many theorists have accounted for and sought to define exploitation in the labor market. Here, we briefly analyze these approaches and identify their utility in operationalizing *exploitation* in this book, including concepts of ownership and the extraction of profit from one person by another. These approaches range from modern slavery studies (Allain 2012) to accounts of trafficking and forced labor reported by the European Commission (Fundamental Rights Agency [FRA] 2015) and ILO (2012), as well as Marxist theories of exploitation (e.g., Marx [1867] 1887, Vol. 1, Chapter 9; Brass 1986). These approaches all have their significant contributions to an understanding of exploitation; however, they are often difficult to operationalize empirically. Further, most accounts lack consideration of at least some aspects of what could constitute the full ambit of exploitative workplace behavior; for instance, modern slavery accounts focus on the more egregious forms of slavery, thereby limiting consideration of frequent but less pronounced exploitation such as routine underpayment (Davies 2019). Marxist approaches are commonly pecuniary in focus (wage underpayment in particular) and, arguably pay insufficient attention to the full ambit of safety and gender- and identity-based forms of discrimination considered in the database, which may not have any immediate or even future pecuniary gain to the employer but are still forms of workplace abuse. (For a full discussion of this topic, see Boucher 2022.) In light of the limitations of alternative definitions of exploitation, in this book we focus on a positivist legal approach, informed by the historical development of labor laws across the four jurisdictions (and, to a lesser extent, other areas of law that shape workplace conditions). In particular we use the legal norms in place in the chosen jurisdictions as the best empirical basis to measure exploitation, although we also acknowledge some of the potential limitations of this approach.

This section focuses predominantly on the development of labor law, given this is a chief area that regulates workplace behavior, although additional legal fields are also considered insofar as they connect to the workplace. Labor law emphasizes a *pacifying* role for the law, against a background of conflict between workers and capital (Hepple and Veneziani 2009, 5; Hepple 1986, 6–12). Under such an approach, labor law can be seen as a way to partially rectify existing economic inequality between employers and employees in a legal sense: to detach work from property law, to avoid treating humans as chattels (Kahn-Freund 1981, 78), and to differentiate employment contracts from other types of contracts (Hepple 1986, 11). Alternative perspectives are that labor law's central purpose is intended to protect workers from the market, to democratize workplaces, and to protect against managerial prerogatives when they interfere with these rights (Fudge 2011b, 123). A further account is that it addresses market failures caused by an unregulated market, such as information asymmetry between worker and employer (Collins 2000).

To identify the constituent parts of exploitation in a classification schema, we must understand the evolution of labor law historically, as the development of this area of law was intended as an antidote to workplace exploitation. To evince what workplace exploitation is, we must identify what it is not by examining legal standards over time. Within this history, we can locate changing norms over what is considered exploitative in the workplace and the progressive identification of the vagaries of exploitation and appropriate remedies for breaches. It is important to note that these evolving standards affect not only migrant workers but native workers as well. Many of these ideas stem from the development of master and servant laws and the subsequent rise of trade unionism, which followed the expansion of the factory as a site of production and the struggles of working people for protections there (Gray 1987).

Master and servant laws in England, from 1747 onward, mobilized people into work, created employment rules, and elevated the role of employees over that of subcontractors, artisans, and laborers (Anderson, Brodie, and Riley 2017, 10; Veneziani 2009, 3). Gradually protective laws emerged for employees, including the restriction and, ultimately, the abolition of child labor, the creation of health and safety laws in 1802, and the extension of worker protections through the Factory Act (1833) and the Factories and Workshops Act (1878). These acts sought to address some of the social and economic crises presented by large-scale industrial factories and agitation by workers, as well as vigorous debate among employers, experts, and public intellectuals about appropriate workplace conditions (Gray 1987, especially 145, 167). Over time the so-called *Condition of England*, as the issue of workplace standards came to be known, extended outside of the factory "into mines, child and female labor generally, the weavers, out-work and sweating, and urban conditions" (171). Concepts such as unreasonable overtime and the need for uniform working hours developed through the Factory Act (1847) (also known as the Ten Hours Act). The tactics of collective organizing, including strikes, took shape in this period. These late nineteenth-century developments are the bridge between the indentured labor that preceded them and the array of labor rights in the contemporary workplace, including those affecting migrants. Of course, these developments were not without their critics—including Marx ([1867] 1887, Vol. 1, Chapter 15) himself, who viewed the Factory Act as concentrating the power of capital. However, they were clearly an improvement on the prior absence of regulation.

As noted, a central philosophical rationale behind the development of labor and industrial laws was that human welfare was primary to property, not secondary (Alfred 1857, 1:118). These laws were separate from the law of commercial contract and from historical master-servant relationships, which preceded them, and were collectively conceived of as employment relations. Part of this evolution involved a new ideological vision of the relative power of individual workers when compared with their employers and the dissolution of laws that used criminal law to enforce the contractual obligations of workers to their masters (Deakin and Wilkinson 2005, Chapter 2). The rise of universal male suffrage also brought democratic force to the claims of workers and furthered the efforts of trade unionists for greater protections in the United Kingdom (McClelland 1987, 200). Similar trends occurred at this time in Australia, Canada, and the United States (Deakin and Wilkinson 2005, 42). While the distinction between employees and subcontractors was clarified over time, it was in the United Kingdom in 1942 with the Beveridge Report on social insurance that the distinction was finally established (42).

In the period after World War II, recognition of the diversity of the workforce contributed to a raft of antidiscrimination laws being passed in the 1960s and 1970s (Gordon 2019, 925).[1] As Judy Fudge (2011b, 122) notes, this period can be viewed as the high watermark of the maxim "Labor is not a commodity" and its differentiation from the regulation of commercial matters. In the contemporary era, some of the sectors that are most subject to exploitation—domestic service and agricultural labor—have seen either the retention or revisitation of master-servant patterns (Veneziani 2009, 46; Collins and Mantouvalou 2016). This brief sketch is useful insofar as it demonstrates how concepts of acceptable and unacceptable conditions developed in workplace and industrial settings over an extended historical period.

A continuum approach to exploitation?

How, then, to conceive of exploitation in the workplace? One approach is to consider exploitation as a continuum ranging from decent work through to slavery. Indeed, some critics of modern slavery theory argue that exploitation is best conceived not as a slave/free dichotomy but rather as stages or degrees of freedom varying from enslaved to fully free (Costello 2015, 191). Leading policy reports, such as the "Independent Review of the Overseas Domestic Worker Visa" by James Ewins in the United Kingdom, also place exploitation on a continuum, from "slavery and forced labor at one end to more minor breaches of employment and health and safety law at the other" (Ewins 2015, 12; see also Metcalfe 2018, 5). As Scott (2017, 45) notes, a defining feature of the continuum approach is that as forms of exploitation worsen, the wage labor relationship moves from relative control to full coercion.

A continuum approach allows for more specificity and clarity in identifying different components of exploitation (Skrivankova 2017, 113). A continuum approach is also more easily translated into policy, as a gradated understanding of exploitation can run parallel to corresponding levels of regulatory response. At the same time, a continuum approach is also more expansive than a purely criminal lens that would view modern slavery as the anomaly in need of criminal sanctions, set against otherwise compliant wage labor relationships (see Davies and Ollus 2019, 89; Scott 2017, 5). And yet, a continuum approach still does not assist us in identifying the categories of exploitation; it merely brings attention to the fact that exploitation can vary in its extremities. The question of categories takes us back to first principles of where and how such exploitation can occur. For this reason, an additive classification of exploitation based on labor and other legal standards that differentiates between types of offenses is adopted.

It is important to note potential criticisms of the use of law as a metric for interpreting abuses and exploitation in the workplace. Theoretically, one might argue that law merely reflects functional legalism or, indeed, furthers the ideology of the dominant ruling class and, therefore, is ill-equipped as a source to objectively define these terms. Here, we draw attention to the work of critical political economists, including E. P. Thompson (1975, 262), who, in his chapter on the rule of law, identifies the separateness of labor law from the ideology of capitalism.

We might also look to existing empirical studies of migrant worker rights, based on surveys with migrants, to ascertain the types of workplace rights they focus on. The instruments allow us to see whether migrant-initiated complaints match the types of issues framed legally in this book. There are limited studies of migrant workers that use sufficiently large samples to address this issue, but those that do, identify the key areas: In Australia, a large survey of migrant workers commissioned by the Departments of Home Affairs and Employment identified the following grievances in descending order of frequency: underpayment and denial of other wage entitlements; racial discrimination; verbal, physical, or psychological abuse; pressure to violate an immigration visa condition; and sexual harassment or violence (Hall and Partners 2016, 5). These features mirror the violations raised in the MWRD coding frame that we set out below. Other studies focus mainly on underpayment and overtime work, and therefore capture a smaller array of violations than does the MWRD, or they are sometimes accompanied by qualitative or focus group research that is necessarily limited in its inferences due to nonrandom sampling (e.g., Berg and Farbenblum 2017; Bernhardt et al. 2009). In conclusion, the additive schema of exploitation presented below has advantages over alternative methods that are narrower in their treatment of possible species of "exploitation" or less amendable to quantitative empirical analysis.

Major variations in labor law and industrial settings across the jurisdictions

We have defended the reliance on legal standards, and labor law in particular, as a measure of exploitation. It is important to note that labor laws and their broader industrial settings do differ across the jurisdictions in a variety of ways. This variation, as we argue throughout the book, drives variation in the patterns of exploitation observed in the legal cases analyzed. As such, an appreciation of cross-country industrial and labor laws is crucial to understanding the core findings of this book. Here, we set out major differences—but also their similarities—before moving on to the method and presentation of some of the key findings of the MWRD.

Australia

Australia's industrial relations system was built upon a clear, legislated settlement between labor and capitalism, with a strong role for trade unions and collective bargaining at the occupational level. As Francis Castles (2004) notes, the Australian welfare state was based in an industrial form of welfare that focused on a fair minimum (male) wage, tariffs that protected against trade in exchange for high wages, a relatively closed border (up until the mid-1940s at least), high rates of male employment, and a collective and compulsory centralized arbitration and wage-setting system (see also Hancock 1984; Cooper and Ellem 2008, 534, 535). These qualities contributed to comparatively higher minimum wages in Australia than in the other four countries (OECD 2021b) and a focus on occupational level rather than individual or enterprise level, setting minimum labor standards, known as awards (Wright and Kaine 2021). Traditional characteristics of the Australian system, while heavily diluted today—and strongly attacked in the short period from 2006 through to 2009 during which Conservative labor laws known as Work Choices[2] were in place—have been retained in some ways compared with other jurisdictions considered in this book. Under the Australian Constitution, s51(xxxv), the federal level has predominant power over industrial relations, and this centralizing tendency of policy design has increased over time through reliance on the corporations' power as a basis for employment and industrial law reforms (Wright and Kaine 2021). In addition to award wages, there are ten National Employment Standards that set a minimum for employment conditions nationally and a base for negotiation of awards that set minima across different industries (Fair Work Act (2009 (Cwth), Part 2(2)), s61(2)). Further, the Australian system can be viewed as more interventionist on the part of government, both regarding wage setting through the central award-setting body—the Fair Work Commission—but also through enforcement by a government agency, the Fair Work Ombudsman, which is increasingly involved in litigation. While trade unions remain active in Australia, they have seen a diminished power in recent decades, overlapping with the period of this book's analysis (Wright and Kaine 2021). These features are explored further below, particularly in Chapters 7 (trade unions) and 8 (enforcement).

Canada (provinces of Alberta, British Columbia, and Ontario)

In contrast to Australia, Canada has a decentralized employment and industrial relations system with powers delegated to its ten provinces for 90% of its workforce. Only federal employees are covered by the federal jurisdiction (Canadian Constitution Act, 1867 to 1982, ss91 and 92(10); Walsworth, O'Brady, and Taras 2021).[3] Due to this decentralized setting, provincial political and social cultures at particular points in time influence the employment and industrial settings in each province differently (Walsworth, O'Brady, and Taras 2021). The election of the leftist National Democratic Party is correlated with more pro-worker policies in these various provinces, while pro-business Conservative governments have been more likely to enact pro-employer policies (Walsworth, O'Brady, and Taras 2021). There are also differences across the provinces in unionization rates; of the three provinces considered in this book, Alberta has the lowest rates of union density in 2017, although rates have stabilized since across all three provinces (Statistics Canada 2022b). The Canadian Charter of Rights and Freedoms (1982) generally protects the right to strike and associate; however, as we will see in Chapter 7 (trade unions), there are some limitations regarding migrant workers employed in particular occupational sectors in some provinces. In terms of its management of unions, government policy across the provinces is influenced by the U.S. National Labor Relations Act (Wagner Act) (1935) that focuses on conciliation (generally at the local or enterprise level), decentralized management of employment relations, and enforcement of bargaining relations through a quasi-judicial labor relations system. This system has been viewed as less supportive of workers than other, more centralized systems (Walsworth, O'Brady, and Taras 2021). Labor laws differ across the provinces. Trade union density varies over time (Martinello 1996), and incumbent political parties (Martinello 2000) may be sources of this provincial variation.

United Kingdom

The United Kingdom can be described as having a traditionally voluntarist industrial and employment law system based in contract law and individual bargaining. However, this changed with the election of New Labor in 1996 under the Blair government and the increased incorporation of European social policy into British law through the EU Maastricht Social Protocol (Johnstone and Dobbins 2021). A national minimum wage was introduced in 1999. With the United Kingdom's admission into the European Union in 1973 up until Brexit in 2020, EU law, especially in the areas of antidiscrimination, human rights, equal opportunity, and reasonable working hours, played an important role in shaping British employment law practices (Howell 2020). As we discuss in the conclusion in more detail, Brexit and ensuing dissolution from EU directives could hold important implications for the extent of labor and industrial protections offered to workers in the future. That said, even before Brexit there was evidence of "light touch" adoption of EU directives (Coulter and Hancké 2016). Many regulatory aspects of industrial law reform during the Conservative era from 1979 through to 1997 can be characterized as permissive toward employers and inactive toward employer noncompliance (Baccaro and Howell 2017, 58). Arguably these aspects of soft compliance continue in the contemporary period with wage enforcement, as we discuss in Chapter 8, and this attribute affects migrant workers in particular ways.

While England is the birthplace of unionism, trade union membership has declined since 1990, when compulsory union membership was rendered illegal (Johnstone and Dobbins 2021), coupled with restrictions on unions' capacity to bring industrial action under the Conservative era from 1970 through to 1997 and then again in 2016 (Bogg 2016). Since the 1970s, the United Kingdom has also moved away from industry- or sector-wide collective bargaining to workplace negotiation of wages in the private sector. At present only 16.8% of the private sector is covered by collective bargaining, and most private-sector employers unilaterally negotiate conditions with their employees (Johnstone and Dobbins 2021; Baccaro and Howell 2017, 52, 68–69). The operation of unions at the enterprise level was crucial to earlier protections of workers' rights in the United Kingdom. However, once union membership declined, the unions' influence was further weakened as they lacked centralized organizing. This encouraged further employer permissiveness in labor and industrial regulation in the United Kingdom (Baccaro and Howell 2017, 52, 79).

United States (California)

The United States is commonly viewed as having the most deregulated and voluntary industrial and labor law system of the four countries. It is characterized by low levels of trade unions, a focus on enterprise or individual-level bargaining, and low minimum wages in comparative perspective (Katz and

Colvin 2021; OECD 2021b). However, there is considerable variation within the United States, where labor laws are determined at the state level in most instances, outside of labor relations regarding collective action rights, which are set federally under the National Labor Relations Act (NLRA) (1935), the "Wagner Act." As noted in the introduction, California is often viewed as having among the most liberal and progressive labor and industrial settings across the American states (Shin and Koenig 2018).

The NLRA requires certification of a union by the affected workplace through a secret ballot before the union can represent workers as the exclusive "bargaining agent" (see Katz and Colvin 2021). This unusual aspect of collective organizing in the United States has both advantages and disadvantages from a worker rights' perspective, but certainly, in comparison to other jurisdictions, it can result in localized patterns of employment protection that do not have the reach of sector-based bargaining, such as that which occurs in Australia (e.g., Katz 1993). It also leaves far lesser standards for those enterprises that are not unionized (Freedland 2013, 87). Federal civil rights legislation provides protections against race and other forms of workplace discrimination (Civil Rights Act (1964)). America is also unique in having a stronger focus than the other jurisdictions on nonconventional forms of representation, such as workers centers, which are discussed in Chapter 7 (trade unions). These can be particularly important for migrant workers, who may feel greater affinity with migrant or workplace-specific centers than large-scale trade unions (Fine et al. 2018).

Methodological challenges in measuring "exploitation"

Having sketched the key traits of employment and industrial relations systems in which varying labor standards are situated, we move now to a discussion of some of the methodological challenges in measuring and operationalizing "exploitation" as a concept. In quantifying court cases to ascertain patterns of exploitation, the MWRD draws upon the tradition of quantitative legal studies as innovated by studies of U.S. Supreme Court cases (Spaeth and Segal 2001; Spaeth et al. 2015). Studies that quantify multiple court cases have been criticized for not appropriately selecting the full array of cases (Hall and Wright 2008, 79). To address this concern, for the MWRD we coded all available court cases in each jurisdiction and cross-searched across legal databases and search terms to maximize the number of cases selected, thereby avoiding omissions (see online Codebook for further details: annaboucher.org).

A second concern with legal databases is that they are seen as attempting to construct legal facts as "data" when these are constructed or subjective fictions (Hall and Wright 2008, 79). In some regards, this presents a challenge to quantitative methods generally, which can be seen as lacking interpretive framing (Yanow and Schwartz-Shea 2006). One possible response to these challenges is to use statistical methods such as intercoder reliability to ensure that coders interpret legal facts in a similar fashion across cases. This was the approach to coding for the MWRD, where high rates of intercoder reliability were achieved and where all coders were law graduates or lawyers who ensured similar levels of coding aptitude (see online Codebook). Another criticism of quantitative legal approaches, particularly those undertaken by political scientists rather than lawyers, is that coding may occur along thematic lines selected by the researcher rather than legal concepts, thereby overlooking legal themes identified by courts (see Shapiro 2008, 486–488). We overcame this challenge by undertaking coding based both on legal findings in the cases (e.g., the legal determinations regarding types of workplace violations) and sociolegal indicators such as the gender, ethnicity, occupational sector, and visa type of migrant litigants. In his analysis of the coding of constitutional court cases, Thomas Keck (2017) makes several suggestions to improve data quality. These include bringing qualitative dimensions into the coding to maximize its application (this was achieved for the MWRD through a combination of binary and nominal variables) and refinement of the coding instruction over time (this was gained the MWRD through multiple pilot codes and the recoding of some nominal variables into different groupings after the coding phase is complete). (See Methods Annex at annaboucher.org for further details.)

The fact that the database contains four countries and six separate labor law jurisdictions raises potential comparability issues as lawful minima vary across countries and subnational regions and even across time within each country. We undertook several inclusion decisions to minimize the risks associated with such variation. First, employment protections that were available in only one jurisdiction were not included for comparative purposes; an example of this is the adverse action protections under the Australian Fair Work Act (2009), s342. To the extent that similar protections exist under dismissal and antidiscrimination or retaliatory dismissal provisions in other jurisdictions, adverse action was included under these indicators. Second, in the case of workplace rights that are themselves contested for all workers or that have been reduced over time, such as a blanket right to strike or compulsory unionism, such indicators were excluded from coding. A series of intercoder reliability tests were undertaken to ensure that indicators worked across jurisdictions and time and were reliable in their construction.[4]

Setting out the MWRD

Having defended the quantitative analysis of court cases adopted in this book and its methodology, we now move to define some of the key components of the database design and its core operationalized definitions. First, we set out some core components of the database in terms of the types of court cases covered. Second, we determine the remit of the concept of "exploitation" as individual in nature and generally excluding collective action, with several notable exceptions. Third, we clarify who is a possible violator and what constitutes an "employer." Fourth, we define "exploitation" as happening to employees and note the exclusion of analysis of the rights of independent contractors, although misclassification of workers as contractors is a relevant area of litigation. Finally, we clarify that the relevant benchmark for the analysis of exploitative practices is existing lawful minima and not normative ideals of *best practices*. In the following section, we set out the five-group classification schema of exploitation comprised of (1) criminal infringements against the body and mind; (2) economic violations against wage and hour entitlements; (3) safety violations; (4) leave and other workplace entitlement violations, aside from overtime; and (5) discrimination.

The MWRD

The MWRD comprises 907 legal cases brought by migrant workers seeking to enforce their rights in Australia, Canada (Ontario, Alberta, and British Columbia), the United Kingdom, and California. For ease of analysis in this chapter, the three Canadian provinces are combined. This database covers all published cases brought in these jurisdictions between 1996 and 2016, from low-level tribunals through to the highest courts of appeal.[5] It covers employment law violations but also a variety of other claims (criminal, tortious, human rights, antidiscrimination claims—outlined in more detail below) brought by migrants seeking to enforce their workplace rights. A key selection criterion for the case list was that the migrant's alleged violation occurred in the workplace and not outside the course of their employment. Each individual alleged violation is called a "claim," and a successful claim is called an "event." It is also possible that migrants can suffer multiple, concurrent claims across different violation areas, so each of these was coded individually for each migrant. Collectively, across the six labor law jurisdictions, we captured 907 cases involving 1,912 migrants who alleged 2,640 different violations, or claims.

Does exploitation include physical abuse and discriminatory behavior?

We may practically question whether exploitation can include nonpecuniary violations. In a Marxist sense, we may view exploitation as centrally related to the extraction of surplus value from labor and therefore excluding physical abuse or discrimination. However, insofar as physical abuse, sexual assault in the workplace, discrimination, or even holding a visa instead of a passport can increase employer control, these violations are consistent with a working definition of exploitation. Gary Dymski (1992) has argued that domination on racial or gender grounds can operate after an employee has been hired to increase the rate of financial exploitation that is already occurring. As such, domination and exploitation are bound through a reinforcing nexus[6] (see also Robinson and Kelley 2000). Empirically it is useful to explore whether this is the case in the immigrant worker area through an assessment not only of labor law legislation but also antidiscrimination and workplace health and safety laws and the likelihood of concurrent claims.

Individual or collective exploitation?

A separate issue arises as to whether exploitation is individual or collective in nature. For instance, the right to strike is a collective right that is generally violated at either the enterprise or sector level rather than individually. Given that the cases analyzed were primarily brought by individuals or groups of individuals rather than trade unions or worker associations, we focused our attention on discrimination on the basis of trade union activity against individuals rather than the violation of collective rights.

Exploited by whom?

In selecting a population of possible court cases where acts of alleged exploitation are adjudicated, it is necessary to consider who is responsible for these claimed acts. At times, it is clear it is the employer. However, at other times additional issues of intersecting liability arise. This can occur either through a contributory role played by recruiters or through subcontracting arrangements, meaning that liability is split. Recruitment agencies are often identified as key players in the exploitation of migrant workers (Davies 2019; Skrivankova 2017, 115). However, while recruiters may contribute to exploitation, their behavior is independent from breaches by the employer, unless their fees are unlawfully passed on to the employee by the employer (Faraday 2014). Naturally, depending upon one's perspective, governments may also be seen as one of the actors enabling exploitation through their laws or immigration policies. However, rarely do migrants bring governments to court as employers, and as such, cases involving governments as defendants or respondents are not the central focus of the analysis in this book.[7] More commonly in this space, governments seek to protect migrant workers, as legal representatives in court actions.

Further, it is not uncommon for a series of subcontractor arrangements to be used to minimize liability of the actual employer for their exploitative behavior. This phenomenon is sometimes known as *cascade subcontracting* (Frances, Barrientos, and Rogaly 2005). So-called letter box companies, or shell companies without employees or assets, are sometimes used to avoid contractual liability (Rusev and Kojouharov 2019, 22). Alternatively, a sequence of companies can engage in subcontracting arrangements that obscure one another's liabilities and reduce the end payment to employees (Davies and Ollus 2019, 99, 1010). To address this situation, we coded all employers who were listed in the court case as employers, at times requiring multiple defendants/respondents to be coded for each case.

Who is an employee?

The question "Who is an employee?" goes to the heart of labor law and distinguishes between employees and independent contractors. This determines whether labor or contract law governs a dispute. As such, the definition of who is an employee was driven by the coding of case law and whether decision-makers themselves determined the status of individuals as employees or subcontractors. Misclassification as a subcontractor was identified as a violation indicator (Codebook, Indicator 51).

A classification of exploitation

We now set out the component parts of our operationalized definition of exploitation, drawn from the scholarship discussed above. The classification of exploitation can be viewed as a series of five additive classes, with more and less serious violations within each of the constituent classes rather than a single continuum ranging from minor through to serious infringements.[8] These classes are based on the areas where violations can occur or the issue or the violations are centrally affected, from bodily and psychological integrity through to freedom from criminal violations against one's personhood, economic rights, safety, the right to leave, and freedom from discrimination.

Criminal infringements

Harm to the individual and an unwillingness on the part of the victim to be harmed are intrinsic to constituting criminal violations (Skrivankova 2017, 111). This unwillingness separates a criminal offense from an instance of informed choice on the part of the victim. Yet sometimes such choice is itself compromised. For instance, a migrant worker may voluntarily enter into a forced labor arrangement due to a lack of choice (Davidson 2015, 136). This inability to leave consensually can be viewed as part of what constitutes force and renders the arrangement criminal (ILO 1930, Article 1(3); see also CEACR 2022). There are also crimes for which there is strict liability on the part of the accused, irrespective of the actual or constructed consent on the part of the employee, who is also a victim. Physical harm may comprise part of criminal violations, such as sexual assault and assault; however, the crimes can sometimes occur without any form of physical harm, such as psychological or economic offenses that carry criminal sanctions.

Another aspect of criminal infringements is that sometimes the allegations against the employer are so serious—attempted murder, sexual assault, grievous bodily harm, etc.—that they can include self-protective cross-claims on the part of the defendant. In these instances, the migrant may be accused by the employer of having themselves committed a criminal offense, having broken other laws, or being vicariously liable for commissioning the criminal offense (Skrivankova 2017, 116). Instances such as these were considered on the legal facts in the cases where they arose.

Some forms of violations have both criminal and monetary components, for instance theft. The question is whether these are best classified as criminal or economic infringements. For instance, forced labor is a concept originally defined by the ILO in 1930 to include "abuse of vulnerability, deception, restriction of movement, isolation, physical and sexual violence, intimidation and threats, retention of identity documents, withholding of wages, debt bondage, abusive working and living conditions and excessive overtime" (ILO 2012). This concept can include both criminal violations (physical and sexual violence) and economic violations (withholding of wages), combined with a lack of consent by the victim. Given that forced labor is often criminalized under domestic laws, it is included under the criminal infringement component of the classification schema. The key violations identified for the criminal infringement section are being subjected to various infringements, such as visa fraud or assault or battery by the employer, or another agent if the employer is vicariously liable. False imprisonment or unlawful restraint by the employer as one of the elements of the crime of trafficking is also included in this category. There is some overlap here with the broader concept of trafficking, which also involves restraint; however, this category of imprisonment is differentiated as it does not involve movement across borders. Forced or compulsory labor without the employee's consent and harassment by an employer or a colleague where the employer should have intervened and is vicariously responsible are also included. Sexual misconduct, which includes sexual harassment and other sexual misdemeanors short of sexual assault (rape), is considered separately under its own classification category, both by the employer or where the employer, again, is vicariously responsible for an employee's actions. Being subjected to sexual assault (rape) and sexual servitude[9] are considered as individual criminal categories given their severity. Also included are the severe modern slavery offenses, including being trafficked by the employer and being a victim of industrial manslaughter or industrial homicide. These two latter crimes require either death deliberately caused by the employer or their direct liability for the death. Further, the death must occur in the workplace, not outside of it. Manslaughter and homicide are differentiated on the basis of the general legal requirement that homicide necessitates both the act and the mental state, whereas negligence alone causing death constitutes manslaughter.[10]

Economic violations of wage and hour entitlements

The second major category of exploitative behavior is economic violations of wage and hour entitlements. This component of the classification covers what Jon Davies (2018, 295, 305) refers to as "routine exploitation" through "civil, regulatory or labor law" that might frequently include underpayment. Included here are fraudulent independent contractor arrangements when the person is in fact an employee. Such arrangements, which may be used to circumvent employment laws, often appear in the migration and modern slavery setting (Jokinen and Ollus 2019; Davies 2018, 298).

The key violations identified for this section are unpaid wages, which covers (1) insolvent employer, (2) unpaid leave, (3) superannuation, (4) minimum wage requirements, (5) wage penalty rates, (6) meal and rest period violations, and (7) unlawful business practices.[11] Being required to work inhuman hours, including the denial of meal breaks, is included as a separate variable. This is distinguished from other work, health, and safety issues that are considered under safety violations. It is important to note that while failure to provide paid leave is included in underpayment, the denial of other forms of leave (parental, sickness, etc.) are coded as separate variables and combined into the denial of leave and other entitlements category. We also included the employee being denied severance pay at the point of dismissal or redundancy or being dismissed unfairly, unlawfully, or wrongfully and being incorrectly defined as a contractor. Finally, for this category, we included as a variable where the employee is subjected to breach of contract, such as where a contractual requirement in the migrant worker's individual contract related to wages goes unfulfilled, and being subjected to misrepresentation at the point of contractual agreement, where the employer falsely induces a person to enter a contract.

Safety violations

Workplace safety issues have been raised in other studies on migrant worker exploitation (Davies 2018, 305) and can include injuries, overwork, and other unsafe work practices. For this component, we included the single but important variable of whether the migrant worker was denied workplace safety. Depending upon the severity of these violations, they may be better categorized as criminal infringements. However, as this is rare, workplace health and safety issues are treated as an independent category in the classification, separate from criminal violations. Where industrial oversight leads to homicide or manslaughter, these are considered under the criminal category, discussed above.

Leave and other workplace entitlement violations

This battery of indicators encompasses the denial of forms of leave to which the employee is entitled that include being denied caregiver's leave, holiday leave, maternity leave, paternity leave, sick or personal leave and not being informed about pension (retirement) rights upon the commencement of employment. These forms of leave are distinguished from overtime work (which is included under economic violations) as overtime relates to day-to-day pay, whereas these leave characteristics are generally for longer periods of time or are connected to special conditions or characteristics of the worker (such as pregnancy or illness). The separation of leave from overtime is consistent with case law from Australia that found that leave entitlements could not be cashed out for payment, highlighting the exclusivity of these two concepts (e.g., *AFMEPKIU v. Tweed Valley Fruit Processors Pty. Ltd.* (1995) 61 IR 212; *Arrowcrest Group Pty. Ltd. re Metal Industry Award 1984* (1994) 36 AILR 402).

Discrimination violations

Discrimination can be divided into discrimination related to access, expressive discrimination, and physical discrimination. While most workplace discrimination is expressive (Bleich 2003, 9) rather than physical, this does not reduce its severity. Further, it can be viewed as a form of exploitation insofar as discrimination can further other pernicious goals, such as underpayment. In this section we included being denied the right to privacy through surveillance and monitoring, but note that this is a negative right, a freedom from interference, rather than protection against behavior, so it is a little different from the other rights against discrimination. We also included being discriminated against on the basis of age, family or caregiver responsibilities, impairment or disability, relationship status, political conviction, pregnancy, sex, race, religious activity, sexual orientation, and gender confirmation. Being denied freedom of expression is also included, as is being discriminated against on the basis of trade union activity and freedom of association. When a worker was denied rights of expression unrelated to freedom of association, these generally related to political expression in the workplace, stemming from denial or obstruction of activities by members of trade unions, or those attempting collective action.

Empirical analysis

In the remainder of this chapter, we set out the findings of the most common violations in each of the four jurisdictions, comparing alleged claims that are made against successfully substantiated claims. We remind the reader that these data include only finalized cases and therefore exclude any cases that were initiated but settled. Table 1.1 sets out the substantiated (successful) violations according to the five major classes of exploitation, across the four countries (all three Canadian provinces are collapsed into one country for ease of analysis). As is clear, in all jurisdictions, claims related to economic interests are the largest grouping of substantiated violations, ranging from 92% of all successful claims of events in Australia down to 53% in England. Next come discrimination-based claims, followed by criminal infringements, safety violations, and, finally, leave and other workplace entitlements. In short, consistent with expectations, a large majority of the patterning of workplace violations is economic in nature, related to wages and conditions; however, this does not capture the entire landscape of possible violations. It is also unsurprising that substantiated criminal cases are so infrequent given the greater burden of proof for the plaintiff in criminal than civil cases.[12]

Economic violations are the most frequent substantiated claim, as is clear from both Table 1.1 and Figure 1.1. Yet they also intersect with other

Table 1.1 Number of successful claims of violations, by violation category and jurisdiction (reported as a percentage of country cases and overall)

Violations Category	Australia	Canada	United Kingdom	California	Overall
Criminal infringements	29 (4%)	8 (2%)	14 (18%)	32 (8%)	83 (5%)
Economic violations	698 (92%)	213 (54%)	41 (53%)	415 (84%)	1,367 (81%)
Safety violations	28 (4%)	30 (8%)	1 (1%)	5 (1%)	64 (4%)
Leave and other workplace entitlements	0	1 (0.3%)	0	1 (0.2%)	2 (0.1%)
Discrimination	4 (1%)	140 (36%)	21 (27%)	12 (3%)	177 (10%)
Total	759	392	77	465	1,693

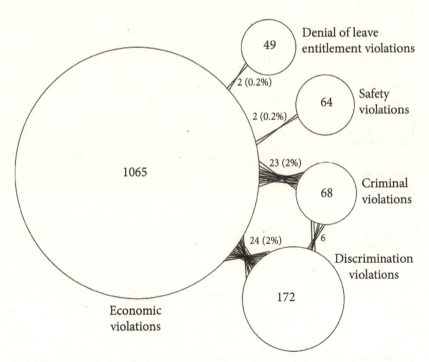

Figure 1.1 Number of migrants bringing successful violation claims, including intersecting claims, as a proportion of all successful MWRD claimants

Table 1.2 Intersections of successful violation claims, reported as N claimants and as percentage of migrants bringing that claim type

Successful Claim Type	Criminal Violations	Economic Violations	Safety Violations	Denial of Leave Entitlements	Discrimination Violations
Total claimants of this violation type	68	1,065	64	49	172
No intersections (% of total claimants)	44 (65%)	1,019 (96%)	62 (97%)	47 (96%)	147 (85%)
Intersecting criminal violation claim (% of total claimants)	-	23 (2%)	0	0	6 (3%)
Intersecting economic violation claim (% of total claimants)	23 (34%)	-	2 (3%)	2 (4%)	24 (14%)
Intersecting safety violation claim (% of total claimants)	0	2 (0.2%)	-	0	0
Intersecting denial of leave entitlement claim (% of total claimants)	0	2 (0.2%)	0	-	0
Intersecting discrimination violation claim (% of total claimants)	6 (9%)	24 (2%)	0	0	-

Source: MWRD.

violation areas. This is in the form of multiple claims by migrants and their representatives within each legal case that are then validated judicially or administratively. In Table 1.2, we list successful violation claims by type and the concurrent claims that are brought, as percentages across the entire database. In 34% of criminal violations an economic violation is also substantiated, demonstrating that criminal infringements against the body often correlate with wage and hour infringements. In 9% of successful criminal cases, there are also discrimination violations. Economic violations do stand alone 96% of the time; however, in 2% of these cases they are combined, successfully, with criminal and discrimination violations. This supports the argument that violations can reinforce one another in compounding ways, such as racial discrimination by an employer exacerbating or reinforcing economic deprivation. In a third of discrimination-based cases, the discrimination type is race (which covers race, ethnicity, nationality, and national origin). The next highest concurrent violations are economic violations and discrimination on the basis of trade union membership, which again relates to the view that exploitation is not only economic but often also has a political basis (see Meiksins Wood 2009).

There is only a very small overlap of 3% between safety-based violations and economic claims. This is most likely because often safety-based claims happened as stand-alone actions or also within specific workers compensation tribunals. For instance, 59% of substantiated safety violations are brought in workplace-specific tribunals.[13] Leave entitlement violations are raised less frequently across the database (see Table 1.1 and Figure 1.1), and there is less overlap. As noted, discrimination-based violations cross over with economic and criminal infringements. On this basis, we can see that while the bulk of substantiated claims for workplace violations are in the economic area (81%), not all are, and there is sometimes overlap with the other areas of the classification schema, especially discrimination. This provides some support for the argument that exploitation, while predominantly an economic phenomenon, has other components.

To ensure clarity, we now dive further into each jurisdiction separately as the overall number of claims differs dramatically across each location. We also compare, in the following tables, claims against substantiated violations to explore the extent of migrant success and failure in the cases. As such, this covers claims that have been adjudicated by a judge or other legal decision-maker as successful rather than simply made out by a migrant.

Australia

Australia has the largest number of cases of any of the four jurisdictions. Within these 355 cases, there were 1,123 claims in total. Underpayment was the largest area of claims and accounted for 47% of the total number. This was

38   PATTERNS OF EXPLOITATION

Table 1.3 Most common violation type claims in Australia, arranged by N claims

Violation Type	Claims Filed (% of total claims)	Successful Claims (% of total claims)	Success Ratio
Unpaid wages	531 (47%)	506 (45%)	95%
Dismissed unfairly, unlawfully, or wrongfully	144 (13%)	40 (4%)	27%
Subjected to misrepresentation	122 (11%)	116 (10%)	95%
Subjected to visa fraud	101 (9%)	2 (0.2%)	2%
Not informed about pension (retirement) rights commencing employment	62 (6%)	47 (4%)	76%
Subjected to breach of contract	44 (4%)	31 (3%)	70%
Subjected to unsafe work conditions (leading to injury, not death)	39 (3%)	28 (2%)	71%
Subjected to sexual servitude	25 (2%)	16 (1%)	64%
Incorrectly defined as a contractor	22 (2%)	14 (1%)	64%
Subjected to forced or compulsory labor	8 (1%)	5 (0.4%)	62.5%
Required to work inhuman hours, including denial of meal breaks	4 (0.4%)	5 (0.3%)	80%
Victim of industrial manslaughter	3 (0.3%)	3 (0.3%)	100%
Total	1,123	670	60%

followed by dismissal in its various forms (13%), being subjected to misrepresentation (11%), and visa fraud (9%). The remaining categories are listed in descending order in Table 1.3. Successful violations vary somewhat from claimed violations, as is clear from the third and fourth columns of Table 1.3, which sets out the claims that are most often successful. Again, underpayment is a top claim (45%), followed by being subjected to misrepresentation (10%), dismissal (4%), and breach of contract (3%). Comparing the two tables demonstrates that claims for unpaid wages have a high success rate, while for other categories, such as dismissal, they appear hard for migrants to win. Most of the Australian claims, and substantiated violations, are in the economic infringement category of the exploitation classification. Wage underpayment claims had the highest success rate, along with misrepresentation (95%).

Canada

Canada has the second largest number of cases in the database. The Canadian data combine the provinces of Ontario, British Columbia, and Alberta. Within the 276 Canadian cases, there were 626 claims in total. The largest number of claims were for discrimination on the basis of trade union activity and freedom of association (28%), unpaid wages (20%), discrimination on the basis of race (14%), and subject to breach of contract (12%). The remaining most common violation claims are listed in Table 1.4. If we also consider the claims that were successful, they are similar to the alleged claims: discrimination on the basis of trade union activity and freedom of association (21%), unpaid wages (18%), subjected to breach of contract (11%), and subjected to unsafe work conditions, leading to injury but not death (5%). Unlike Australia, where the top claims (and violations) are economic infringements, the top Canadian infringements are discrimination (trade

Table 1.4 Most common violation type claims in Canada, arranged by N claims

Violation Type	Claims Filed (% of total claims)	Successful Claims (% of total claims)	Success Ratio
Discriminated against on the basis of trade union activity and freedom of association	176 (28%)	131 (21%)	74%
Unpaid wages	123 (20%)	112 (18%)	95%
Discriminated against on the basis of race	89 (14%)	2 (0.3%)	2.2%
Subjected to breach of contract	76 (12%)	71 (11%)	93%
Dismissed unfairly, unlawfully, or wrongfully	58 (9%)	26 (4%)	45%
Subjected to unsafe work conditions (leading to injury, not death)	58 (9%)	30 (5%)	52%
Subjected to visa fraud	8 (1%)	2 (0.3%)	25%
Discriminated against on the grounds of impairment or disability	5 (1%)	2 (0.3%)	40%
Subjected to misrepresentation	5 (1%)	0 (0%)	0%
Discriminated against on the basis of sex (distinguished from pregnancy)	4 (1%)	2 (0.3%)	0.5%
Subjected to harassment by the employer	3 (0.5%)	3 (0.5%)	100%
Incorrectly defined as a contractor	3 (0.5%)	3 (0.5%)	100%
Total	626	392	63%

union and racial discrimination) and economic (unpaid wages and breach of contract). The high number of claims around discrimination on the basis of trade union membership reflects several very large class actions in British Columbia; 160 of the 330 claims in that province related to trade union and freedom of association matters.[14] Notably, racial discrimination claims comprise a far larger component of cases in Canada than in Australia, although most often claims are unsuccessful (see Table 1.4).

California

Table 1.5 shows that in California, the leading claims were economic infringements: unpaid wages (41%), subjected to breach of contract (20%), subjected to misrepresentation (12%), and required to work inhuman hours, including being denied meal breaks (7%). Table 1.5 shows that successful claims followed a similar pattern, although with lower ratios of success than actions brought: unpaid wages (31%), subjected to breach of contract (16%),

Table 1.5 Most common violation type claims in California, arranged by N claims

Violation Type	Claims Filed (% of total claims)	Successful Claims (% of total claims)	Success Ratio
Unpaid wages	269 (41%)	202 (31%)	75%
Subjected to breach of contract	129 (20%)	104 (16%)	81%
Subjected to misrepresentation	76 (12%)	66 (10%)	87%
Required to work inhuman hours, including denial of meal breaks	44 (7%)	28 (4%)	64%
Discriminated against on the basis of race	42 (6%)	9 (1%)	21%
Dismissed unfairly, unlawfully, or wrongfully	25 (4%)	15 (2%)	60%
Subjected to unsafe work conditions (leading to injury, not death)	15 (2%)	5 (1%)	33%
Trafficked by the employer	9 (1%)	7 (1%)	78%
Subjected to visa fraud	8 (1%)	8 (1%)	100%
Subjected to forced or compulsory labor	6 (1%)	6 (1%)	100%
Subjected to sexual misconduct	6 (1%)	2 (0.3%)	33%
Total	654	465	71%

subjected to misrepresentation (10%), and required to work inhuman hours (4%). These events are split over 125 cases. Many of these claims were brought by migrant farm laborers or factory workers. Furthermore, the overall low number of claims in California (654), despite its large population, is reflective of the low levels of claim-making among undocumented migrants, who comprise a large percentage of the immigrant population overall. We return to these themes in Chapter 5 on undocumented migrants.

The United Kingdom

The United Kingdom had a total of 237 claims, spread across 146 separate cases. An important observation is that, generally, there were fewer claims brought in each legal case in the United Kingdom than in other jurisdictions, where class actions were more common. This is related in part to narrower court procedure rules around class actions in the United Kingdom (Samuel 2019). From Table 1.6 it is clear that the majority of cases were economic infringements: 28% for dismissal, 18% for unpaid wages, and 8% for breach of contract. However, discrimination on the basis of racial vilification was also a crucial component of claims (24%). When we compare against successful claims and successful ratios, substantiated claims are also largely economic in nature, including unfair dismissal (11%) and unpaid wages (5%); however, racial discrimination (4%) and trafficking findings (4%) are also present in the top categories of substantiated claims. Generally, the violation percentages are far lower than the claims, indicative of low success rates for claimants in the United Kingdom across many criteria (see success ratios, Table 1.6).

Overview of a new method to understand exploitation in the workplace

Mapping exploitation as a theoretical and empirical concept defines the outer boundaries of what this book explores. Clearly, economic injustice is a significant component of any working definition of "exploitation." For this reason, our classification of exploitation includes economic violations, but it also contains other forms of abuse: criminal violations, safety, leave, and discrimination. It considers how these can exacerbate or reinforce economic

Table 1.6 Claims in England arranged according to number of claims by violation type and success ratio

	Claims Filed (% of total claims)	Successful Claims (% of total claims)	Success Ratio
Violation			
Dismissed unfairly, unlawfully, or wrongfully	67 (28%)	26 (11%)	39%
Discriminated against on the basis of race	58 (24%)	10 (4%)	17%
Unpaid wages	42 (18%)	11 (5%)	26%
Subjected to breach of contract	20 (8%)	3 (1%)	15%
Trafficked by the employer	14 (6%)	9 (4%)	64%
Discriminated against on the basis of sex (distinguished from pregnancy)	11 (5%)	4 (2%)	36%
Discriminated against on the grounds of impairment or disability	7 (3%)	1 (0.4%)	14%
Discriminated against on the basis of religious activity or belief	4 (2%)	2 (1%)	50%
Subjected to sexual misconduct	4 (2%)	4 (2%)	100%
Discriminated against on the basis of age	3 (1%)	1 (0.4%)	33%
Total	237	77	33%

infringements or exploit a worker in economically irrational but still deeply problematic ways. For instance, an employer may not extract a financial benefit through harsh racial discrimination—it may even lead to financial loss for the employer—and yet, the effect upon the migrant employee may be very damaging and nonetheless exploitative. Moving beyond a purely economic conception of exploitation to consider these other violations is important not only to capture the full scope of workplace exploitation but also because it paints a more accurate picture of the scope of what is accurately occurring in the cases considered in this book.

This book identifies different types of vulnerabilities experienced by migrant workers that may render them more likely to be exploited than domestic workers. These include the migrant's gender, ethnicity, and concentration in occupations located in key sectors. We can also consider a migrant's visa status—whether it is short term, long term, or lapsed (undocumented)—as an influence on the extent of a migrant's vulnerability. Workplace representation in various guises, especially through trade unions and workers centers, can mitigate the vulnerability that migrant workers may experience, as can the extent of government enforcement of labor laws. There are also potential underlying legal, social, and cultural reasons in each country (and in the case of subnational systems, each labor law jurisdiction) for variation in forms of exploitation. Chapters 2 through 8 will explore the distinctiveness of each of the four countries and the six labour law jurisdictions through qualitative case studies focusing on specific legal cases and a particular jurisdiction in each chapter. They take a deep dive into a variety of possible patterns of exploitation: gender, ethnicity (country of origin), sector of employment, the impact of undocumented visa status, immigration visa design, trade union engagement, and government enforcement.

2
"A Member of the Family"?
Gender, Domestic Work, and Violations

Binti Salim Udin was a female Indonesian domestic care worker who had been employed as a maid in Mokaram Kaylani's house in Saudi Arabia before migrating to London in 2004, after her employer died. She then worked for Mrs. Kaylani's daughter in the Chamsi-Pasha family for five years, until 2009. The Employment Tribunal described Mr. Chamsi-Pasha as "a member of a famous Syrian family, well known particularly in the textile trade for many generations," and Mrs. Chamsi-Pasha as also coming from "a well-to-do Syrian family" (*Udin v. Chamsi-Pasha*, Employment Tribunal 2203182/2009, para 2).[1] At the start, the Chamsi-Pashas and Ms. Udin lived in "a very large flat in Portland Place" in central London. However, after the family experienced a decline in its financial situation, they moved first to Hallam Street and then to Thurloe Street. In the words of Employment Tribunal Judge Snelson, "there was no disagreement that, relative to the accommodation in Portland Place, conditions in Hallam Street and Thurloe Street were cramped" (*Udin v. Chamsi-Pasha*, para 74). Upon moving, Ms. Udin no longer had her own room and was instead required to sleep on a mattress on the floor of either the two youngest boys' room or in the dining room (para 78). From here the two versions of events in the Chamsi-Pasha house diverge.

According to Ms. Udin, she was trafficked, overworked—up to seventeen hours per day, seven days a week—bullied, exploited, deprived of her passport, falsely accused of theft, strip-searched, sexually harassed, and humiliated to the point that she drank drain-cleaning acid in a suicide attempt and in doing so destroyed her esophagus and some internal organs. Through a series of connections, she sought out the legal support of Kalayaan and then the Poppy Project, two organizations that represent abused migrant domestic care workers. They made a successful application to the UKBA (United Kingdom's Border Agency) that Ms. Udin was a victim of human trafficking and on this basis secured her ongoing residency in the United Kingdom (*Udin v. Chamsi-Pasha*, paras 8, 12, 14).[2] Mrs. Chamsi-Pasha was arrested at her home on suspicion of unlawful imprisonment, assault, and threats to kill, before being released on bail (para 10). Ultimately, Ms. Udin was left unemployed, with "impaired health" and "facing an uncertain future" (para 1).

The Chamsi-Pashas provided an entirely different version of events: they asserted that Ms. Udin was treated kindly and with respect, as a *member of the family*, until she stole "a string of valuables from them including jewelry, a Louis Vuitton handbag, a Harvey Nichols store card, phones, an iPod, CDs and silk scarves," whereupon she was promptly dismissed (*Udin v. Chamsi-Pasha*, paras 17; 149; Wright 2010). The suicide attempt was an act of shame (Bushra Ahmed, counsel, Interview UK 1, via Dubai). Mrs. Chamsi-Pasha was innocent, and one of the United Kingdom's most formidable criminal defense barristers, Jonathan Goldberg QC, was employed to defend her, which he did successfully: the charges against Mrs. Chamsi-Pasha were dropped.

The facts of the case were clearly deeply contested. Ms. Udin won on her immigration claim, lost on the criminal issues, and then lodged a claim in the Employment Tribunal for unfair dismissal, racial discrimination, unauthorized deductions in her pay, and other claims under the Working Time Regulations (*Udin v. Chamsi-Pasha* 2009, para 11). Her counsel argued that she had been erroneously classified as a "member of the family," leading to her being paid far less than owed under the National Minimum Wage Act (1998) (UK). Yet, the Tribunal came down in favor of the Chamsi-Pashas on most grounds. They found that "Ms Udin's attempt to paint a picture of herself as excluded, overworked, bullied, exploited and ultimately humiliated was . . . a travesty of the truth." Further, no evidence of the strip-search was found (*Udin v. Chamsi-Pasha* 2009, paras 164, 167). Overall, Ms. Udin was judged "a witness who could not be believed" (at para 183).

The issue of whether a domestic care worker can be considered a "member of the family" is the focus of this chapter and goes centrally to gender equality and the treatment of gendered work and the pursuit of gender equality through law.[3] We begin this chapter by clarifying the statutory exemption under English law, for what is meant by "a member of the family" and its interpretation in litigation; the potential for gender discrimination inherent in this provision; the treatment of domestic care work *as work*, along with its regulation; and normative questions that the "member of the family" exemption implies for family life and the emotional character of familial relationships both in England and in other jurisdictions. The potential nexus between domestic servitude, trafficking, and sexual violence is also raised.

We then move to the quantitative findings of the MWRD.[4] First, are female migrants more or less likely to raise workplace claims than male migrants, factoring in their representation within the broader migrant population? Second, are women more likely to experience underpayment than men, given—or perhaps exacerbated by—gendered wage gaps? Third, the rate of claims brought around sex-specific issues (e.g., discrimination on the grounds of sex, sexual orientation, and experiences of sexual violence in the workplace) are discussed. We conclude by considering the intersection of gender, ethnicity, and social class as a compounding obstacle in the experience of migrant women when raising claims of workplace violations, and providing some potential policy recommendations.

A member of the family

Regulations to the National Minimum Wage Regulations (2015) 57 and 57(3) that wages can be excluded from the requirements of the national minimum under the following conditions:

(1) [that] the worker resides in the family home of the employer for whom he works;
(2) that the worker is not a member of the family but is treated as such, in particular as regards to the provision of accommodation and meals and the sharing of tasks and leisure activities;
(3) that the worker is neither liable to any deductions, nor to make any payments to the employer, or any other person, in respect of the provision of the living accommodation or meals; and
(4) that, had the worker been a member of the employer's family, it [the work] would not be treated as being performed under a worker's contract or as being work because the conditions in sub-paragraph (b) would be satisfied.

The conditions of subparagraph (b) are:

(1) that the worker is a member of the employer's family,
(2) that the worker resides in the family home of the employer,
(3) that the worker shares in the tasks and activities of the family,
(4) and that the work is done in that context.[5]

A central issue for the Employment Tribunal, and subsequent appellant courts in the *Udin* case, was how to interpret these regulations and what was meant by "not a member of the family but is treated as such." Under her contract, Ms. Udin was entitled to £400 per month, which was significantly less than she would have been owed under national minimum requirements given the long hours she worked. There was evidence that she was underpaid (*Udin v. Chamsi-Pasha* 2009, paras 67, 71); therefore, there would have been financial benefits to her, had she not been viewed as a "member of the family." The Tribunal made clear that for a domestic worker to be "treated as though a member of the family," there did not need to be a perfect division of tasks between worker and family:

> The concept of sharing tasks, must, it seems to us, be interpreted in the context of what it is that the worker is employed to do. If a primary employment duty of the worker is to get children ready for school in the morning, the exemption clearly does not depend on that task being shared in the morning, the exemption clearly does not depend on that task being shared with other members of the family. To put it another way, the domestic worker does not need to share her role with other members of the family in order to fall within the exemption. (*Udin v. Chamsi-Pasha*, para 213)

Minute and detailed accounts of daily life in the Chamsi-Pasha household were furnished to track Ms. Udin's daily activities and integration into the family. This included whether she ate meals with the family or alone: she ate alone; if she was invited on family outings to the country: she was; whether household tasks were shared or segregated: they were shared; who met the cost of travel and expenses: the Chamsi-Pashas; where she slept: on a mattress on the floor of either the two youngest boys' room or the dining room; and whether she socialized with family members: she did. On balance, it was found by a 2–1 majority that the exemption was not met, as the shared room she was afforded would not have been what a biological Chamsi-Pasha in their late thirties would have been given (*Udin v. Chamsi-Pasha*, paras 214, 217). On this basis, Ms. Udin was owed wages for overtime, rest periods, and annual leave. The case was remitted for the first-instance Tribunal to determine remedies. However, before this could occur, the case was appealed to the Employment Appeal Tribunal, where it was subsumed into the cases of two other domestic care workers, Ms. Jose and Ms. Nambalat (*Jose v. Julio* UKEAT 0553_10_0812, 8 December 2011). Although the facts of their cases were not as alarming as those alleged by Ms. Udin, all employers had at first instance lost on the "member of the family" exemption.

The Employment Appeal Tribunal clarified the correct construction of Regulation 2(2)(a)(ii): the worker's place in the household must be considered holistically and will differ across families. Accommodation alone does not determine whether they are treated as a family member; the provision of meals, the sharing of tasks, and "the degree of privacy and autonomy" are also relevant. Further, general household tasks may be shared but cannot include work where the worker would otherwise be employed—namely and often child care.[6] Sharing tasks equally with family members was not required. The real issue was one of integration into the family structure (*Jose v. Julio*, paras 46, 50, 56). On this basis, the three claimants were found to be members of the respective families and were not owed unpaid wages (*Jose v. Julio*, Ms. Jose at para 50; Ms. Nambalat at para 53; Ms. Udin at paras 56–58). Ms. Udin's initial case was overturned. In particular, the fact that the Chamsi-Pasha's daughter—but not their sons—was also required to sleep on a mattress on the floor, rather than in a bed, gave weight to the finding that Ms. Udin was not singled out as a nonfamily member (*Jose v. Julio*, para 57).[7]

In the Court of Appeal in 2012, the matter was appealed by Ms. Nambalat and Ms. Udin (*Nambalat v. Taher and Anor.* (2012) EWCA Civ 1249) given similarities across these cases and the broader policy issues at hand. Again, the case turned on the correct construction of then Regulation 2(2)(a)(ii). Counsel for the migrants argued that a narrow interpretation of the exemption should be applied to avoid differentiation between industrial sectors and to avoid discrimination, in this case against ethnic minorities, women, and young people (para 7). The argument that shared tasks should include those tasks within the remit of the employment contract was reiterated by Counsel for the claimants (para 14) but rejected by the Court (para 41). The Court found that the first-instance Tribunal had erred in determining that accommodation was a central factor in whether someone was a member of the family. Instead, the issue was to be treated holistically. It was not necessary to construct a hypothetical family member and consider their sleeping arrangements (para 37). Ms. Udin and her co-claimants lost their appeal.

It is important to note that since 2016 (the end point for the MWRD), a case brought by a domestic worker was successful in challenging the Regulations. In this case of *Ajayi v. Abu & Abu* (2017) EWHC 3098 QC, the employer was found to have breached the regulations because they had kept a ledger of earnings and had made unlawful deductions for accommodation and food, among other things. For this and other reasons, the relationship was deemed to be employment-based and not that of a family member, and remedies were payable for unpaid wages. However, the provision itself still stands, and this successful case can be viewed as an anomaly.

The gendered effects of workplace regulations

Workplace regulations can operate to reinforce gender stereotypes in a variety of ways. In this chapter, we treat "gender" primarily as the socialized and, in many instances, biological differences between men and women, while acknowledging that gender discrimination in law can also relate to discrimination on the basis of intersex and fluid gender identity. However, given that such cases arose infrequently in the MWRD, the focus in this chapter is on gender discrimination on the basis of ascribed female or male gender. For instance, in the United Kingdom, overtime payments of 1.5 times minimum salaries are present in male-dominated sectors, such as horticulture, but not in female-dominated ones, such as care work (Exemptions, Special Rules and Establishment of Minimum Wage Regulation [UK], cf. ss 13–18, 1, 23). Domestic workers in the United Kingdom, both British and overseas-born, are excluded from maximum weekly working times, occupational health and safety legislation, and duration of night work requirements (Working Time Regulations 1998, reg 19; Health and Safety Act 1974, s 51, discussed in Mantouvalou 2012). Previously, domestic workers were also excluded from the British Race Relations Act, which limited their capacity to bring racial discrimination claims, although this was changed in 2003 and their inclusion was retained when the Race Relations Act was incorporated into the Equality Act 2010 (Butler 2018, I.8, para 3). At the other end of the labor market, certain trainee areas and higher-level occupations, such as surgeons, are also exempt from the Working Time Regulations (1998, regs 2, 21).

Gendered effects in labor law regulations are also apparent in other jurisdictions. In Ontario, the Employment Standards Act (2000) exempts home care employees, liquor servers, and agricultural employees from key provisions of protection (Vosko 2019b; Ontarian Exemptions, Special Rules and Establishment of Minimum Wage Regulations (2019), ss 2, 8, 11, 23 para 61, s 201, para 61, s 213, s 11); sectors that are highly gender segregated with either a preponderance of men or women. In the United States, domestic workers are excluded from protections under the NLRA, but some states, such as California, have passed the Domestic Workers Bill of Rights (2013) to partially fill some of the gaps; however, they are still excluded from the Occupational Safety and Health Act (OSHA), and campaigns to extend these health and safety regulations to domestic workers continue. In Australia, no such exclusions exist at the federal level, although they do in several states.[8] That said, as Laurie Berg (2015, 7) has noted, the regulation of au pairs in Australia may lead to de facto exclusion from basic minimums in some instances, depending upon whether their work is viewed as employment or as a cultural experience (see also Berg and Meagher 2018, 34–37). Similar arguments have been made about au pair programs in the United Kingdom (Cox 2012, 38).

Gendered care work

These regulatory exclusions across the different jurisdictions operate on the basis that in-home care work is somehow different from other types of work or exempted in some way. Some of these exemptions may be practical in their motivation. For instance, there are difficulties in quantifying household work or challenges in assessing the work contribution of a sleeping person "on standby" for a child or disabled person. Such individuals are not working, but are not completely at rest either.

There is also a deeper normative issue: whether in-home domestic care work is the same as the unpaid domestic work that women have historically performed and therefore is less deserving of regulated minimums. Susan Himmelweit (1995, 9) has argued, "Activities remaining in the home are the more personal aspects of domestic life . . . and therefore retain the characteristics of invisibility that [are] used to characterize all unpaid work" (see also Cox 2012, 49; Fudge 1997, 119). Viewed in this way, domestic work may be considered different from other work and subject to separate regulation, given the porous boundaries between home and market, private and public. For instance, slippages in when an employee is required to work or not may be more prone to misinterpretation in live-in situations (Sitkin 2017, 228). Care work may even be seen as primarily motivated by altruism, given its linkages to motherly tasks, or as motivated morally, or "psychically," rather than by economic incentive (Folbre 2003, 216, 291, citing Thurow 1978, 219). This relational and emotional quality of care can contribute to a sense of selflessness being erroneously attributed to care workers and provide an intellectual justification for low—or no—pay.

There are broader issues pertinent to a discussion of care, particularly the way that some work is viewed as *skilled*, and thus worthy of compensation, and some is not. This argument is well established in feminist critiques of human capital theory (McLaren and Dyck 2004, 43; Boucher 2016). Attributing altruism to care work, and women's specialization in the sector, often devalues such positions, which can further contribute to under- or nonpayment (Tronto 1993, 114).

Women may also be more likely to be chosen as domestic workers due to employer perceptions that women are better at domestic work or to unfair stereotypes about male caregivers as pedophilic (Anderson 2007, 251). Existing studies of the occupational distribution of migrant workers show that women are more likely to be placed in care, cleaning, hospitality, and food-processing work (WEstJustice 2016, 219; Boucher 2016, Chapter 6). The human capital perspective argues that rational specialization follows women's experience gained through their reproduction and child rearing (Becker 1991, 37–38, cited by Hewitson 2003, 269). By contrast, feminists argue that global inequality and gendered pay gaps give rise to women's predominance in global care chains (Anderson 2000). As such, notions of "skill" are clearly gendered. In the case of migrant women, these gendered distinctions are exacerbated by the intersecting role of economic differences between sending and receiving countries. Global inequality motivates migrants to take up opportunities overseas (Fudge 2011a, 239; Hochschild 2000). The *Udin* case exhibited such a class difference. Justice Snelson compared Ms. Udin's very different social background from the respondent's: "It is perhaps no surprise given their backgrounds that Ms Salim Udin and Mr and Mrs Chamsi-Pasha had little in the way of common interests, but a shared religion which they practiced together (all three are committed Muslims) served to some extent as a levelling force" (*Udin v. Chamsi-Pasha* 2009 at para 4).

Gender stereotypes may also play into what is judged an appropriate division of labor—and even what is considered *work*. In accepting that a person could be treated as a "member of the family" even where they had full responsibility for specific tasks, a certain idea of family was implied in the *Udin* case. At times, this argument was cited in defense of an uneven division of household tasks. For instance, Mr. Goldberg QC, acting for the Chamsi-Pasha family, argued that "it was necessary to look at the actual family and its circumstances. In a family with an Asian background, women may customarily do more of the household work" (*Nambalat v. Taher*, at para 31).

The emotional nature of care

The *Udin* case raises an interesting question around the level of respect and cordiality owed to workers who are to be treated as a "member of the family," and in doing so, it raises normative assumptions about family life. Inherent in the "member of the family" exclusion is the notion that family relationships are somehow different from other relationships, requiring different rules, behaviors, and exclusions. Assumptions of emotional attunement and cordiality that underpin domestic work differ from standard employment relationships and may create arguments in favor of casting the employment as atypical.

But eliding its emotional nature runs contrary to a fundamental principle of care. As many scholars have argued, care is fundamentally relational. Quality of care is judged not only in terms of the tasks performed but also on the way they are performed and in terms of the relationship with the care receiver. As Marin Jochimsen (2003, 236) puts it, "[t]he performance of the caring activity is not separated from life and self, but constitutive of the caregiver and not separate from his or her relations with other people." Emotional attunement is a fundamental feature both of good caregiving and, it would seem, good family life. Therefore, to remove notions of emotion from evaluations of family-like relationships is both to rid families of their true—or at least ideal—character and to overlook the fundamental emotional labor inherent in quality care work.

In arguing, in the *Udin* case, that the adjudgment of family life draws centrally upon *tasks performed*, the judges failed to consider the potential for exploitation within biological families. The rationale behind the regulatory exclusion would seem to be that biological families are nonexploitative, and therefore being a "member of the family" means that the work is inherently nonexploitative. However, as feminist economists have demonstrated (e.g. Folbre 1982, 324), biological families themselves are rife with sexual and economic violations, especially where women and children lack independent economic means.[9]

Some of these concerns around the emotional quality of familial relationships in domestic care situations arise in the cases considered above. The general position of the employers and also the judges in the Court of Appeal decision of *Nambalat v. Taher* was that relationships did not have to be perfectly harmonious for a worker to be viewed as a "member of the family." Nonetheless, mutual respect was needed. As Bushra Ahmed, counsel for the Chamsi-Pashas, said:

> [N]o relationship is going to be perfect. You have ups and downs even in family relationships. I'm not saying that there wasn't a cross word said, that it was all perfect, not at all. I'm just saying that the reality of family life is that there are going to be ups and downs. So Yoyoh [Ms. Udin] comes over, and, you know, we see photographs wherein she is at family get-togethers and she is, you know, eating as part of the family. You know, the children are hugging and kissing her. (Bushra Ahmed, Interview 1, UK; see also *Nambalat v. Taher and Anor.*, para 30)

Nor must there be parity in the distribution of work among members of the biological or constructed family (*Nambalat v. Taher*, para 42). Counsel for the migrants argued that the Tribunal had construed the exemption too broadly. Julian Milford, counsel for the three claimants, explained, "We were saying 'look at what this was conceived for, it was conceived for au pairs and people who come and live with a family and do twenty to twenty-five hours of work a week and spend the rest of it going out, learning English, having a nice time. It was not meant for people who are here to work, which is what, in effect, it was applied to in these cases'" (Interview 14, UK). Milford and fellow barrister Oldham QC relied upon material from the House of Commons, when the exemption was enacted by Minister of State of the Department of Trade and Industry Ian McCartney, and a focus was placed upon au pairs: "The regulations provide an exemption for work undertaken by people who work and live as one of a family [sic] in their employer's home. That could, for example, include many au pairs" (cited in *Udin v. Chamsi-Pasha*, at para 211).

Domestic work or domestic servitude?

This brings us to the threshold question of when domestic work becomes domestic servitude. As argued in Chapter 1, exploitation can be viewed as a classification schema, comprising different components. The risk of exploitation is heightened in domestic care work, especially where the worker is trafficked or their visa is tied to their employer. Rights violations in these instances can include underpayment, suboptimal living conditions, physical threats, sexual abuse, and illegal recruitment and visa fees (Anderson 2007; Berg and Meagher 2018; Hafiz and Paarlberg 2017, 6, 22, 25; Human Rights Watch 2014; Kalayaan 2013; Mantouvalou 2015; Moore 2019, 45–51; Fudge 2011a, 255). Domestic work is also at a higher risk of trafficking than other jobs. Its private, familial nature can render it invisible or hard to detect (Fudge 2016a, 154). These issues have previously been considered by the European Court of Human Rights in the *Siliadin v. France* (Application No. 73316/01, 2005) case and were raised again in the *Jose v. Julio* case. Further, aspects of this case were incorporated into British law through the Modern Slavery Act (2015) (UK).

Notwithstanding the regularity of such domestic servitude, it is often difficult for domestic worker advocates to make out these claims, given that sex trafficking is more commonly viewed as a classic form of slavery. As Judy Fudge (2016c, 160) notes of the Canadian experience, the focus of antitrafficking and human slavery campaigns is on sexual exploitation and prostitution. Similarly, British barrister Kathryn Cronin, who frequently works on trafficking cases, argues:

> I think . . . very often you have to fight to get them to see domestic service as an extreme form of exploitation. And so, I think there is an array of domestic worker provisions, some where you get sexual abuse and some where you get very severe mistreatment and violence exacted, or very extreme privations. (Interview 3, Garden Court Chambers, London, 28 January 2018)

There is also a gray line between trafficking, exploitative labor standards, and permissible employment standards. This point was clear in the *Zarkasi v. Anindita & Anor.* (2012) decision, where a finding of trafficking into domestic servitude was not reached, despite a high-risk environment and seeming threats from the employer:

> We accept as an almost inevitable fact that the Claimant at least initially had limited social contact. She did not speak much English and was in a poor financial position. We do not accept that the Claimant was imprisoned in the Respondents' house in the sense of being locked in. However we do find that she was discouraged from going out, and that the word "dangerous" was used in that connection. Indeed it was potentially dangerous for the Claimant to have a social life, dangerous to the Claimant and

to the Respondents, because of the Claimant's status in the UK. (*Zarkasi v. Anindita & Anor.* (2012) 0400_11_1801, at para 6)

The line between legitimate domestic care work and illegal domestic servitude can be blurry. The policy context around the time of the *Udin* and *Nambalat* judgments was not immaterial. Passage of the entire Modern Slavery Act within the House of Lords turned on commissioning a government inquiry into the overseas domestic worker visa (James Ewin, barrister, Interview 9, UK). The Modern Slavery Act (2015) (UK) consolidates existing criminal offenses (slavery, servitude, forced and compulsory labor, and trafficking for labor exploitation) into a singular piece of domestic legislation, thereby drawing heightened attention to these offenses (Fudge 2018b, 426). The act has been criticized on a number of grounds, including limitations in the identification of trafficking within the United Kingdom and insufficient victim protection (Fudge 2018b, 427; Robinson 2015, 140). Further, following critique that the act focuses only on the most egregious forms of gendered violence, missing other unlawful acts, such as those in less regulated employment law areas (Robinson 2014, 7), we might argue that there is also a subsequent underrecognition of less serious but far more common *gendered* employment breaches, such as gendered differences in wage underpayment.

The National Referral Mechanism that the act established does create a context for achieving immigration status and regularization for victims of human trafficking. While the grounds for this are narrow, the provision does not exist in the other jurisdictions and has been used to protect domestic workers.[10] There are also some options to extend visas for an additional six months in the event that a trafficking claim is successful for overseas domestic workers brought in by foreign nationals (Modern Slavery Act (2015), s 53; Immigration Rules, s 151I, 159K; Home Office Guidelines 2017). However, the provisions are narrow and arguably insufficient to protect against trafficking and exploitation (Ewins 2015; Human Rights Watch 2014; Mantouvalou 2015, 353).

Visa regulation often compounds the trafficking risk faced by domestic workers. Limitations placed on overseas domestic worker visas in the United Kingdom since 2012 can reduce the time a worker can stay, from two years down to six months, and close down opportunities for conversion to permanent residency (Sitkin 2017, 228; Mantouvalou 2015, 355; Immigration Rules 159A–159H). Critics have argued that these changes increase the risk of abuse and the potential for migrant women to fall into undocumented status as they have no options to apply for permanent residency (Moss 2015, 72–73; Sitkin 2017, 230; Fudge 2016c, 12).[11]

In the other jurisdictions, similar issues have been raised. For instance, in the United States, the federal government enacted the Trafficking Victims Protection Reauthorization Act, which provides statutory protections for A-3 and G-5 workers.[12] However, there are no mechanisms to enforce contractual violations (Hafiz and Paarlberg 2017, 22). Similar protections exist for trafficked domestic workers under the Support for Trafficked People Program in Australia, although again they have been criticized for being too narrow (Moore 2019, 17). In Canada, the Live-in Caregiver Program (now defunct) provided opportunities for a caregiver to work for two years for a family. The vast bulk of applicants were women (Fudge 2011a, 248). This program received frequent complaints of abuse from domestic worker activists and in academic reports over many years (e.g. Bakan and Stasiulis 1997a, 1997b), eventually leading to the program being closed (Citizenship and Immigration Canada [CIC] 2014, 169).[13]

In the *Udin* and *Namabalat* cases, counsel for the migrant workers drew attention to the risk of exploitation of domestic workers inherent in the "member of the family" provision. They cited Perrins and Osman (2001) (at B1(B)(8), para 178): "In keeping with the general scheme of the legislation it would appear that this exception should be constructed narrowly and particular attention should be paid to ensure that the au pair relationship is not a simple shield for exploitation" (cited in *Jose v. Julio*, at para 40). Counsel continued that a broad interpretation of the regulation would raise the risk of forced labor, which was identified as a prohibition in *Siliadin v. France* (2006) 43 EHRR 16 (*Jose v. Julio* at para 41). While this argument was not addressed in full in the Court of Appeal, Justice Pill also identified the inherent risk in too broad an interpretation of the "member of the family" provision: "Tribunals will need to be astute when assessing whether an exemption designed for the mutual benefit of employer and worker is not being used as a device for obtaining cheap domestic labor" (*Nambalat v. Taher*, at para 48). This slippage reveals one of the key risks of the broader interpretation of the "member of the family" exemption.

Michelle Brewer, a barrister who has worked on trafficking cases involving domestic workers, made the following argument about gendered work:

> I've had cases where I've appealed judgments where they've said, "Well, she was just washing dishes" and these kinds of things. So, for us, it's incredibly

important when we do domestic worker cases to really set out the framework by which they are working. And if it's children, important things would be access to schooling, access to GPs, what kind of hours they're working, where they're sleeping, sanitary stuff, where are they eating? What kind of food are they getting? All of those things illustrate the conditions of work and how plainly that doesn't suggest that it's for pocket money or that it's within the family household and they've just taken on particular responsibilities.... But I think it's a real problem to allow that narrative to continue, because it essentially creates a justification for what is always exploitation. But I think there's a significant problem with cultural prejudices; the gender prejudices that arise make understanding where domestic work becomes exploitative much more difficult than in, for example, sexual exploitation.... But in domestic worker cases it can be really tricky, and I've found that in employment tribunal cases, it tends to go badly wrong. (Interview 4, UK)

The issue here is not only the way that care work is read as *nonwork* but also the power differential between employee and employer. This is interpreted differently in care work and sexual exploitation cases. Relatedly trafficking, care work, sexual violence, and discrimination may be more common in domestic work than in other sectors of work (outside of sex work) because of the hidden nature of the work and the difficulty of intervening, or even having third-party witnesses to sexual violence. A study of twenty-four domestic worker cases in the United Kingdom found that sexual abuse was alleged in at least two cases and that safeguards against this were ineffectual (Mantouvalou 2015, 341–342). In the *Udin* and *Nambalat* cases, the domestic workers claimed some form of sexual violence or discrimination, although neither claim was substantiated by the courts. How do these particular features of the current cases reflect broader trends across the MWRD?

Quantitative findings

We now move on to quantitative findings drawn from the MWRD of 907 cases to build upon the qualitative picture above. The first issue is whether men or women are more likely to bring workplace violation claims. We can adjudge this by comparing claim statistics against gender-disaggregated migration flow data. It is necessary to benchmark these data against disaggregated

58 PATTERNS OF EXPLOITATION

Table 2.1 Gender representation in claims across the population, by jurisdiction and migrant sex

Jurisdiction	Female	Male	Unknown	Increased Coverage after Imputation
Australia	168 (18%)	318 (34%)	463 (49%)	68 (7%)
California	73 (22%)	192 (58%)	66 (20%)	174 (53%)
Canada	75 (15%)	129 (26%)	284 (58%)	2 (0.4%)
United Kingdom	78 (54%)	64 (44%)	2 (1%)	0

migration flow data, as these findings could simply reflect the lower number of women overall in the migrant population, where women have been consistently found to be underrepresented, at least in highly skilled work categories (Boucher 2016; Dauvergne 2000). Occupational gender segregation that is apparent for the standard domestic population is often amplified for migrant workers (ILO 2018; Boucher 2016, Chapter 6), so exploring the gendered make-up of complaints is important.

Table 2.1 outlines the key differences in claims, disaggregated for gender. There was a large amount of missing data for gender, especially for Australia, as class actions without first and second names were more common there; imputation improved this somewhat, but not for all jurisdictions.[14]

Across all jurisdictions, other than the United Kingdom, it is clear that female migrants make fewer claims. There is a gap of between 11% (Canada) and 36% (California) in claims brought by men over women. In the United Kingdom, women bring 10% more claims, which could relate to high rates of actions brought by domestic workers and sexual trafficking offenses, an issue we return to below. It is also necessary to benchmark these data against disaggregated gender migration flow data, as these findings could simply reflect the lower number of women migrants in the overall migration intake populations, where women have been consistently found to be underrepresented, as noted above.

We also consider the gender ratios within the MWRD when compared with the broader immigrant population. Analysis is somewhat stymied by the high levels of missing data for gender in the database. For this reason, we average the data ratios after having removed missing data and compare these against the averages of male and female immigration flows over the twenty-year period of 2006–2016. As is clear from Table 2.2, in Australia

Table 2.2 Gender disaggregated immigrant entrants and representation in the MWRD, adjusted percentages

Jurisdiction	Male MWRD (adjusted) %	Male Immigration %	Female MWRD (adjusted) %	Female Immigration %	Unknown MWRD %
Australia	65	50.6	35	49.4	49
California	72.5	44.2	27.5	55.8	20
Canada	26	54.7	15	45.3	58
United Kingdom	44.8	47.9	55.2	52.1	1

male and female immigration entry when averaged across the twenty years and the various visa categories[15] is roughly even, yet men bring two-thirds of claims in the MWRD and women only one-third. This means that women are heavily underrepresented as claimants. In California, women actually have slightly higher rates of immigration when averaged over twenty years (55.8% compared with 44.2% for men); however, men make up 72.5% of claimants in the database, again indicating that women are underrepresented as claimants. In England, immigration and claimant rates are more similar. In Canada, there are 11% more claims by men than women, which is roughly consistent with men's overrepresentation in immigration entry data. A key inference to make from these figures is that to the extent that available data from the MWRD can be viewed as reliable and demonstrative of the broader missing data, women are underrepresented as workplace claimants outside of Canada. This could relate to lower levels of experienced violations and by association, lower levels of engagement in paid employment. However, an alternative and perhaps more likely possibility is that women more commonly experience types of violations for which legal action levels are very low, such as sexual violations, a point we return to below.

Differences between men and women do not appear to reflect differences in knowledge of workplace abuses. For instance, a large survey of temporary migration commissioned for the Migrant Worker Taskforce (2019, Appendix D, 27, 34–35) in Australia did not find significant differences between male and female temporary migrant workers in their knowledge of workplace laws, though women were almost twice as likely as men to say they needed information about workplace laws. Whether this related to a greater

60 PATTERNS OF EXPLOITATION

Table 2.3 Migrants bringing successful underpayment claims, as a percentage of the gender/jurisdiction MWRD population

Jurisdiction	Female	Male	Unknown
Australia	69 (43%)	120 (44%)	317 (69%)
Canada	20 (27%)	18 (14%)	74 (26%)
United Kingdom	10 (13%)	1 (2%)	0
California	18 (25%)	121 (63%)	63 (95%)
Total	117 (30%)	260 (37%)	454 (56%)

quantum of grievances, more serious grievances, or more interest in these issues is not reported.

Across the MWRD, male migrants raised more successful claims for underpayment, both in absolute terms (349 compared to 159 for female migrants) and as a proportion of the population (see Table 2.3). Fifty percent of male migrants raised a successful underpayment claim, compared to 40% of female migrants across the jurisdictions. This is in large part due to the gender discrepancies for these claims in Australia and California; the two jurisdictions that bring the highest number of underpayment claims. That said, Australia also has a large number of migrants whose gender was not recorded.

Differences in claim-making could also relate to gendered differences in the types of violations experienced by men and women and their reporting rates. For instance, forms of sexual violence are more often experienced by women, and there are low rates of reporting of sexual harassment in the workplace. One survey of 1,000 women, though not specifically migrant workers, found that only 34% reported sexual harassment, perhaps due to a sense that it was normalized. We might expect even lower rates for migrant workers, given their often precarious visa status and other forms of vulnerability. Evidence suggests that perpetrators target victims of sexual harassment based on their vulnerability and isolation, and visa status could be viewed through this lens (Uggen and McLaughlin 2004, 648).

Rates of sexual discrimination

We now look at gender-specific violations in the MWRD. First we consider issues of sex discrimination, which women in the broader population

Table 2.4 Successful sex discrimination claims, by jurisdiction and migrant sex

Jurisdiction	Female	Male	Unknown
Australia	1 (0.5%)	0	0
Canada	2 (2%)	0	0
United Kingdom	4 (5%)	0	0
California	0	0	0

Table 2.5 Migrants bringing successful sexual orientation discrimination claims, as a percentage of the gender/jurisdiction MWRD population

Jurisdiction	Female	Male	Unknown
Australia	0	0	0
Canada	0	0	0
United Kingdom	0	1 (1%)	0
California	1 (1%)	0	0

experience disproportionately. It is not only women in low-skilled caregiving positions who may perceive themselves as facing discrimination; sex discrimination has also been reported by migrant women in highly skilled occupations (Grigoleit-Richter 2017, 2745; Charpentier and Quéniart 2017). However, within the MWRD, it is clear that there were very few experiences of sex discrimination reported (Table 2.4). Similarly, across the entire database, there were only two instances of discrimination on the grounds of sexual orientation (Table 2.5).

Rates of sexual violence

Table 2.6 reveals that a small number of successful sexual violence cases were brought by women—and none by men. Sexual violence here covers sexual assault, sexual misconduct (includes sexual harassment), and sexual servitude. Across the MWRD, 6% of female migrants brought successful claims, although this did range from 10% of female migrants in Australia down to 1% in Canada. The percentages in the table show the number and proportion of claims that were successful for each violation. These claims had a high rate

Table 2.6 Migrants bringing successful sexual violence claims, as a percentage of the gender/jurisdiction MWRD population

Jurisdiction	Female	Male	Unknown
Australia	17 (10%)	0	0
Canada	1 (1%)	0	0
United Kingdom	4 (5%)	0	0
California	3 (4%)	0	0
Total	25 (6%)	0	0

Note: This combines sexual assault, sexual misconduct, and sexual servitude claims.

of success in all jurisdictions except Canada. Overall, 63% of sexual violence claims brought by female migrants were successful.

It is important to apply the broader scholarship on sexual violence and harassment in the workplace to contextualize the low incidence of sexual violence cases in the MWRD. As has been noted elsewhere, sexual violence is marked by low reporting rates, whether it occurs inside or outside the workplace (Graycar and Morgan 2005; UK Office for National Statistics 2015, cited in Ewins 2015). Further, underreporting sexual acts, such as harassment, may be viewed as a coping mechanism (Handy 2006, cited in Barmes 2015a, 17). There may also be cultural barriers to bringing sexual harassment claims, especially against members of one's own ethnic community (WEstJustice 2016, 215). Only 2%, or 41 of the 1,912 migrants in the MWRD, brought cases concerning sexual offenses and 25 were successful. This low number of claims may also reflect the higher rate of nondisclosure agreements and settlements in sexual offenses than in other areas of workplace violations (Prasad 2018).

Sexual harassment and violence come up as an issue in all jurisdictions. Visa conditionality may also play a role in the area of sexual violence. In Australia, international students are at a higher risk of sexual violence because their visas limit them to work no more than twenty hours a week. This limitation can be used either accurately or falsely by employers to threaten visa cancelation in the event that sexual favors are not performed (Kingsford Legal Centre et al. 2019, 41–43; Interview 6, Sharmilla Bargon, Redfern Legal Centre, Australia). Au pairs coming through the Working Holiday Maker program in Australia may also be at greater risk of sexual violence, given the live-in arrangement (Berg and Meagher 2018, 21), although there were no successful claims on the grounds of sexual violence brought by au pairs across the MWRD. In short, visa design—which we discuss further in Chapter 6, on regulation—can influence the nature and rate of sexual violence experienced by migrant workers, its reporting, and its punishment.

Rates of trafficking

The MWRD includes a small number of trafficking claims, 18 of which were successful. Female migrants raised trafficking claims more often than male migrants, both in absolute terms (18 compared to 10 claims) and proportionally (5% compared to 1%). However, the success rate for male migrants was higher than for female migrants: 100% of trafficking claims brought by men succeeded, compared to 44% for women. Table 2.7 shows that there is larger number of successful claims for male migrants *overall* (10, compared to 9 for women). Male claimants were generally exploited in the hospitality sector but also as housekeepers (*Attorney Generals' Reference (Nos. 37, 38 and 65 of 2010) (Shahnawaz Ali and Others)* (2010) EWCA Crim 2880; *R v. K(S)* [2011] ECWA Crim 1691). It is also relevant that a claim made by a female domestic worker *analogous* to the successful claim of a male domestic worker was rejected (*Zarkasi v. Anindita & Anor.* (2012) UKEAT 0400_11_1801).

Intersectionality

Intersectionality is complex but essentially turns on multiple types of disadvantage that can compound and heighten the risk of exploitation. In the context of migrant workers, it is important to consider nationality and race as

Table 2.7 Migrants bringing successful trafficking claims, as a percentage of the gender/jurisdiction MWRD population

Jurisdiction	Female	Male	Unknown
Australia	2 (1%)	0	0
California	6 (8%)	1 (1%)	0
Canada	1 (1%)	0	0
United Kingdom	0	9 (14%)	0

forms of discrimination that intersect with gender.[16] Critical race feminists argue that this is crucial. A.K. Wing (2003, 2), for example, suggests that it is necessary to consider those women of color who might otherwise "become, literally and figuratively, voiceless and invisible under so-called neutral law or solely race-based or gender-based analyses." By way of example, in Canada arrivals under the Foreign Domestic Worker program (predecessor to the Live-in Caregiver Program), since the 1950s, had come predominantly from the Caribbean states of Jamaica and Barbados (Arat-Koc 1997, 74; Fudge 2016a, 155; Stasiulis and Bakan 2005). It is also notable that the women in the *Udin* and *Nambalat* cases were also women of color. Mapping intersectionality is challenged by the missing gender and country of origin data. Nonetheless, in Table 2.8 we map the percentage of total claimants comprised of men and women for each region, and then compare that with representation in total migration flows across the six jurisdictions.[17] Therefore, this table collapses all data in the MWRD into one table. It is clear that some regions of the world are overrepresented as claimants compared to immigration flows, in particular Africa, Latin America, and Asia. Europe and Oceania are underrepresented. With regard to gender, the data are not weighted, but it is clear that outside of Europe, women comprise a far smaller percentage of claimants than men (between half and one-third), depending upon the region.

Table 2.8 does not capture all aspects of intersectionality, but it does hint at some possible reasons for women's lower representation as migrant worker claimants: the preponderance of women in lower income occupations and on transitory visas provides a further form of intersectionality—between gender, country of origin, and social class. It is clear from other research that lower income people are the least likely to pursue litigation in the first place, either from a sense of powerlessness or out of concern about the cost of such action (Genn 1999, 101, cited in Barmes 2015a, 31). The general class bias that exists within the legal system is amplified for women of color, with even lower wage earnings—particularly in the case of migrant women. One study on sexual harassment cases found that resources influenced successful outcomes (Rosenthal and Budjanovcanin 2011). Access to effective counsel could therefore appear to be important here in influencing these patterns.

Finally, domestic care work, in which women predominate, is also underorganized by trade unions. As such there is a potential intersection of gender, sector of work, union representation, and the experience of workplace violations. This could relate to the difficulty of organizing across private

Table 2.8 MWRD claimants, by gender and region of origin, compared with overall immigration flows

Region	Female*	Male*	Total*	Migration Flow**
Africa	2%	4%	6%	3%
North Africa	0%	1%	1%	0%
Sub-Saharan Africa	2%	3%	5%	1%
Americas	8%	22%	30%	27%
Latin America and the Caribbean (including Spanish imputed)	7%	20%	27%	22%
North America	1%	2%	3%	0%
Asia	19%	28%	47%	36%
Central Asia	0%	0%	0%	0%
West Asia	0%	1%	1%	0%
East Asia	9%	11%	20%	22%
South Asia	2%	10%	12%	2%
Southeast Asia	8%	6%	14%	4%
Europe	7%	8%	15%	27%
Eastern Europe	3%	2%	5%	0%
Western Europe	1%	1%	2%	9%
Northern Europe	2%	3%	5%	6%
Southern Europe	1%	2%	3%	12%
Oceania	0%	1%	1%	7%
Australia and New Zealand	0%	0%	0%	0%
Melanesia	0%	0%	0%	0%
Polynesia	0%	0%	0%	0%

*Percentages are of the number of migrants where the country of origin and gender are known (N = 850). All numerals rounded to full numbers, hence Total column is 99%.

**Percentage of total average intake for Australia, California, the United Kingdom, and Canada (Alberta, British Columbia, and Ontario). Stateless and unknown country of origin excluded. Subregion totals may not add up to region totals where migration flow data failed to specify a country or subregion.

households; there may also be limited contact between workers in disparate locations and subsequent distrust of trade unions (Anderson 2010b; Mantouvalou 2015, 347; Mundlak and Shamir 2014; Albin and Mantouvalou 2015). While attempts have been made by organizations like Kalayaan in the United Kingdom to organize domestic workers, such developments are not consistent across the jurisdictions. We return to the issue of how workplace location can affect sectoral-based discrimination, collective action, and enforcement in Chapters 5 and 7. Unions are also more often active in male-dominated sectors, which could reflect the higher claimant rates for men in some regions, in particularly Latin America, which sources high rates of farm laborers, especially in California.

Summary

The idea that care work should be valued as work is central to feminist understandings of social processes (Power 2004, 10). This chapter has used the case of *Udin v. Chamsi-Pasha* to explore the ways in which work is gendered for migrant workers. It has considered gendered differences in the types of violations that can arise and their success rates. While the *Udin* and associated cases demonstrated that migrant women received low remuneration for long hours of work, they lost on the "member of the family" statutory exclusions. Though some of their arguments were difficult to prove, they were ultimately discredited as witnesses. The more recent case of *Ajayi v. Abu & Abu* stands as an exception to the general observation that domestic workers often lose such cases when they seek higher payments and formal recognition of their employment status.

These qualitative cases demonstrate the granular detail embedded in the quantitative findings of the MWRD. Female migrants bring fewer underpayment cases than male migrants, though they have similar success rates: 74% of cases for both genders succeed. Further, successful findings for gender-specific discrimination and violence are very low, and in trafficking cases more male than female litigants win. The database both reveals the challenges of making out claims and exposes some of the outright obstacles to claim-making that migrant women experience.

The findings of this chapter generate a number of important policy findings regarding migration and gender. First, they demonstrate the limits of "member of the family exemptions" within labor law and the risks this can pose for the underpayment of domestic workers. It is recommended that such rules be removed, or more narrowly redrafted, as was intended in the initial first-reading speech of the national minimum wage reforms. Second, the chapter makes clear that women are underrepresented as claimants, even when factoring in their lower representation within immigration statistics. This reality highlights the need for legal counsel to pay particular attention to the obstacles that can pose limitations on access to justice, particularly around sexual violence claims. Finally, there is scope for further education of judges around the broad nature of trafficking and forced labor so that exploitative care work is more readily included within these categories. Arguably, strategic litigation in this area may assist in this regard.

3
Ethnicity, Race, Country of Origin, and the Challenges of Antidiscrimination Claims for Migrant Workers

Mary Hounga was fourteen years old when she was flown from Lagos, Nigeria, to the United Kingdom in January 2007. She was informed that she would receive an education and £50 each month in exchange for providing a small amount of child care. Ms. Hounga entered on a tourist visa rather than a work permit. Prior to her departure, she falsely told the Nigerian High Court that her employer was her grandmother, when in fact the employer, Adenike Allen, a British Nigerian woman, bore no relation to her (*Hounga v. Allen* (2012), EWCA Civ 609, para 34). Court documents suggested that Ms. Hounga was vulnerable and had little choice but to leave Nigeria. She overstayed her visa and worked for Mrs. Allen until 17 July 2008, when she was dismissed. The English Employment Tribunal found that her dismissal was racially motivated (*Hounga v. Allen & Ors.*, ET, 2201467/2009).

Ms. Hounga received no education in the United Kingdom, there was no payment, and the work extended well beyond basic, occasional child care. Mrs. Allen also threatened Ms. Hounga that she would be imprisoned if she was found by police, as she was in the United Kingdom illegally. The Tribunal accepted Ms. Hounga's claim that she was physically abused by Mrs. Allen, including being smacked and beaten and having water thrown at her. The full extent of the physical abuse and whether the acts also involved a knife attack, attempted asphyxiation, and death threats was disputed (*Allen v. Hounga*, UKEAT 0326/10, paras 19–21). Nonetheless, the conclusion was that she had been subjected to serious physical abuse. On 17 July 2008, Ms. Hounga was evicted from the house and told to "die" by Mrs. Allen. She slept in the Allens' garden and was discovered by a stranger, a Dr. Cummings, in a distressed state in a Sainsbury's shopping center carpark the next day. Dr. Cummings took her to a charity that helped her secure housing (*Hounga v. Allen & Ors.*, paras 13–15; *Allen v. Hounga*, UKEAT 0326/10, para 25). A separate case was successfully brought and afforded her immigration status on refugee grounds (Kathryn Cronin, barrister, Interview 3, UK).

Despite her win on immigration grounds, the question remained as to what, if any, redress Ms. Hounga could seek for what she claimed was racial discrimination during her employment and a racially motivated dismissal. She also made additional claims for unfair dismissal, breach of contract, unpaid wages and holiday pay, and use and mistreatment of a trafficked domestic worker. All were rejected by the court as the contract to which she was a party was illegal and Ms. Hounga was aware of that illegality (*Hounga v. Allen & Ors.*, at paras 4, 49). She was, however, awarded damages for unlawful racial discrimination under the Race Relations Act (UK), with the Tribunal at first instance finding that because she was "Nigerian or a resident in [the United Kingdom] illegally, [she] was vulnerable and could be treated less well because of her inferior status." A British national would not have been treated in this way, the Tribunal found (*Hounga v. Allen & Ors.*, at paras 51, 53).[1] However, the employer, Mrs. Allen, successfully appealed the damages for racial discrimination to the Court of Appeal, arguing that Ms. Hounga's engagement in illegal behavior vitiated her claims for damages in torts as well as the contractual claims that had already been dismissed (*Hounga v. Allen*, Court of Appeal (2012), at para 63). This was despite the finding that the entire illegal entry itself had been "masterminded" by the Allen family (*Hounga v. Allen* (2009), at para 42). The Court of Appeal's judgment was finally overturned in the Supreme Court in 2014. The latter court found that the illegality defense "should give way to the public policy to which its application is an affront" (*Hounga v. Allen* (2014) UKSC 47, para 52). In other words, the illegality of Ms. Hounga's entry was less germane than the public policy rationale of protecting against the trafficking of underage children into employment as illegal maids.[2] There was no parity in the illegal acts of employer and employee (paras 38–39).[3] Crucially, Anti-Slavery International intervened in the case, arguing that Ms. Hounga had in fact been trafficked from Nigeria by the Allen family and was not an au pair, as earlier judgments had claimed, but rather an exploited child. Direct reference was made to the Palermo Protocol to Prevent, Suppress and Punish Trafficking in Persons, Especially Women and Children (per Lord Wilson, at para 47). Indeed, it is possible that the severity of the facts encouraged the judges of the Supreme

Court to draw in public policy despite Ms. Hounga's knowing fabrication. As counsel to Ms. Hounga argued:

> Someone's beaten someone. There's effectively, someone who is more or less a child, and there's evidence of that. And you're complicit in some way, because you've promised them schooling, and so it felt wrong that because they were in some way complicit in what you did that they could then avoid liability. I think the idea that it encouraged wrongdoing by people just didn't apply here.... [I]t would encourage employers to be abusive: just bring children in and make them complicit. (Counsel to Hounga, Interview 1, UK)

Illegality of contract has been explored elsewhere in the migration setting, such as the "unclean hands" doctrine in United States (*Salas v. Sierra Chemical Co.* 2014, No S196568, para 432) or the fact that working without a valid visa is considered an offense in Australia (Migration Act (1958), s 235(1)). Furthermore, recent English case law suggests that the migrant worker must have "knowingly participated" in the illegality in order to block their claims. Where the illegality is the responsibility of the employer (e.g., they fraudulently sign false papers on the migrant's behalf), it will not block claims on public policy grounds (*Okedina v. Chikale* (2019) EWCA Civ 1393, at para 48).

For current purposes, the key issue is less the precise legal understanding of illegality of contract and more what the case reveals about the role of ethnicity in migrant worker violations. Ms. Hounga's case is a very sad one. Despite her positive outcome before the Supreme Court, she withstood seven years of litigation for a small amount of compensation to remedy serious racial discrimination against her that included physical, emotional, and verbal abuse (*Hounga v. Allen* (2014) UKSC 47, para 4). The case highlights the challenges migrants face in bringing claims for racial discrimination, challenges that are explored in detail below. This is true not only in England but also in the other jurisdictions featured in this book. The case also demonstrates similar challenges to domestic worker cases relating to gender that we considered in Chapter 2. Claims of discrimination based on race or country of origin, like those of gender discrimination, are often hard to make out forensically in closed, domestic households, where independent third-party witnesses are limited or nonexistent. That said, not all racial discrimination claims occur in private employment environments; they can occur in any number of workplaces, as the examples in this chapter illustrate.

Chapter overview

In this chapter, we focus on several key issues that the *Hounga* case reveals about ethnicity, country of origin, and race as bases for migrant workplace violations. It includes interviews with barristers who worked at various levels of the *Hounga* appeal, as well as reference to the secondary literature. First, we distinguish between the key concepts of *ethnicity, race, country of origin, immigrant (as opposed to national) status,* and *social class,* which are distinguishable both at law and in the social science scholarship, but also interact in important ways. Second, we consider the ways that antidiscrimination law, a feature in all the jurisdictions, can limit the capacity of immigrants to bring claims. A central limitation here is the notion of a *comparator,* which is central to indirect antidiscrimination cases but at the same time arguably ill-fitted to the migrant worker setting. Third, we look at other violations that can occur based on country of origin, including the heightened vulnerability of certain migrant workers from certain countries to workplace relations and the role played by language barriers. Fourth, coethnic exploitation, an emerging issue in all the jurisdictions, is also considered, alongside the fifth issue of intersectionality between race and other violations.

The chapter then moves on to a discussion of quantitative data drawn from the MWRD. We investigate how country of origin interacts with the frequency and nature of workplace violations: Are migrants from certain countries more likely to bring claims than others, even once their relative weighting within immigration flows is factored in? We compare claimant rates in the database against immigration statistics to analyze this point. These issues are outlined to provide insights on the key issues that the data present around ethnicity, race, and nationality as bases for migrant worker exploitation. While discrimination against minorities on these bases is a key area of concern in this chapter, it is not the only one. We also demonstrate how ethnic, racial, and national status correlate with other forms of discrimination.

Defining ethnicity: Nationality, ethnicity, race, immigrant status, country of origin, or social class?

"Ethnicity" is not a simple term to define. A classic distinction exists between those who view ethnicity as an immutable, primordial attribute based on shared beliefs about a common ancestry and culture (Geertz 1973; Glazer and Moynihan 1975, 1) and those who see it as a socially constructed opposition to another (Barth 1969; Horowitz 1985; Hylland Eriksen 1993). This latter approach emphasizes the subjective nature of "ethnicity" and proposes that all people exhibit some degree of "ethnic" status. As Thomas Ericksen Hylland (1993, 4) argues, ethnicity is centrally about "aspects of relationships between groups which consider themselves, and are regarded by others, as being culturally distinctive." Therefore, he continues, "majorities and dominant people are no less 'ethnic' than minorities."

This distinction between race, ethnicity, and immigration status has been debated at length in the immigration scholarship. While Michael Banton (1983, 106) argues that there is a strict distinction between race and ethnicity, with "race" referring to the categorization of people and "ethnicity" to group identities, the disrepute of early twentieth-century eugenic characterizations of fixed racial typologies clearly undermines such a clear distinction. Some scholars (e.g., Anderson 2017, 1532, 1534; Virdee and McGeever, 2018, 1808) have argued that discourse around immigration is actually more about race and class than migration status. On the other hand, discussions of migration and migrant status can be employed to either exacerbate or obfuscate racism. For instance, in *Hounga*, the Employment Tribunal accepted that Ms. Hounga's status as a Nigerian immigrant working in the United Kingdom allowed her to be "treated less well because of her inferior status having no rights to be in the country and no legal right to be employed" (2009, at para 51), thereby bringing the focus to the issue of visa status rather than her ethnicity or race.

Legal interpretations of the remit of ethnicity, race, and nationality have changed over time in antidiscrimination cases in the United Kingdom. While *Hounga*'s scope is potentially broad, the subsequent *Taiwo v. Olaigbe and another: Onu v. Akwiwu and another* ((2016) UKSC 31 (2016) all ER (D) 134) decision has limited racial discrimination claims to instances where nationality rather than immigrant status is the key source of discrimination. This is because immigration status is not a protected characteristic under the United Kingdom's Equality Act (2010). In *Taiwo*, speaking for the Supreme Court, Lady Hale (at para 26) noted that while immigration status is a function of nationality, the two are distinguishable, and the real issue at stake in *Taiwo* was the vulnerability caused through immigration status (at para 22). Barristers working in this area argued that the *Taiwo* decision has rendered it very difficult—if not impossible—for a migrant without a visa to bring a racial discrimination claim in the United Kingdom because the discrimination would at least ostensibly be on the basis of visa status rather than race or ethnicity, and visa status is not a protected statutory ground (Counsel, Interview 2, UK; Laura Prince, barrister, Interview 8, UK; Julian Milford, barrister, Interview 14, UK).

Similarly, race and ethnicity may point to differences that are more accurately socioeconomic in nature. While social class, ethnicity, and race are often related, they are distinguishable. As Hylland Ericksen (1993, 7) argues, "[b]oth class differences and ethnic differences can be pervasive features of societies, but they are not one and the same thing and must be distinguished from one another analytically." Many analysts of immigration, particularly of postwar immigration to Europe, have characterized the experiences that immigrants have faced primarily through a class rather than a racial lens (Castles and Kosack 1973; Miller 1981; Miles and Phizacklea 1977). Yet, this is not reflected legally within British equality law, where class alone is not a ground for bringing a discrimination claim. The exclusion of class and immigrant status grounds for discrimination claims may be intentional on the part of policymakers. As Lisa Rodgers (2017, 118) notes, "the aim of setting out the protected characteristics of the Equality Act was to limit freedom of contract in very narrow circumstances only, namely, to groups that had suffered historical labour market disadvantage."

Racial antidiscrimination law

Racial antidiscrimination law, in its different variants, holds limitations for protecting migrant workers against racial violations in the workplace. Under English law, while there is protection under general principles of legality and direct discrimination, this latter protection is only against protected classes; otherwise discrimination is "largely unregulated." As noted, immigrant or visa status is not one of these classes. A second problem with using antidiscrimination law as a means to address migrant worker violations is that the law looks at the individual rather than broader racialized structures that may prefigure the individual's situation and experiences of racism.

The adoption of race relations and antidiscrimination laws in England was located within a global trend that individualized race as an attribute (Robinson et al. 2017). In some ways, such an approach provided "containment" of more radical approaches to tackling racism through structural redress. Eric

Bleich (2003, 36) sees the development of the Race Relations Act (1968) in the United Kingdom as a response to riots against new commonwealth migrants in Nottingham in 1958. The legislation can be viewed as a weak antidote to some of the anti-immigration regulations that were introduced under the Conservative government in 1962 (Hansen 2000, 137–139, 225). Furthermore, more radical recommendations in the Street Inquiry that preceded the Race Relations Act would have allowed for systemic forms of change around racial inequality (e.g., affirmative action), but these were not accepted by the government (Monaghan 2013, 33, citing Street, Howe, and Bindman 1967, para 47.1).

Similarly in Australia, antidiscrimination law has been criticized both for being individualized and for reacting to events that have already occurred rather than preventing future discrimination (Allen 2009, 796, cited in WEstJustice 2016, 212). In Canada, s15(1) of the Canadian Charter of Rights and Freedoms at least theoretically contains the potential to address structural change, although whether this has been achieved in the migrant area is debatable (Denike, Faraday, and Stephenson 2006). Further, provincial human rights laws in Canada are quasi-constitutional and apply to private and public actions, including against private employers (who form the majority of respondents/defendants in the MWRD) (Howe and Johnson 2000, Chapters 1, 2).

In the United States, the Civil Rights Act's (1964) Title VII provides the basis for discrimination claims on the grounds of race, color, religion, sex, or national origin. Other federal legislation extends protection to disability, gender discrimination, sexual orientation, and pay equity, among other grounds. Title VII actions, which can result in damages to a discriminated employee, bind both public and private employers and can apply both directly and indirectly (Oppenheimer et al. 2020, 79). There is some capacity for group claims under the concept of "disparate impact" that compares one group against another; however, these claims can be difficult to win (113). Further, while the modern federal class action provision has been used to seek remedial structural reform, including on the grounds of race, this provision has with time been interpreted tightly through court jurisprudence with additional evidentiary barriers to identify a coherent class, and some limitations on the seeking of monetary relief, thereby limiting its breadth and application (Malveaux 2017).

The construction of a necessary "comparator" in indirect antidiscrimination law in most of the jurisdictions considered in this book demonstrates the limitation of racial discrimination claim-making for addressing widespread and structurally entrenched workplace experiences of racism by migrant workers. Originally developed in the United States as a response to civil rights law in the *Griggs v. Duke Power Co.* (1964) decision, the notion of a comparator was brought into the United Kingdom through the Sex Discrimination Act (1975) and the Race Discrimination Act (1965) (now consolidated under the Equality Act (2010)) by labor lawyers exposed to American race relations policies (Bleich 2003, 53; Monaghan 2013, 31, citing Street, Howe, and Bindman 1967, para 22.1). Within any indirect antidiscrimination case (e.g., where there is not immediate discrimination between two workers in the same workplace), it is necessary to construct a comparator and to demonstrate that they would not have been discriminated against in contrast to the aggrieved person. Thus, the protected attribute is the "relevant circumstance" leading to discrimination (Equality Act (2010 UK), s 23). However, this construction is often impossible to evince, as the condition which led to the discrimination is distinctive to a particular group. Karon Monaghan QC, a leading authority on British equality law, provided the following example from the migration setting:

> Let's say you brought a case by a Nigerian very, very poor woman brought over on a domestic visa and abused, and she said, "You treated me differently because I was Nigerian, my status was irregular, I was vulnerable. You wouldn't have treated a British domestic worker like that." The tribunals will find ... that, well, it wasn't to do with the fact that you were Nigerian, it was to do with the fact that your visa status was different, so they would have treated anybody whose visa status was equivalent to yours, in the same way because you were vulnerable. So, they will say that the visa status was a material circumstance, whereas that doesn't arise in the case of a British domestic worker, so they're not comparable. Which fundamentally exposes the difficulties in our antidiscrimination scheme. It relies on a constructed comparator which often completely obliviates the very basis for the disadvantageous circumstance. (Interview 10, London)

Comparator status can be hard to establish where sector-wide inequality is so embedded that a constructed comparator may be viewed as implausible by the court or tribunal. In the *Zarkasi* decision, involving a migrant domestic worker, highlights this point. The Tribunal (*Zarkasi v. Anindita & Anor.* (2012) UKEAT 0400_11_1801, at para 129), found that "a British national is not in our judgment an appropriate hypothetical comparative because such a person must share the same characteristics as the Claimant apart from nationality." Even when system-wide discrimination is evident through statistical data for instance, the individual focus of the comparator test may render this information unimportant (Monaghan 2007, 1.28l, 1.42).

Referring back to Ms. Hounga, we can ask whether it was the views of the employer, the underlying vulnerability of domestic care workers in the United Kingdom, her ethnicity, her gender, or even the broader societal treatment of undocumented migrants that permitted the racist attacks against her to occur. The answer is probably multifarious, but antidiscrimination law requires the compartmentalization of the issue into the experiences of an individual claimant. In Canada, there may be some basis to challenge structural disadvantage through provincial human rights codes, such as the Ontario Human Rights Code, which have provided an importance resource for migrants making claims against their employers and also allow for pecuniary damages in addition to other courses of action (Allen 2009, 85, 86). Further, there is a strong tradition of using class actions in Canada under its human rights codes. The B.C. Human Rights Tribunal has the power to issue collective orders such as the implementation of employment equity programs. While these human rights frameworks are not perfect—there are, for instance, still financial obstacles to bringing class actions in Canada—they do provide advantages over the other jurisdictions in the pursuit of race discrimination claims (Allen 2009, 85, 98; Bhuyan and Smith-Carrier 2010).

There is also the question of how much power different government agencies have to address systematic racialized abuse against migrant workers. The now defunct Commission for Racial Equality in the United Kingdom did have the capacity to audit systemic race relations (Bleich 2003, 100). The Equality and Human Rights Commission that replaced it in 2007 lacks that power and has not been that active in the migrant worker space—it was involved in only one of the 907 cases considered in the MWRD.[4] It could be that the Commission has been active in other areas of equality enforcement or through more active policy-driven means, but in the area of migrant worker litigation, there was very limited evidence of engagement.

Available survey evidence indicates that migrant workers of color are far more likely to experience racial discrimination than either Anglo-Celtic migrants or nonmigrants of color. While comprising a nonrepresentative sample, a survey of migrant clients by the WEstJustice Legal Centre (2016, 210) in Melbourne found that discrimination against migrants in the workplace was common. Bullying and discrimination arose in 7% of the Centre's caseload, and discrimination in 8% of cases. The only representative sample undertaken in Australia of temporary migrant workers found that 9% had experienced racism at work and 7% had been subjected to verbal, physical, and psychological abuse. Experiences of racism were elevated for migrants from Southern and Central Africa (Hall and Partners 2016, 113, 114). Catherine Barnard and Amy Ludlow's (2015, 10) study of migrant claims in the Employment Tribunal of England found that 10.7% of claims were related to racial discrimination. There was an overrepresentation of discrimination claims among migrants when compared with British nationals.

Other workplace violations against migrant workers

The discussion above should not suggest that racial discrimination is the only violation experienced by migrant workers. In jurisdictions such as Australia, where antidiscrimination law is more restricted than in the United Kingdom, other areas, such as underpayment, have been the focus of litigation. Unpaid wages were the single highest category of both alleged and substantiated violations in the MWRD for Australia for underpayment. At times, a migrant's country of origin has also informed judicial decision-making around the extent of awards in Australia. Several high-profile cases in the Federal Court of Australia have drawn attention to the linguistic vulnerability that can accompany migrant origin, contributing to wage theft. For instance, in *Ram v. D&D Indian Fine Food Pty. Ltd. & Anor.* ((2015) FCCA 389, at para 76), Justice Driver found:

> Mr Ram, a man who was functionally illiterate, spoke virtually no English and had no contacts in the Australian community, was brought from India to work 12 hours per day, seven days per week in the respondent's restaurant. Over 16 months, Mr Ram was not paid, beyond the small foreign exchange transfers sent to his wife and received no leave.

Mr. Ram's illiteracy was a relevant factor in the court's determination because it challenged some of the assertions made by the employer, such that Mr. Ram could operate a bank account set up in his name (paras 113–115). Flowing on from this, a common argument arising in the court cases and the policy literature is that country of origin can influence either language abilities, knowledge of the legal system, or acceptance of illegality, which predicates the vulnerability that migrant workers experience. For instance, Hall and Partner's (2016, 113) study in Australia found that migrants for whom English was not their first language were more likely to have experienced workplace violation than native English speakers (see also Fels Commission 2019, 13). A survey of employment violations experienced by over four thousand workers across several major U.S. cities, including Los Angeles, found that Latin American and Black migrants experienced aggravated levels of minimum wage violations compared to white workers and that those with lower English-speaking skills had higher rates of violations compared with those who spoke it well or very well (Bernhardt et al. 2009, 42). However, a perspective that focuses on language ability alone as the major source of racial discrimination overplays the role of individuals in preventing their own experiences of racism and underplays the role of government to effectively protect against this occurrence. It also overlooks nonlinguistic forms of racial discrimination.

Coethnic exploitation

Exploitation of ethnic minority migrants by citizens of the same ethnic background is a theme that emerges across the jurisdictions and in the scholarship. Coethnic exploitation arose in the *Hounga* case, where both claimant and respondent were Nigerian, or at least of African background.[5] This finds broader resonance in a study of Brazilian, Chinese, Turkish, Ukrainian, and Zimbabwean undocumented workers in the United Kingdom that demonstrated high levels of exploitation in coethnic workplaces, particularly for those with undocumented status. Lack of visa status may feed into a fear of expanding social networks beyond one's own ethnic group (Bloch 2013). This status in turn can limit vertical progression in workplaces and lead to ethnic and sectoral clustering—an issue we explore further in Chapter 4.

There is qualitative evidence from Australia that labor exploitation may be more common (and characterized by worse conditions) in "ethnic restaurants" where there is a "shared ethnicity" between employer and worker than where identity is not shared (Campbell, Boese, and Tham 2016, 293; see also Li 2017; Migrant Worker Taskforce 2019, 39). That said, separating coethnic status from broader questions of irregular visa status and its role in worsening labor violations is difficult.

A strong argument that comes through in the literature is that community or familial connection with the employer, as in the *Hounga* case, can have a chilling effect upon people's willingness to enforce their rights for fear of broader cultural or social ramifications (see also Fels Commission 2019,

37–38, citing Industrial Relations Victoria 2016, 308). Cultural proximity, or social capital created through shared ethnic status, can be used to establish a trust relationship that is then breached (van den Broek and Groutsis 2017; Bloch 2013, 925). Finally, coethnic exploitation can take on a structural quality. Li (2015, 922) argues that at times coethnic employers offer lower wages in anticipation of the inability of migrant workers to find work elsewhere, precisely because of race-based labor market discrimination. This approach has been called "opportunity hoarding," where "employers hoard opportunities within a particular sector, distributing them within a carefully maintained ethnic boundary, excluding outsiders from the resource." This behavior also creates the conditions for broader toleration of poorer conditions than would otherwise be acceptable (Velayutham 2013, 356–357).

The issue of coethnic exploitation arose frequently in the interviews with British barristers in racial discrimination claims. There was a perception among the barristers that, while it is possible legally for a person to bring such a claim against an employer of the same ethnic or racial background, it might be difficult to establish the comparator if employee and employer share ethnic status (e.g., Christopher Stone, Interview 13, UK; Karon Monaghan QC, Interview 10, UK). Yet, according to Kathryn Cronin, a barrister who works at the interface of immigration and antitrafficking, "they [employer and employee] nearly always come from the same home country" (Interview 3, UK).

The intersectional relationship of ethnicity to other bases of exploitation

As with gender-based discrimination, race-based discrimination can often have an intersectional quality and coexist with other forms of discrimination. This was apparent in the *Hounga* case. Ms. Hounga's status as a person of color, undocumented, a migrant, a child, and female all played out in her abusive treatment. At present in the United Kingdom, discrimination claims must be brought on singular grounds (Monaghan 2013, 5.10). When claims are brought for various forms of discrimination, they must be made separately and distinctively, meaning that the decision-maker cannot consider compounding and intersecting forms of discrimination (*Tilern de Bique v. Ministry of Defence* (2009), cited in Atrey 2009, 119).

In Canada, intersectional bases of discrimination have been more commonly recognized in jurisprudence, including by the Supreme Court

(Monaghan 2013, 5.33–5.34, citing *Corbire v. Canada* (1999) 2 SCR 203), by virtue of the Equality provision of the Charter of Rights and Freedoms, s15(1). However, the majority of cases in Canada are brought against private citizens not through the Charter but under the various provincial human rights codes, and here the robustness of intersectional analysis has been critiqued (e.g., Steinberg 2009). The Australian Human Rights Commission, which handles the vast bulk of first-instance discrimination claims in that country, can address multiple areas of discrimination within a singular complaint, but complainants must still choose the primary basis upon which they wish to make their complaint (Mansour 2012, 539). Title VII Anti-Discrimination claims under the Civil Rights Act (1964) in the United States often work on a single-discrimination basis (Crenshaw 1989), and intersectional jurisprudence remains underdeveloped (Mayeri 2015, 730).

A second form of intersectionality relates to ethnicity and visa status. As we will discuss further in Chapter 5 on undocumented migration and Chapter 6 on visa regulation, visas that tie a migrant to a single employer raise a greater risk of subsequent undocumented status than untied visas. Certain ethnicities and countries of origin are also more or less likely to be admitted on particular visas. This fact renders the relationship between visa design and ethnicity potentially racialized in its outcomes, even if this is not an intentional dimension of its design. This issue has been observed in detail in the now defunct overseas domestic worker visas in the United Kingdom, discussed in the prior chapter (Kalayaan 2013, 2). Such tied visas may exacerbate or heighten existing racialized treatment given the vulnerability they can create for migrants relying on their employer. A survey by the domestic care worker advocacy group Kalayaan demonstrated that those workers on tied visas experienced worse conditions than those with mobility across employers, and that migrants from certain countries are more likely than others to be represented on these visas (4).

Quantitative findings

Methodology

In this second part of the chapter, we present key data from the MWRD, using nationality of origin as a proxy for race and ethnicity. In many instances, nationality of the migrant was mentioned in the cases. In the event of dual nationality, this was also coded. There were cases where nationality was missing, but due to visa status, mentioned in the judgment, we were certain that the claimants were migrants and not nationals in the host society. In these instances, we increased the range of nationality data through imputation, using claimants' surnames. In some instances, we were unable to discern the exact country of origin via imputation. Instead, only a region of origin was imputed, especially in California, where migrants with Hispanic surnames could have arrived from across Latin America.[6] With these methodological issues addressed, we move to the empirical analysis.

Country of origin in the MWRD

A first issue to canvass is whether migrants from certain nationalities are under-or overrepresented in the MWRD compared with their representation in immigration flow statistics. Documentation of this issue is stymied by the fact that temporary and permanent immigration permit data are collected differently. While permanent admissions are collected on an annual basis, temporary admissions may reflect visa renewals or fresh allocations; there is therefore an associated risk of overcounting temporary admissions (Boucher and Gest 2018, 189). To address this issue, we used global immigration intake figures that combine temporary and permanent flows in each country (and province or state for Canada and California) and average them over the twenty-year period of data collection. As such, the percentages simplify variation across time and visa category (see further Methods Annex, annaboucher.org).

Australia had the largest number of cases and claimants of any of the countries in the MWRD. It is clear from Table 3.1 that Australia also presents a diverse array of countries of origin. Several key countries are overrepresented among claimants, compared with their representation within immigration flow data. These include Afghanistan, with only 0.05% of intake but 0.5% of claims; the Philippines, with 1.3% of migration intake but 5.4% of claims; and Thailand, with 1.3% of migrant intake but 3% of claims. Some countries, particularly European- and Anglo-Celtic-majority countries, are underrepresented in the data proportionate to immigration flows: France, Germany,

82 PATTERNS OF EXPLOITATION

Table 3.1 Percentage of claimants in MWRD by country of origin compared with immigration flow intake (Australia, 1996–2016)

Country of Origin	% of Claimants	% of Total Intake
Afghanistan	0.1%	0.05%
Bangladesh	0.1%	0.3%
Brazil	0.1%	0.7%
Bulgaria	0.2%	0.0%
Canada	0.1%	2.6%
Chile	0.1%	0.2%
Chinese ethnicity (including China, Hong Kong, Taiwan, Singapore)	13.5%	19.4%
Colombia	0.1%	0.2%
Denmark	0.4%	0.5%
Egypt	0.3%	0.1%
Fiji	0.4%	0.4%
Former Yugoslav Republic of Macedonia	0.1%	0.0%
France	0.4%	3.0%
Germany	0.3%	3.8%
India	4.3%	4.4%
Indonesia	0.9%	2.0%
Iran	0.4%	0.2%
Iraq	0.1%	0.1%
Ireland	0.5%	1.5%
Italy	0.3%	1.5%
Japan	11.7%	8.6%
Republic of Korea	13.2%	5.1%
Malaysia	2.4%	4.9%
Nepal	0.1%	0.4%
Netherlands	0.1%	0.0%
Pakistan	0.2%	0.3%
Peru	0.1%	0.1%
Philippines	5.4%	1.3%
Poland	0.1%	0.2%
Romania	0.1%	0.1%
South Africa	0.3%	1.0%
Sri Lanka	0.1%	0.5%
Switzerland	0.1%	0.8%
Thailand	3.0%	1.3%
Timor-Leste	0.3%	0.0%
Tonga	0.1%	0.1%

Table 3.1 Continued

Country of Origin	% of Claimants	% of Total Intake
United Kingdom	2.6%	14.4%
USA	0.7%	9.3%
Zimbabwe	0.1%	0.1%
Spanish (imputed)	0.5%	
Unknown, after imputation	38.7%	
Total	100.0%	89.7%

Sources: Temporary data: DHA 2006–2017; permanent data: DIMIA 2001–2004; DIAC 2002–2009; DHA 2013–2017.

Ireland, Italy, South Africa, the United Kingdom, and the USA. And several notable countries outside of this grouping are also underrepresented: China, Korea, and Malaysia. Finally, a number of countries have either negligible or equal representation as claimants and immigration intake: Fiji, India, Iraq, Tonga, and Romania.

Canada

Canadian data focuses on entry only into the three provinces considered in this book, as national intake varies regionally. In Canada, the Seasonal Agricultural Worker Programme has traditionally featured agreements with Mexico and the thirteen Commonwealth Caribbean countries, although other countries since have been included (Hennebry and Preibisch 2012, 20). As is clear from Table 3.2, migrants from Costa Rica and Mexico are heavily overrepresented as claimants when compared with their representation in overall immigration flows. Immigrants from Costa Rica comprise 0.1% of flows but 10.09% of migrants making claims, while for Mexico the figures are 4.1% and 16.4%. For countries like the United States, the relationship is inverted: U.S. citizens comprise 8.7% of entrants but only 3.3% of claimants. Similarly, British people are 4.3% of immigration flows but only 1.2% of claimants.

Table 3.2 Percentage of claimants in MWRD by country of origin compared with immigration flows (Alberta, Ontario, and British Columbia, 1996–2016)

Country of Origin	% of Claimants	% of Total Intake
Argentina	0.2%	0.2%
Bangladesh	0.2%	0.8%
Bosnia and Herzegovina	0.4%	0.1%
Caribbean	0.2%	n/a
Canada	0.2%	n/a
Chinese ethnicity (including China, Macau, Hong Kong, Taiwan, Singapore)	10.2%	14.2%
Colombia	1.4%	0.7%
Costa Rica	10.9%	0.1%
Croatia	0.2%	0.1%
Czech Republic	0.2%	0.2%
Dominican Republic	0.2%	0.1%
Ecuador	0.4%	0.1%
El Salvador	0.2%	0.2%
Ethiopia	0.8%	0.3%
Fiji	0.2%	0.1%
France	0.6%	0.9%
Germany	0.2%	1.4%
Ghana	0.4%	0.2%
Guatemala	0.2%	0.2%
Guyana	0.2%	0.3%
Haiti	0.2%	0.1%
Hungary	0.2%	0.2%
India	2.7%	11.1%
Iran	0.8%	1.8%
Ireland	0.2%	0.8%
Israel	0.4%	0.6%
Italy	0.8%	0.4%
Jamaica	1.6%	2.1%
Japan	0.4%	2.4%
Korea (imputed)	0.2%	4.5%
Lebanon	0.6%	0.4%
Mexico	16.4%	4.1%
Morocco	0.2%	0.1%
Nepal	0.2%	0.2%
Netherlands	0.2%	0.4%
Pakistan	0.2%	2.8%

Table 3.2 Continued

Country of Origin	% of Claimants	% of Total Intake
Philippines	12.3%	9.0%
Poland	0.8%	0.5%
Portugal	0.6%	0.3%
Romania	0.6%	0.6%
Russian Federation	0.8%	0.9%
Saint Lucia	0.4%	0.1%
Spain	0.2%	0.2%
Spanish (imputed)	1.4%	
Sri Lanka	0.2%	1.0%
Thailand	0.2%	0.3%
Trinidad and Tobago	0.2%	0.5%
Tunisia	0.2%	0.04%
Ukraine	0.4%	0.7%
United Kingdom	1.2%	4.3%
USA	3.3%	8.7%
Uzbekistan	0.4%	0.03%
Unknown, after imputation	23.6%	
Total	100.0%	79.3%

Sources: Temporary data: IRCC 1998–2016; permanent data: IRCC 1996–2016.

England

Table 3.3 shows that immigrants from certain countries to England are heavily overrepresented in the database. It should be noted here that these data are for the entire United Kingdom rather than just England. However, England represents the vast majority of the United Kingdom's immigrant intake (Kone 2018, 3).[7] A first notable trend is that new European Union migration (EU-8), while comprising the single largest component of migrant flows (27%), comprises proportionally less of the claimant figures (21.6%). Certain former British colonies are overrepresented as claimants: Malaysia, Nigeria, and Pakistan. India is underrepresented, proportionate to flow intake. Flow data are missing from some of the older EU countries over this period, reflective of free movement and previously poor data collection, but generally the claimant percentages are very low (e.g., Italy and France) and may overlap with the EU-8 data.

Table 3.3 Percentage of claimants in MWRD by country of origin compared with immigration flows (United Kingdom, 1996–2016)

Country of Origin	% of Claimants	% of Intake
Algeria	0.7%	0.6%
Angola	0.7%	0.2%
Belgium	0.7%	NA
Benin	0.7%	0.02%
Brazil	0.7%	0.3%
Canada	0.7%	0.7%
China	1.4%	10.9%
Democratic Republic of the Congo	0.7%	0.2%
Egypt	0.7%	1.6%
EU8*	21.6%	27.0%
France	0.7%	NA
Ghana	0.7%	1.3%
Grenada	0.7%	0.01%
India	11.1%	18.0%
Indonesia	2.8%	1.3%
Iran	0.7%	1.3%
Italy	1.4%	NA
Japan	0.7%	0.5%
Jordan	0.7%	0.6%
Malaysia	2.1%	0.4%
Mauritius	1.4%	0.2%
Morocco	0.7%	0.6%
Nepal	0.7%	0.6%
Nigeria	13.2%	5.5%
Pakistan	6.9%	5.1%
Palestine	0.7%	0.2%
Philippines	2.1%	2.3%
Russia	0.7%	7.3%
Saint Vincent and the Grenadines	0.7%	0.01%
Serbia	0.7%	0.6%
Sierra Leone	0.7%	0.2%
Somalia	0.7%	0.4%
Sri Lanka	0.7%	1.4%
Sudan	1.4%	0.3%

Table 3.3 Continued

Country of Origin	% of Claimants	% of Intake
Thailand	0.7%	2.4%
Uganda	0.7%	0.4%
Ukraine	0.7%	1.7%
United Republic of Tanzania	0.7%	0.3%
USA	0.7%	2.7%
Zimbabwe	1.4%	0.6%
Spanish (imputed)	1.4%	
Unknown, after imputation	12.5%	
Total	100.0%	97.7%

Source: Temporary immigration data: Home Office 1997–2016; Permanent data: Home Office 1996–2003, 2004–2016. EU8 data has been calculated using National Insurance Numbers (Salt 2018; U.K. Home Office 2020).

California

The number of migrant claimants in California varies depending upon country of origin, even once their presentation within immigration flow data is accounted for. Missing country data was dealt with through name imputation, meaning that countries were combined into a Hispanic grouping. Mexican migrants make up nearly a third of all immigrants to the United States and half of its eleven million undocumented population (Krogstad et al. 2017, cited in Gleeson and Xóhitl 2019, 10). Migrants with Spanish surnames account for 36.2% of immigration into California but 52.9% of claimants in the MWRD, as Table 3.4 shows. This is a significant overrepresentation. Other overrepresented countries of origin are Indonesia, Nigeria, Kenya, the Philippines,[8] and Turkey, but at a lower percentage than Hispanic migrants from the Americas. In contrast, some countries are underrepresented as claimants. These are mainly European nations, like France, Germany, Italy, and the United Kingdom, but not exclusively: the Chinese surname grouping, Australia, Japan, New Zealand, and Korea, are also underrepresented. Finally, there is a small grouping of nations where claim and intake representation is almost identical, including India and Russia.

Table 3.4 Percentage of claimants in MWRD by country of origin compared with immigration flows (California, 1996–2016)

Country of Origin	% of MWRD Claimants	% of Total Intake
Australia	0.3%	4.1%
Chinese ethnicity (including China, Macau, Hong Kong, Singapore, and Taiwan)	3.3%	7.3%
France	0.3%	4.2%
Germany	0.3%	4.4%
India	2.4%	2.4%
Indonesia	3.9%	0.5%
Italy	0.3%	1.9%
Japan	0.6%	7.6%
Kenya	0.3%	0.03%
Naturalized U.S. citizen "Arab heritage"	0.3%	NA
New Zealand	0.3%	1.2%
Nigeria	0.3%	0.1%
Philippines	2.7%	1.6%
Poland	0.3%	0.2%
Republic of Korea	0.9%	3.6%
Russian Federation	0.6%	0.5%
Trinidad and Tobago	0.3%	0.05%
Turkey	0.9%	0.3%
Ukraine	0.3%	0.1%
United Kingdom	0.3%	7.3%
Unknown, after imputation	28.1%	n/a
Spanish	52.9%	36.2%
Total	100.0%	84%

Sources for immigration flow data: Temporary: DHS 2020; permanent DHS 1997–2017. For definition of the "Spanish" grouping, please see Methods Annex.

Percentage of claims around racial discrimination

As noted earlier in this chapter, racial discrimination is one of several violations that can be experienced by migrant workers—and a particularly important one. Here we consider at the event level the number of recorded racial discrimination events in each country (how many instances of racial discrimination are claimed) and the number of successful claims by migrants by jurisdiction on racial discrimination grounds. The first thing to note is that racial claims comprise varying percentages of overall legal claims in each of the jurisdictions; as noted in Chapter 1, Australia has a small number of events (5 of 949 claims by migrants);[9] England has more (58 of 144 claims), as do Canada (89 of 488 claims) and California (68 of 331 claims). There are also differences in the success rates across the four jurisdictions on racial discrimination. Australia and England have similar success rates at 20% and 17%, respectively, although for Australia the low total number of cases is itself startling and reflects the limited nature of its antidiscrimination law (Rees, Rice, and Dominique 2018, 63; Gaze 2000; Gaze and Smith 2017, 176–177). In contrast, the success rate in Canada was lower, 2.4% (2 of 89 cases), but it had more cases overall; again, the success rate in California was higher than in Canada, 16% (11 of 68 cases), but it had fewer cases. These differences could represent the differences in the ease of bringing antidiscrimination claims across the various jurisdictions, a theme that we return to in the conclusion.

There are also differences in the migrants most likely to bring racial discrimination claims across the four jurisdictions. These data, presented in Tables 3.5 through 3.8, provide aggregate figures and are not weighted against the representation of migrants within overall immigration flow data, in part as the figures are slight. In Australia, the overall number of cases for racial discrimination is so small that the higher representation of Bulgarian, Iraqi, and Filipino migrants is not statistically meaningful. In Canada, rates of claims brought by Costa Rican workers are high, reflecting

Table 3.5 Events of racial discrimination in Australia (total and successful) as number

Country of Origin of Migrant	N	Success
Bulgaria	2	1
Iraq	1	0
Philippines	2	0
Total	5	1
Success Rate		20%

Table 3.6 Events of racial discrimination in Canada (total and successful) as number

Country of Origin of Migrant	N	Success
China	1	0
Colombia	5	0
Costa Rica	53	0
Ecuador	2	0
El Salvador	1	0
France	1	0
India	1	0
Ireland	1	0
Israel	1	0
Mexico	4	0
Morocco	1	0
NA	4	0
Nepal	1	0
Netherlands	1	0
Philippines	7	1
Saint Lucia	1	1
Trinidad and Tobago	1	0
Tunisia	1	0
Ukraine	1	0
USA	1	0
Unknown, not specified in judgment	4	0
Total	89	2
Success Rate		2.4%

their large proportion—almost one-third—of all temporary workers in Canada (see CIC 2020), though only one of these claims was successful. In England, there is no single country of origin that stands out significantly in terms of racial discrimination claims. Both more recent EU countries, the Czech Republic and Poland, and New Commonwealth countries, India and Zimbabwe, feature. In California, there were high rates of migrants with Spanish surnames bringing racial discrimination claims. Unsurprisingly,

Table 3.7 Events of racial discrimination in the United Kingdom (total and successful) as number

Country of Origin of Migrant	N	Success
Algeria	1	0
Angola	1	0
Canada	1	0
China	1	0
Croatia	1	0
Czech Republic	3	0
Democratic Republic of the Congo	1	0
France	1	0
Ghana	1	0
Hungary	1	0
India	4	3
Indonesia	3	0
Iran	1	0
Italy	1	0
Jordan	1	0
Latvia	1	0
Lithuania	1	0
Mauritius	1	1
Nigeria	14	2
Pakistan	1	1
Philippines	2	1
Poland	8	0
Saint Vincent and the Grenadines	1	1
Sudan/Ethiopia	1	0
Zimbabwe	2	0
Unknown, not specified in judgement	4	1
Total	58	10
Success Rate		17%

given the racial discrimination experienced by Hispanic workers in California (Guerin-Gonzales 1994; Pitti 2002; Sabo et al. 2014), they comprise the majority of claimants, though they are successful only 29% of the time (3 of 17 cases).[10]

92 PATTERNS OF EXPLOITATION

Table 3.8 Events of racial discrimination in California (total and successful) as number

Country of Origin of Migrant/Region	N	Success
Australia	1	0
China	3	0
Hong Kong	1	1
India	1	0
Italy	1	1
Japan	1	0
Mexico	3	2
Naturalized U.S. citizen of "Arab heritage"	1	0
Nigeria	1	0
Republic of Korea	1	1
United Kingdom	1	0
Spanish (imputed)	15	3
Unidentifiable Chinese (imputed)	2	0
Unknown nationality, after imputation	11	0
Unknown nationality, not identified in judgment	27	3
Total	69	11
Success Rate		16%

Percentage of intersecting discrimination claims

We are also interested in the relationship between racial and other discrimination claims. Concurrent actions may be one way to address intersectional disadvantage in workplaces legally. Table 3.9 shows that, in almost all cases

Table 3.9 Events with the same outcomes out of cases bringing concurrent discrimination claims, where racial discrimination and another discrimination claim were brought*

Discrimination Claim Other Than Race	Australia	Canada	United Kingdom	California	Overall
Age	0	2/2	0/2	0	2/4
Caregiver	0	2/2	0	0	2/2
Disability	0	2/2	2/2	2/2	6/6
Sex/Gender	0	3/3	6/6	0	9/9
Pregnancy	0	0	0	0	0
Religion	0	1/1	3/3	2/2	6/6
Sexual orientation	0	0	0	0	0
Union	2/2	30/30	0	0	32/32

* Australia includes both federal and state antidiscrimination cases, across time.

where a racial discrimination claim was brought concurrently with another discrimination claim, the findings were the same for both actions. Success on one discrimination ground often correlates with success on another. The only exceptions are two U.K. cases, where concurrent age and racial discrimination claims resulted in different findings.

Coethnic exploitation

Coethnic exploitation is identified as a potential ground for exploitation in the migration scholarship. We therefore attempted to quantify the ethnic background of all employers after having removed any corporate employers, without human surnames, from the data set.[11] Looking at the percentage of cases where this was possible to measure, Table 3.10 shows that coethnic cases make up a small percentage. In California, coethnic employers comprise around 47% (54/116) of total human employers, but only 15% (62/414) in Australia, 5% (2/46) in England, and 4% (3/63) in Canada. The largest single coethnic grouping in California is Hispanic, which could relate to high numbers of Hispanic owners of horticultural businesses there (U.S. Department of Agriculture 2020). Therefore, while there is some evidence that people of the same national background exploit each other, based on available employer and employee data, 86.4% of cases across the database do not involve coethnicity, challenging generalizing statements made in the qualitative scholarship and policy documents.

Table 3.10 Frequency of coethnic exploitation across the MWRD (N of coethnic exploitation)

Jurisdiction	China*	India**	Spanish***	Japan	Thailand	Korea	Total	Total Human Employers
Australia	48	2	0	0	11	1	62	414
Canada	1	2	0	1	0	0	3	63
England	0	2	0	0	0	0	2	46
California	1	0	52	0	0	2	54	116
Overall	20	12	52	1	11	2	86	632

*Includes migrants where the country of origin is China or Taiwan.
**Includes migrants where the country of origin is India or Pakistan.
***Includes migrants from any Spanish-speaking country.

Summary

This chapter outlined the racialized treatment of migrant workers, through the *Hounga* case and others, and through broad quantitative data drawn from the MWRD. The results are more nuanced than might be anticipated. While the data from 907 court cases do demonstrate patterns of overrepresentation of migrants from some countries, with the exception of California, where Spanish-speaking migrants are heavily overrepresented, and Canada, where Mexican migrants are somewhat overrepresented, the percentages are in single rather than double digits. Perhaps more noticeable is the underrepresentation, across all jurisdictions, of Anglo-Celtic and European migrants. The emerging theme is therefore more about comparative white privilege in workplace treatment than violations against key ethnic groups (with the exception of Spanish-speaking migrants in California and Mexican migrants in Canada). Further, the argument that most workplace exploitation is coethnic in nature is simply not supported by the data. Averaged across the database, only 13.6% of cases involve coethnic exploitation; the vast bulk of natural person employers who violate their migrant workers' rights are either of different nationalities or they are corporations to which no single nationality or ethnicity can be easily attributed, at least not based on the evidence available in the judgment and tribunal decisions.

There are several important policy implications that flow from the findings in this chapter. First, the data make clear that a focus in the scholarship on coethnic exploitation can overlook the broader bases of race-based discrimination that migrant workers face. While some exploitative employers are coethnics with their workers, outside of California this is the minority of employers. As such, a broader analysis that considers the ways in which racial discrimination reflects existing racial inequality in the workplace is needed. Second, refusal of courts to examine the intersection of race- and visa-based discrimination stymies claim-making in this area. This relates in part to restrictive statutory regimes for bringing antidiscrimination-based claims, which do not sufficiently acknowledge visa status as a potential source of vulnerability and discrimination. Statutory reform in this area is recommended.

Returning to Ms. Hounga, while her claims were successful, after the *Taiwo* decision they would likely now be rejected. As noted, a racial discrimination claim by a migrant worker is, since *Taiwo*, rendered effectively impossible in the United Kingdom as visa status and race are generally comingled. In Chapters 4 through 8, we move away from migrant attributes and focus upon the structural and regulatory conditions that frame migrants' workplace experiences. Chapter 4 turns to economic sectors and begins with a case study from a construction site in downtown Toronto.

4

A Fatal Fall

Workplace Death, Injury, and Employment Sector

On Christmas eve 2009, workers at a Toronto construction site were rushing to complete already overdue work. Balconies on the building at Kipling Avenue were supposed to have been restored by 30 November, and Metron Construction Company was offered a C$50,000 bonus if the work was completed before Christmas. Safety steps were skipped and a swing stage supporting six workers on the fourteenth floor collapsed. Foreman Fayzullo Fazilov, Aleskey Blumberg, Vladimir Korostin, and Shohruh Tojiddinov fell to their deaths. Dilshod Marupov survived but was rendered disabled. The sixth worker, who alone wore a lifeline, survived. They were all migrants on visas from the former USSR; Blumberg was a refugee claimant, and another was on an expired student visa, without a work permit.

At the original sentencing, the director of Metron, Joel Swartz, pleaded guilty to four counts under the Ontario Health and Safety Act and was fined C$200,000, with an additional per victim surcharge of C$30,000 (*R v. Metron Construction Company* 2012). The Crown had sought a harsher penalty of C$1 million, but this was rejected at first instance (*R v. Metron Construction Corp.* (2012) 1 CCEL (4th) 266, para 44). It then appealed on the basis that the trial judge had erroneously applied lesser health and safety penalties to a more serious criminal case. The Ontario Court of Appeal agreed and imposed the higher penalty and, applying sections of the Criminal Code, stated that there had been a "wanton and reckless disregard for the lives or safety of others" (*R v. Metron* 2012, paras 37, 50, 80–81).[1] It found that numerous oversights had allowed the tragedy to occur. There had been pressure to complete the job. There had been insufficient safety training, and it was unclear whether all workers could understand English sufficiently to have adequately completed the training or to appreciate the appropriate use of the swing stage. As noted, six men were standing on the swing stage when

Patterns of Exploitation. Anna K. Boucher, Oxford University Press. © Oxford University Press 2023.
DOI: 10.1093/oso/9780197599112.003.0005

it collapsed, though the regulations stipulated only two, and only one was secured with a lifeline (para 11). No precautions had been taken to ensure the swing stage was safe, and it was later found that the swing stage itself was poorly constructed; a separate action was brought against the swing stage company by the surviving worker (*Marupov v. Metron Construction* (2014) ONSC 3525; *R v. Kazenelson* (2015), para 61). Forensic examination concluded that the faulty design of the swing stage and the absence of sufficient lifelines were crucial in causing the deaths (*R v. Metron*, para 14). Toxicology showed that three workers had consumed marijuana before they fell, meaning their brain function was impaired during the accident, and Fazilov, the acting manager, had not undertaken necessary drug testing (para 13). This was relevant to the issue of Metron's allowing employees under the influence of drugs to work on the project (para 15).

Alongside these hearings, there was a statutory push for Metron's managers to be individually tried for the deaths. In 2004, the Canadian federal government introduced corporate criminal liability laws, creating criminal offenses—including manslaughter offenses up to full life imprisonment—for senior management who fail to protect workers from death. They are known as the "Westray Laws," after the Westray mine explosion in Nova Scotia in 1992, where twenty-six miners were killed. Drawing parallels with the Metron case, civil society, the police, and the trade union movement argued that the Westray Laws applied to this tragedy. Verne Edwards from the Ontario Federation of Labour described the momentum leading up to criminal charges being pursued by the Crown:

> We had a vigil for the workers killed on the job and we had something down at city hall. We had the one survivor from the tragedy, the young guy [Marupov], he was there in a wheelchair and was recognized, and that was the incident where we launched our "Kill a Worker, Go to Jail" campaign. Because we had been trying to push for investigations by the police around the criminal code amendments . . . since 2004 and nothing had really happened. So that began our campaign, which we continue today, reaching out to police. (Interview, Toronto, 2 April 2019)

The union movement reached out to the police with a package of material about the Westray Laws regarding the Metron tragedy. Following concurrent efforts by the Toronto Police Service to engage with the Crown prosecutors regarding possible criminal action, the Crown decided to pursue criminal action for negligence leading to manslaughter. Metron's manager, Vadim

Kazenelson, was prosecuted for a 3.5-year prison sentence, as he was the immediate superior of the deceased (*R v. Kazenelson* (2015), ONSC 3639, para 11). It was submitted by the Crown prosecutors, and accepted by the presiding judge, that Kazenelson should have ensured that the swing stage was safe, and he had failed to by not finding additional lifelines and by not preventing excess workers from boarding it. His failings led directly to the workers' deaths (paras 16, 21, 23, 124).[2] The workers' contributory negligence through boarding the faulty swing stage was not found to be decisive (para 147). The case was appealed by Kazenelson but was rejected and the prison sentence upheld (*R v. Kazenelson* (2018) ONCA 77). Furthermore, given the seriousness of the incident and the affected sector, a coronial inquest was ordered and was underway in 2022, leading to further safety recommendations (*Canadian Press* 2022).

The *Metron Construction* case is important for a number of reasons. It was the first time that the Westray Laws had led to the imprisonment of a manager in Canada. The case also raises important questions about corporate responsibility for workplace deaths and serious injury, as well as how far up the corporate chain that responsibility should be pinned. The case also encourages consideration of less examined issues about the rights of migrant workers in high-risk occupations. First, there are economic sector-specific attributes:[3] the case occurred in the construction sector, which had been identified as an at-risk sector prior to the accident. It also raises broader issues over whether the sector or particular industry in which migrant workers are employed affects the likely violations workers will experience, particularly bodily injury leading to disability or death. Construction work is emblematic of the so-called 3-D jobs (dangerous, dirty, and degrading) in which migrant workers may be overrepresented (Caviedes 2010; Piore 1979). Second, evidence from the *Metron* litigation revealed insufficient levels of safety training of the workers, possibly doctored training completion certificates, and, as noted, low knowledge of English among workers to adequately complete the training (Sylvia Boyce, United Steelworkers Union, Interview, Toronto, 26 March 2019). This is a common theme in migrant worker cases that involve injury. Third, the vulnerable visa status of the workers increased their precariousness and meant that they were less likely to complain about dangerous conditions at the site. The workers were also remitting much of their wage to family members in Uzbekistan and Ukraine, further increasing their reliance on the dangerous work. These issues are explored in detail below.

Note that, though the primary focus in this chapter is on economic sector as a source of workplace safety and injury, there are important points of connection with other parts of this book. For instance, as considered in the Chapters 2 and 6 case studies, severe overwork may be primarily an underpayment issue, but it can also intersect with work, health, and safety issues, as such work can lead to mental health problems or physical illness. This became apparent in an inquiry into mining work in Australia, where it was revealed that some Filipino migrant workers worked as many as fifty-two days straight and had experienced resultant psychological damage (Hagemann 2014). The vulnerability of the sector of employment can also intersect with class and other bases of discrimination, including ethnicity and gender. For instance, many of the migrant workers in Canada employed in the agricultural sector are also visible minorities, creating layers of vulnerability (Vosko, Tucker, and Casey 2019, 235). Sector and country of origin or ethnicity may intersect with visa status to reinforce vulnerability to workplace injury. For instance, migrant workers on the Seasonal Agricultural Worker Programme (SAWP) in Canada employed in the high-risk horticultural and agricultural sectors are disadvantaged through the short-term, circular nature of the visa, an issue explored further in Chapter 7 on trade unions and SAWP workers. All of these factors combine to worsen migrants' risk of health and safety violations (Preibisch and Otero 2014). The timing of visa issuance can also compound these factors: those who are still paying off immigration costs may be more likely to be burdened with unsafe work conditions as they are not in a position to decline employment (Kosny et al. 2012; Yanar, Kosny, and Smith 2018).

In the following section, we outline some of the key themes related to economic sector and workplace safety as they affect migrants. In particular, we consider two key industries where injury is prone to occur: construction and agriculture. We then discuss some of the common themes of dangerous sectors, including the physical isolation of migrants, business structures and independent contracting, piecework, inadequacy of safety training, and the depth or dearth of government policy. We also consider the regulatory setting in each of the labor law jurisdictions (as work, health, and safety is set provincially, not federally, in Canada). Finally, we address the issue of lapsed or temporary visa status and how this can interact to reinforce sectorial vulnerability.

In the second part of the chapter, we turn to the quantitative data from the MWRD, as well as immigration flow data from public agencies to analyze how occupational sector can inform the frequency of violations and the success rates across different types of physical workplace injuries, sexual assault, and workplace death. Given the range of issues considered, we focus on injury (physical, sexual, and resultant in death) rather than the broader array of violations considered more commonly across the database. Further, we analyze how the reported injuries sustained by migrant workers compare with the rest of the population in each of the countries under examination.

Sector and nature of work

It is well established that particular economic sectors are more or less at risk of injury, safety concerns, and other workplace violations. The risk in some sectors over others can relate to the business structures common in these industries and also to the fiscal pressure that business owners face, which increases the risk that costs shift from the company to workers (Rosewarne 2019; Reilly et al. 2018, 4). Inadequate sector-specific regulation could also be a factor.[4] Government policy can affect the relative safety of sectors, in particular the prevalence of safety inspections and the way that visa policy interacts with precarious sector practices to increase the vulnerability of migrant workers. And the work in some sectors is simply more dangerous. As such, the economic sector of employment is a useful unit for analyzing violations and for understanding the relative precariousness of workers (Weil 2020). Focusing on sector as a unit of analysis resonates with some areas of the industrial relations scholarship that emphasize that sector rather than country may more powerfully predict many employment outcomes (Bechter, Brandl, and Meardi 2012).

In this chapter, the construction and agriculture sectors are considered in detail, though this analysis is by no means exhaustive and excludes several important areas that are often identified as high risk, in particular beauty (e.g., nail salons), cleaning (e.g., car washes), hospitality, meat processing, and care work (Underhill et al. 2019; WEstJustice 2016, 77; McGregor 2007). Where possible, we consider the full array of jurisdictions, while focusing in detail on the *Metron* case and Ontario. As work, health, and safety laws differ at the state and provincial level in Australia, Canada, and the United States, we consider the sub-national level in those countries.

Construction

Construction is an at-risk sector for workplace injury. The financial structures underpinning its operation and the inherently dangerous nature of the work increase the risks to migrant workers. Metron Construction was under pressure from another company to complete its work the day the accident occurred; the owners of the building at Kipling Avenue, Fishman Holdings, wanted to refinance the property before Christmas (*R v. Kazenelson* (2015), para 48). Safety concerns were raised about the Metron Construction project prior to the tragedy, including about the swing stage, by Korostin, who was among the dead (Edwards 2010). Time pressure and poor safety standards were endemic to this case. Construction is viewed as unsafe and potentially exploitative in other jurisdictions as well. For instance, the reduction in union membership in construction in Australia has seen a concomitant reduction in labor standards there (Bray and Underhill 2009, 383–384; see also WEstJustice 2016, 77). In the United Kingdom, construction is identified as a sector where migrant workers are at risk, with the deaths of migrant workers occurring at twice that of domestic workers (Meardi, Martín, and Lozano Riera 2012; Tutt et al. 2013, 516), while in California, the sectors with the highest incidence of use of trafficked workers are construction and janitorial services; workers in these sectors also have high rates of incidence of leukemia and lung cancer (Zhang et al. 2014).

Agriculture

Agriculture is identified as another sector with high workplace risk across all of the jurisdictions, coupled with high levels of employment of migrant workers. Writing of the Canadian case, but applicable more broadly, Preibisch and Otero (2014) consider agriculture dangerous in part due to work characteristics. These include "piece rates, no overtime or contracts, low rates of unionization and illegality to unionize," the location of the work (including the fact that work may be split across various sites), "risks of exposure to agrochemicals, plants, soil, insects, sun and climatic extremes," as well as "hazards posed by machines, vehicles and confined spaces" (180). The seasonal nature of agricultural work can also render it short term and unpredictable with respect to workplace conditions (Underhill and Rimmer 2016, 615).

Agriculture has been identified as a sector with high rates of exploitation in Australia (Underhill et al. 2019; Reilly et al. 2018, 22; Krivokapic-Skoko and Collins 2016; Underhill and Rimmer 2016). There have even been some workplace deaths in this sector among Pacific Island workers (Field and Marsh 2017). A study of employers in the horticulture sector in Australia found that 39% were noncompliant with regard to labor standards (Reilly and Howe 2019, 95). The Howells Report into employer sanctions in Australia found that undocumented migrant workers in the sector were "underpaid, misled about what they were doing, undernourished, beaten and threatened" (Howells 2010, 56).

In California, it is well-established that migrant farm workers are exposed to risk of heat stress, chronic kidney disease, and death, as well as being diagnosed with hypertension at a far higher rate than the general population (Horton 2016). Irma Morales Waugh (2010) found that 80% of the female migrant farm workers she surveyed in California had experienced sexual harassment. Female workers in the sector are also vulnerable to sexual assault and underpayment and due to ineligibility for workers' compensation and reliance on the employer to supply housing (Human Rights Watch 2012, 18). Different rules around unionization of agricultural workers under the Agricultural Labor Relations Act (1975), when compared with other workers in California, emphasizes the historical vulnerability of these workers to various workplace infringements, including around safety (Martin 1983).

Events such as the Morecambe Bay cockling disaster in the United Kingdom, in which twenty-three Chinese migrant workers were killed in 2004, are regarded as the impetus for the establishment of the Gangmasters Licensing Authority, designed to prevent exploitation of agricultural labor (Consterdine and Samuk 2018, 1016). It is clear that sectors heavily employing migrants in the United Kingdom are also more at risk of injury. For instance, agriculture, a migrant-heavy sector, employs 1.5% of the working population in the United Kingdom but produces between 15% and 20% of fatalities (U.K. Health and Safety Executive [HSE] 2012). This overrepresentation of migrants within the agricultural sector could also relate to employer control over labor, housing, and wages in the case of migrant agricultural workers (Scott 2015).

Common themes of dangerous sectors

In this section we consider some of the key shared attributes of dangerous sectors, including the isolation of worksites, business structures in these sectors, a tendency toward piecework,[5] and, frequently, inadequate safety training.

Isolation

Sector location can heighten risk through a variety of mechanisms. An isolated location can minimize contact with trade unions and other worker advocates. In the mining sector in Alberta, physical isolation by virtue of an on-site living requirement creates distance and segregation from local communities, and in turn undermines worker solidarity (Foster and Taylor 2013, 174). Movements of workers across locations can also increase the risk of accidents en route, as has been the case in Canada with various bus injuries involving overloaded vehicles (Lynch 2015; Preibisch and Otero 2014, 180). Isolation can also reduce access to necessary healthcare in the event of an accident (Basok, Hall, and Rivas 2014; Preibisch and Otero 2014, 191). Regional location has been found to play a role in increasing the exploitation of migrant agricultural workers in Australia (Fels 2019, 36). According to one representative survey of migrant workers, working over fifty hours per week was most common in Australia in agriculture, forestry, and fishing, followed by mining; sectors that are generally geographically isolated (Hall and Partners 2016, 108).

Physical isolation presents different issues for male than female migrant workers. Isolation is an issue for domestic workers given they work in the private sphere, and even in agency-based care work across a variety of workplaces. Domestic work is also a physically high-risk sector, especially for forms of sexual violence and harassment. This relates in part to the provision of accommodation by the employer that can limit the connection of workers to friends, family, and, in some cases, collective organizing (Anderson 2018). Sexualized injury can be conceived as a distinctive form of injury. Speaking of farm work and sexual assault and harassment in Australia, Tim Nelthorpe from the National Union of Workers Australia argued that such violence is:

> a really big issues in farms, unfortunately, and particularly among undocumented workers because it's very hard for them [female migrants] to get recourse when they do suffer assault or even just harassment.... The services are not great in the Australian community and the police force response is not always great in regional areas.

He added that the nature of live-in accommodation increased the likelihood of female farm workers experiencing sexual violence:

> [A] lot of workers live in accommodation either provided by the farmer or provided by a contractor, and their employment is dependent on living in that house. So once you're in that environment, and your boss can just walk in and out of your house whenever they want, and you don't have a visa, it just leads to really precarious and unsafe conditions for the workers. (Interview 8, October 2019)

Business structure and independent contracting

The presence of labor hire companies that employ staff on a contract basis and hire them out to third parties can increase exploitation. David Weil (2009, 418–419) finds in the U.S. context that the following business structures can reinforce the vulnerability of low-wage workers:

1. where there are strong buyers sourcing competitive supply chains (such as a company like Wal Mart that has responsibility for the product market but not the employment conditions)
2. central production coordinators managing large contracting networks
3. small workplaces that are linked to large, branded national organizations (such as franchising models of ownership)
4. small workplaces and contractors that are linked together by common purchasers.

In all of these business structures, there is risk of increased hazardous conditions as well as underpayment. Similar findings have been reached in Australia regarding labor hire arrangements in food processing, cleaning, distribution, and construction, with the additional point that vulnerable and low-wage workers may be ill-equipped to understand the legal complexities of these arrangements and their ramifications for working conditions (WEstJustice 2016, 168; Fels 2019, 36, 99). For instance, the report of the Fels Commission (2019, 102) in Australia notes that "in some industry sectors, unscrupulous labour hire operators are accepted as a standard part of the market" and that "[h]aving a complex supply chain structure with multiple layers of contracting can worsen the situation." Australia faces distinctive challenges with franchisee arrangements that several commentators have argued increase exploitative behavior within certain sectors (Fels 2019, 37–40). The Gangmasters and Labour Abuse Authority (2016) in the United Kingdom notes that car washes are a sector that features a high number of undocumented migrant workers, who are forced to do piecework and operate under dangerous and unsafe conditions involving issues with electrical safety, toilet facilities, fire safety, and lack of appropriate protective equipment. These car washes operate through franchise-like arrangements, with some companies requesting a "franchise payment" from their workers and using self-employed workers.

Subcontracting arrangements can increase the precariousness of workers along the supply chain. For instance, one study of the horticulture industry in Australia found that subcontractors were responsible for hiring undocumented workers and for accommodating them in substandard housing (Underhill and Rimmer 2015, 30). Further, when some workers are hired through subcontractors and others are not, this can split the workforce and increase workers' vulnerability (32). Evidence from Australia suggests that when contracting is in place, work practices are intensified, there are fewer breaks, and workers are less likely to be provided with water—important in dry conditions like Australia (38). Subcontracting can also take the form of labor hire companies that recruit workers into key sectors and take deductions from their wages (McGregor 2007, 810). Subcontracting arrangements are common in the construction sector in Ontario and a contributor to poor workplace conditions. Counterintuitively, these arrangements may be preferred by some migrants, as they avoid focusing upon valid visa status (Ontario Construction Secretariat [OCS] 2008, 3).

The British NGO Focus on Labour Exploitation (FLEX 2017) identifies long supply chains as common in the construction industry in the United Kingdom. Complex structures involve subcontracting arrangements that decentralize control and oversight, diminish liability, and therefore heighten risk of injury and exploitation. FLEX found the same problem apparent in the U.K. garment manufacturing industry (32). Subcontracting is also common in the construction industry in Canada and related to the industry's *boombust* character. In this sense, the Metron disaster can be viewed as the logical result of subcontracting practices (Reid-Musson, Buckley, and Anderson 2015, 11).

Piecework

Another common feature of certain sectors with high rates of injury is where work is erroneously treated as piecework. For instance, workers may be paid for the job rather than the hour, as was the case for the Metron foreman, or paid per item, as is often the case in the garment sector. A statistical analysis of injuries in textile factories showed that those paid by the piece were more likely to sustain injuries than those paid by the hour because they were more likely to be under time pressure and suffering fatigue (Wrench 1982, 513; Underhill and Rimmer 2015, 29, 38). In a survey of 650 farm workers in Australia, piecework was found to be common (NUW 2019). These effects can be exacerbated in the context of outworkers who work in their own home, often without sufficient protections (WEstJustice 2016, 183). A dimension of this is *sham contracting*, where the employee is erroneously identified as a contractor and not a worker, leading to a reduction in labor standards and the transferal of costs onto the worker themselves (189).

Inadequacy of safety training

In high-risk sectors, safety training is crucial, yet often inadequate. In the *Metron* case, the supervisor, Kazenelson, had undertaken three days of training, including in the operation of swing stages and lifelines (*R v. Kazenelson* (2015), paras 38–40). However, this alone was not sufficient for him to provide adequate instruction to the workers. Further, the foreman, Fazilov, had not yet undertaken his fall-arrest training course (para 60). There was also evidence that at least one of the employees had not undertaken swing stage training at all and had such limited English that he would have struggled to understand the Construction Association of Ontario manual (Edwards 2010).

It was unclear whether Metron's migrant workers knew they were permitted to refuse unsafe work. Blumberg's widow said that her husband was not aware he possessed such a right (Edwards 2010). At times, the migrant worker may erroneously assume that occupational safety standards in the host country are the same as in the sending country. According to Gerry LeBlanc of the Canadian United Steelworkers:

> [A] homemade scaffolding may not be that unusual in the workplace [in the home country]. Like, you know, they may not be used to using

safety equipment necessarily. I mean, I've been to places in other parts of the world where it's terrifying to go on a mine site or a construction site. (Interview, Toronto, 20 March 2019)

The home country reference point can lead to an underestimation of safety hazards (Yanar, Kosny, and Smith 2018, 8). Language skills may also be an issue insofar as training may be offered only in English and the migrant may be unable to understand complex instructions in English. Speaking of the *Metron* case, a member of the Toronto Police Service said:

[E]ven when it came down to the training aspect of the construction protection training, swing stage training, that was done in English, with English textbooks and test papers, et cetera. So some of these individuals who couldn't speak English obviously couldn't write or read English as well. But, strangely enough, they all passed. (Interview 1, 17 October 2019)

Despite these language obstacles it is clear that the responsibility for safety primarily lies with the employer. A lack of sufficient training is common in studies on migrant workers. A Canadian study of 110 recently arrived workers found that very few had safety instruction, and there was often a lack of personal protective equipment (Yanar, Kosny, and Smith 2018, 6). At the same time, reliance on information sharing among migrants through social media platforms like Facebook or word of mouth, rather than through independent government portals, can lead to misinformation about safety standards (Underhill et al. 2019, 156; Underhill and Rimmer 2015, 38).

Government policy

Government policy can affect the safety of key sectors in two main ways. First, there are work health and safety laws in each jurisdiction that shape the extent to which unsafe work conditions are regulated. Migrants may or may not be covered under such laws, which can sometimes vary along visa lines (see Table 4.1 for further details).

Work, health, and safety laws and their coverage differ across the six jurisdictions. Given the large number of state and territorial workplace safety schemes in Australia, these are included under one column in Table 4.1 rather than separately.[6]

Table 4.1 Work, health, and safety laws across the jurisdictions

Workplace Safety	Australia	United Kingdom	California	Ontario	British Columbia	Alberta
Enforcing bodies	SafeWork NSW, SA Workplace Health and Safety Queensland, WorkSafe Western Australia, Australian Capital Territory, Victoria, Tasmania, Northern Territory Comcare	Health and Safety Executive	Californian Occupational Safety and Health Enforcement Unit	Safe at Work Ontario	WorkSafe British Columbia	Alberta Occupational Health and Safety
Regulating laws	Work Health and Safety Act (2011) (Commonwealth), Work Health and Safety Act (2011) (New South Wales), Occupational Health and Safety Act (2004) (Victoria), Work Health and Safety Act (2011) (Australian Capital Territory), Work Health and Safety Act (2011) (Queensland), Work Health and Safety Act (2012) (Tasmania), Work Health and Safety (National Uniform Legislation) Act (2011) (NT), Work Health and Safety Act (2012) (SA), Occupational Safety and Health Act (1984) (Western Australia), Workers' Compensation Act	Health and Safety at Work Act, (1974)	California Occupational Safety and Health Act (1973) California Occupational Safety and Health T8 Regulations California Labor Code	Ontario Occupational Health and Safety Act (1990)	Occupational Health and Safety (Occupational Health and Safety), Regulation of British Columbia (1998)	Alberta Occupational Health and Safety Act (2017), Occupational Health and Safety Regulation (2009), Occupational Health and Safety Code

(continued)

Table 4.1 Continued

Workplace Safety	Australia	United Kingdom	California	Ontario	British Columbia	Alberta
Number of inspections	New South Wales Inspectors: 299 Inspections: 12,349 (2018–2019) Western Australia Inspectors: 174.4 (2018–2019) Inspections: 8,217 South Australia Inspectors: 89 Inspections: 15,510 Northern Territory Inspectors: 33 Inspections: 3,684, concentrated on construction Victoria Inspections: 48,652: more than a quarter in the construction sector Queensland Inspectors: "over 250" Australian Capital Territory Inspectors: 30 (2018) Inspections: 4,204	Inspectors: 1,059 (FY 2019) Inspections: 13,300	Inspections: 7,571 (FY 2019) Inspectors: 221	Inspections: 89,188 (2018–2019; up from previous years) Inspectors: 354, of which 126 construction, 198 industrial, 21 mining	2005–2012: 34,000 inspections per year 2018: 44,576 (including phone calls etc. that are "counted" as inspections even if they do not involve a worksite inspection) Inspectors: 300	Inspectors: 130, 2018 Inspections: 10,365

Tasmania
Inspections: 1,064
Inspectors: 43.5

Comcare
Inspections: 1,120 (lowest in min 5 years)
Total—FY 2018 149,793 inspections
Inspectors: 1,136 FY 2018

| Inspectors per million workforce | 1,136/13.3 = 85.4 | 1,059/34 = 31.1 | 221/19.4 = 11.4 | 354/7.94 = 44.6 | 300/2.67 = 112.5 | 130/2.5 = 52 |

Sources: HSE (2020, 13, 75); WorkSafe Tasmania (personal communication, 2020) DOC/20/78445 Query – Staff Level Research for University of Sydney; WorkSafe B.C. (2018, 77); WorkSafe B.C. (personal communication, 2020); Zussman (2020); McLeod (2019); Barnetson and Matsunaga-Turnbull (2018); Ontario Government (2020a); Government of Alberta (2019); Department of Mines, Industry Regulation and Safety (2019, 53, 54); SafeWork SA (2019, 17); Independent Commissioner Against Corruption South Australia (2018, 50); NT WorkSafe (2019, 4, 18); WorkSafe Victoria (2019, 2); Comcare (2019, 51); WorkSafe; Queensland (2019); Nous Group (2018, 57); Department of Justice (Tasmania) (2019, 46); SafeWork Australia (2020, 8); Ontario Government (2020b). Inspections figure is only proactive. Inspections can include phone calls and document reviews but are included in the total inspection count.

Next, we consider in detail the regulatory settings in each of the jurisdictions.

Australia

Work, health, and safety laws apply to all workers in Australia regardless of their visa status. By contrast, workers' compensation schemes cannot be accessed by employees without a visa because legally there is no contract of employment in place in these cases (Guthrie 2007). Federal (Comcare) and state insurers make workers' compensation payments to visaed migrants. Comcare also conducts enforcement, including audits, inspections, and investigations under the Work Health and Safety Act for Commonwealth employees. Each of the state-based schemes is listed in Table 4.1.

Canada

Occupational health and safety regulations apply to all workers in the Canadian provinces considered in this book. On the sector level, Alberta allows variances or deviations on regulations, which tends to occur in coal mining. These must "provide for equal or greater protection than specified in the regulations" (Bryce and Heinmiller 1997, 1). Similarly, British Columbia's Mines Act contains a variance provision, which allows variation to be made in the best interest of the health and safety of an individual mine (Ministry of Energy and Mines 2017). Draft legislation in train in 2020 would create a more comprehensive compliance system with greater auditing and more proactive investigation (Ministry of Energy, Mines and Resources Petroleum 2020).

The Workplace Safety and Insurance Board (WSIB) of Ontario is *no fault*, and all workers, including migrants, can access the scheme's full benefits. However, in practice migrant workers face many barriers to accessing WSIB, including employers' reluctance and attempts to avoid reporting injuries; fear that reporting will lead to job loss; being laid off after injury; and difficulty being viewed as credible, particularly those migrants experiencing invisible or chronic injuries (Kosny et al. 2012). In Alberta and British Columbia, the body administering the Workers Compensation Act is known as the Workers' Compensation Board.

United Kingdom

Migrant workers in the United Kingdom are entitled to the same occupational safety and health protections, if not employment protections, as citizens. As such, there is no clear exclusion of workplace health and safety laws for migrants (Sargeant and Tucker 2009). There is not a distinctive workers' compensation body.

California
In California, health and safety regulations apply to all workers regardless of immigration status. Undocumented workers can file complaints with the Californian Division of Occupational Safety and Health (Cal/OSHA) and are required to have their status protected. However, in practice, undocumented workers are less likely to report unsafe working conditions to Cal/OSHA, as they can face employer threats, intimidation, and retaliation (California Labor Federation 2013). All workers, including undocumented workers, can access workers' compensation, but undocumented workers cannot always access retraining benefits (Legal Aid at Work 2020).

Frequency of inspections

The frequency of workplace inspections also has a direct influence on the safety of key sectors. Table 4.1 shows that there is significant variation among locations, as inspection rates differ depending upon workforce population size. Inspection rates range from 11.4 inspectors per million in California to 112.5 per million—almost tenfold higher—in British Columbia. There is also variation across the states and territories of Australia; for instance, southern Australia has the highest number of inspections and inspectors proportional to its small population size.

The interaction of migrant characteristics with the nature of the work and the workplace inspection laws can render migrants more vulnerable to injury. The migrant workers in *Metron* were covered by workplace health and safety laws, and there had been workplace inspections at the site in the months leading up to the accident—yet this did not prevent their deaths. A central issue that arose in the subsequent government inquiry into the Metron tragedy was whether there had been sufficient checks of the construction site prior to the accident. An Ontario Ministry of Labour inspector had attended twice in October 2009 and had issued a Stop Work Order, in part related to improper use of the swing stage; however, this was lifted and work was allowed to continue (*R v. Kazenelson* (2015), paras 43–44). There was evidence from some of the interviewees that the inspection was insufficient in capturing the faults with the swing stage, but this issue was not directly addressed in the litigation. According to Verne Edward from the Ontario Federation of Labour:

> [I]f the inspector had actually done a walk-about, anybody who works on construction would have looked at the swing stage and said "That's not right." It wasn't designed properly, and there were cracks in the wells. So a closer examination, just sort of walking up to it and looking at it closely, would [have] seen that that swing stage was not safe. (Interview, Toronto, 2 April 2019)

According to a policy officer in the Ministry of Labour in Ontario there were some changes to safety inspections after the *Metron* deaths:

> We definitely increased our focus on swing stage applications. So, in the construction and industrial program, going out there and making sure we examined as many locations that we became aware of. And also, because of the media surrounding that incident, we started to receive a lot more reports of swing stages applications.... [P]eople were calling in. (Interview 6, 27 March 2019)

The U.K. HSE conducts workplace inspections based on intelligence gathered about high-risk sectors. In 2019, for example, the greatest proportion of inspections was conducted in the construction sector. The offshore oil and gas sector is also identified as very hazardous, but difficult for inspectors to access (HSE 2020). The HSE has been criticized for engaging in a steady degradation in regulation and enforcement, moving to a "light touch" approach that prioritizes inspections targeted by sector over random inspections (Tombs and Whyte 2010). The number of inspections between 1999 and 2009 for health and safety has been more than halved (James, Tombs, and Whyte 2013).

Reduction in proactive inspections is a trend reflected in the other jurisdictions as well. On the one hand, in some jurisdictions, there has been a concurrent increase in reactive inspections. For instance, Safe at Work Ontario has seen a fall in its proactive inspections, from 76,561 in 2007–2008 to 41,319 in 2016–2017, but the number of reactive inspections has increased during those time spans, from 24,714 to 38,530 (Ontario Government 2019; Ministry of Labour, Ontario 2017). Multiple state-level Australian health and safety inspectorates have been criticized for understaffing. A 2018 review of WorkSafe Tasmania, with a focus on construction and stone production, found that, outside of the mining sector, the inspectorate was capable of conducting only reactive inspecting (Sherriff 2018). As of 2020, half of all workplace fatalities in Tasmania were not investigated (Bolatti 2020). A similar review found that WorkSafe Australian Capital Territory committed only 10% of its activities to enforcement, with use of notices declining by 59% to 75% across 2015–2018, and over half of inspections targeted to construction (Burgess 2018). Given the high rates of migrants in these sectors, these downward trends are worrisome.

In some jurisdictions, governments have focused their meager resources on at-risk migrant populations. For instance, WorkSafe B.C. targets inspections to sectors where vulnerable workers, including migrants, tend to be employed, such as agriculture. A dedicated team conducted 4,720 worksite inspections and issued 3,928 orders in 2018–2019. They have partnered with the Consulate of Mexico and the Mexican Ministry of Labour to create an occupational health and safety education program for seasonal agriculture workers coming in from Mexico. WorkSafe B.C. (2019, 35–36) estimates that, in 2018, 5,800 workers took part in training, which, while significant, still represents a small number of the 81,295 SAWP permits issued across Canada (Immigration, Refugees and Citizenship Canada 2020).

Like the other jurisdictions, a large proportion of California's activities focus on problematic sectors, namely construction, followed by agriculture and tree trimming. Nearly 40% of all inspections target these three sectors. On the U.S. federal level, OSHA has been shrinking systematically, with half as many inspectors available now as in the 1980s (Smith 2018). In California, although there are 270 authorized inspector positions, only 221 are filled (Zou 2020). Of Cal/OSHA's 221 safety inspectors, 28 are bilingual in community languages, suggesting a focus on migrants and those of migrant background (Wenus 2020).

Visa status

Visa status can interact with economic sector to compound the vulnerability of migrant workers. Temporary visa status is often viewed as an exacerbating feature in risky sector-based violations, as it increases the likelihood that migrant workers will not speak out about their experiences. In Australia, the requirement for Working Holiday Maker visa holders to work eighty-eight days in regional Australia in order to extend the visa for a second year has been identified as a potential source of vulnerability for workers, leading them to work that was exploitative or with deficient safety standards (Reilly and Howe 2019, 98; Underhill and Rimmer 2016, 619). The number of available migrant workers in a particular sector may also be a component here; when a worker is considered disposable, it may be more likely for work conditions to be lowered (Howe et al. 2017). Migrants on tied visas are viewed as more vulnerable to occupational health and safety issues in the United Kingdom than those enjoying free movement and portability across employers (Sargeant and Tucker 2009, 61). We explore the vulnerabilities that can arise through visa tying further in Chapter 6, on regulation.

In the *Metron* case, the temporary visa status of some of the workers was identified as a contributing factor to their vulnerability. Verne Edwards from the Ontario Federation of Labour noted:

> Because they [migrants] are tied to one employer, and if they have disputes with that employer then they can be repatriated within 24 hours. . . . And we know there have been cases where somebody's been injured, and they go from a hospital to a plane and they're gone. They may be miles from the nearest hospital, so they're not continuing with any sort of medical treatment, and they're cut off from workers compensation. (Interview, 2 April 2019)

All of the deceased Metron workers were migrants from Central or Eastern Europe. The judgment made some note of this: Blumberg had been in Canada for four years, since 2005. Another of the deceased, Aleksandrs Bondarevs, was a permanent resident for seven years at the time of his death. Fazilov had been in Canada for two years; his family was in Uzbekistan. The remaining injured worker on the swing stage accident, Dilshod Murapov, who survived the accident but with a serious disability, was from Uzbekistan and was on an expired student visa and had no right to work in Canada. He had been invited by a friend to the Metron site (*R v. Metron Construction* (2013), para 18). All but Murapov had been recruited to work on the site through the Russian-speaking media in Toronto and were not fluent in English (*R v. Kazenelson* (2015), para 32; interviews with Toronto Police Service, 2019). Visa issues also shaped the evidence collection in the case: at least one of the witnesses appeared concerned about giving evidence because of possible deportation (*R v. Kazenelson* (2015), para 74). Furthermore, the judgment noted that all four workers were economically vulnerable, that they and their families "were of limited financial means," and that "[n]one had life insurance" (*R v. Metron Construction* (2013), para 23). The reliance on work, not only to maintain visa status but also to support families back home through remittances, operates as a deterrent to speak out against unsafe conditions (Reilly and Howe 2019, 95). Media reports indicate that most of the deceased in the *Metron* case were sending money back to relatives (Edwards 2010).

Lapsed visa status or undocumented status can be an additional compounding aspect in informing vulnerability to injury. In the United Kingdom, changes to visa policy, including the closing down of visa routes for low- and semi-skilled care workers in 2008, rendered some undocumented (McGregor 2007, 807). A report by the OCS (2008, 2) found that 22% of the workers in the construction sector in 2008 worked cash-in-hand and that undocumented status eroded occupational health and safety. In Australia, recent estimates suggest that between one-quarter and one-third of the total horticulture workforce are undocumented workers and that in some locations of Australia, such workers comprise a majority of the workforce (Underhill and Rimmer 2016, 2016, 609).

The lack of a stable visa can significantly increase the precariousness of these workers (Underhill and Rimmer 2015, 29, 40; Underhill and Rimmer 2016). Undocumented migrants may be particularly unlikely to report a workplace injury out of fear of deportation (Bloch and McKay 2016). While the number of undocumented migrant workers is generally high in the United States, they are particularly common in certain sectors: service occupations (e.g., maids, cooks, and groundskeepers), construction, and especially farming (Pew Research Center 2014; Passal and Cohen 2007, cited in Trivedi 2018).

Quantitative findings

In this quantitative section, we explore insights from the MWRD regarding how a migrant's economic sector correlates with the types of workplace violations they experience. We used the International Standard Classification of Occupations (ISCO) as the measure here, rather than more aggregate measures of economic sector. ISCO ranks occupations on a scale from 1 to 9, with an additional 0 category for the armed forces. This measure can then be converted into skill level using ILO (2012, 11–12) conversion methods. ISCO Levels 1, 2, and 3 generally involve the top two skill levels, as does ISCO 0 in some instances. Otherwise, the ISCO levels are arranged across the bottom two skill levels, which capture low- and semi-skilled occupations (ILO 2012, 14).[7]

We must briefly defend the use of ISCO rather than a measure of economic sector (such as the International Standard Industrial Classification of All Economic Activities) to assess the broader theme of sector-based organization and related injuries. As the UN Department of Economic and Social Affairs (2008, 38–39) notes, the two concepts are not synonymous. Economic sector, or economic industry, as it is sometimes known, identifies key sectors of the economy, while ISCO measures classification of jobs within those sectors (Mannetje and Kromhout 2013). We opt for ISCO as a measure of occupational clustering and groups rather than a more aggregate measure of economic sector classification for a number of reasons. First, the analyzed judgments predominantly describe a migrant's job but generally not the larger economic sector in which they work, as this is the most common way for a judicial decision-maker to comment on the workplace experience of an individual. Second, job classifications can be standardized cross-nationally using the ISCO scale, which applies in different country contexts and is benchmarked against national scales. This is not the case with economic sector. (Information on the ISCO scale and conversion from national systems is provided in the Methods Annex.) Third, ISCO can be coded at a finer level of specificity than economic sector or industry, allowing us to investigate more fine-grained trends, even if we ultimately analyze the occupational data at the 4-level ISCO scale that is akin to economic sector. Finally, ISCO is the scale most commonly used in studies of workplace injury and health, which is the focus of this chapter (e.g. Mannetje and Kromhout 2013).

In this section, we use ISCO to measure the occupational clustering of migrant workers. First, we look at the representation of immigrants in the MWRD within the broader foreign-born populations of each country, arranged according to ISCO level. Second, we consider how successful claims for violations are distributed across these levels. Third, we focus in on the question of injury—which encompasses personal injury to the body, sexual assault, and death (manslaughter, negligence leading to death, and homicide)—and consider the distribution of these violations across sectors. Finally, we compare the data on injury with the broader domestic populations in each of the jurisdictions. Where possible, we report these data at the provincial/state level as this is the relevant unit of analysis for work, health, and safety laws.

It is important to note that Table 4.2 gives the sector breakdown of foreign-born citizens at the population level. This is not the same reference

Table 4.2 Distribution of occupations of migrants in MWRD compared to in foreign-born population

	Australia MWRD	Australia Pop	Canada MWRD	Canada Pop	United Kingdom MWRD	United Kingdom Pop	USA MWRD	USA Pop*	Total MWRD	Total Pop
Major group 1 (Manager)	4%	11%	2%	12%	3%	16%	1%	9%	3%	10%
Major group 2 (Professionals)	4%	20%	5%	31%	29%	18%	27%	21%	10%	21%
Major group 3 (Technicians and associate professionals)	5%	12%	12%	7%	8%	13%	4%	2%	7%	3%
Major group 4 (Clerical support workers)	1%	12%	0.2%	3%	3%	13%	0%	8%	1%	8%
Major group 5 (Service and sales workers)	35%	13%	24%	22%	22%	16%	8%	30%	27%	28%
Major group 6 (Skilled agricultural, forestry, and fishery workers)	1%	1%	0.4%	2%	0%	0%	0%	2%	1%	2%
Major group 7 (Craft and related trade workers)	16%	11%	3%	N/A	3%	5%	2%	3%	9%	3%
Major group 8 (Plant and machine operators and assemblers)	1%	7%	18%	13%	1%	7%	1%	15%	5%	14%
Major group 9 (Elementary occupations)	27%	12%	33%	10%	26%	10%	57%	13%	33%	13%
Major group 10 (Armed forces occupations)	0%	0.1%	0%	N/A	1%	1%	0%	N/A	0.1%	0.05%
Unknown	5%	2%	1%		4%	5%	0%		3%	0.1%
Total (N)	949	1997517	488		144	2327892	331	27502000	1912	34853524

*Totals add up to more than 100% due to overlap in occupation classifications.

Sources: OECD 2000; U.S. BLS 2019. N/A indicates ISCO major group not distinguishable in national occupation classification. See Methods Annex for occupation conversions.

category as in other chapters (where average immigration flow data are used), but it is the most readily available sector-level data. Generally, Table 4.2 demonstrates that migrants are overrepresented within the MWRD in the lower-skilled ISCO levels, even while they are underrepresented in the general foreign-born population. For instance, averaged across the database, 33% of claimants are in the elementary occupations (ISCO Level 9), but only 13% of the population of migrants. In contrast, only 10% of the database population are professionals (Group 2), while 21% of immigration flows are comprised of this group. There is, in short, a positive relationship between lower skill level and overrepresentation in the database. Those in higher-ranked occupations are also less likely to make workplace complaints in the database.

The next question is whether the clustering of injury-based violations in particular in the database is similar to the sector-based distributions of foreign-born populations in each country. Table 4.3 shows the recorded injury violations in the database at the state or provincial level for each jurisdiction and arranged according to ISCO code, while Table 4.4 examines injury figures in the standard population.

The first thing to note from these data is the low number of successful actions against workplace injury and death by migrant workers. Across the MWRD, there are sixty-nine successfully substantiated violations in this area. When we considered that the estimated total migrant population represented here is an aggregate of all flows (Chapter 6),[8] this is an exceedingly low level of claims. The success rate for injury is 56% for personal injury, 50% for sexual assault, and 100% for homicide and manslaughter claims, for a total of sixty-nine successful claims. Therefore, success rate alone does not explain the very low numbers of substantiated injuries within the MWRD (see Table 4.5). In all likelihood, the scale of reported injuries is low, even factoring in the underreporting of other violations, for a number of reasons. First, workers may be concerned that raising complaints about workplace injury could lead to dismissal (WEstJustice 2016, 208). One study of injured migrant workers in Canada found that none filed complaints to the Canadian workers' compensation system due to fear of job loss (Kosny et al. 2012, 279). The truncated time required to report injuries could be an impediment in some jurisdictions, especially where migrants are physically isolated or unaware of their rights (Kosny et al. 2012, 281; see also IAVGO 2009). The nature of injury can also influence underreporting. Deaths may be underreported if infectious diseases, pesticide exposure, occupational

Table 4.3 Number of successful injury claims, by sector and jurisdiction (N migrants)

ISCO Group	Australia NSW	NT	SA	Tas	Vic	WA	N/A	Canada (Ontario)**	United Kingdom	USA	Total
Major group 1 (Manager)	0	0	0	0	0	0	0	1	0	0	1
Major group 2 (Professionals)	1	0	1	0	0	0	0	0	0	0	2
Major group 3 (Technicians and associate professionals)	0	0	1	0	1	1	0	0	0	1	4
Major group 4 (Clerical support workers)	1	0	0	0	0	1	0	0	0	0	2
Major group 5 (Service and sales workers)	0	0	0	0	0	0	1	2	0	0	3
Major group 6 (Skilled agricultural, forestry, and fishery workers)	2	1	1	0	1	0	0	0	0	0	5
Major group 7 (Craft and related trade workers)	5	0	1	0	1	0	1	3	1	0	12
Major group 8 (Plant and machine operators and assemblers)	4	0	2	0	0	0	0	3	0	0	9
Major group 9 (Elementary occupation)	0	0	0	1	1	0	0	21	0	6	29
Major group 0 (Armed forces occupations)	0	0	0	0	0	0	0	1	0	0	1
NA	1	0	0	0	0	0	1	1	0	0	3
Total	14	1	6	1	4	2	3	32	1	7	71

*Injury claims include sexual assault, manslaughter, murder, and unsafe working conditions causing injury. Percentages indicate distribution of injury claims in the jurisdiction by sector.

**No successful injury claims in the other Canadian provinces in the MWRD.

Table 4.4 Traumatic fatalities and injuries of domestic population

	Australia	United Kingdom	California	British Columbia	Alberta	Ontario
Traumatic fatalities (per 100,000)	2018 1.1	2015–2019 0.42	2008–2018 2.32	2013–2017 2.8	2013–2017 3.7	2013–2017 1.3
	Top 3 sectors Agriculture: 11.2 Transport, postal, and warehousing: 5.9 Mining: 3.7	Top 3 sectors Agriculture: 7.73 Waste and recycling: 7.71 Construction: 1.64	For Latinx workers: 3.7 (2016) 20% of fatalities are migrants in 2016 (2016)	Top 3 sectors: Construction Manufacturing Transportation		Top 3 sectors Construction: 4.73 Transportation: 6.32 Mining: 7.05
Injuries (per 100,000)	2019 910	2016–2019 1,803	2016–2018 1,433	2013–2017 2,230	2013–2017 1,310	2013–2017 950
	Agriculture: 1,670 Manufacturing: 1,520 Construction: 1,500	Agriculture Construction Accommodation and food service	Hospitals: 8,000 Logging: 5,500 Meat processing: 5,800			

Sources: Ontario Government (2019); SafeWork Australia (2019, 7, 15); Tucker and Keefe (2019, 16, 22); U.K. HSE (2016, 2018, 2019, 2020, 6); Worksafe (2018, 14); Worksafe (2020, 8); U.S. Bureau of Labor Statistics (2018); WorkSafe B.C. (2018, 15).

Table 4.5 Comparison of success rates of different injury types and death, by ISCO grouping

	Unsafe Workplace			Sexual Assault			Death (Manslaughter or Murder)		
	Claims	Successful Claims	Success Rate	Claims	Successful Claims	Success Rate	Claims	Successful Claims	Success Rate
ISCO 1	2	1	50%	0	0	N/A	0	0	N/A
ISCO 2	1	1	100%	0	0	N/A	0	0	N/A
ISCO 3	4	2	50%	0	0	N/A	0	0	N/A
ISCO 4	6	3	50%	1	1	100%	0	0	N/A
ISCO 5	2	2	100%	0	0	N/A	0	0	N/A
ISCO 6	8	3	38%	0	0	N/A	0	0	N/A
ISCO 7	4	4	100%	0	0	N/A	1	1	100%
ISCO 8	18	11	61%	1	0	0%	1	1	100%
ISCO 9	14	8	57%	0	0	N/A	1	1	100%
ISCO 10	51	26	51%	1	1	100%	2	2	100%
NA	4	3	75%	1	0	0%	0	0	N/A
Total	114	64	56%	4	2	50%	5	5	N/A

toxins, and cancers are not accurately causally linked to the employment experience (Gerry LeBlanc, Interview, Toronto, 20 March 2019; IVAGO 2009; Bittle, Chen and Hébert, 2018). Further, driving accidents between locations, such as to different farms, may not be recorded as workplace fatalities rather as general accidents; even when they are linked to the course of employment (Verne Edwards, Interview, 2 April 2019).

A second observation of the injury data relates to skill level. There is a clear clustering of injury in the ISCO levels generally classified as lower skilled. ISCO Level 7 (craft and related trade workers), ISCO Level 8 (plant and machine operators and assemblers), and elementary occupations (ISCO level 9) comprise the bulk of substantiated violations. Further, there is variation across the jurisdictions. The vast bulk of cases are in Ontario, and mainly at ISCO Level 9 (21, or 66%). Within Australia, there is variation across the cases, with the highest number in New South Wales, Australia's most populous state.

It is also useful to consider how the scale of injury experienced by migrant workers as represented in the MWRD compares with the general population. The scales are different across the jurisdictions in the original data but can be standardized per million workers, as is undertaken in Table 4.4. Further, the domestic population includes reported fatalities and time-loss injuries (injuries related to inability to work) rather than only successful litigation violations. Still, the differences between the figures are interesting to explore. Considering traumatic fatalities, it is clear that the United Kingdom has far fewer incidences than the other jurisdictions, and Alberta has a particularly high rate (connected to its focus on mining) among its domestic population. It is possible to measure the danger of a sector based on the number of reported injuries as a percentage of the population of workers (Bellés-Obrero, Bassols, and Castello 2020).

Focusing on injury, there is also variation across the jurisdictions from very low levels of 5.5 injuries per million in Australia up to 2,230 in British Columbia. While these numbers are small, they are still far higher than the figures suggested by the MWRD, which records only sixty-nine injury claims across the entire database. In short, although employed in high-risk sectors, migrant workers are less likely than domestic workers to report such injuries.

With regard to the types of injuries experienced by migrant workers, the numbers are too small to divide according to jurisdiction. However, we can divide the injuries according to workplace (health and safety), sexual assault, and death (either negligent manslaughter or homicide) claims. Aggregated across the MWRD, we can see that the vast bulk of claims for injury is related to unsafe workplaces, with 114 claims and 64 successfully substantiated violations, and 5 substantiated death claims. Most of these are in the lower-skill ISCO levels, confirming the established relationship between low-skill level and sector. Claims for sexual assault and death are in the single digits, but there too the cases are in the lower-skill level (see Table 4.5 for details).

The small number of death claims is reflective of the challenges of bringing actions for workplace deaths generally. This relates to the limited resources to prosecute such crimes, as well as the higher standard of proof for criminal compared to civil trials (Bittle, Chen, and Hébert 2018). Sexual injuries present particular types of harm. However, as noted in Chapter 2, reporting, prosecution, and success of sexual-based harms is low in the MWRD, and this is reflective of broader challenges in the wider population in bringing sexual assault actions, such as a reticence among survivors to report such injuries.

Summary

This chapter has explored how sector can influence the potential for workplace violations against migrants related to injury, whether it be bodily injury, sexual assault, or death. Generally, it finds a relationship between lower-level sectors and more pronounced rates of violations. British Columbia has the highest number of substantiated injuries sustained of any of the jurisdictions, related to the high number of agricultural cases there and frequent injury in farmwork. Generally, the number of injuries both claimed and substantiated in court and tribunal cases is low compared with the broader population data; this is related to the challenges of reporting injuries, particularly if the migrant is still employed in the workplace following the injury or has left the country due to short-term visa status.

Unionization may have a protective effect against sector-specific vulnerability. For instance, migrant workers in the construction sector in Australia are viewed as better protected than other migrant workers who have lower levels of trade union membership (Velayutham 2013, 353). However, in some contexts, unions have excluded migrant workers rather than protected them.[9] Not all trade unions are active in these vulnerable sectors for reasons of isolation coupled with the temporary nature of the work (Reilly et al. 2018, 10). Alternatively, in some sectors in some of the jurisdictions, trade union membership is restricted to citizens or those on permanent residency visas. We explore these issues further in Chapter 7, on trade unions.

Enforcement policy may also affect the relative risk of injury and its apprehension. Such government bodies are particularly important in protecting the rights of migrant workers in key sectors such as agriculture and construction. For instance, speaking of agricultural migrant workers in Ontario, Leah Vosko, Eric Tucker, and Rebecca Casey (2019, 254) argue, "Given the multiple layers of vulnerability that inhibit complaints in the first instance, emphasis must be placed on building a proactive public enforcement regime." While we have considered workplace health and safety inspection in this chapter, we assess the broader scope of enforcement policies in Chapter 8. There are several important policy implications that flow from the core findings in this chapter.

Finally, this chapter has made clear that those without valid visa status are also more likely to fall through the additional cracks of workplace protections against injury. For instance, in one case in the United States, an undocumented worker was not granted social security protections after he was injured at work (*Salas v. Sierra Chem Co.*, 129 Cal. Rptr. 3d 263 (2011)).[10] That said, even with these formal protections, there have been immigration reprisals in recent years on undocumented migrants as they seek to bring workers' compensation claims in California courts, further diminishing any positive changes to enforcement policy (Dooling 2019). We discuss these issues further in the next chapter, on undocumented immigration, with a case involving workers in a factory in Southern California, *Hoffman Plastics*.

This chapter leads to a number of important policy recommendations, which must be contextualized within the data limitations canvassed already: that we do not have injury-reporting data for migrants in all of the jurisdictions and that occupation rather than economic sector is used as the principal measure in the MWRD. First, it is clear from the data presented that low-skilled migrants experience disproportionately higher rates of injury and death than those in higher-skilled occupations. Across the database, 33% of claimants are in the elementary occupations (ISCO Level 9), but only 13% of the population of migrants. This finding emphasizes the need for specialist inspection focused on key low-skilled sectors. Changes to enforcement policies, such as greater regulation of labor hire operators with a licensing authority, can also be part of a package of changes to improve conditions in certain sectors (Fels Commission 2019, Recommendation 14). Second, the highest rate of successful injury claims are in Ontario, which does not have the lowest rate of workplace inspection (the United Kingdom does; see Table 4.1). Nor is Ontario the most dangerous or prone to fatalities of the six jurisdictions (in fact Alberta is; see Table 4.4). This demonstrates that both the rate of injury and fatality of migrant workers and appropriate remedies are driven by a variety of factors, including the inherent unsafety of the workplaces and sectors, the capacity and support for migrants to bring claims, and their rights to seek remedies offshore. As such, enforcement in the work, health, safety space is important but must not be considered independently from other factors that drive workplace safety rights, including legal representation in claim-making. The facts of the *Metron* case demonstrate the need for detailed, close-up inspections to adequately assess risk. As the case narrative reveals, the earlier inspection of the swing stage was from afar and failed to identify the inherent structural issues with the swing stage that contributed to the workers' deaths, alongside the negligent actions of the employers themselves. Especially in a context where migrant workers may lack both the structural power and language skills to raise their concerns over workplace safety, it is imperative that workplace inspections act as an appropriate safety check. We return to these issues insofar as they intersect with funding of enforcement bodies in Chapter 8. Finally, the relationship between temporary and precarious visa status and also injury—especially in contexts where undocumented visa status is tightly regulated—demonstrates that addressing injury adequately requires an understanding of the role of lapsed visa status, a topic to which we now turn in Chapter 5.

5
Labor Rights or Immigration Enforcement?
Conflict in Protecting Undocumented Migrant Workers

In 1989, Samuel Perez, an undocumented Mexican migrant worker employed by Hoffman Plastics, a factory in Orange County, California, was fired for his trade union activities. In 1988, Perez was marginally involved in a failed organizing campaign at the plant led by the AFL-CIO's United Rubber, Cork, Linoleum and Plastic Workers of America, having given out forms that encouraged others to join the union. When his employers became aware of this, he was interrogated about his relationship to the union and summarily fired. Perez had used a fraudulent document—the birth certificate of a friend, to purport that he was born in El Paso, Texas—to gain employment at the plant (Fisk and Wishnie 2005, 361). His undocumented status was revealed many years after his entry into the United States, during deposition in subsequent court proceedings and based entirely on additional discovery work by the employer's attorney (Cleeland 2002; Fisk and Wishnie 2005, 363).[1] As such, his undocumented status, while irrelevant in the early stages of legal proceedings, addressing his dismissal for trade union organizing, became pivotal in subsequent litigation.

Under the National Labor Relations Act (NLRA) (1935) of the United States, there are several remedies for unlawful dismissal. These include reinstatement, posting a notice in the workplace advising employees that there has been a breach by the employer, and the back payment of wages for the period the employee should have been employed, or settlement of these wages by judgment. Perez sought back payment of US$67,000 following unfair dismissal for the seven-month period he had worked at the plant and was denied this by Hoffman Plastics. In the preliminary administrative law judgment, before the National Labor Relations Board (NLRB), it was found that Perez had been fired unlawfully on the basis of his union activity and was entitled to back pay (*Hoffman Plastic Compounds, Inc. v. 306 NLRB 100* (1992)). It was in the deposition hearing from the 1992 case that the employer raised the issue of Perez's unlawful immigration status. This elevated the case to a question of public policy over whether an undocumented worker was entitled to back pay at all. Hoffman Plastics appealed the case to the D.C. Circuit Court, where the decision of the NLRB was affirmed (*Hoffman Plastic Compounds, Inc. v. NLRB*, 208 F.3d 229 (D.C. Cir. 2000)). The employer then contested the decision. The ambiguity over the implications that Perez's unlawful status held for employment law entitlements was perhaps the reason that discretionary leave was granted by the Supreme Court of the United States to hear the matter.

The case before the Supreme Court was not litigated by Perez himself but by the NLRB, which sought to enforce back pay on behalf of workers generally (*Hoffman Plastic Compounds Inc. v. NLRC* 535 U.S. 137 (2002) 237 F3.d. 639). The central question that arose was whether the NLRB had the statutory authority to enforce this back pay on his behalf, given that in doing so it might conflict with other government obligations under immigration legislation, specifically the Immigration Reform and Control Act (IRCA) (1986), which made it illegal to knowingly hire unauthorized workers.[2]

The Supreme Court found for Hoffman Plastics by a 5–4 majority. Chief Justice William H. Rehnquist, speaking for the majority, vacated the back pay award. Defending the majority's decision, he said, "Allowing the Board to award back pay to illegal aliens would unduly trench upon explicit statutory prohibitions critical to federal immigration policy" (*Hoffman Plastics* (2002), at 1278). He continued that doing so "would encourage the successful evasion of apprehension of immigration authorities, condone prior violations of the immigration laws, and encourage future violations" (at 1278). Rehnquist distinguished the case from precedent set in *Sure-Tan, Inc. v. NLRB* (467 U.S. 883, 892 (1984)), as well as other lower-level cases that had permitted back pay to undocumented workers, on the basis that it had occurred before the IRCA was enacted. The majority reached its conclusion even though the IRCA contains no explicit restrictions on the employment rights of undocumented workers (Ho and Chang 2005, 482).

At the same time as the *Hoffman Plastics* case was advancing in the courts, the political climate was worsening for undocumented migrants in the United States. In 1986, Congress legislated the IRCA, which, under section 1324(b)–(c), rendered illegal the hiring of unauthorized workers by employers. Prior to the IRCA, employers were not required to verify the immigration status of employees.[3] Section 1324(a)(h)(3) of the IRCA defined an "unauthorized alien" to encompass both those who overstayed their visas and those who entered the United States illegally. This single amendment had the effect of calling into question an array of rights attached to the employment of undocumented migrants, including their right to seek legal remedies for labor law breaches. Between the enactment of the IRCA and the *Hoffman Plastics* case coming before the Supreme Court, "the issue of illegal immigration had become even more salient in the national political consciousness" (former U.S. government lawyer, Interview, 20 November 2019). In 1996, President Bill Clinton cut welfare provisions for new permanent migrants, increased detention and deportation for certain immigrants, and restricted deportation protection for some categories of asylum applicants. This period also corresponded with a sharp increase in the undocumented population in the United States, particularly in California—and especially in Southern California, where Hoffman Plastics was located (Fisk and Wishnie 2005, 354, 356, citing Lopez and Feliciano 2000). In this sense, the outcome of the *Hoffman Plastics* case can be read as a political decision as much as a legal one that spoke to prevailing debates about undocumented immigration into the United States more broadly and the best ways to stem it.

The policy and political implications of *Hoffman* were considerable, perhaps informing the close 5–4 decision before the Supreme Court. In his dissent on behalf of the minority—with Justices Stevens, Souter, and Ginsburg concurring—Justice Breyer argued that the decision for *Hoffman Plastics* could lead to an increase, rather than a decrease, in employer demand for undocumented migrants, thereby vitiating the policy intent of the IRCA, which was to reduce the magnet effect of a lack of employment regulation upon unlawful immigration flows. He wrote, "[T]o deny the Board the power to award backpay, however, might very well increase the strength of th[e] magnetic force [of immigrant labor]" (*Hoffman Plastics* (2002), at 1287). In contrast, the majority's position, as stated by Justice Rehnquist, was that "awarding backpay [would] not only trivialize the immigration laws, it also condones and encourages future violations" (at 1284).

The case was notable in involving numerous amici briefs, including some co-drafted by multiple organizations. These included large players such as the American Civil Liberties Union (ACLU), but also smaller bodies such as Make the Road, a community organization run out of New York City that focused on worker and welfare issues, especially for undocumented populations.[4] Unusually, the amici briefs in support of the NLRB's claim also included an alliance of business groups—employers and employer associations that were motivated to represent those employers "doing the right thing" and not using undocumented migration to undermine wages. These organizations argued that a judgment in favor of Hoffman Plastics would see a race to the bottom in terms of illegal business practices, that would be particularly aggravated in the garment, meat packing, and agricultural sectors and could advantage "outlawed 'sweatshops' and other scofflaw businesses that hire undocumented workers."[5]

Overview of the chapter

In the next section of this chapter, we consider the legal reach of *Hoffman* across a variety of areas of labor law in the United States. We address the concept of "unclean hands" and how the illegality of immigration status can be seen, through case law, to limit access to employment law remedies in some instances. This is true not only for the United States but also for the other jurisdictions considered in this book, as we noted in our discussion of illegality of contract in Chapter 3 and its detailed discussion of the *Hounga v. Allen* case. In this chapter in particular, we consider how undocumented migrants suffer from aggravated concerns over access to justice, amplifying those raised in Chapter 1, by virtue of their unauthorized presence in their host societies and how, in turn, they could suffer higher employment law infringement risks because the likelihood that they will bring action against their employer is heavily reduced. Finally, we look at the phenomenon of immigration retaliation, where employers who are the subject of labor law complaints by their undocumented workforce will invite raids or immigration investigations from government authorities to push back against such complaints. In the quantitative section, we draw upon available national statistics to examine the levels of predicted undocumented immigration in each of the four countries (we collapse Canada as immigration is a federal issue there, and subnational data are not available). Finally, we use the Migrant Worker Rights Database MWRD to present key findings with regards to what percentage of cases are brought by migrants without visa status and the key violation areas for such complaints. We also consider the percentage of such complaints that are substantiated.

The stretch (and limitations) of *Hoffman Plastics*

The impact of *Hoffman* was broad legally but also culturally. The most immediate effect was to restrict undocumented migrants' access to back pay and other actions brought under the NLRA. The case of *Mezonos Maven Bakery* (Board Case No. 29-CA-025476, 2013) tested whether Hoffman still applied in instances where the employer knowingly hired an illegal migrant worker. It found that its application was "broad" and that it did reach to such instances where the employer had engaged in a different form of illegality, such as a breach of immigration and work authorization rules. A concurrence before the NLRB (see *Mezonos Maven Bakery, Inc.*, 357 NLRB 376, 376 (2011)) found that such a reading was necessary given the Supreme Court precedent. In this way, a migrant's entering the United States unlawfully, and gaining employment on this basis, was viewed as a more severe breach than the employer's unlawful hiring of the same undocumented worker.

There were questions over whether broader employment rights, such as access to the Fair Labor Standards Act's (1938) minimum wage entitlements, would be barred by virtue of an undocumented status. But this was rejected because it would have denied access to payment for work performed, raising slavery concerns under the U.S. Constitution (Justice Ginsburg in oral hearings, *Hoffman* (2002), 18; Cleeland 2002). Civil Rights Act (1964) Title VII provisions, which provide compensation and preventive awards in instances where nonwhite employees and other protected groups are discriminated against, were insulated from the effects of *Hoffman*, as were other antidiscrimination protections and common law negligence (*Salas v. Sierra Chemical Company* (2014) 59 Cal. 4th 407; see also Ho and Chang 2005, 509; *Tyson Foods Inc. v. Guzman*, 116 S.W. 3d 233 (2003)). It was also clear that damages would still be owed to undocumented workers for work already performed, if the pay had been withheld due to engagement in union activities (*Tuv Taam Corp.*, 340 NLRB No. 86, at 4 & n. 4 (2003) WL 22295361). This stands in contrast to *Hoffman*, where the work was not performed, as there had been a dismissal.

Practically, Hoffman also had an impact upon the question of whether an undocumented migrant worker's visa status could be raised in deposition or discovery during court proceedings. Ana Avendaño, previously legal counsel at AFL-CIO, pointed out:

> Prior to Hoffman, when we were litigating . . . employers would often ask in discovery, when you were in court . . . interrogatory or in deposition,

whether a worker was documented or not. And because that question was not relevant, either for coverage [or] some form of remedy, we were often able to get protective orders or instructions from the judge that that question should not be asked of the worker, because it had a chilling effect. When *Hoffman* came down, it was harder to argue that, because employers had more leverage to say "Well, it's absolutely relevant to remedy." (Interview, 22 November 2019).

That said, the case of *Rivera v. Nibco Inc.* (384 F.3d 822 (9th Cir. 2004)) restricted the grounds for discovery against undocumented workers to one of relevance. Christopher Ho, head of the Immigrants' Rights Program at Legal Aid at Work in San Francisco, said that any court would have to first clarify that such discovery was justified given "[t]he huge deterrence effect that this sort of discovery would have on the willingness of private plaintiffs to come forward and exercise their rights" (Interview, 1 November 2019). As such, some commentators, including Professor Benjamin Sachs, who helped the ACLU draft its amicus brief in *Hoffman*, have argued that the worst possible effects of *Hoffman* were constrained and that the case "did not lead to a wholesale evisceration of formal legal rights for the undocumented" (Interview, 4 November 2019). At the same time, the potential for invasive discovery on undocumented grounds that it created "would likely deter many... plaintiffs from taking any legal steps at all" because "[t]he risk of retaliatory or other severe, far-reaching consequences is, much too often, quite real" (Ho and Chang 2005, 523).

Culturally, *Hoffman* had a deeply quieting effect upon litigation by undocumented migrant workers, their collective action, and their broader claim-making. A lawyer at the AFL-CIO commented on the case, "[I]t has a chilling effect for sure, because once everyone understands the rules of the game, it structures their behavior" (Interview, 20 November 2019; see also Ho and Chang 2005). In their article "Iced-Out," Rebecca Smith, Ana Avendaño, and Julie Martinez Ortega (2009, 6, 10) consider how *Hoffman* and subsequent court cases informed employers' use of immigration raids to cease migrant workers' organizing efforts or during ongoing workplace disputes. This trend, they argue, has coincided with an increase in federal funding for immigration enforcement and a decrease in labor inspection.[6] Further, even if the scope of *Hoffman* has been fettered by judges and litigators in progressive states like California, it is still raised to dispute the enforcement of protections for undocumented workers.

Hoffman's bleeding into discovery practices to permit questions about visa status has also had a chilling and potentially discriminatory effect upon legal migrants—and even citizens with "foreign sounding surnames" or who have "membership of an ethnic minority group" (Chung 1995, 267, 279). Indeed, Christopher Ho and Jennifer Chang (2005, 495) argue that these effects could go so far as to discourage some minorities from bringing national-origin antidiscrimination claims because they fear invasive and stereotyping questioning.

In the following section, we consider several key themes that arise from the *Hoffman Plastics* case and the position of undocumented migrant workers more broadly. First, the tension between enforcing labor rights and the fact that the rights-holders have breached immigration law raises ethical, legal, and legislative issues. Second, undocumented states increase the potential rate of labor rights infringements for migrants and their access to justice within the legal system. And third, migrant workers face risks in terms of immigration retaliation and protections against such retaliation.

"Unclean hands" and employment rights

A central conflict in *Hoffman Plastics* and in the area of undocumented migrant rights more broadly is the concept of "unclean hands," which was also raised in Chapter 2 (*Hounga v. Allen*). This phrase refers to the concept that because the migrant has "unclean hands" by virtue of their breach of immigration laws, they are denied entitlements under other areas of law—here, labor law. The puzzle of "unclean hands" requires us to weigh the relative importance of rights and responsibilities under either immigration or labor law. The *Hoffman Plastics* case is useful to an examination of the inherent conflict raised by the enforcement of the labor rights of undocumented migrants: whether someone who has breached immigration law is entitled to remedies under another area of law. These issues can be canvassed in three main ways: (1) morally; (2) legally, in terms of judicial interpretation of the rights of undocumented migrants to labor law enforcement, both in *Hoffman* and in court cases in the other countries—in short, how labor law conflicts with immigration law; and (3) legislatively and administratively, in terms of how governments decide to address this issue through statutory enactment but also resource allocation for enforcement policies.[7]

Morally

In the *Hoffman* case, a clear line in the Supreme Court majority's reasoning was that an individual who had breached a basic condition (immigration status) should not be entitled to an equitable relief like back pay that paid the individual from the point of dismissal or discriminatory treatment up until the point of legal judgment. Such moral assumptions were apparent in *Hoffman* in Justice Scalia's cross-examination of lawyer Paul Wolfson, where Scalia insinuated that undocumented migrants would exploit and benefit from the award of back pay provisions:

SCALIA: If he's smart he'd say, how can I mitigate, it's unlawful for me to get another job.
MR. WOLFSON: Justice Scalia—
SCALIA: I can just sit home and eat chocolates and get my back pay.
(*Hoffman Plastics* (2002), legal transcript at 32–33)

Undocumented immigration also raises moral questions about whether liberal states have a legitimate claim to limit the rights of individuals who are not naturalized and have committed an offense—here, the breach of immigration laws (Ferracioli 2021, Chapter 8). It demands consideration of the issue of how severely we judge immigration violations and whether we view them as necessitating the denial of other bundles of rights, such as the socioeconomic rights associated with labor law enforcement. Ayelet Shachar (2007) calls this the policing of the "internal borders." How governments choose to clamp down on undocumented migration, and the extent of it, is an important part of border management. While some have argued that any form of enforcement may be discriminatory (e.g., Mendoza 2014), Luara Ferracioli (2021) argues that there are instances when the enforcement of visa status is permissible and morally compellable, but that certain limits need to be put in place, for instance that states should not engage in racial profiling in pursuing such enforcement claims and that agencies engaged in immigration deportation should overrepresent ethnic minorities in their workforces. These are useful policy suggestions, but they do not centrally address the issue of whether immigration law does indeed trump employment law, which was so central in *Hoffman*. In fact, navigating this challenging ethical question of "unclean hands" is central not only to the *Hoffman Plastics* case but in any area of law where entitlements are owed to someone who also breaches other areas of law—for instance, a thief who is injured by a third party while stealing something.

Legally—a conflict between labor and immigration law?

Hoffman can also be viewed as a case about the legal conflict between two statutes—the National Labor Relations Act and the IRCA—and whether the two can be reconciled or not. Speaking for the majority, Justice Rehnquist argued, "Where the Board's chosen remedy trenches upon a federal statute or policy outside the Board's competence to administer, the Board's remedy may not yield" (*Hoffman Plastics* (2002), at para 147). In short, the immigration statute would prevail over that regulating labor.

Professor Sachs of Harvard Law provided an alternative interpretation:

> We have [in *Hoffman*] two canons that are supposed to guide judges in precisely this situation when you have two federal statutes. . . And one of those says you don't read a latter enacted statute as overruling a formerly enacted statute unless the latter enacted statute especially says that it does this.[8] The Court didn't engage with this traditional canon in its opinion. . . . And this is consistent with a history of courts reading immigration law to trump labor protective legislation without much reasoning at all.

He added that this decision elevated immigration law in a way that was not necessarily legally required but perhaps politically expedient:

> I think that this became a very politicized question, more than a legal one, and that the case was decided largely . . . on partisan lines at the Supreme Court and was, ultimately a question about employer versus worker power, and was a question about the justice's ideas of the deservingness of undocumented workers and not really about what the Congress meant when they enacted the IRCA and the National Labor Relations Act. (Interview, 4 November 2019)

There was no real legal reason why the IRCA was seen by the justices to trump the operation of the NLRA. Under U.S. administrative law, both were federal statutes, and no reason existed why one should have preemption over another. One lawyer involved in the *Hoffman Plastics* case argued that the illegality of the claimant was central to the Supreme Court's decision to not award back pay:

> I think they [the Supreme Court justices] just couldn't get past the fact that pay was being awarded to somebody who wasn't eligible to work. You know, they just found it incongruous that ... it wasn't so much a question of letting the employer escape as it was, I think, a point of—it seemed like a windfall to the worker who wasn't entitled to it. (Interview, 20 November 2019)

The case law on this topic in the other jurisdictions is less advanced, probably in large part because the undocumented migrant populations there are smaller. In Australia, some cases view the employment contract of undocumented migrants as unenforceable or void due to immigration breaches. For instance, in the cases of *Australia Meat Holdings Pty. Ltd. v. Kazi* (2004) (2 Qd 458, 466, at paras 32–34) and *Smallwood v. Ergo Asia Pty. Ltd.* (2014, 964), the judges held that workers' compensation could not be provided to migrants in Australia who were working without a valid visa and thereby without a valid employment contract. This case can be compared with *Nonferral (NSW) Pty. Ltd. v. Taufia* (1998) (43 NSWLR 312, 316 (Cole JA)), where workers' compensation was awarded to a migrant who was unlawfully present in Australia.[9] In the area of unfair dismissal, the case law is mixed, but generally it appears that remedies will not be available to migrants who are working in breach of their visa conditions (Berg 2015, 185, citing *Wei Xin Chen v. Allied Packaging Co. Pty. Ltd.* (1997) 73 IR 53). That said, equitable remedies may be more likely to be available than statutory remedies to undocumented workers (*Midya v. Sagrani* (1999) NSWCA 187; *Masri v. Santoso* (2004) NSWIRComm 108) (see Berg 2016).

In the United Kingdom, the common law's illegality of contract principle, explored in Chapter 3, limits claim-making in this area. While some carve-outs around this rule have been developed for undocumented migrants who have been unlawfully trafficked or victims of human slavery, and therefore enjoy a public policy protection under torts law (as we saw in *Hounga v. Allen* (2014) UKSC 47), generally undocumented migrants do not fit this exemption or alternately, do not have the necessary evidence to make out a claim of slavery (Fudge 2018b, 572). Further, because the individual in some way consented to their unlawful contract, modern slavery protections may not apply (see Tataryn 2019, 135; Fudge 2018a). Furthermore, as was discussed in Chapter 3, there is no species of antidiscrimination claims in the United Kingdom based in the visa or undocumented status of the complainant

(*Taiwo v. Olaigbe* (2016) UKSC 31). As a result of this statutory framework and accompanying case law, undocumented migrant workers who have experienced workplace infringements may more often be viewed as unlawfully engaging in illegal work rather than as deserving of labor rights enforcement (Fudge 2016c, 2).

Legislatively

Across the countries studied in this book, legislative frameworks are mixed on the rights of undocumented migrants under labor law. In Australia, the Migration Act (1958), Section 235 renders working on an invalid work visa or while unlawfully present in Australia a criminal offense. The interpretation of this section by the courts has been mixed as relates to the imposition of employment rights. On this basis, some commentators have argued that Section 235 needs to be reformed to clarify that undocumented migrant workers do indeed enjoy minimum employment standards (Segrave 2017, 8).[10] This provision has been interpreted to limit the capacity of an unauthorized migrant to enforce their labor rights, including workers' compensation and unpaid work undertaken while in immigration detention (Berg 2015, Chapter 6).[11] Australia prohibits employers from hiring unauthorized individuals and includes a series of sanctions, ranging from administrative to criminal in nature (Migration Act 1958, s 245AB; see Fels 2019, Figure 4.3 for an overview). Further, hiring an illegal migrant and exploiting them can result in imprisonment of up to two years. The Australian legislative framework, in a more balanced approach than in the other jurisdictions, also penalizes employers who gain some benefit—including free labor—from paying a visa charge (Migration Act 1958, ss245AR, 245AS). As a product of these provisions and activities of the Australian Border Force, in recent years there has been an increase in fines issued to employers who illegally hire migrant workers (Fels Commission 2019, 71).

Further, Australia at times has offered informal settings for claim-bringing around employment law, such as the Wage Repayment Program following the 7-Eleven scandal that, at least in its early stages, made it easier for applicants to avoid concrete focus on their visa status and protected them from adverse deportation actions (Berg and Farbenblum 2018, 1066; Fels Commission 2019, 41). In California, the Labor Commissioners Office has provided a similar function and does not pose questions about visa status in first-instance decisions (California Department of Industrial Relations, Labor Enforcement Task Force 2019). In Canada, where immigration laws are determined federally, Laurie Berg (2016, 157–158) argues that departure orders are less stringent and applied with more discretion than in Australia (citing Immigration and Refugee Protection Regulations, SOR/2002-227, s226). In the United Kingdom where the Immigration Act (2016), Sections 34–38 now renders both the hiring of undocumented workers and their engagement in work a criminal offense, there is limited capacity for judges to explore such discretion (Fudge 2018a).

Infringement risk and access to justice for undocumented migrants

Undocumented status affects access to justice in several ways. There is strong evidence that migrants without legal status experienced lower adherence of their labor rights than those on visas. For instance, one study of several U.S. cities found that 37.1% of undocumented immigrant workers experienced minimum wage violations in the week prior to their being surveyed, compared with 21.3% for unauthorized immigrants and 15.6% for U.S.-born citizens (Bernhardt et al. 2009).

In Australia, the Howells Report into undocumented migrants found that undocumented workers are frequently "underpaid, misled about what they are doing, undernourished, beaten and threatened" (Howells 2010, 56). In their study of undocumented migrant workers in the harvesting sector in Australia, Elsa Underhill and Malcolm Rimmer (2016, 615) found:

> Undocumented workers . . . appear to be the most vulnerable segment in the harvest workforce. The available evidence (mainly anecdotal) suggests this vulnerability rests upon a set of interlocking characteristics—their lack of any legal right to work (and to claim employment rights); total dependence on contractors to supply work; social isolation from other workers and the wider community; disorientation created by moving from job to job; and the lack of English language skills that might help them understand and break away from their conditions of bondage.

Underhill and Rimmer's research makes it clear that undocumented status may compound or interact with other factors to increase the vulnerability of undocumented workers as relates to pay, working time, propensity for overwork, and the intensity of work. Maria Segrave's (2017) study of undocumented migrant workers in detention in Australia for visa infringements similarly finds high rates of underpayment and unlawful deductions, but also forms of indebted servitude—such as the provision of sexual favors to employers to pay off debts—for those working without valid visas.

These higher rates of infringements are compounded by the fact that migrant workers without valid status are less likely to bring litigation to enforce their rights due precisely to their unlawful status. They may also face legal impediments in enforcing such claims. Barrister James Ewins QC, commenting on the challenges of bringing migrant cases in the British context, said:

> And how do you empower someone who is being told explicitly, "You are illegal, you should not be here. Put your head above the parapet, even to complain about something legitimate, we will treat you first and foremost as an illegal immigrant, before we acknowledge your victimization in the U.K., and therefore with the right to access remedies and criminal sanctions under U.K. law." (Interview, 13 February 2019)

That said, as noted above, in some jurisdictions, migrants can seek access to justice without declaring their visa status, and this increases the likelihood that they will have their grievances addressed. These include underpayment claims before the Labor Commissioner's Office in California and underpayment claims with the Fair Work Ombudsman in Australia, although these do not lead to enforcement. The obstacles in bringing claims on behalf of undocumented workers can increase challenges for their lawyers, and thereby reduce the likelihood that they will take on such cases at all. According to Christopher Ho of Legal Aid at Work in San Francisco:

> Litigating these cases requires . . . more than the usual level of risk, both for the client and in terms of any legal fees. So it's not surprising to me that nonprofits or any kind of lawyers would think twice about that. And that's partially because the law's not very clear. (Interview, 1 November 2019)

Furthermore, in contexts where the courts are viewed as hostile to undocumented migrants, such as the current U.S. Supreme Court, lawyers may deliberately seek to limit litigation to avoid worsening the situation. Professor Sachs provided the following example from the case *U.S. v. Agri Processor*

Co. v. NLRB (2008 U.S. App. LEXIS 101 (D.C. Cir. 2008) (Supp. 32)), where the minority judgment of Brett Kavanaugh—now a Supreme Court judge—threatens to widen *Hoffman* to limiting collective bargaining rights more generally for undocumented workers:

> *Agriprocessor* involved a union election. The union wins the election, the employer says "We don't have to bargain because undocumented workers can't be employees." That would have gone further than the court did in *Hoffman Plastics*. The Court of Appeal for the D.C. Circuit says "That's not right. Undocumented workers are still employees within the meaning of the National Labor Relations Act." So the employer loses. The problem is, and the reason the case is significant, is it was a 2-1 vote, and the judge in dissent said, "This is an easy question. You can't possibly be an employee if you're not authorized to work in the United States." Almost as a matter of logic. That judge's name was Brett Kavanaugh. (Interview, 4 November 2019)

Governments have the scope to provide legislative frameworks to assist undocumented migrants in bringing workplace complaints. This can include creating legislative amendments that support undocumented migrant workers. However, in some instances, such legislation may be politically unpopular and not implemented, as has been the case in the United Kingdom, which was (formerly) one of three EU member states that did not implement the EU Directive 2009/52/EC that provided minimum standards on sanctions against employers of "illegally staying third country nationals." A decision not to implement such policies may have been motivated by other factors, including a political desire to seem tough on illegal immigration and to focus on immigration breaches over wages and employment rights (Bloch, Kumarappan, and McKay 2015, 148). Similarly, though undocumented migrants can bring claims under provincial employment law statute in Canada, including payment for unpaid wages, fear of exposure remains a factor in discouraging them from commencing litigation (Marsden 2018).

Immigration retaliation and protections against it

Another risk faced by undocumented migrant workers in enforcing their rights is that of retaliation by the employer on immigration grounds. Undocumented migrant workers fear that if they complain about their conditions, their employer will report them to immigration officials. The statutory rules around the permissibility of immigration retaliations by employers is therefore another important part of the rights puzzle. In some of the jurisdictions, there are protections in place against such retaliation, either by criminalizing the behavior of employers who engage in it, through noncooperation between enforcement and immigration officials, or through judicial action to limit the revelation of undocumented status during the discovery process of litigation.

In the United States, retaliations are rife and have increased since *Hoffman*. The Immigrant Defense Project in New York City estimated that the number of Immigration and Customs Enforcement (ICE) arrests in courthouses had increased tenfold between 2016 and 2017 (Costa 2018, 14). The Tahirih Justice Centre (2017) argues that these activities have had clear deterrent effects on the willingness of survivors of violence to enforce their rights where employment law has also been breached. Further, under the Trump administration, the nature and scale of these ICE inspections increased considerably, as Ana Avendaño noted:

> When I say "robust enforcement," it's militarized enforcement. These workplace raids are not just the Department of Homeland Security, it's the drug administration, it's like five or six different agencies that come down. And it's terrifying, agents with guns . . . and surrounding plants; and it's a family separation mechanism that nobody talks about, because for the four million U.S. citizen kids who have undocumented parents, for the most part, their parents disappear. (Interview, 22 November 2019)

Some efforts have been made over the years to manage the potential effects of immigration retaliation by employers in the United States. A memorandum of understanding was signed in 1998 between the Department of Homeland Security and the Department of Labor to guide communication in instances of immigration retaliation by an employer against a purported unfair labor practice. Essentially, the memorandum dictates that, other than in a few limited instances, if there is an open labor investigation, ICE will not pursue a concurrent immigration investigation (U.S. Department of Labor 2018, para IV[A]). Further, an *Operating Instruction* published by the Immigration and Naturalization Service (INS) is intended to guide field officers in addressing undocumented immigration claims in the event of a competing purported labor offense.[12] Scholars argue that these documents are not always watertight (e.g., Smith, Avendaño, and Martinez Ortega 2009).

That said, these instruments have been used by legal counsel to protect undocumented migrant workers in the event of retaliatory immigration actions (National Immigration Law Centre, Lawyer, Interview, 9 January 2020).

Further, in California, courts have also been sympathetic to migrants by providing protections from deportation when they are bringing labor claims (Smith, Avendano, and Martinez Ortega 2009, 16).[13] There is a precedent there of enforcing labor standards even after employer retaliation to federal immigration officials has occurred (e.g., *Contreras v. Corinthian Vigor Ins. Brokerage, Inc.*, 25 F. Supp. 2d 1053, 137 Lab. Cas. P 33795, 4 Wage & Hour Cas. 2d (BNA) 1793, 1998 WL 791597 (N.D. Cal. 1998)). As noted above, in *Rivera v. Nibco Inc.* (2004) the court considered the risks of retaliation if migrant visa status is revealed through discovery. The potential chilling effect of such discovery upon litigation by migrants was seen in this case to "burden the public interest," and therefore a limit was placed upon possible discovery around a migrants' visa status that could occur at the outset of the case.

California has taken legislative steps to limit the reach of *Hoffman* and retaliatory action by employers more broadly. Immediately following *Hoffman*, an amendment to the California Labor Code was passed that directed state and civil rights remedies, except those provisions exempt by federal law (Senate Bill 1818, c1071). Separately, Bill 524 (2013) required that threats by employers to report migrants to ICE be classified as "criminal extortion" under California law. Further, there is a requirement under the California code that employees be informed when their employer is being audited for immigration compliance. Over the period 2013 through 2018, California passed seven major statutory reforms to protect undocumented migrants in instances of retaliation (see Costa 2018). It was widely acknowledged in the interviews undertaken for this book that California is more protective of undocumented immigrants from a regulatory and case law perspective than any other comparable U.S. state.

Some of these protections were challenged legally by the Trump administration in its filings against sanctuary cities, although most protections have been upheld by the courts (see *US v. California* 314F. Suppl. 3d 1077, 1104; *US v. California* (No. 18-16496), 9th Circuit 2019). This is because while California cannot trespass on federal immigration powers to lawfully arrest unauthorized migrants, it does have the right to protect migrants from retaliation and discrimination on immigration grounds that are not preempted by federal powers (Costa 2018; Motomura 2018, 459). The federalist conflict between the two levels of government over their appropriate remit in protecting borders or protecting workplace rights infringements is therefore central to current policy on this issue. It relates to the constitutional question under the U.S. Constitution, Article VI, Clause 2 of presumption, or whether federal law prevails due to an implied "Supremacy Clause" in federal statute or an implied intention that state law would state as an obstacle to the operation of Congress's intention (citing *Hines v. Davidowitz*, 312 US. 52 67 (1941)). As Kati Griffith (2017) notes, California in particular has been a "laboratory of progressiveness" in this regard, with various attempts made to protect undocumented migrant workers' rights through state-based legislative initiatives.[14]

In the United Kingdom, the legislative framework provided by the Immigration Act (2016) introduced a series of provisions that made it more difficult for employers to hire undocumented workers and rendered engagement in work without a valid visa a crime. These provisions increase rather than reduce risks of retaliation. Focusing on the restrictions on employers, these replicated a requirement under the prior legislation that employers check their workers' immigration status and their entitlement to work. However, there are now potential jail sentences of up to five years or limitless fines for unlawful migrants (U.K. Home Office, Department of Innovation and Skills 2016). Reflective of the seriousness with which the British state views undocumented visa status, it has high levels of deportations of migrants (47,000 in 2013, although the number did plummet to 7,952 during COVID-19) (Walsh 2022). The ultimate effect of the new immigration provisions is to increase the potential for retaliation in the event of unauthorized immigration status. Since 2016 there has also been an uptick in prosecutions of employers hiring unauthorized migrants (see further Fudge 2018a, 576; Griffiths and Yeo 2021). Alice Bloch, Leena Kumarappan, and Sonia McKay (2015, 135) argue that, over time, the focus of employer sanctions under immigration law has shifted government resources and policy attention from improving conditions for migrant workers to creating a hostile environment for undocumented migration in the United Kingdom. This means that the provisions under the Immigration Act may perversely have had the effect of pushing migrants into even more exploitative conditions with longer hours and rendering them less likely to make complaints.

Some protections for certain types of migrant workers do exist in the United Kingdom under the Modern Slavery Act (2015), Section 45; for example, those undocumented migrants who are also recognized as victims of slavery can be protected from deportation. These individuals can make complaints to the National Referral Mechanism (NRM) and, if found to be victims, will not face immigration penalties. However, the risks associated with making an unsubstantiated complaint to the NRM are considerable, and the threshold for demonstrating slavery as opposed to lower forms of exploitation is difficult to reach.

This situation presents challenges within British regulatory design. As A. C. L. Davies (2016, 444) notes, the question of whether labor enforcement agencies enjoy a firewall with immigration authorities to not report undocumented workers directly influences the relative regulatory power of these two competing areas of law. She quotes the British Labour Enforcement Directorate, demonstrating that some information sharing still occurs:

> We do not intend that preventing illegal working should be a focus of the Director or the labor market enforcement strategy. Where illegal workers are the victims of exploitation, we will still take action against the rogue businesses that are committing these crimes, and we will continue to increase our efforts to support victims of modern slavery. However, the Government has concluded that it is still appropriate for labor market enforcement agencies to work with Immigration Enforcement (as they do now) to share information about illegal workers. (U.K. Home Office, Department of Innovation and Skills 2016, para 86)

In Australia, the Fair Work Act (2009), s434 includes adverse action protections that could, at least theoretically, be used to protect against immigration retaliation by an employer reacting to an employment law complaint by an undocumented worker. However, as Berg (2016, 187) argues, it is unclear whether "'adverse action' includes terminating unauthorized employment." With regard to protections that migrants enjoy during the complaints process, questions have been raised about the robustness of an agreement between the Fair Work Ombudsman (FWO) and the Department of Immigration and Border Protection (DIBP) to not share information about visa status between the two departments. While this agreement was struck as a protection for migrant workers who bring complaints, commentators have argued that it is not watertight. According to Laurie Berg and Bassina Farbenblum (2018, 1082–3):

> [T]he protection remains partial: it leaves visa-overstayers and tourist visa holders unprotected. Indeed, it is unclear whether it will offer sufficient

comfort to enable those visa holders with work rights to come forward and report exploitation. It does not appear to give rise to any [legal] rights on the part of a visa holder to appeal a visa cancellation on the basis of unauthorized work. Nor does it establish a firewall between the FWO and the DIBP such that the FWO can guarantee the confidentiality of information provided by migrant workers requesting assistance. To the contrary, it *requires* that the FWO notify DIBP of the migrant worker's visa status to obtain the visa cancellation dispensation.

There are similar concerns that Taskforce Cadena—a collaboration between the FWO, the Australian Federal Police, and other government agencies to detect criminal syndicates that exploit migrant workers—might act as a deterrent to claim-making by migrant workers (Fels Commission 2019, 52). Furthermore, an anonymous reporting line called "Border Watch Online Report" allows citizens, including coworkers and employers, to report suspected undocumented migrants to the Department of Home Affairs, with no consideration of current employment-based claims those individuals may possess. That information can then be used by border enforcement to deport the individual, and there has been an increase in deportations in Australia over the past two decades (see Walsh 2020, 286 for a critique). Inquiries have called for legislative reform to make coercing a migrant worker into breaching their visa conditions an offense (Fels Commission 2019, Recommendation 19).

Canada has no specific protections for migrant workers against reprisal; however, it does have broad employee protections against reprisals, including in human rights, collective bargaining, and labor law statutes. For instance, in Ontario, the Occupational Health and Safety Act (1990), s50 includes protections against reprisals for a complaint against unsafe work conditions.

Quantitative analysis

Having considered some of the key ethical, legal, and policy dimensions of the *Hoffman Plastics* case, as well as undocumented migration policy and law in other countries, we move now to the quantitative dimensions of the chapter and consider the broader array of statistics on undocumented populations in each of the jurisdictions covered.

Undocumented populations

California has the largest number of undocumented workers of any of the U.S. states. Estimates of the undocumented population across the United States are placed at around 11.3 million, accounting for one-quarter of all immigrants in the country (López and Bialik 2017). Up to 50% of this undocumented cohort are Mexican (Hoefer, Rytina, and Baker 2009, cited in Gleeson and Xóchitl 2019, 10) and 2.3 million reside in California as of 2021 (Table 5.1 provides averages of all undocumented migrants over time, rather than 2021 alone). In fact, 6% of California's labor market is comprised of undocumented migrants, and the vast bulk of them are in paid employment (Pew Research Center 2016; Passel and Cohn 2016, cited in Costa 2018). While there is evidence that the proportion of the undocumented Mexican population in the United States has declined, from 6.9 million in 2007 to 5.8 million in 2014 (Krogstad, Passel, and Cohn 2017), the overall undocumented population has remained relatively stable over this period. This is because while Mexican representation has decreased, new flows from Central America's Northern Triangle countries—El Salvador, Guatemala, and Honduras—have increased. As border crossing has become more challenging, there has also been an increase in those arriving legally but then remaining on lapsed visas (Lopez, Passel, and Cohn 2021). These figures explain the elevated importance of understanding the undocumented migration question in California when compared with the other jurisdictions in

Table 5.1 Undocumented migrants, in MWRD and as total population

	Australia	Canada	United Kingdom	California
Undocumented migrants in the MWRD (N)	5	6	3	13
Proportion of migrants that are undocumented in MWRD (%)	0.5	1.2	2.1	3.9
Estimated undocumented population (2006–2016, average)	710,600	948,000	7,040,000	1,880,250

this book, and why the issue of the rights of undocumented workers has been given much more attention in the U.S. context than elsewhere.

There are few good estimates of the size of the undocumented population in Australia. This could in part relate to the fact that the size of this group will vary depending upon lapses and whether there have been subsequent visa renewals. As such, individuals may move in and out of illegality quite fluidly. Official estimates vary between 50,000 and 100,000 (Howells 2011), and visa overstayers have been estimated at 62,700 (Berg 2015). However, these data are now dated and are probably a vast underestimation. Some research by Underhill and Rimmer (2016, 614) suggests that up to a third of the workforce in the harvesting sector in Australia is undocumented and come from countries as wide ranging as the United Kingdom, Estonia, Afghanistan, and South Korea. Most recent estimates presented before the Australian Parliament revealed that there were 64,000 noncitizens who overstayed their visas and approximately 20,000 of whom had worked (Segrave 2017, 56). However, according to Tim Nelthorpe of the National Union of Workers, whose union principally represents horticultural workers, the figure could be as high as 500,000 (Interview, 8 October 2019).

In the United Kingdom, 2009 estimates by the London School of Economics put the undocumented population as ranging between 417,000 and 863,000 (Gordon et al. 2009). Estimated undocumented flows in Canada have grown from 4,000 people in the early 1980s to a very large range of between 50,000 and 800,000 by 2009 (Marsden 2009, 213, 220).

The MWRD

We now consider the representation of undocumented migrants in the MWRD. Table 5.1 captures the number of migrant workers with a clear undocumented status in the database as a number and as a percentage of total migrants. It should be noted here that stock data (total present undocumented migrants) are used for the undocumented population, while flow data are used for the total migrant population, as stock data that are also arranged according to visa status are not available.[15] As is clear, the numbers in the database are very small; apart from California, they are single digits. And while the database generally has low numbers compared to the estimated reference population, they are even smaller for undocumented migrants. This is consistent with what this chapter has demonstrated about the challenges

Table 5.2 Violation type, claims brought, and claims substantiated, by jurisdiction and undocumented or visaed migration status

	Australia		Canada		United Kingdom		California	
	un.	visa	un.	visa	un.	visa	un.	visa
Criminal								
Brought claim (N)	0	140	0	19	0	19	3	22
Substantiated claim (N)	0	29	0	8	0	14	3	14
Success rate (%)	0	20.7	0	42.1	0	73.7	100	63.6
Economic								
Brought claim (N)	2	799	0	187	3	88	11	285
Substantiated claim (N)	2	665	0	143	1	32	9	213
Success rate (%)	100	83.2	0	76.5	33.3	36.4	81.8	74.7
Safety								
Brought claim (N)	3	36	6	52	0	2	1	14
Substantiated claim (N)	1	27	3	27	0	1	0	5
Success rate (%)	33.3	75	50	51.9	0	50	0	35.7
Denial of leave and other workplace entitlements								
Brought claim	0	63	0	2	0	0	0	1
Substantiated claim	0	48	0	1	0	0	0	0
Success rate (%)	0	76.2	0	50	0	0	0	0
Discrimination								
Brought claim	0	11	0	240	2	71	5	41
Substantiated claim	0	4	0	137	0	20	3	8
Success rate (%)	0	36.4	0	57.1	0	28.2	0.6	19.5

Note: un. = undocumented; visa = all migrants on substantive visas.

undocumented migrants face in bringing claims, particularly where they also face potential immigration reprisals from their employers.

Table 5.2 includes information on the types of claims undocumented migrants do bring and how these compare with the remainder of the MWRD claimants who have visas. Migrants, undocumented or visaed, are most likely to bring claims of economic violations, as noted in Chapter 1, compared to other violation types. Undocumented migrants generally have success rates in these cases on par with or higher than those claimants with visas. This is unsurprising, given that it will only be undocumented migrants with the strongest cases that will risk deportation orders to bring employment-based claims. Leave- and discrimination-based claims are infrequent, which reflects the fact that undocumented migrants may be focusing upon more immediate needs—such as cash repayments of wage entitlements—in the rare instances where legal action is brought.

Summary

The central challenge to bringing workplace claims for undocumented migrants is whether they are entitled to employment protections at all while also being unauthorized to work. This question is first and foremost a normative one—both for the courts and for policymakers. It relates to the classic issue of where the limits of entitlement should extend to and where they should cease. Judy Fudge (2016c, 3) summarizes the dilemma: "Jurisdiction sets the outer boundaries of the process of legal characterization, and it is an outcome of social and political contestation. It functions to allocate social relations and social activities into different legal domains or regulatory contexts." The rights of undocumented migrants touch on broader public policy concerns about courts having to implement laws that would sanction other forms of illegality, here immigration breaches (for a detailed discussion, see Berg 2016, Chapter 6). And it goes to the qualitative judgment of how seriously we view undocumented status: Is it a serious civil or even criminal offense or more akin to littering in a public park, to use the analogy of Hiroshi Motomura (2014, 21).

Establishing effective workplace protections for undocumented migrant workers is therefore an ongoing issue of political and legal contention. For some, such workers do not deserve any rights by virtue of their unlawful status within the host societies. However, this remains predominantly an anti-union and antiworker perspective, such as that espoused by Justice Kavanaugh in Agriprocessor. Such a hardline position may not even be supported by those otherwise opposed to migration but mindful that the economic benefits of such workers may be worth retaining. A more moderate position is to provide some protections for such workers when investigating their employment claims or during the court discovery process and later dealing with the regularization of their immigration status. As such, the two issues of labor and immigration can be disentangled from one another and treated as separate rights—or infringements—issues.

The most liberal perspective is offered by those who propose amnesties. The United States offered the most high-profile amnesty in 1986, which granted legal status to over three million people (Orrenius and Zavodny 2001). However, even in Australia, where the government has historically taken a tough stance on lapsed visa holders and undocumented migrants, there are increasing calls during the COVID-19 pandemic for an amnesty to address the growing undocumented population working on Australian farms (Love 2021). A more moderate position would be to offer amnesties on most breaches of ongoing valid visas, excluding serious crimes, but no amnesties for undocumented status (WEstJustice 2016, 226). As such, the way that visa cancelation rules and immigration laws operate to indirectly affect the capacity for undocumented migrants to enforce their employment rights is important here.

Several recommendations flow for governments and legal advocates from the findings of this chapter. First, it is clear from the analysis that government data on undocumented populations across the four countries is poor. Even in the United States, the best estimates are driven by the Pew Research Center rather than government agencies themselves. In the other countries, the estimate ranges are broad and the data themselves dated. There is a strong need for better data in order for government to have a more accurate sense of the scale of the issue it faces with undocumented workers, from a labor rights but also, arguably, an enforcement perspective. Insofar as this issue also intersects directly with visa regulation, as we will see in detail in the next chapter, the need for an empirical baseline for analysis is hugely important.

Second, it is recommended that, where possible, government remove information sharing or minimize as much as possible the lack of firewalls between labor enforcement and border enforcement bodies. This chapter has provided several examples where such information sharing has created a "chilling effect" upon litigation by undocumented migrant workers, contributing to the low litigation rates we see in Table 5.1. Such information sharing could be removed except for the most egregious cases of visa violations and associated criminality by a migrant worker. It should be noted that while California has made important inroads in this regard (Griffith 2017), this is less the case in the other jurisdictions or across other American states, and there are significant reforms that could be achieved.

Third, it is clear that most legal claims on behalf of undocumented workers are economic in nature. It could be useful for community legal centers and migrant worker centers to be provided by governments with more guidance on the use of antidiscrimination law in this area, given that workplace violations may often have intersecting discrimination dimensions.

Finally, in the United States, any future deliberations on comprehensive immigration reform should incorporate reform of the IRCA to clarify that the legislative intent of the 1986 reforms was not to deny undocumented migrants recourse under the NLRA, and that this be explicitly clarified statutorily. Secondary material from the passing of the IRCA did make this point clear, but was not taken into account by the majority of the Supreme Court in *Hoffman Plastics* (2002). Given there was a Republican majority in both houses after the *Hoffman* decision, no such legislative reform was proposed at this time (former U.S. government lawyer, Interview, 20 November 2019).

Focusing on the rights of undocumented migrant workers encourages us to consider how migrants become undocumented in the first place and where the supposed fault for this lapsed or undocumented status may lie. While unlawful border crossing has historically been a common source of undocumented migrants in the United States, lapsed visa status or working on a visa that does not include working rights is more common in the other jurisdictions. Sometimes this breach can occur unwittingly on the part of the migrant. As such, the design of visa regulation is an interconnected component for understanding the rights of undocumented migrant workers. For instance, Joo-Cheong Tham, Iain Campbell, and Martina Boese (2016) note that the design of temporary labor migration programs can encourage noncompliance by the employer—and sometimes also the worker—that can in turn contribute to breaches of immigration law. In this way, temporary visa programs can provide their own pathways to undocumented status, which can in turn increase the vulnerability of workers. We consider this issue further in Chapter 6, on immigration regulation.

6
Regulation and Migrant Vulnerability

The Role of Visas in Workplace Violations

Between 2007 and 2010, Ronald Kheong Huat Choong and, his wife, Kim Choong, hired ten workers from the Philippines as chefs and managers for their restaurants and cafés in Darwin, in Australia's Northern Territory. The workers were all paid significantly less than legally required in Australia, and they received neither overtime nor penalty rates for weekend or holiday work. They often worked over sixty hours per week in the dry season and less in the wet session. No attempts were made by the two employers to account for these discrepancies. During the bulk of their employment, the workers were paid between $12 and $13 per hour—far below the national minimum wage. The level of underpayment came to a net loss of between $9,200 to $11,000[1] for each worker (*Minister for Immigration and Border Protection v. Choong Enterprises Pty. Ltd.* (2015) FCA 390, 27 April 2015, paras 8, 98, henceforth *Choong Enterprises*).

The workers were employed on 457 Temporary Work (Skilled) visas that enabled Choong Enterprises to bring them into Australia for the specific purpose of employment at their businesses. It is clear that the workers were grossly underpaid for their work. However, the particular legal issue in the case was whether the employers had breached the Migration Act (1958) (Cwth) (Australia), s140Q, which sets out a variety of sponsorship requirements, including, through an associated regulation, paying a migrant worker no less than that paid to Australian workers. The Temporary Skilled Migration Income Threshold (TSMIT) was introduced into the Migration Act in 2011[2] to ensure that migrant workers were protected from underpayment and, in turn, that they did not undercut Australian workers. The Department of Immigration and Border Protection was empowered to enforce the act and seek restitution for the workers. This is a rare case where an immigration department, as opposed to a wage enforcement agency, brought a claim for an employment breach on behalf of migrant workers.

Patterns of Exploitation. Anna K. Boucher, Oxford University Press. © Oxford University Press 2023.
DOI: 10.1093/oso/9780197599112.003.0007

Choong Enterprises was fined a total of $39,000 for the contraventions. In addition to underpayment, there was also evidence of poor record keeping by Mr. Choong and the imposition of agency fees on the employees, for which Choong Enterprises was also fined $30,000 and $4,000, respectively.[3] An additional fine of $120,000 was imposed for breaching the TSMIT rules under Regulation 2.79 of Migration Regulations (1994). The company was also fined $10,000 for inappropriately deflecting costs onto the workers, under Regulation 2.87; this was because recruitment fees had been passed on to the workers by deducting between $200 and $300 per week from their pay over several months of their employment (*Choong Enterprises*, para 32). The total penalties and remedies for Choong Enterprises was $335,017—the highest to date in Australia and the largest penalty pursued by the Department of Immigration and Border Protection up to that point (Daly 2015).

The assistant minister for immigration and border protection, Senator Michaela Cash, noted the public policy rationale behind the litigation: "The stiff penalty this company has received should send a warning to other sponsors: if you fail to meet your requirements, my [d]epartment may impose administrative sanctions, issue an infringement notice, execute an enforceable undertaking, or apply to the federal court for a civil penalty order" (cited in Pendlebury 2015).

There are several legal complexities to this case. One was the correct interpretation of the "totality principle," or how reductions in penalties could be achieved when imposing penalties upon employers. Another was the interaction of the protections created through the TSMIT and broader employment law protections. Here, Justice Mansfield noted that the relevant reference point was the Migration Act's TSMIT rather than employment law's industrial awards. This made it clear that a migrant worker must be paid at the TSMIT level,[4] which could differ from an award (*Choong Enterprises*, para 24). In a separate restitution penalties hearing, he wrote, "[A]s the Pay As You Go (PAYG) tax adjustment in each case is different, the total claimed by way of reimbursement of regulation 2.79 fixes the entitlement, the total reimbursement sought by the Minister is $125,956 compared to $52,480 if the Award is the appropriate starting point" (*Minister for Immigration and Border Protection v. Choong Enterprises No. 2*, FCA 553, 4 June 2015, at para 9). This statement underlies the protective function of the TSMIT in requiring a higher level of payment than the award in some instances and thereby also acting as a disincentive to hire migrant rather than Australian workers. Although not foremost in the judgment, the vulnerability of the workers by virtue of their visa status is a latent theme in this case. For instance, there is evidence that Choong Enterprises was advised that it was not paying the workers at the TSMIT; however, they "did not take heed of these reminders" (para 63). The interaction of immigration and employment law was also a key feature of the judgment. This case offers insights into the role of immigration visa design in shaping the rights and entitlements of migrant workers. For instance, the fact that workers were directly sponsored by the Choongs meant that they had limited capacity to change jobs. If they wanted to change jobs or were dismissed, Migration Regulations (1994), Schedule 8, Condition 8107 (3)(ii)(C)(b) gave them only twenty-eight days to seek another employer before they would be deemed unlawfully present in Australia.[5] An agent was used to bring the workers to Australia from the Philippines, and their visas charges were inappropriately deflected onto the workers. Further, the migrants' area of employment limited their opportunities to transition onto permanent skilled visas, increasing their dependence on their employer for ongoing sponsorship, whereas permanent visa holders or highly skilled temporary migrants might have readily found employment opportunities elsewhere. The *Choong Enterprises* case invites analysis of the intersection of regulatory design, sector of employment, and employment law in shaping patterns of migrant workplace violations.

In this chapter, we consider two key dimensions of regulation. The first is how the regulation of immigration law can shape the conditions of migrants and thereby their likelihood of experiencing workplace violations. For example, this can occur when a migrant is tied to a particular employer, which increases a relationship of control, or through the conditions that immigration law places upon migrants on dependent visas. Second, we consider how the interaction of employment and immigration law can compound the effects of each regulation. We consider both of these regulatory dimensions before turning to a quantitative analysis of visa status drawn from the MWRD and key policy recommendations.

Immigration law regulation

Much of the scholarship on regulation deals with the particular vulnerabilities of temporary migrants compared to permanent migrants. There are several aspects to this that implicate visa design.

First, tying migrants to employers can negatively affect migrants' workplace rights. Some authors have argued that this visa design can increase the likelihood of noncompliance by employers in certain industries (Tham, Campbell, and Boese 2016). Speaking of the overseas domestic worker visa, but with broad application to the issue of visa tying, British barrister James Ewins (2015, 20) asks, "What is the rationale for imposing the tie? Does the tie result in any increased risk of abuse? And if so, is the increased risk of abuse created by the tie sufficient to outweigh the rationale for imposing it?"

Second, a visa that limits employment portability can also limit migrants' rights. For instance, the ILO (2017b, 20) has argued that restrictions on visa mobility "not only hinder the protections of migrant workers' rights, they also result in inefficient labor markets and contribute to high recruitment costs ... which are exacerbated by the inability of businesses to promptly obtain workers with appropriate skills from a local labor pool." In the opinion of the ILO, revising temporary visas to allow portability "has great potential to ameliorate the rights of migrant workers" (ILO 2017b, 7). Judy Fudge (2016c, 3) goes further and labels temporary forms of visa regulation a form of "unfreedom." The increased risk posed by temporary immigration visa design relates largely to the control of the migrant by their employer; limitations on free choice through a lack of portability is a key component of the risk presented by temporary visas (ILO 2019, 9).

Third, visa conditions can create differences between the rights given on either temporary or permanent visas. Even if a migrant has the opportunity to change employers, visa conditions can effectively control them. For instance, if a breached condition can lead to an illegal status, the vulnerability of the migrant is increased. A permanent migrant, who already enjoys security of residency, is less likely to be affected by such provisions. Summarizing some of the risks faced by temporary migrants in bringing claims, Matt Kunkel from the Migrant Worker Centre in Victoria, Australia, argued, "Worker exploitation in temporary visa cohorts is just so underreported because people fear the prospects of deportation. So, even coming in our door to talk about their problems or calling us on the phone is a really courageous first step" (Interview, Melbourne, 2019). The precarity of temporary status also affects to the potential of cases being brought. Temporary status can mean that by the time a court date arrives, the migrant's visa status has lapsed. As employment lawyer Gabrielle Marchetti, noted:

> Up until about April or May [2019], it was a three-month wait time from when you issued a small claim application in the federal circuit court to when you got your final hearing.... But now, it's out to six months. So, I just

think that is going to have a huge impact on temporary migrant workers who file their application but then have to wait six months for a hearing date. (Interview, Melbourne, 2019)

On the basis of the existing literature and policy critiques of temporary migration schemes, a strong line of scholarship finds that there is a "rights versus numbers trade-off": more migrants are brought in on temporary visas with fewer rights, while fewer migrants are brought in on permanent visas with more rights (Ruhs 2013). At times, this argument looks not only at the type of visa but also its intersection with skill level; for instance, those with lower skills are more likely to be brought in on temporary visas with fewer rights than those on high-skilled permanent visas (see Reilly et al. 2018, 5, citing van den Broek, Harvey, and Groutsis 2016; Green, Atfield, and Purcell 2016). The rights versus numbers argument has been criticized as defending a reduction in labor standards (Tham and Campbell 2011) when it merely provides an empirical map of existing regimes; it is not a normative preference for temporary migration.

An alternative perspective, from political economy, posits that the effects of temporary immigration on workplace rights relates to the overall scale of migration, not just visa status. The fact that in many jurisdictions temporary visas are uncapped can lead to a reserve army of labor forming, with a larger number of workers enjoying fewer rights. A government decision to increase low-skilled temporary immigration, but not permanent migration, suggests a preference for "a docile labor pool" (Foster 2012, 37). As such, the reserve army effect can impact the size of this temporary workforce as well as the conditions it enjoys.

Finally, an argument that focuses on the role of regulation in shaping violation outcomes operates from the assumption that even small regulatory changes can influence both employee and employer behavior. Iain Campbell and Joo-Cheong Tham (2013, 251–252) suggest that governments possess a variety of regulatory tools that can increase protections for temporary visa holders; these include

> caps and quotas (which limit the supply of migrant labor according to the extent of the shortages), specification of the areas . . . where there are skill shortages and labor market testing requirements. They could also include mechanisms aimed at sending a price signal to employer sponsors that the engagement of migrant workers will be more expensive than comparable

local workers (for example, high application and sponsorship fees, specific taxes on engagement of migrant workers, or a requirement that migrant workers be paid a higher wage than local workers).

As is clear from the discussion below, some of these changes have been considered for some of the visas profiled, but not across all four countries. Given that immigration policy is set federally in the countries covered in this book, we consider each jurisdiction at the national, not provincial level.

Australia

A shift toward temporary immigration over the 2000s has transformed Australia's immigration settings and, some have argued, migrants' labor rights (Tham and Campbell 2011, 2; Boucher 2016, Chapter 7). Survey data suggest that there are higher rates of underpayment of temporary migrants than among permanent migrants (Fels 2019, 5, 112; Hall and Partners 2016), although such analyses are stymied by lack of a clear reference category or robust sampling methods or low response rates.

Flawed data limitations aside, there are regulatory features of some temporary visas in Australia that could contribute to greater risks of exploitation. The first visa to consider, and the one profiled in the *Choong Enterprises* case, is the 457 visa. Some aspects of worker vulnerability are built into this visa design. For instance, employer control over the migrant's visa status can lead in some instances to "employers extracting inappropriate advantage from obtaining a visa" (Fels 2019, 123). The 457 visa has been subject to a series of deregulatory moves, followed by re-regulation and ultimately its rebadging in 2018 as the Temporary Skills Shortage visa; this process permitted the migration of lower-skilled workers into regional areas in 2003 and then expanded the definition of "regional" in 2007. In that same year, a provision was introduced that a salary paid to a 457-visa holder be no less favorable than the salary of an analogous domestic worker (under a now superseded version of Migration Regulations (1994), (Cwth), reg2.72(10)(cc)).[6] In 2009, some restrictions were introduced following a government inquiry to provide new protections from competition both to migrant workers and to domestic workers (Campbell and Tham 2013, 258). Further, the visa is now split between short- and medium-term streams with different rights to remain in Australia (Migration Regulations (1994), Schedule 2, Subclass 482). This division has been criticized for entrenching low-skilled workers' vulnerability (see Boucher et al. 2017, 9–10).

The working holiday maker (WHM) visa program in Australia has also been criticized for creating workplace risks for migrant workers (e.g., Reilly 2015; Tan et al. 2009; Tan and Lester 2012). According to one survey of temporary migrant workers, the WHM visa raised the most reports of negative migrant worker experiences of all the temporary visa categories in Australia (Hall and Partners 2016, 113). Although formally a travel and tourism visa, since its creation in 1997 the WHM visa includes working rights; visa holders are primarily employed in agriculture and horticulture, hospitality, and au pair work. Over time, the "working" component of the visa has been extended to the time permitted with each employer across a total number of employers (Reilly et al. 2018, 2–3, 14).

One aspect of the visa is the eighty-eight-day rule, requiring WHM holders to work in farm or other related work in regional Australia for eighty-eight days to extend their visa for a second year (Migration Regulations (1994), Schedule 2, Subclasses 417 and 462).[7] A key motivation for this extension was to increase the number of workers in harvest periods (Reilly et al. 2018, 15). The rule has been identified as creating particular vulnerability: a "cultural mindset amongst employers wherein the engagement of... visa holders is considered license to determine the status, conditions and remuneration levels of workers . . . without reference to Australian workplace laws" (Australia, FWO 2016b, 33). As Reilly and Howe (2019, 96) note, dependence on the employer is built into the design of the WHM.[8]

Some legal representatives of migrants noted the challenges that the structure of the WHM visa presents to bringing legal claims. Tarni Perkal of the WEstJustice Legal Clinic in Melbourne states:

> I think they [migrants] are a particularly difficult cohort to target. They move a lot. Often by the time they're in a position to enforce their rights, they're off the farm, they may then be focused on trying to get the second-year visa or . . . rather than dealing [with the legal issue] they just want to move on from it. (Interview, Melbourne, 2019)

The risk of illegality is another way that employers can exercise control over certain visa holders. This was raised by the Australian Council of Trade Unions (ACTU) before a Senate inquiry in 2017, when it noted that "there is evidence that certain employers exert pressure on temporary visa holders to breach a condition of their visa in order to gain leverage over the employee because the Fair Work Act does not apply when a person has breached their visa condition."[9] One example of this is the forty-hour rule in Australia, which prevents international students from working more than forty hours over a fortnight. This condition is a strict liability offense, meaning that its breach can lead to deportation (Migration Act (1958) (Cwth), ss116(1) and 235).[10]

On the basis of the precariousness created by visa rules, changes have been recommended that would either remove the forty-hour rule (WEstJustice 2016, 229; Fels 2019, 122) or make employers that have coerced their workers into breaching their visa conditions guilty of an offense (Fels Commission 2019, Recommendation 19). Others recommend replacing the WHM visa with a specific agricultural visa (Reilly and Howe 2019), although it is unclear how that would address worker vulnerability if it were also temporary. None of these recommendations has been introduced to date, although work is currently underway to finalize the policy design of a new agricultural visa category under the so-called Pacific Australia Labour Mobility Scheme (Australian Department of Foreign Affairs and Trade 2022)

Although they constitute a small percentage of migrant flows, the reinforced economic and political vulnerability of asylum seekers with pending applications for status warrants particular attention here. While not all of those on asylum seeker visas can or do work, some do, and this puts them at risk of exploitation, as Tarni Perkal notes:

> They're going to find it very difficult to get a job for a variety of reasons, including the fact that they're on a bridging visa. And they are desperate for work, and there's not enough employment. Because there's a group [of asylum seekers] now which are getting no government support at all, so they are totally reliant on [employment] places. (Interview, Melbourne, 2019).

United Kingdom

Prior to Brexit in 2020, the majority of the United Kingdom's temporary immigration came through general EU entry rather than immigration permits. The 2007 decision to suspend low-skilled third-country national migration by blocking Tier 5 visas has meant that, at least formally, the United Kingdom did not accept low-skilled labor until 2020. However, there are several important exceptions here.

First, migrants from new accession states (EU8) could enter the United Kingdom with very few restrictions, and many took up low-paid work (see Boucher and Gest 2018, Chapter 4). Between 2004, when EU8 controls were lifted, and 2009, the number of EU8 nationals living in the United Kingdom increased from 115,000 to 700,000. This largely uncapped form of free movement had significant effects on the immigration composition of the United Kingdom and increased the population by a full 1% (Migration Advisory Committee 2014, 57). Second, although low-skilled immigration outside of the EU was formally closed in 2007, many non-EU migrants employed in low-skilled work were already present in the United Kingdom, having entered through spousal, asylum, or international student visas, as well as open work permits (49, 55). This meant that a variety of visas contributed to the stock of migrants that could face potential workplace violations.

Second, there were several exceptions to the exclusion of Tier 5 temporary low-skilled immigration before 2021 when changes were made to the Immigration Act. The most notable of these is the Overseas Domestic Worker visa. Chief among the concerns with this visa is its temporary nature (Human Rights Watch 2014), which in 2012 was shortened from twelve to six months (Immigration Rules 159A(iv); 541 Parl. Deb. H.C. (6th ser.) (27 February 2012–8 March 2012) col. 35WS). Another important feature is lack of portability (Mantouvalou 2015; see also Anderson 1993; Costello 2015). Other than in very restricted instances when an overseas domestic worker leaves the employment relationship and meets the requirements of the National Referral Mechanisms under the Modern Slavery Act (s50(2)(b), 53(4)), they are rendered undocumented when they choose to leave their employer. Since 2012, permanent status cannot be applied for from this visa and the individual is tied to one employer with limited portability to a different employer during their time in the United Kingdom. Concerns over the temporary and precarious nature of this visa persist (Mantouvalou 2015, 340ff.). As barrister Ewins (2015, 20), who conducted a review of this visa, noted:

> The argument has been fiercely debated. On the one hand parallels are drawn by various groups within the kafala system of sponsored/ bonded labor present in some Gulf States. . . . On the other hand, the Government remains unconvinced that there is sufficient evidence to show that by adding the tie in 2012, there has been any more abuse than before 2012.

Canada

Temporary status has been found to create migrant vulnerability in Canada. The vast bulk of the temporary migrant workers in Canada enter through the Temporary Foreign Worker Program (TFWP). This scheme comprises both high- and low-wage positions as well as a broad overarching category for the Seasonal Agricultural Worker Program and the Live-in Caregiver Program (defunct since 2014).[11] The genesis of the TFWP visa may itself relate to lobbying from the mining sector for a ready supply of workers (Foster and Barnetson 2015). For a period, the "4-in-4-out rule" required that a temporary foreign worker be in Canada for no more than four years before they were required to leave for at least four years. Heavily criticized for increasing the vulnerability of temporary migrant workers (and contributing to their undocumented status), and the rule was rescinded in 2016 (Faraday 2016, 49). Despite the removal of this odious provision, the continued tying of the TFWP migrants to a key employer may increase the likelihood of workplace complaints.

The supply of temporary migrant workers into the TFWP is also affected by the extent of the nature of labor market testing, which has changed over time (Faraday 2016, 7; Boucher 2016, Chapter 7). While labor market testing may not appear to be directly related to migrant rights, insofar as labor market testing can affect the number of entrants into the program and thereby the size of the migrant workforce, it can affect the overall availability of workers who can be subject to breaches.[12] A second subtle but important regulatory change in 2016 was the recharacterization of some occupations from "high wage" to "low wage." This had the effect of changing entry rights for certain migrants and excluding low-skilled workers in most instances from access to subsequent permanent residency routes. Further, the definition of "low skilled" encompasses those on hourly wages below the median provincial rate, which reinforces wage inequality in certain sectors and arguably penalizes those in low-paid jobs, even if the associated work is skilled in nature (Boucher 2016, Chapter 7; Faraday 2016, 22–23). Circling back to the topic of visa status and ensuing rights, it is clear that such a recharacterization could potentially have important implications for the extent of employer control over a migrant.

Within Canada's TFWP, there are several specific subcategories that warrant particular attention from a regulatory perspective. The Live-in Caregiver Program Visa originated in the Canadian Foreign Domestic

Movement Visa and provided domestic work and refugee status to migrants from Eastern Europe during and after World War II. This was later expanded to the Temporary Employment Authorization Program in 1973. In 1991 some moves were made to transition these workers onto permanent residency visas (Bakan and Stasiuslis 1997a). In 2014, following many controversies surrounding this visa,[13] it was dissolved as a separate visa category (see Chapter 2; Boucher 2016, Chapter 7). The debates and ultimate demise of this visa reveal some of the broader tensions in temporary visa design that are hard to avoid, even with worker-friendly policy design, namely the tension between requiring a person to stay in a sponsored position and granting them the freedom to move, and the tension between low-paid work and the desire of an individual to improve their situation and transition upward in the labor market (Boucher 2016, Chapter 7).

The Seasonal Agricultural Worker Program has been the focus of particular criticism in Canada. Some argue that it is insufficiently regulated, suffers persistent issues with housing and healthcare access, and that migrants have limited recourse to remedies (Hennebry and Preibisch 2012, 30–31). Aspects of its design that could increase the vulnerability of workers include lack of flexibility in the length of the visa, some limits (although not exhaustive) on employer portability, forced deductions on pay to cover flights, agent and employer control over the return of migrants each season, and limitations on conversion to permanent status (Hennebry and Preibisch 2012). Further, as we will see in Chapter 7 on trade unions, there are limitations under this visa on collective action and, in some provinces, prohibitions on collective organizing.

California

Temporary migration has grown rapidly in the United States since the 1990 Immigration Act. This so called nonimmigrant migration is nine times greater than permanent economic immigration there (Costa 2020, 24). And temporary states may be a particular source of vulnerability. For instance, one comparison of temporary and permanent visa holders found that while temporary migrants earned less than U.S. citizens, once they adjusted to permanent status they earned more (Lowell and Avato 2014, 93). Temporary migrants who are granted a legal Temporary Protected Status (preventing deportation for a finite period) also find it easier to obtain better-paying jobs (Orrenius and Zavodny 2015) than those on a strictly temporary status.

Instances of slavery-like conditions have resulted even in some formally high-skilled temporary visas, such as the F1 student visa for work in the information and communications technology sector (Swaminathan 2017). The temporary H-2A visa used for agricultural workers has been linked to experiences of exploitation (Costa 2020, 30). Under the temporary H-1B and L-1 visas, employers also have control over the process of migrant workers' applications for permanent residence (Costa 2021). There are even some bespoke visas, such as the Q1 visa that allows the Walt Disney Company to bring in workers for their fun parks and keep them on site with no health insurance or pension plans (Johnson 2018). Across many of these visas, the power of the employer to sign off on a job offer (and thereby control ongoing visa status), coupled with restrictions on portability across employers, increases the vulnerability of these temporary migrants. In contrast, those on permanent visas can change employers and are not subject to either the reductions in labor standards that exist on some temporary visas or to retaliatory removal (Costa 2020, 31, 36).

Employment law regulation

The interaction of visa design and employment law shapes the rights of migrant workers. Employment laws vary across countries and subnational labor law jurisdictions, not only in the relative strength of protections conferred upon workers and employers but also in how these protections are extended to or exclude migrant workers. We consider each of the major countries in turn, with specific reference to subnational variation in Canada and the USA. First, it is important to reiterate that all countries examined are liberal market economies, characterized by lower worker protections, rather than coordinated market economies, with higher rates of unionization and more frequent collective bargaining claims (Hall and Soskice 2001; Soskice 1999). A study by the OECD found that, after New Zealand, the United States, Canada, Great Britain, Chile, and Australia had the lowest worker protections against individual and collective dismissal protections across OECD member states (OECD 2022). That said, it is important to consider how specific dimensions of employment law can affect migrants in particular, both as they interact with immigration law and independently, given that the vulnerability of migrants in the labor market is established, outside of unfair dismissal laws.

Australia

Formally, all migrant workers in Australia enjoy the same protections as Australian citizens and permanent residents.[14] As such, the large-scale legal carve-outs that exist in other countries and which disadvantage migrant workers do not operate in Australia (as we discussed in detail in Chapter 4). However, there are still areas of confusion, which led the 2019 Migrant Worker Taskforce to call for greater clarity in legislation on this point (Fels Commission 2019, Recommendation 3). Further, as noted in Chapter 5 on undocumented migration, migrants with lapsed status are restricted from bringing legal actions in some areas of law. However, even without large-scale carve-outs, there are other ways that employment law can affect migrant workers differently than domestic workers.

Subcontracting, labor hire, and franchising arrangements are gray areas of protection. According to the Fels Commission (2019, 99, 1030ff.), labor hire operators can "exploit migrant workers [and] often create complex operating environments that make it harder to ensure compliance with the law. This can include involvement in the shadow economy, the use of intermediaries ... and potential acts of money laundering, human trafficking and modern slavery." Further, labor hire companies can be connected to the immigration system in ways that pose specific risks for migrant workers, such as expensive migration agents and debt bondage. These arrangements can increase the risk of employment breaches (Fels 2019, 92). However, there are very few instances of prosecution of this type of breach in Australia, highlighting the difficulties for migrant workers in bringing claims, even with the new accessorial powers provided to prosecuting agencies introduced through the Fair Work Act Protecting Vulnerable Persons amendments of 2017 (Hardy 2017).

Employment law restrictions on bringing a legal action can also create challenges for migrant workers in Australia. For instance, being required to be employed for at least six months before bringing an unfair dismissal claim, under s383 of the Fair Work Act (Cth) 2009, can be difficult for international students or working holiday makers who often work for shorter periods of time (Howe et al. 2017, 10). The restriction of unfair dismissal laws to those with permanent, though not fixed-term, positions further limits temporary migrant workers whose positions are often not permanent, resulting in low levels of reinstatement (10, 18–19).

United Kingdom

As noted in Chapter 1, increased Europeanization of British employment law over the 1990s had the effect of introducing general protections to workers, such as minimum wage rules, laws around working hours, and parental leave. It also included the introduction of migrant-specific laws, such as the EU Directive on Temporary Agency Work 2008/104/EC that binds employers to treat agency workers the same way as those directly recruited into such positions. Despite the protective effects of EU law, however, the United Kingdom is still deemed to have a more flexible and less protective employment structure than comparable European countries (OECD 2014, cited in Migration Advisory Committee 2014, 60). In addition to this, there are exceptions in British protections for migrant domestic workers, such as the minimum time and wage regulations (Mantouvalou 2015, 333). The effects that Britain's exit from the EU in 2020 will have on workers, and migrant workers particularly, are yet to be fully realized, but early indications are that they could be harmful (O'Connor 2020; Yong 2019; Polak 2019).

In 2016, new protections in the labor enforcement area were introduced in the United Kingdom, including the creation of a Labor Market Enforcement body. These changes are discussed further in Chapter 8 on enforcement and can be seen to shift the responsibility for enforcement of some labor rights, such as the National Minimum Wage, away from individual litigants toward a public body (Davies 2016, 440). In this regard, these changes can be viewed as protective. However, it is important to note that while these provisions were sought in part to address some of the perceived deficiencies in protections for migrant workers earlier in the United Kingdom, they brought with them provisions that criminalize undocumented workers and increase government powers to conduct workplace raids.[15] The double-edged dimension of these reforms "is a tendency to build, rather than break down, connections between labor law enforcement and immigration enforcement" (Davies 2016, 444).

Canada

As discussed in Chapter 4, some areas of provincial employment law in Canada create carve-outs for some migrant workers in certain occupations. For instance, in Ontario, agricultural workers are denied access to some protections, such as restrictions on maximum hours of work, breaks, and overwork (Vosko, Tucker, and Casey 2019, 237). These exemptions can reinforce the precariousness of already vulnerable workers whose visas may be about to lapse. According to one estimate, up to 61% of employees in Ontario are subject to some kind of carve-out or special exemption, and recent migrants are more likely to lack coverage than others (Vosko 2019c, 2, 6; see also Vosko, Noack, and Thomas 2016, 4, 66). Protections vary widely by violation type: 8% of workers are excluded from minimum wage protections, compared to 15% from overtime pay standards and 60% from severance pay protections (Vosko, Noack, and Thomas 2016, 4).

California

In California, state labor laws and the Federal Labor Standards Act (FLSA) (1938) do not distinguish between migrant and nonmigrant workers. However, under the FLSA agricultural workers are excluded from some protections, including overtime pay and, on small farms, the minimum wage guarantee. Indeed, when the FLSA was first enacted as part of the New Deal, agricultural workers were wholly excluded from its protections (Linder 1987). Much of this exclusion has been removed through state legislation. In 1975, California enacted the Agricultural Labor Relations Act, making it the first state in the United States to create a right to collective bargaining for agricultural workers (Martin 2003). Since 1976, the Industrial Welfare Commission Wage Order No. 14 (Agricultural Occupations) has required overtime pay for agricultural workers in California for work exceeding sixty hours in one week. In 2016, the state legislature passed reforms that will gradually reduce the minimum hours required for overtime to forty hours, in line with other workers under the FLSA (Ulloa and Myers 2016).

In several respects California leads the way for labor protections for migrant workers in the USA (Costa 2018). As we discussed in Chapter 5 on undocumented migration, laws enacted between 2013 and 2018 have created civil penalties for employers who retaliate against workers with threats based on their immigration status, such as reporting undocumented migrants to police or federal bodies (Costa 2018). Several laws passed during this period also prohibit ICE from entering government buildings and courthouses. The prohibition seeks to end the practice of ICE using court proceedings to identify and arrest undocumented migrants, which discourages migrants from seeking legal redress for employment breaches (Kitroeff 2017).

Quantitative findings

In this section, we consider the relationship between visa type and number of substantiated violations. It is important to reiterate here that the number of complaints by temporary migrants is likely underrepresented within the MWRD, when compared with permanent migrants, due to the obstacles they face, including concerns over immigration reprisals or waiting periods for court hearings. Nonetheless, it is useful to consider the broad trends in the MWRD, while taking these caveats into consideration. For purposes of analysis, the visas considered in the database are divided into nine major visa categories:[16]

1. Family
2. Humanitarian
3. Other
4. Student
5. Temporary work
6. Tourist
7. Unavailable
8. Undocumented
9. Work

We consider first the distribution of migrants across time and then the number of migrants holding these categories both within the MWRD (M) and within each country. We also consider how their representation in the database is weighted against their proportions within migrant flows averaged over the period 2006 through 2016 (P).[17] We also consider whether migrants on some visas are more likely to be successful in their claims than those on other visas. As immigration policy is set nationally, we consider the data at the national, not the subnational, level.

Table 6.1 sets out the distribution of migrants in the database according to the visa categories identified above and then compares this to the overall migrant population averaged over the period of analysis. Figures are given for each of the four countries, although for Canada and the United States proportionate shares are taken, since the selected jurisdictions do not represent the entire migrant population.

In some areas migrants are underrepresented as claimants in proportion to their representation in flows. This is most common for tourist visas, where

Table 6.1 Distribution of visa types, by migrants in the MWRD (M) and total migrant flows (P) 2006–2016

	Australia		Canada		United Kingdom		USA	
	M	P	M	P	M	P	M	P
Family	1%	1%	0%	0.4%	1%	0.1%	0%	1%
Humanitarian	1%	0%	2%	0.2%	3%	0.0%	0%	0.2%
Other	10%	0%	15%	0.0%	13%	0.4%	7%	0.1%
Student	6%	2%	1%	0.4%	5%	1%	1%	1%
Temporary worker	55%	5%	68%	1%	10%	1%	67%	1%
Tourist	2%	90%	0%	97%	1%	97%	0%	93%
Unavailable	9%	-	13%	0%	54%	0%	21%	-
Undocumented	1%	1%	1%	1%	2%	2%	4%	4%
Work	15%	1%	0%	0.4%	11%	0%	1%	0.1%
Total	949	76,666,827	488	153,973,270	144	355,925,214	331	525,554,757

Note: M = Migrant Worker Rights Database; P = General population.

migrants comprise a large percentage of flows but very low percentages of claimants—between zero and 2% of claimants. This outcome no doubt reflects the fact that most tourists are present in the country for only short periods and generally do not have access to either working rights or opportunities to work, let alone the capacity to enforce workplace breaches when they do occur. Nonetheless, we retain them in Table 6.1 for comparative purposes and also to acknowledge the reality that some tourists do work unlawfully and are present in the database. (In fact, surprisingly, more tourists bring successful claims than those on valid family reunion visas.) In contrast, other visa types are overrepresented in the database. This includes temporary workers: 55% of claimants, but only 10% of flows in Australia; 68% of claimants, but only 1% of flows in Canada; 10% of claimants, but 1% of flows in the United Kingdom; and 67% of claimants, but 1% of flows in the USA.

In all the jurisdictions, except for the United Kingdom, it is clear that the single largest category of claimants is temporary migrant workers, and in most jurisdictions their representation in the MWRD heavily eclipses their representation in migrant flows. Permanent migrants on work visas are also a larger percentage in the database than in migration flows, although, outside of Australia, the percentages are very small when compared with temporary migrants. This reinforces the point that regulatory theorists make: visa design may in and of itself increase the risk to exploitation, putting aside other possible factors.

Aside from the preponderance of work-based visa holders as claimants, a second observation is that those on visa categories less commonly associated with work (humanitarian, family members, tourists, and secondary work applicants) are also bringing workplace claims, although at lower rates than work-based visa holders. Except for the general observation that temporary work visa status features in the background of workplace claims, other shared features do not emerge as consistently important. The key reasons for variation are considered in the conclusion to this book and relate primarily to differences in industrial relations and employment law systems across the various jurisdictions.

Summary

Regulatory scholars argue that visa design matters for the capacity of workers to craft convincing legal arguments in their favor. Good regulatory design might make a difference to the rights of working migrants, and even small regulatory changes can have an impact on outcomes. As Fudge (2016b, 156, citing Bianchi 2011) argues, "the process of legal characterization is 'not a neutral' one since 'legal categories are not immutable abstractions into which sets of facts can be squeezed regardless of whether or not they fit.'" On this basis, scholars such as Manolo Abella (2006) and Graeme Hugo (2008) have included visa design in their criteria for evaluating best practices for temporary migration schemes, including flexibility in the length of stay and the portability of jobs across employers. In other words, temporary programs can be designed to minimize exploitation. This chapter demonstrates that, overwhelmingly and disproportionate to their overall representation within populations, notwithstanding some regulatory variation across the jurisdictions, temporary migrant workers suffer more workplace violations than those on temporary visas. It would appear that it is centrally temporary visa status rather than the details of those temporary visas that drives this outcome. Further, as we demonstrate and argue in this book's conclusion, these features of immigration regulation themselves are a product of broader industrial relations systems rather than the central driving force behind the variation present in the data.

This leads to a central policy recommendation for designers of immigration law regulation. If visa design does influence workers' propensity to bring violation complaints and, in some instances, to succeed as complainants, it is at the very aggregate level of visa design: whether the visa is temporary or permanent, rather than the level of fine regulatory detail, seems to matter the most. Small features of visa design do not appear, at least on the available evidence, to make a substantial difference to complaint rates. From a policy perspective, the core question is the number of temporary work visas permitted within an overall immigration program and whether they permit portability and pathways to permanent status. Finally, temporary visa status often correlates with low-skilled jobs, which are themselves more susceptible to exploitation. As such, the effects of visa design need to be separated out from the occupation and related economic sector where the migrant works. Our next chapter explores another feature of the migrant worker experience that may be important for the rate and nature of workplace violations: the presence or absence of trade unions and broader forms of worker representation that can assist migrant workers in their claim-making.

7
Decertification, Blacklisting, and Circular Migration

The Challenges of Trade Union Representation for Migrant Workers

In the series of cases known as *Floralia Plant Growers Ltd. v. United Food & Commercial Workers Union* (2008, 2015, 2016, 2017), a group of Mexican farm workers in British Columbia was involved in almost a decade of litigation to enforce organizing rights in their workplace. The workers had been employed on the Floralia farm on the interprovincial highway in Abbotsford through Canada's Seasonal Agricultural Worker Programme (SAWP) visas. Over several decades at Floralia, the union argued, management attempted to limit collective organizing by decertifying the United Food and Commercial Workers Union (UFCW), having union members blacklisted by the Mexican consulate in Vancouver, and recruiting other workforces directly from Mexico to replace unionized workers, although Floralia contested these points. There were also attempts, some of which were successful, to change the legal definition of the workforce in order to dilute its trade union component. Many of the actions of the UFCW were strongly contested by the employer, but in most cases the union was successful in its claims, even if a clear finding of unlawful interference by the employer in blacklisting was not made out before the British Columbia Labour Relations Board.[1]

The *Floralia* litigation allows us to consider some of the key themes regarding the relationship between trade unions and migrant workers. These include whether trade unions help or hinder migrant workers and whether migrants have the right to unionize at all. In the second part of this chapter, we explore these themes and use comparative data from the MWRD across its six labor law jurisdictions to explore the types of claims brought by trade unions and their relative success.

Attempts by migrant workers to unionize at Sidhu and Sons Nursery, Greenway Farms, and Floralia Plant Growers were triggered by concerns over the dismissal of SAWP workers in the summer of 2008 (Jensen 2013, 72). The Floralia farm was owned by Gurjit Sandhu. The farms had been hiring workers through SAWP since 2005, and the Mexican consulate in Vancouver was involved in recruiting workers on their behalf (*Re Floralia Plant Growers Ltd. v. UFCW, Local 1518* (2008) CarswellBC, para 9). Many workers returned to Canada each season on a rotational basis. In 2008, all but one of thirty workers at the Floralia farm was a migrant. Of these thirty, sixteen were returning after prior seasons and fourteen were new; fourteen workers were also returned to Mexico after receiving the union's application for certification (Vosko 2014, 463; *Floralia* 2008, paras 12, 14). Management argued that this was related to environmental conditions that led to the loss of a significant number of crops, resulting in a reduced harvest, a downturn in business, and the fourteen workers being sent back (*Floralia* 2008, para 14). In this case, the Labour Board decided for Floralia and agreed that the sending back of the workers was bona fide and motivated by economics rather than anti-union animus (para 90).

At the same time, the UFCW was attempting to gain certification and thereby permission to represent the workers at the enterprise level. The UFCW also raised questions about whether the dismissal following the harvest downturn had been unfair, whether workers were intimidated into agreeing to their own dismissal, and whether dismissal had been in part motivated by "anti-union animus" (*Floralia* 2008, paras 61, 64). Heather Jensen (2013, 72), in her discussion of the *Floralia* litigation, argues that the certification processes lodged by UFCW on behalf of the farm workers resulted in increased fears of reprisal and repercussions for workers on the farms. This was in part because the certification process creates a lag between when employees join the union and when the British Columbian Labour Relations Board certifies the workplace. Jensen writes that "employees who have taken steps to join a union and begin collective bargaining may face months or years of working for an employer who refuses to recognize or bargain with the employees' union, while legal processes unfold in front of the Labour Board" (71). At Floralia, certification occurred but was hindered over the medium term by layoffs that changed the workforce composition and which complicated the construction of the group seeking union representation (see also 92–94).

The institutional structure of trade union organizing that underpinned the *Floralia* cases was also important in this early case. UFCW-funded worker centers, such as the Abbotsford Agricultural Workers Alliance, first established in Canada in the early 2000s, were involved in the case. Floralia workers attended the Abbotsford center to raise their grievances about their workplace and to become unionized (Felix Martinez, Interview, 18 June 2019). What followed were anti-union activities:

> When [the workers] went to the office and started signing union cards... the employers sent most of the supporters back to Mexico. And even after that, the union still wanted to vote, so the vote has to be won by a majority. It was won, but right after that, once the union was certified, there was a ton of issues. It was both farms, both Sidhu Sons and Floralia, going together and appealing, saying that it was not possible to unionize foreign workers at the time. (Felix Martinez, Interview, 18 June 2019)

Ultimately, the Labour Relations Board found that the dismissal was not motivated by anti-union animus but was bona fide and related to a downturn in business. Further, it did not find, contrary to UFCW arguments, that the more vocal union supporters had been sent back to Mexico first (*Floralia* 2008, para 80). As such, the Labour Board accepted neither the arguments about opposition to trade union organizing nor those about unfair labor practices at Floralia.

In 2014, the UFCW brought a case arguing that Floralia had failed to rehire those SAWP workers with union affiliations and that this had led to the decertification of the union, as they no longer held the majority vote (*Floralia Plant Growers Ltd. v. UFCW, Local 1518* (2015)). In this case, union representatives also argued that the Mexican consulate in Vancouver was blocking SAWP applicants with union membership. Felix Martinez, a former official at the Mexican consulate who now works for the UFCW, testified in support of this claim.

In 2015, the UFCW brought an additional case relating to whether the seasonal workers were entitled to holiday pay under their collective agreement with Floralia. It argued that the reason it did not bring this action earlier was due to its members' vulnerability as foreign workers. Floralia refused to pay vacation leave and also disagreed about the time period over which such pay was retroactively due. Martinez again provided evidence that there had been discussions in the Mexican consulate as to the risks of having unionized SAWP workers (*Floralia Plant Growers Ltd. v. UFCW, Local 1518*, (2015), CarswellBC 3852, No 135, 2015, 4). Ultimately, arbitrator Paul Devine decided in favor of the union's evidence and accepted that its workers had raised concerns about vacation pay but delayed doing so due to fears of deportation or the nonrenewal of their visas. This in turn sent what he referred to as a "chilling message" to workers. In this context, holiday pay was awarded (paras 14–15). Factoring in wage differentials between Canada and Mexico, Devine found that "[w]hile the amount of money that [Floralia] would be required to pay . . . [w]ould not be large, it would have a very significant and disproportionate impact on them [the migrant workers] because of the fact that all of their earnings are required to sustain their famil[ies] in Mexico" (at para 20). The delay in the union bringing claims was linked back to the inherent vulnerability of migrant workers, and the general time limitation to claim-making was waived (para 20).

Between 2016 and 2017, a fresh case involving allegations of unfair labor practices at Floralia was brought by the union (*Floralia Plant Growers Limited & S&G Fresh Produce Limited v. UFCW, Local 1518*, B17/2017). This time the issue was the recall practices the farm employed across seasons. Under the collective agreement signed by Floralia and the UFCW, the employer was required to request that SAWP workers be recalled on the basis of seniority on the farm, rather than other factors, such as union membership (Floralia Collective Agreement, Article 20.05, para 14). Naturally, employers themselves could not mandate this as entry of foreign workers was subject to approval by the Canadian government, which regulates all immigration entry. Recall of migrants on an annual rotational basis is also a condition of the SAWP visa; employees are generally offered a minimum of four months' work but are required to leave by December of the year they are employed. They could then be recalled for subsequent years based on their seniority (para 12). In 2016, there was evidence that Floralia had departed from the prior standard recall practices; in 2017, only two workers were on the seniority list and the other seven were new (paras 19, 52). This was achieved by Floralia delaying its request for workers, leading to workers from prior years being reassigned to other farms (para 52). The UFCW put forward evidence that Floralia was motived by anti-union animus, although the employer again denied this.

This case also involved Floralia arguing that a connected farm, S&G, was separate and therefore should not be bound by the same collective agreement, including the same rules regarding worker recall. Martinez described this process:

Gary from S&G opened a farm . . . and that same year we saw a drop in workers requested by Floralia. It fell to about one-third of what they would usually request in number. And we started going and visiting the farm and we saw workers that we didn't recognize. So basically what they were doing ... was bringing workers from the nonunion farms and using them on the union farms. (Interview, 18 June 2019)

Ultimately, the Labour Relations Board found that Floralia and S&G had a "common purpose," were intimately linked through shared family relations across the two farms, that they were in frequent communication with one another, and that the workers on the two farms were commonly affected (paras 73, 113). It decided, in the union's favor, that there had been unfair labor practices regarding the recall of key workers across the two farms.

The issue of blacklisting unionized migrant workers arises repeatedly in the *Floralia* litigation. Through concurrent litigation, including *Sidhu & Sons Nursery Ltd.* ((2010) B.C.L.R.B.D. No. 64), the UFCW discovered evidence that Mexican consulate officials were being instructed not to renew the SAWP visas of pro-union workers and that a list of such workers was maintained (for a detailed overview, see Vosko 2019a, 65–83). While the Mexican government enjoyed state immunity and could not be called as a witness in these cases, it was still possible to hear evidence related to events in Mexico and the activities of officials involved in the alleged backlisting (Jensen 2013, 106). Still, the state immunity argument meant that the Labour Relations Board had no power to outlaw blacklisting practices on the part of the Mexican government (Vosko 2015, 12). Furthermore, the impact of the Mexican government stretched beyond the action of blacklisting to broader roles such as concealing the existence of Canadian unions as well. Martinez summarized:

When the workers arrived, there was always a consular official that would receive them, that would basically tell them what to do and what not to do and give them a brief idea of what to expect here in Canada. But in doing those lectures, they would be told not to approach anybody from the union.

He also noted that the employer sometimes attempted to keep unions away:

Most of the people [the workers] ... didn't even know what a union was, and we didn't even have a chance to talk to them before the vote. So basically, when they arrived in Canada, we tried to reach them that night. The employer kept them away from us, so we weren't able to tell them

"Tomorrow in the morning there is going to be this important union vote, you're going to be deciding ... whether you will stay with the union or just leave." (Interview, 18 June 2019)

The UFCW's lack of access to workers at Floralia, blacklisting by the Mexican consulate, and the temporary nature of the SAWP visa all stymied the union's efforts to build its membership among migrant workers.

An overview of trade union organizing and migration

In this section, we provide a general overview of the historical and contemporary relationship between migrants and trade unions, and we consider the challenges that trade unions face in organizing migrants, some of which are exemplified in the *Floralia* litigation. We consider the tension between trade union representation of migrants and concomitant concerns among some domestic workers that migrant labor undermines their wages, both historically and in more recent periods. We also canvass the role of autonomous workers' centers and alt-unions as alternatives to formal trade union representation of migrants. Finally, we address challenges to trade union representation of migrant workers, in particular restrictions on migrant workers' rights to unionize, sector-specific factors that can stymie representation, and the challenges presented by temporary, lapsed, or undocumented visa status that can make migrant workers reluctant to act collectively in the workplace.

As noted in Chapter 1, trade unions were an important player in the evolution of labor standards within capitalist systems through their attempted reconciliation of the demands of employers and workers. The role of trade unions in protecting workers' rights is two-fold: pushing for legal protections in the workplace and enforcing such protections once they exist. Evidence suggests that unions are important for both aspects of workplace culture (Webb and Webb 1898, discussed in Colling 2012, 191). Further, Trevor Colling (2012, 198) adds an inspirational role for unions in validating a sense of workplace injustice and the capacity of unions to "radiate" from a singular example of behavior to broader cultural change. These characterizations of the role of unions are also applicable to migrant workers. Quantitative studies reveal that there is a general relationship between trade union power and greater equality in the treatment of migrants and citizens (Boräng, Kalm, and Lindvall 2020, cited in Wright et al. 2022). This has particularly been the case since the end of World War II, when unions increasingly engaged in a wider array of social democratic policies (Boräng, Kalm, and Lindvall 2020). Further, many unions that do represent migrant workers view them first and foremost as workers rather than migrants. This universalist framing of workers joined in common purpose has the benefit of undermining discrimination against migrants. But it can also overlook migrants' particular needs (Alberti, Holgate, and Tapia 2013) as well as intersectional forms of disadvantage that they may also face—due to race, gender, or visa status (Piore and Safford 2006, cited in Wright et al. 2022).

This general theme of inclusivity exists in tension with the possibility of migrant labor undermining domestic workforces. This is particularly the case when migrant labor is oversupplied, raising the potential of pushing down domestic wages. Lower-skilled sectors, where migrant workers often predominate, are where union representation is most needed to counter low wages and poor working conditions and where union density is lowest (Afonso, Negash, and Wolff 2020, 529). As such, anti-migrant positioning and wage-based protectionism have historically been features of trade union organizing. As Chris Wright and collaborators (2022) note, "For much of the 20th century, unions were generally reluctant to represent and advocate for migrant workers because of a fear that increased labor supply via immigration would erode wages and working conditions. Racist assumptions that migrants would not join unions or that they were 'unorganizable' were also prevalent" (see also Milkman 2000; Haus 2002).

Trade unions' historical and contemporary positions toward migrants

Such tensions play out in the various jurisdictions featured in this book. In the United Kingdom, unions have historically focused on British workers (Virdee 2014). There has been a refusal to engage with posted workers and a belief that collective agreements are undermined by foreign workers (Meardi, Martín, and Lozano Riera 2012, 17). Randall Hansen (2000, 130) makes a similar observation about the Trades Union Congress in the 1960s, noting that it "viewed race relations legislation as an interference in free collective bargaining, and the workers at the grass-roots level instinctively viewed New Commonwealth immigrants, the majority of whom were unskilled, as a threat to their standard of living." More recently, trade unions have been less inclined to oppose immigrants and, at least prior to Brexit, support free movement of new accession state migrants from the European Union. Across the EU member states, British unions were therefore relatively open to migrant workers (Afonso, Negash, and Wolff 2020, 538–539) and supportive of most aspects of the Blair Labour government's immigration program (Wright 2017, 363).

In Australia there have been differing positions within the trade union movement on the question of whether to support migration and which kinds of migrants to include. Michael Quinlan and Constance Lever-Tracy (1988, 28) argue that the entry of migrant workers into Australia after World War II "has never been a major problem." They attributed this to the conciliatory approaches successive federal governments had taken toward unions, which provided assurances that increased immigration would not undermine unionism or workplace conditions. The entry of new migrants into unions was also facilitated by the fact that most joined sectors with high levels of unionization, including some with compulsory union membership. Part of these conciliatory approaches, however, involved an initial commitment by government to unions that postwar immigration would not undermine a "White Australia," which excluded non-European immigrants (25). From 1975 to 1983 the Australian Council of Trade Unions (ACTU) promoted an antiracist platform, and a number of unions emphasized outreach to non-English-speaking workers (29–30). However, it is important to note that these steps took place in the context of a largely permanent migration program, which is no longer the case. Tim Nelthorpe of the Australian National Union of Workers explained:

> The ACTU takes a kind of protectionist approach by trying to stop people coming into Australia on temporary visas. They support permanent migration. We support permanent migration as well, but we also think that you shouldn't attack the visa path that the migrant has been given. So, our view is that . . . people should be able to move where they want, when they want, and the union's job is to represent who ends up here. (Interview, 8 October 2019)

In recent times, the capacity of unions to shape immigration policy in Australia has been heavily shaped by the presiding government in power, with more power exercised over Labour than Liberal (Conservative) governments (Wright 2015, 324).

In some instances, positions that appear to be anti-migrant may be motivated primarily by concerns over the diminution of rights for all workers. One example is the case of HD Mining (2012) in British Columbia, where a mine that was operational in Vancouver but owned by Chinese investors tried to deploy only foreign Chinese workers by advertising exclusively in Mandarin. In this case, the local union brought litigation arguing that the mining company had failed to consider eligible Canadians in its hiring of the migrant workers and that the Canadian government had failed in its assessment when offering the temporary foreign worker permits to these migrants. The union also argued that the mine was offering lower wages to these new workers, although HD Mining contested this. The union and the company argued over whether the foreign workers were hired because they possessed skills that the domestic workers did not, or whether the intent was to displace the domestic workforce (Stueck 2013). The union's case was ultimately rejected by the courts, but it did highlight the tensions that can emerge between domestic and migrant workers (Woo 2013).

American unions have historically opposed open immigration policies and did not support the large-scale amnesty granted to migrant workers under the 1986 Immigration Reform and Control Act. This opposition may have been due to the perceived conflict that large-scale migrant labor would create with the domestic workforce (Milkman 2011; Fisk and Wishnie 2005, 353). In the *Floralia* case, we can see this playing out in calls for particular protections for SAWP workers in the UFCW agreement alongside the condition that Canadian workers would be hired, retained, and recalled over the same SAWP workers (Jensen 2013, 98). As such, inequality between migrant and domestic workers can be enshrined not just culturally or organizationally but also contractually in the agreements that unions negotiate.

More recently, unions, in all of the jurisdictions considered in this book, have focused upon reaching out to migrant workers and have begun to view migrants less as a threat and more as an opportunity. Several factors motivate this. First, international solidarity coupled with the increase in migrant labor compounds the need for attention to immigration issues; second, declining domestic trade union membership motivates increased attention to migrant workers as a new potential source of membership; and finally, trade unions increasingly take the position that limiting legal immigration might increase undocumented immigration, especially given the rise in temporary migration programs, and thereby further undermine labor standards (Wright et al.

2022, citing Avci and McDonald 2000; Cachón and Valles 2003; Haus 2002; Watts 2000). In this sense, supporting legal immigration is beneficial for contemporary unions when compared to the hardline anti-migrant position that may have been adopted in the past.

Alt-unions

Alt-unions have emerged recently to address concerns about racism or a lack of attention to intersectional challenges within the traditional trade union movement. Migrants may also come from countries where unions are embedded within corrupt or criminal government systems and may not have an accurate picture of unions and thus actively eschew them while seeking alternative forms of worker-led representation. This has been the case with domestic workers in the United Kingdom, for instance, who have preferred small nongovernmental organizations over unions, such as the domestic worker group Kalayaan discussed in Chapter 2 (Mantouvalou 2015, 347).

Alt-unions can take different forms. As an example, in Los Angeles workers may select people from their own communities to stand on labor inspection boards where they are empowered to enforce wages on projects funded by construction bonds (see, e.g., Connolly, Marino, and Martinez Lucio 2019, 7; Fine et al. 2018). Such organizations may create new ways of regulating or protecting worker rights. In Florida, the Coalition of Immokalee Workers—a grassroots alt-labor organization representing mostly migrant tomato growers—implemented privately regulated standards of conduct by lobbying large tomato purchasers to refuse to buy from growers unless they signed on to those standards (Dias-Abey 2018, 2019). This network addressed issues of exploitation not in courts but on the production and supply side (Dias-Abey 2018, 2019). There have also been partnerships between state agencies and the community sector (Vosko 2013, 886–887; Dias-Abey 2018). These hybrid forms of representation are a fusion of traditional trade union models and government-led enforcement that we consider further in the next chapter.

There are also alt-unions based in sending countries that act on behalf of migrant workers prior to departure. These include organizations such as the Institute for Mexicans Abroad and Justice in Motion. Unions in the home country can provide support and legal advice (Bada and Gleeson

2015, 42; Bada and Gleeson 2019, 95–96; Dias-Abey 2018). Sending-country governments may also lobby for changes in the host society. For instance, in Singapore nongovernmental organizations campaigned for the government to push for rest breaks for its citizens employed as domestic workers abroad (Ford 2019). Foreign consulates can also take on some roles of traditional trade unions; such as the Mexican consulate providing basic legal advice in the Fresno region of California, where there are no migrant worker centers (Bada and Gleeson 2015, 40).

Alt-unions have in many instances proven more effective than traditional trade unions in providing protections and have also engaged in litigation, including before the National Labor Relations Board in the United States (Fisk and Wishnie 2005, 383). The activities of alt-unions can be more grassroots than is the case with unions, such as protesting outside an employer's church on a Sunday to force payment (immigration and employment law attorney, Interview, 9 January 2020) or hosting vigils to recognize killed, injured, or underpaid workers, as was the case in the *Metron Construction* case considered in Chapter 4. At times due to legal impediments on trade union organizing, these informal networks may achieve more at a local level or with greater publicity than large umbrella structures can accomplish at a provincial or national level.

In the *Floralia* case, a UCFW-funded worker center in Abbotsford was central to the workers eventually gaining an agreement. Worker centers distribute grants and funds and sometimes provide legal advice to support migrant workers (Connolly, Marino, and Martinez Lucio 2019; Fine et al. 2018). Such centers are particularly prevalent in the United States and to a lesser extent in Canada, the United Kingdom, and more recently Australia.

All this suggests that the relationship between organized labor and migrant workers is at least in part becoming more supportive and positive than in the past. Certainly in all of the jurisdictions considered in this book, there are also examples of successful campaigns run by unions to protect the rights and conditions of migrant workers. These include the Justice for Cleaners campaign in the United Kingdom that improved migrant cleaners' wages and addressed issues of union recognition and holiday and sick leave (Alberti, Holgate, and Tapia 2013, 4141) and campaigns to change legislation around the overseas domestic worker visa, discussed in Chapter 2. Research demonstrates that when migrants have the support of the union as a whole, rather than a particular section of the union, campaigns are more likely to be successful (Alberti, Holgate, and Tapia 2013, 4144).

The importance of unions as legal representatives

Unions can and do play an important role in representing migrants who are pursuing their workplace rights in legal venues. However, there are differences across jurisdictions in this regard. For instance, in Australia, unions may be seen as quite protectionist of domestic (native) workers' rights (Quinlan 1979), whereas in Canada and the United States, the UFCW has been involved in litigation to protect vulnerable migrant workers' rights since the U.S. civil rights era. This can be linked back to a history of civil rights activism in which unions were involved in representing migrants (e.g., Ontiveros 2009), particularly in Los Angeles in the labor rights area (Higbie 2021). We explore in the quantitative section the rates of union representation within the MWRD.

It is also important to note that there are several potential impediments to trade unions representing migrants legally. First, there are differences across economic sectors or sometimes even occupations in the right to organize collectively. At times those sectors where migrants predominate are also those where there are legal or practical obstacles to unionism for migrant workers, and thereby legal funding of unions. Second, lapsed visa status and, to a lesser extent, temporary visa status can have a chilling effect upon migrants' willingness to unionize, thereby creating barriers for union engagement in court cases. Finally, industrial laws regulating unionism more broadly can present important obstacles for the representation of migrant workers.

The right to unionize can differ for migrants across sectors

One of the clearest impediments to trade unions formally representing migrant workers is a legal exclusion from collective bargaining for certain occupational sectors. This is most common for migrant workers on agricultural visas. In the United States, agricultural and domestic workers were historically excluded from the protections of the National Labor Relations Act ((1935) 29 U.S.C. §§151–169), otherwise known as the "Wagner Act," legislation considered in Chapter 5 as it relates to the rights of undocumented migrants. So influential was this legislation that it developed a form of industrial relations, known as "Wagnerism," marked by key collective bargaining requirements, in particular a need for majoritarianism in bargains, centralized bargaining systems, and prohibition of strikes when agreements are in force (Tucker 2014, 2). Another, less acknowledged feature of Wagnerism is a tendency toward sector-based exclusions, particularly of agricultural workers (Barnetson 2012; Tucker 2012; Jensen 2014). Similar Wagnerian exclusions apply in some Canadian provinces, including Ontario, where agricultural workers continue to be excluded from the right to bargain (Fudge 2008, 124; Colvin and Darbishire 2013; Faraday, Migrant Worker Alliance and Change Caregivers Action Centre 2017).[2] Analysis suggests that these so-called carve-outs were viewed as "economically practicable" to employers (Vosko 2019, citing U.S. Department of Labor 1967; Vosko, Tucker, and Casey 2019, 254). There may also be a regulatory basis for this related to the nature of farm work as intensive and with low profit margins (U.S. Department of Labor, Interview 3, 27 March 2019).[3] Given the large number of migrant workers in agricultural work, these exclusions have differential effects upon migrant workers.

Domestic workers have also been historically excluded from rights to collective bargain in Canada. Although these rights were returned to them in Ontario after Charter of Rights and Freedom–based challenges (Fudge 1997), the exclusions were reintroduced and currently remain operative (Ontario Labour Relations Act, 1995, S.O. 1995, c. 1, Schedule A, s 3(a)). In British Columbia, care workers and agricultural workers have historically been excluded from rights to collective bargain, in part motivated by the high level of industrial disputes in the agricultural sector. However, such exclusions are no longer in operation (Jensen 2013, 17; Vosko 2014, 458)[4] and in fact were removed in 1975. Where such limits on trade union organizing continue to operate, they radically limit the capacity of unions to attract migrants as members and to represent them legally.

Some economic sectors create conditions that are more negative for mobilization than others

Our focus on economic sectors in Chapter 4 emphasized the importance of the sector-level unit of analysis in understanding migrant worker exploitation. Such a lens is vital for the analysis of trade union behavior as well. As noted in Chapter 4, certain sectors are more isolated than others, and this can pose challenges to access for trade unions as well, resulting in low rates of union density among migrants. The private care sector is typical of this, with each worker isolated within an individual household (Mantouvalou 2015; Anderson 2010b; Fudge 1997, 121). In the agricultural sector, unions face difficulties in entering employer premises, which can also be due to the remote locations of farms. This in turn increases employer control over workers (Jensen 2013, 80; for Australia, see Wright and Clibborn 2020, 18).

Fissured corporate structures that dominate within particular sectors can also affect union organizing. Leah Vosko (2014, 460) notes that when a contractor is understood to be an employer but is in fact only an intermediary, the identification of an appropriate bargaining unit for collective agreement purposes can be frustrated. These obstacles were apparent in the *Floralia* litigation in 2016–2017 where the Floralia and S&G farms used the same workers but split them across the two farms, which made it difficult for the UFCW to demonstrate that the workers were employed by a "common employer" for the purposes of certification of the union as their representative (see also Vosko 2019a). Brett Matthews, who represented the union in court proceedings, commented more broadly on the use of subcontracting arrangements as a common strategy to reduce the costs and red tape of employing workers:

> I think for larger corporations, and this is where we see it a lot, I don't think it's necessarily a deliberate attempt to avoid unionization. But it's a way of saying "Look, I don't have to deal with these hassles. You, the labor control supplier, can deal with employment and all the things that go along with that, including unionization, and I don't really care because I'm just going to pay you a fixed rate." (Interview, 6 August 2019)

Some of the trends toward fissured workplaces that we observed in Chapter 4 on sector can in turn influence unionization patterns of migrant workers.

Visa status or lapsing can be important

The precarious nature of short-term visas, a topic covered in detail in Chapter 6, increases the risk of exploitation. It also places limits on trade union organizing, insofar as union engagement can increase the risk of deportation. Vosko (2015, 4) refers to this as "deportability," which she defines as "the threat and act of not being permitted to return to the host state in a response to workers exercising their labor rights" (see also de Genova 2005). As Vosko (2015, 4) notes, deportability affects not only undocumented migrants but also those on temporary visas who occupy "a more liminal space shaped by the temporalization of borders." In this way, deportability can be viewed as a potential threat of collective dismissal that can lead to a loss of visa status and a reduction in rights. This concept was powerfully demonstrated in the

Floralia cases and the associated reluctance among the migrant workforce to organize. Matthews, the former UFCW lawyer, explained:

> One of the difficulties in pursuing these cases was finding people who would stick their necks out even when you had the union representing folks. Just to prosecute any kind of breaches of collective agreements, we need grievers who were there to say "Hey, I was entitled to this pay and I wasn't paid it." But to find people who are willing to stick up their hand, and to bring a case on their behalf, it's difficult even when the facts were there, because there is a fear of being labeled a troublemaker, mostly from the side of the Mexican consulate. The folks who are deciding where to go and, you know, whether you stay in the program. (Interview, 6 August 2019)

In the *Floralia* cases it was difficult for legal counsel to find migrants who were willing to testify against the employer out of fear of nonrenewal of their SAWP visas. Indeed, one of the migrants, Honorio Corona-Martinez, testified for the employer and against his own interests; his claims were later found by the Labour Relations Board to be misrepresentations (Brett Matthews, Interview, 6 August 2019). The guarantee of reinstatement that might be sought in unfair dismissal actions is more tenuous for migrant workers. While a domestic worker who is inappropriately fired often has an immediate action under unfair dismissal laws (and potentially a remedy of reinstatement, if not back pay or compensation, depending upon the employment law system), a temporary migrant worker whose visa is not renewed may have no direct action as their status was temporary from the start. In such instances, reinstatement could be viewed as a breach of immigration law and therefore not awardable by a court. This explains why worker complaints in the *Floralia* litigation centered not around dismissal, but the prioritization of return based upon seniority.

Undocumented migrant status can also threaten the viability of workplace solidarity, posing compounding challenges to unions. Employers that employ both unionized and legal workers but also partially undocumented and nonunionized workers may call raids on their own workplaces as retaliation against collective organizing. In the United States, where there is a greater undocumented migrant population than in the other jurisdictions considered in this book, there can be a higher potential cost to the employer from a unionized workforce than that posed by immigration fines for hiring unauthorized workers. On this basis, employers sometimes use immigration raids to retaliate against unions and unionization efforts (Trivedi 2018, 14–15).[5] A senior official from the American AFL-CIO gave an example of the effect of such raids upon organizing in the USA under the Trump administration:

> So it's clear—you see it, you hear it in the threats of supervisors who say, "I'll call Immigration and Customs Enforcement if you pass that union paper around, that petition around seeking signatures for the union," or, you know, "You'll be out of here in a second." And there's nothing that can be done. It may be that many workers think that the government wouldn't help them anyway, given the status of things currently, but even during good governments that are more friendly to labor unions, undocumented workers know that they don't have an effective remedy. (Interview, 20 November 2019)

As a result of cases limiting the rights of undocumented workers in the United States, most prominently *Hoffman Plastics*, trade unions have been dissuaded from organizing once they become aware that a section of the workforce is unauthorized (Trivedi 2018, 383). As such, the effects of *Hoffman Plastics*, itself a case motivated, as we saw in Chapter 5, by anti-union animus, can extend to diluting the rights of all workers, including those on valid visas, or even domestic workers. Rita Trivedi describes this overall effect as a "chill on authorized employees," as well as specifically on undocumented migrants (387). Furthermore, migrants themselves, especially short-term migrants, may be less likely to pay union dues as they are in the country for only a truncated period.

Despite these challenges, in some cases unions will formally represent migrant workers even if they are not members, although this does somewhat reduce the types of workplace claims that can be brought and often leads to a focus on more modest and basic claims. As a senior representative of the AFL-CIO argued, reflecting on matters under the Trump administration:

> In a way, in a very rough sort of way, [representation of nonworkers] is reflective, I think, of both the amount of informality in the economy, some of which has to do with our immigration system and the fact that you have so many folks who are undocumented and therefore vulnerable, and then partially the weakness of the traditional labor movement. You have less people covered by collective bargaining agreements and so you end up with

litigation over basic standards as a way of enforcing things. (Interview, 20 November 2019)

Labor laws regulating union organizing more broadly
Industrial laws govern how trade unions are managed and can organize within broader legal systems. These laws vary across the jurisdictions and are an important component of the general framework affecting migrants' right to organize. For instance, in British Columbia, where *Floralia* occurred, a requirement under industrial law to demonstrate that workers are of a "common bargaining unit" with shared characteristics when seeking union representation at the enterprise level has historically been difficult for migrants to meet, given their heterogeneous qualities and rotational migration patterns. In the case of *Sidhu & Sons Nursery Ltd. v. UFCW Local 1518* (November 2010), the Labour Relations Board accepted, after some contestation and reconsideration, that migrant workers on seasonal agricultural visas did have a common interest—known under the rules as a "community of interest"—to seek union certification, but the Board defined this interest narrowly around collective bargaining and refused to create a unit that combined both foreign and domestic workers (see Vosko 2014, 453–454, 479; Jensen 2013, 78). As in *Floralia*, changes to corporate structures across or within organizations can also be used by the employer to dilute the union component of a workforce; such changes are more common in sectors where migrants are employed.

In Ontario, employment standards have been historically "subordinate . . . in relation to regulations governing collective bargaining" (Vosko 2019b, 5, 13–14). However, as trade union membership dropped and there was more reliance on employment standards as minima, this created a low floor for those not covered by a union-negotiated enterprise agreement. Clearly, the extent to which collective bargaining is permitted under industrial laws affects all workers but may play a particularly vital role for migrants and other vulnerable workers in creating a baseline for workplace protection. Changes in legislative rules around union organizing and density can have this effect as well. One example is Bill 47 in Ontario, passed in 2018, which removed unions' right to access employee lists on achieving 20% workplace density, their right to collective agreement arbitration, and their right to remedial certification where unfair labor practices frustrated their ability to reach a 40% approval vote in a workplace (Making Ontario Open for Business Act, 2018, S.O. 2018, c. 14).

Some jurisdictions have sector-wide collective regulations that can benefit all workers within a sector, including migrants. In Australia, "awards" that set minimum standards at the sector level provide a safety net for that sector, below which (at least legally) norms cannot drop (Wright and Landsbury 2014, cited in Wright and Kaine 2021, 116). While enterprise-level agreements also exist, awards provide an important minimum against which such negotiation at the enterprise level can occur. The other jurisdictions considered in this book, including the United Kingdom, Ontario, British Columbia, and most of the United States, including California, are restricted to enterprise-level bargaining, and in Ontario, to the workplace level. Quebec is the only province that provides sector-level bargaining (Carter et al. 2002, para 267). Such a decentralized approach to bargaining makes the reach of each agreement narrower than in Australia and it places more pressure on individual unions to negotiate conditions within each workplace (Brett Matthews, Interview, 6 August 2019; Colvin and Darbishire 2013). In the conclusion to this book, we consider the implications of these differences across the various Anglo-American industrial relations systems for how migrant rights are protected or undermined.

Quantitative findings

In this section, we draw on the MWRD to consider the breadth of union activity within each of the jurisdictions and their representation in migrant worker court cases. It is clear that there are some limitations to examining the role of trade unions in this area through the database. First, it reflects only published judgments and decisions, as noted in the introduction. Second, the goal of trade unions in many cases is to contain and settle disagreements with employers rather than to litigate them to completion (Guillaume 2018, 233–235). As such, we can expect trade unions to be underrepresented as legal representatives in the litigation stage of migrant worker rights enforcement compared with law firms and clinics. However, if trade unions are underrepresented as legal representatives, this does not mean they are not involved in protecting migrants' rights; they may be involved in other ways that the database cannot capture, such as campaigns that precede litigation. Further, as noted in Chapter 1, the database focuses largely upon individual workplace rights (with the exception of discrimination against the right to organize collectively). This means that cases involving negotiation of collective agreements are generally excluded from the database, unless they involve individual claimants.[6] As such, a range of cases brought by trade unions are necessarily excluded by selection criteria.

In this section, we first provide data on overall levels of trade union coverage across the jurisdictions arranged by economic sector. This is important to consider because trade union membership rates differ substantially across sectors. Union density might in turn affect levels of union representation in migrant worker cases. Second, we compare this with data on the percentage of migrants within each occupational grouping. Third, we consider the level of trade union representation as legal counsel within the MWRD, focusing on cases where unions have brought actions on behalf of migrant workers. Finally, we consider whether trade unions are more likely to bring successful or unsuccessful cases.

Trade union coverage and density across the jurisdictions

Most unions do not collect specific data on the visa status of their members, in part because the sector of work rather than immigrant status is often seen as centrally important within trade union organizing, and data may be arranged by occupation rather than sector (Matt Kunkel, Interview, 17 July 2019). Yet, insofar as visa status does directly affect the vulnerability of migrants, it does seem to be a relevant data point. The failure by many unions to collect such data might reflect an underappreciation of the significant implications of visa status for migrants' workplace rights when compared with citizens. Alternatively, unions may elect not to ask questions about visa status so as to not deter undocumented migrant workers or those working in breach of their visa conditions. Where unions do collect data on migrant background, there are differences across and within sectors (Berg and Farbenblum 2018, 1049–1050). As we do not have consistent data on migrant membership of trade unions either by sector or jurisdiction, we instead revisit the data from Chapter 4 on the representation of the foreign-born within each occupational group, alongside the overall union density of each of those occupations. We were unable to acquire subnational trade union density data for Canada, so instead we provide figures for all of Canada.

Table 7.1 makes clear that trade union density for all workers varies significantly across the jurisdictions. For instance, Australia and California have

Table 7.1 Percentage of union density and foreign-born population, by occupation and jurisdiction

	Australia		Canada		United Kingdom		California	
	Union Density (%)	Foreign-Born Population (%)	Union Density (%)	Foreign-Born Population (%)	Union Density (%)	Foreign-Born Population (%)	Union Density (%)	Foreign-Born Population (USA) (%)
Total union density	14.3	–	29.4	–	23.4	–	14.7	–
Manager	6.9	10.6	19.1	11.7	12.1	16.3	5.9	9.2
Professionals	21.4	19.8	41.3	31.4	39.9	17.7	21.7	20.8
Technicians and associated professionals	11.6	11.6	27.1	6.9	21.3	13.0	9.2	1.5
Clerical support workers	9.0	12.9	24.5	2.6	17.6	12.8	12.6	7.8
Service and sales workers	13.7	12.6	21.5	22.2	19.8	16.3	11.6	30.2
Skilled agricultural, forestry, and fishery workers†	*	0.6	21.1	2.2	18.1	0.4	3.4	1.7
Craft and related trade workers	13.5	11.3	32.5	*	*	5.4	21.1	2.6
Plant and machine operators and assemblers	16.8	6.9	33.5	12.8	26.7	7.0	16.7	14.7
Elementary occupation	11.4	12.3	24.1	10.2	16.2	10.3	21.1	13.4
Armed forces occupations	*	0.1	*	*	*	0.7	*	*
Unknown	–	2.3	–	–	–	–	–	–

Notes: * = Missing data; see Methods Annex for further discussion. Foreign-born occupation data replicates data in Chapter 4.
† = Nonskilled agricultural workers, which forms the bulk of agricultural jobs among migrant workers and includes farm laborers, are classified under elementary occupations (ILO 2012, 47).

the lowest average trade union density at 14.3% and 14.7%, respectively. The jurisdiction with the highest average is Canada, at 29.4%, followed by the United Kingdom, with 23.4%. It is also clear that there is considerable variation across occupational groups. For instance, managers generally have the lowest levels of membership in trade unions. This is not surprising, as they are often excluded from the scope of collective bargaining by virtue of their position. In the occupational groupings where foreign-born workers predominate, services and elementary occupations, there are lower levels of coverage than the averages across all sectors. This is especially the case in sectors where there are high numbers of foreign workers, such as in California, where 30.2% of the services group is comprised of a foreign-born population but only 11.6% are unionized. Similarly, in the United Kingdom, 16.3% of this group is foreign-born but only 19.8% of workers in that sector are unionized. These data reflect some of the challenges in trade union organizing in the service and horticulture sectors.[7]

Unions as legal interveners and their success rates
Generally, we find that unions are not very involved as legal representatives for migrants within the MWRD. There is variation across the six labor law jurisdictions, as Table 7.2 shows. In Australia, trade unions are involved in representing only sixteen migrants across fifteen cases. In Alberta, trade unions represented twenty migrants across seven cases. In British Columbia, 215 migrants were represented in 15 cases. However, several of these cases involved large class actions, including *Re Sidhu & Sons Nursery Ltd.* (2010) (seventy-three migrants), a case concomitant with *Floralia* and raising similar facts, and *C.S.W.U., Local 1611 v. SELI Canada Inc.* ((2009) CarswellBC 1858) (thirty migrants), a case involving construction workers who assisted in building Vancouver Airport. In Ontario, there were seventeen migrants across fifteen cases involving trade unions, while in the United Kingdom only two migrant workers were involved in two cases. Finally, in California there was no legal representation by trade unions at all within the database's cases. When we recall that the overall number of migrants workers in the database is 1,912, encompassing 907 court cases, it is clear that unions are involved in a minority of cases and, outside of British Columbia, represent a small number of migrants. Further, while in Australia, British Columbia, and the United Kingdom, unions have success rates in their litigation close to or exceeding the average across the database (70.2%), in other jurisdictions trade unions are more likely to lose cases than win them (e.g., in Alberta) or their success

Table 7.2 Union interventions, by migrants represented

	Australia (2020)	Alberta	British Columbia	Ontario	United Kingdom (2018)	California (2018)
Migrants	16	20	215	17	2	0
Success rate	11 (69%)	3 (15%)	138 (64.2%)	9 (53%)	2 (100%)	0
Claim Type						
Economic violation	14	6	20	12	2	0
Discrimination violation	2	17	196	3	2	0
Safety violation	1	0	0	3	0	0
Criminal violation	0	0	0	0	0	0
Leave and other workplace entitlement violations	0	0	0	0	0	0

Note: Total migrants (workers represented by unions) may be smaller than the sum of claims by violation claim as some actions involved concurrent claims across a variety of violation areas.

rates are far lower than the average across the Database (Ontario). Clearly these figures are only correlations between union representation and success and do not control for other factors that might influence court outcomes, such as the type of violation area that is litigated or the court forum where a case is brought.[8]

The types of cases that trade unions litigate are also considered on the basis of the five-type classification schema presented in Chapter 1. This schema encompasses five main categories: (1) economic violations, (2) discrimination-based violations, (3) safety violations, (4) criminal violations, and (5) denial of leave and other workplace entitlements. We divide the claims within the MWRD into these five categories. It is clear that the bulk of claims are in the area of discrimination and are most frequent in British Columbia.[9] While the bulk of the discrimination claims brought by unions are around discrimination based on trade union affiliation and organizing (180), there are also claims for race (94), disability (7), sex (6), age (2), caregiver/family responsibilities (2), pregnancy (2), and religion (1). The other main area of litigation for trade unions is economic, predominantly underpayment cases. This is unsurprising given that economic violations comprise the bulk of violation types in the database and that the enforcement of wages is a central remit of trade union activity.

Conclusion

There are differing views on whether trade unions and other forms of collective representation overwhelmingly support or hinder migrant workplace claims. Even the quantitative scholarship that suggests a broad and positive relationship between strong trade unions and better protections for migrant workers is premised upon high trade union density, which is no longer the case, particularly in the Anglo-American countries considered in this book (Boräng, Kalm, and Lindvall 2020). Further, such studies are riddled with the challenges of accurately measuring changes in collective rights regimes over time that are not always that amenable to comparison. A variety of studies demonstrate that trade unions may at times oppose migrant workers and instead advance the rights of citizens in a race to the bottom in terms of protection (e.g., Afonso, Negash, and Wolff 2020). At other times, migrants may be blocked from associating with one another collectively due to restrictions on trade union organizing in migrant-dominated sectors, as the *Floralia* litigation demonstrates. Trade unions or their allies can also oppose immigration entirely through opposition to visa design or shifts toward temporary migration programs. The mobility patterns of migrant workers can stymie traditional methods of trade union organizing that may be historically based on stationary and ongoing workforces. We saw such challenges well displayed in the *Floralia* litigation. However, recent innovations, such as training staff in Mexico or seeking allies within the Mexican consulate to reveal blacklisting, demonstrate that unions are adapting to the obstacles presented by temporary labor migration schemes in order to represent migrant workers in new and creative ways and to widen the ambit of their membership base.

Several recommendations flow from the findings in this chapter. First, the analysis of alt-unions demonstrates that they can play important roles in representing migrants where unions are unable to or where migrant union membership is low. While experimentation with alt-unions has occurred at length in California and some parts of Canada, there is more scope for experimentation in Australia and the United Kingdom. The opportunity for government enforcement agencies, which we consider in more detail in the next chapter, working with trade unions to enforce conditions, is also worthy of more attention as it has been proven to facilitate grassroots connections with migrant populations (Vosko 2013, 886–887; Dias-Abey 2018).

Some of the most recent innovations by alt-unions and unions involve engaging with migrants before they leave their country of origin. This can be particularly important in acculturating prospective migrants into best workplace practices, before they leave, so they are equipped with the knowledge to raise their concerns. Again, there is a long tradition of such activity by the UFCW operating in North America (Felix Martinez, Interview, 18 June 2019), but it is beginning to occur more in Australia as well (Tim Nelthorpe, Interview, 8 October 2019). This is a practice that unions more broadly could engage with. Finally, although a harder battle to win, there are strong grounds for pushing for reform to labor laws that exclude migrants from unionizing in certain sectors. Aside from being discriminatory, it is clear that such a practice also removes the opportunities for collective representation and protection. Where possible, governments should seek to remove these exclusions. As noted, there are also alt-unions based in sending countries that act on behalf of migrant workers prior to departure, raising migrants awareness of future risks prior to their departure.

In all of the jurisdictions considered in this book, trade union membership has declined over the past three decades, but other forms of worker protection have increased. Alexandre Afonso, Samir Negash, and Emily Wolff (2020) argue that when trade union density is lower, the need for state regulation to cover the field grows. In particular, the state and its enforcement agencies will need to take on a heightened role in monitoring and enforcing minimum workplace standards. Aside from the alt-unions and autonomous worker centers that have been considered in this chapter, in some of the jurisdictions, in particular Australia and to a lesser extent California, the state has taken on this role through enforcement policy. In the following chapter, on enforcement, we explore this phenomenon in detail across the six labor law jurisdictions.

8
Strategic or General Enforcement of Migrant Workplace Rights

Kazuhiro Kojima and Zhicheng Zhang were directors and part-owners of Bento Kings Meadows, sushi restaurants in Launceston, Tasmania. They also owned the Wan Japanese Restaurant in Launceston. They had met while studying business and tourism at the University of Tasmania (*Fair Work Ombudsman v. Bento Kings Meadows* (2013) FCCA 977, para 47). Over a two-year period, fifty employees across their four restaurants were underpaid $105,738. Litigation was brought by thirteen of these employees, who were each underpaid $9,171 over a two-month period (Australia, FWO 2013).[1] These employees were predominantly migrants, including international students, mainly from Asia, and they spoke limited English (Australia, FWO 2013). Wages were egregiously low. As Judge O'Sullivan wrote, "[S]ome employees . . . were paid as little as $5 an hour for trial shifts . . . and most of the Employees were paid just under $8 an hour for part or all of the [r]elevant [p]eriod" (*FWO v. Bento Kings Meadows*, at para 38). This compared to the then-mandated minimum of over $18 per hour. Additionally, Bento Kings Meadows did not pay penalty rates for weekend, evening, and public holiday work. Record-keeping and pay slip laws were also breached (paras 12–13).

The immigration angle was an important part of this case. In explaining its thinking in bringing the matter, the Australian FWO's (2013) Natalie James said, "Foreign workers can be vulnerable if they are not fully aware of their workplace rights, so we treat underpayment of foreign workers very seriously and will not hesitate to take action in cases such as this one in Tasmania." Judge O'Sullivan also emphasized the importance of enforcement in workplaces involving migrants. He cited the prior FWO case *Go Yo Trading Pty. Limited and Anor.* ((2012) FMCA 865, at 15–16), where the court wrote, "Foreign nationals working in Australia on visas, be they 417 [student] visas or 457 [short-term work] visas or some other form of visa, in my view, represent a particular class of employee who are potentially vulnerable to improper practices by their employers." He cited the defendants as having used Asian community websites to advertise the positions to non-English-speakers as an additional point of vulnerability (*FWO v. Bento Kings Meadows*, para 12).

This case was one of several where the FWO had sought to investigate exploitation in the Chinese and Korean communities, especially among new migrants, where there had been examples of coethnic exploitation or employers offering a "going rate for overseas workers" (e.g., Australia, FWO 2015, 2016a). Through its campaigns the FWO sought to dispel the misapprehension that there were different wage rates for different ethnic groups or visa classes.

The extent of exploitation in Australia in the hospitality and restaurant sector was also a key issue in this case. Justice O'Sullivan wrote:

> In many cases before this Court over the last number of years it has been repeatedly identified that there is a significant risk of underpayments and breaches of workplace legislation in the restaurant and hospitality industries where vulnerable employees such as foreign nationals on visas are employed. This case is yet another example that the risk continues to exist. (*FWO v. Bento Kings Meadows*, at para 1)

As we noted in Chapter 4, on sector, quite a large number of the cases in the MWRD stem from the hospitality and restaurant industries, not only in Australia but also in the other jurisdictions. In this sense, *Bento Kings Meadows* provides useful examples of challenges for the enforcement of wage underpayment of migrant workers in a central sector of concern.

When the matter was heard in the Federal Circuit Court of Australia in Melbourne, Justice O'Sullivan ordered that all underpayments be rectified. This amounted to a total of $105,738, with repayments ranging between $90 and $12,000 and an average underpayment of $700 per migrant worker (*FWO v. Bento Kings Meadows*, para 54). Further, the two co-directors of Bento Kings Meadows were individually fined $27,984.

The case reveals interesting questions about the degree of employer knowledge of underpayment. Justice O'Sullivan was critical of the actions of Kojima and Zhang, stating that they had "displayed a reckless disregard for their obligations." He added, "The respondents' submissions on this issue effectively amounted to a plea of ignorance or an assertion that they were so ignorant they didn't know any better" (*FWO v. Bento Kings Meadows*, para 38, also cited in Australia, FWO 2013). These arguments were rejected by the court in its imposition of fines, which were intended to also act as a form of "general deterrence . . . to ensure employers understand they must take steps to ensure correct employee entitlements are paid." Kojima and Zhang did concede that these events had occurred.

Chapter overview

The *Bento Kings Meadows* case highlights a number of important points about enforcement. It reveals the potential role for government bodies, here the Australian Fair Work Ombudsman, to act as litigators in cases enforcing migrant worker rights. It invites a consideration of the types of enforcement bodies that exist across the six jurisdictions[2] considered in this book, and their fundamental differences. This also encourages examination of the role of self-help for employers to improve compliance with workplace laws and the limits of such methods. In *Bento Kings Meadows*, the co-directors claimed ignorance of workplace and business laws, despite their university training in these areas. The chapter also addresses complaints-driven, strategic, and generalized approaches to enforcement. The role of penalties to deter unlawful behavior by employers is also considered, as is the interaction between broader enforcement and immigration law and the level of government funding for enforcement activities. In all sections of this chapter, the focus is on enforcement of labor laws, while workplace health and safety laws and their enforcement are the focus of Chapter 4, on economic sector. It is important to note here that the funding and regulation of enforcement policy varies not only across the jurisdictions but also within them and over time. The chapter focuses on present-day regulation, with some reflection upon the historical legacy where appropriate, but it cannot consider these issues exhaustively within the space allotted. The quantitative section considers the types of enforcement bodies involved in litigation within the MWRD, their distribution across the six labor law jurisdictions, their reliance upon class action mechanisms, their success rates when involved in litigation, and the use of penalties by the courts as a source of deterrence.

Enforcement approaches across the jurisdictions

An appropriate enforcement policy is necessary for labor law rights to be realized (Creighton and Stewart 2010, 500–501). In this section, we consider the role of enforcement bodies and their differences across the six jurisdictions, the different types of enforcement strategies used, the types and ranges of penalties available, and the extent of government funding for enforcement.

Structure and regulatory design of enforcement bodies

Each of the six labor law jurisdictions considered in this chapter has a different approach to enforcement. In Australia, the Fair Work Ombudsman is centrally responsible for enforcement. Its predecessor, the Workplace Ombudsman, was created in 2004 and was replaced by a more persuasive compliance model—the Office of Workplace Services (Creighton and Stewart 2010, 500–501)—with what has been described as a "cooperative dispute resolution" model (Hardy and Howe 2019). The FWO itself was created in 2009 with the establishment of new workplace laws through the Australian Fair Work Act. The FWO is responsible for an array of tasks, including enforcing anti-retaliation provisions against employers, workplace discrimination, sham contracting, and supervising trade union behavior (Hardy and Howe 2020, 226).

An *enforcement pyramid* operates in Australia. At its base is the FWO's role in education; next are formal mechanisms, such as compliance notices and enforceable undertakings; at the apex are punitive sanctions, penalties, and prosecution (Hardy and Howe 2009, 311). Enforceable undertakings are orders to a person or organization to act in a certain way such as to make a contrition payment or take actions such as undertaking regular audits of their pay systems, or compliance notices that can be issued if a person is reasonably believed to have contravened workplace laws (Fair Work Act (2009), S715(6)(7); s716(1)), followed by proactive compliance deeds. Compliance notes themselves are viewed as a mechanism to address contraventions of labor laws instead of going ahead with litigation (Australia, FWO 2019, 6, citing *Hindu Society of Australia Inc. v. FWO* (2016) FCCA 221, at 30 per Judge Riethmuller), although the FWO does regularly also instigate court actions for breach of compliance notices. Mediation by the FWO, and its assistance in initiating small claims procedures by workers, are other steps that precede an FWO decision to pursue litigation. Generally, mediation does not impose a decision; instead it encourages settlement (Creighton and Stewart 2010, 519). Litigation then follows but is undertaken rarely, and, as discussed in more detail in the strategic litigation section, there are a series of public interest requirements that must be met before it can begin (Australia, FWO 2019, 9–10). While such litigation is important—and a feature of the analysis in this chapter—it should be noted that it accounts for only 10% of the FWO's activities, with 90% achieved through education and dispute resolution (Hardy and Howe 2020, 227). Table 8.1 provides an overview of the various enforcement functions across the jurisdictions, including in Australia.

The United Kingdom has a series of bodies all placed under the leadership of the director of labor market enforcement. These include the Gangmasters and Labour Abuse Licensing Authority; the Employment Agencies Standard Inspectorate, which enforces the rules governing the conduct of employment agencies; and Her Majesty's Revenue and Customs (HMRC), which is responsible for enforcing the National Minimum Wage. As the U.K. context also includes a Modern Slavery Act, the police force and National Crime Agency also form a component of the enforcement structure (Metcalf 2019). The U.K. Gangmasters and Labour Abuse Licensing Authority enforces legislation related to "gangmasters" (an old term to describe labor providers), such as those in agriculture and goods processing. This legislation was prompted by the death of twenty-three Chinese migrant workers in Morecambe Bay in 2004. In 2016, following recommendations from the Migration Advisory Committee (2014), the Gangmasters Licensing Authority was recast as the Gangmasters and Labour Abuse Authority, which in turn expanded its remit to allow public servants to enforce laws against abuses, although calls to extend the system to other sectors have not been accepted at present (Rosa Crawford, Interview, London, 2019). A separate body, the Employment Agency Standards Inspectorate, regulates agency work.

In California, workplace enforcement occurs through the California Labor Commissioner's Office, also known as the Department of Labor Standards Enforcement. It has the following arms: Wage Claim Adjudication, which enforces pay provisions in the California Labor Code; Retaliation Complaint Investigations Unit, which investigates adverse action (general protections) complaints; Licensing and Registration, which manages licensing for the agriculture, entertainment, garment, and car wash industries; a Public Works unit, which enforces wages, apprenticeship standards, and related workplace protections on public works construction projects; and the Bureau of Field Enforcement, which conducts inspections to enforce minimum wage and overtime laws, workers' compensation, insurance coverage, child labor, cash pay, and unlicensed contractors, among other categories (California Department of Industrial Relations 2017).

Table 8.1 Structure of enforcement bodies, in all six labor law jurisdictions*

Enforcement Area	Australia*	Alberta	British Columbia	Ontario	United Kingdom*	California
Wages and conditions	FWO, Wage Inspectorate Victoria (state level)	Alberta Employment Standards (provincially regulated), Employment Standards (Canada) (federally regulated)	Employment Standards Branch (provincially regulated), Employment Standards (Canada) (federally regulated)	Ministry of Labor Employment Standards Program (provincially regulated), Employment Standards (Canada) (federally regulated)	HM Revenue and Customs National Minimum Wage Unit	Wage and Hour Division of the U.S. Department of Labor (federal labor law enforcement), California Labor Commissioners' Office Bureau of Field Enforcement, California Labor Commissioners' Office Wage Claim Adjudication, California Labor Commissioners' Office Public Works Unit,
Licencing and labor market intermediaries	No specialized body†	No specialized body	No specialized body	No specialized body	Gangmasters and Labour Abuse Authority Employment Agency Standards inspectorate	California Labor Commissioners' Office Bureau of Field Enforcement Licensing & Registration
Serious criminal offenses	Australian federal police	Local and federal police	Local and federal police	Local and federal police	Gangmasters and Labour Abuse Authority National Crime Agency	Civil enforcement: Department of Fair Employment and Housing, Local and federal police, California Labor Commissioners' Office Bureau of Field Enforcement Criminal Investigation Unit

(continued)

Table 8.1 Continued

Enforcement Area	Australia*	Alberta	British Columbia	Ontario	United Kingdom*	California
Construction	Australian Building and Construction Commission	No specialized body	No specialized body	No specialized body	No specialized body	No specialized body
Collective bargaining	FWO and the Fair Work Commission that has power to make bargaining orders and approve enterprise agreements	No specialized body	No specialized body	No specialized body	No specialized body	National Labor Relations Board (federal)
Labor inspectors per million workforce	16	28.8	13.8	262	41	

* *Australia:* Before 2007 the major inspectorate body was the Office of Workplace Services, and then the Workplace Ombudsman until 2009. *United Kingdom:* These bodies are overseen by the director of labor market enforcement. Before 2016, the Gangmasters and Labour Abuse Authority was the Gangmasters Licensing Authority and lacked the power to investigate labor abuse across all U.K. industries. This change also created a new position, the labor abuse prevention officer, specialist officers tasked with investigating severe cases of exploitation which the police address in other jurisdictions. Although the previous body already had powers of arrest, the Gangmasters and Labour Abuse Licensing Authority also has powers of search and the ability to apply for Labour Market Enforcement Undertakings and Orders (Clark 2020, 213). The number of labor inspectorate staff overall rather than specifically labor inspectors is provided. There were nine inspectors per million in 2015.

† "State governments in Australia do not have responsibility for enforcing employment standards established under Federal laws. However, in response to one Federal and two State government enquiries, the Queensland and Victorian State Labor governments introduced labor hire licensing schemes in 2018/19" (Underhill et al. 2019, 148).

Sources: FWO, personal communication, 2020 (Australian labor inspectors); Scott 2017, 193 (U.K. labor inspectors); Alberta Employment Standards, personal communication, 2020 (Alberta labor inspectors); B.C. Government 2020; Focus on Labour Exploitation 2017; Ontario Government 2020.

Moving to Canada, in Alberta, the minimum standards espoused by the Employment Standards legislation applies to all employees and employers. Employment Standards legislate hours of work, overtime, payment of wages, vacation pay, general holiday pay, job-protected leaves, and notice of termination of employment for employers and employees in provincially regulated employment. There are exceptions to the minimum standards in certain industries. Employment Standards runs out of the Safe, Fair and Healthy Workplaces program of the Ministry of Labor and Immigration. Sixty employment standards officers conduct inspections, along with twelve officers specifically tasked to vulnerable workers (Alberta Employment Standards, personal communication, 2020). In Ontario, the Ministry of Labor administers the Employment Standards Act (2000) and the Employment Protections for Foreign Nationals Act (2009). In British Columbia, the Employment Standards Branch of the Ministry of Labor administers the Employment Standards Act (1996) with thirty-five employment standards officers. The Canada Labor Code covers federally regulated workplaces.[3] Enforcement happens through Employment Standards (Canada) in these industries (see Table 8.1). As noted in Chapter 4, each province has its own dedicated work, health, and safety inspectorate.

Types of enforcement

Enforcement of workplace laws can take a number of general approaches. It can be considered on a scale of intervention by the state ranging from self-auditing through to criminal prosecution. Approaches include self-help by employers, complaints-driven approaches, strategic enforcement, and more general "responsive regulation." Penalties can range from simple responses like the issuance of summons and tickets and the seizure of employer property to criminal imprisonment. This section considers these various approaches.

Self-auditing
Perhaps the most low-cost form of enforcement is self-auditing by employers. An example of self-auditing is the requirement in several countries for companies to self-audit their compliance with modern slavery rules, including the United Kingdom (Modern Slavery Act (2015) (UK), s54) and Australia at the federal level (Modern Slavery Act (2018) (Cwth), ss5, 6, part 2).

Self-auditing can also include education campaigns on government websites, where employers can educate themselves about workplace laws, or tools such as the Australian FWO's Pay Calculators or Small Business Hotline that allow employers to accurately calculate workplace entitlements and which advise on the various rules for businesses (e.g., Australia, Fair Work 2020a, 2020b; Parker 2019).

Online campaigns exist in some of the other jurisdictions. For instance, Ontario has online videos and print campaigns in a variety of languages (Ontario Government 2020). The United Kingdom has run a holiday pay awareness campaign using social media advertising, video on demand, and train advertisements (BEIS 2019). Similarly, a U.K. National Minimum Wage Campaign was featured in shopping centers and on public transport in order to raise awareness (BEIS 2017).

In Ontario, the Ministry of Labor Education, Outreach and Partnership Program was started in 2009 to increase employee and employer awareness of workplace breaches and encourage self-help among employees. Under this model, employers either voluntarily comply or a compliance order is issued, with the options of repayment, reinstatement, or rectification (Tucker et al. 2019, 9). In California, campaigns in recent years have sought to increase both employer and employee awareness of underpayment. These include the multimedia and multilingual "Wage Theft Is a Crime" under Governor Jerry Brown and former state Labor Commissioner Julie Su (Labor Commissioner's Office 2020).

While important in raising awareness, a central limitation of such methods is that they do not ultimately lead to penalties for noncompliance or the protection of victims, who might be made even more vulnerable by such audits (Robinson 2015, 140). Further, in some ways self-compliance runs contrary to a view of the role of the law as protecting against noncompliance by employers: it assumes that individuals will self-correct and that legal breaches are largely a product of imperfect information flow rather than regulatory failure to legislate against unlawful behavior (e.g., Tucker et al. 2019, 8). Arguably, the law exists not only to set standards but also to provide mechanisms to enforce them when individual employers fail to self-regulate.

Furthermore, the concept of self-auditing relies upon employer awareness of the law, which cannot always be assumed, even with large-scale education campaigns in place such as those listed above. For instance, a study of twenty-four firms in the United Kingdom documented low levels of compliance knowledge by employers (Ram et al. 2017, 36). It found that employers may reject prevailing legal standards and view what is socially acceptable as a more appropriate benchmark for wages (Ram et al. 2019, 3). Another fundamental problem with self-corrective approaches is that they rely on the self-identification of problems by worker and employer, and mutual resolution, at least at first instance. In support of these limitations, a study relying on complaints data in Canada found that most complaints are not voluntarily resolved between employee and employer (Vosko, Tucker, and Casey 2019, 244).

Complaints-driven approaches to enforcement
Complaints-driven approaches to enforcement rely upon the individual who has suffered an infringement raising a complaint and pursuing this in formal settings, sometimes, but not always, with the support of an advocate.

In Australia, the FWO creates an enforcement pyramid, which includes avenues for telephone-based complaints, which can then be either mediated or pursued legally if resolution is not achieved. This includes in-language information to service Australia's linguistically diverse population and a specialist telephone service for visa holders (Hardy and Howe 2020, 229). However, as we note below, the FWO pursues only a fraction of worker complaints, leaving the workers to proceed either individually or through independent legal counsel.

Ontario is largely complaints-focused. Some scholars have argued that this leads to a "deterrence gap" there (Tucker et al. 2019). Using Employment Standards complaint data, Vosko and collaborators (2019, 241; see also Vosko 2013) find that, while there were violations evident in a minimum of 43% of cases, only a tiny fraction of these led to the issuance of tickets and even fewer to prosecutions. Migrant workers in particular are vastly underrepresented as complainants in the agricultural sector, suggesting that those on short-term visas may not have the capacity or knowledge to come forward with legal claims (Vosko, Tucker, and Casey 2019). As with Ontario, the British Columbia Employment Standards Branch previously required complainants to first attempt to resolve their dispute with their employer before they could make a formal complaint (Banks 2015, 22). As of 2019, this self-help precursor has been removed. Although still complaints-driven, industrial relations officers have been empowered to expand the remit of complaints to encompass broader investigations (Parsons 2019). In Alberta, investigators are less likely to enter workplaces for inspections without a formal complaint having been received, and the average time for a complaint resolution was two hundred days. However, most of the employment standards inspections there are triggered by government and focus on employers of young people and migrants (Alberta Federation of Labour 2017; Foster et al. 2018, 2).

The United Kingdom has opt-in forms of compliance that focus on individual complaints. Since 2015, individual claimants must first undertake a pre-claim conciliation process through the Advisory, Conciliation and Arbitration Service before going to the Employment Tribunal. Close to 44% of claims are conciliated in this way (Clark 2020, 209). Further, those efforts that have been made on enforcement, such as the Low Pay Commission's study into compliance with the National Minimum Wage in 2017, hardly mention the distinctive challenges faced by migrant workers. The Director of Labour Market Enforcement has also been criticized on this basis (Fudge 2018b, 429).

In California, complaints-based approaches demonstrate some gaps in deterrence. For instance, research on the Federal Labor Standards violations and Work Health Safety violations generally demonstrate a significant gap between complaints and compliance dependent upon sector. A 2007 study found only three examples where an industry in the top ten of complaints was also in the top ten for substantiated violations (Weil and Pyles 2007, 173). This suggests that self-compliance operates better in some sectors than others. Weil and Pyles conclude on this basis that a central problem with complaints-based approaches to compliance is that they underplay the vulnerability of workers in making complaints: their status as migrants, the costs associated with complaining, access to information related to complaints, and the risk of employer retaliation bear differently on different kinds of workers (178).

Complaints-driven compliance therefore raises a number of concerns. First, it is *reactive* rather than *proactive* and relies upon individuals to make complaints. Second, as discussed in Chapter 5, individuals may be concerned about reprisals if they are still under an employment contract and therefore may not proceed (Clark 2020, 216). Further, complainants are at least partially protected in some but not all jurisdictions. For example, in Australia the Memorandum of Understanding between Immigration and the FWO,[4] and in California, s244(b) of the Labor Code, protects workers against "unfair immigration-related practices." In other contexts, complaints-driven processes may begin only after a person has already lost their job and there is no clear firewall between departments. We return to this issue below when comparing the relative extent of enforcement and immigration funding. On the basis of these inherent weaknesses of complaints-based enforcement, some scholars have recommended strategic targeting of key areas of noncompliance to overcome far lower likelihood of worker-initiated complaints (Weil and Pyles 2007, 129).

Strategic enforcement
Strategic enforcement acknowledges that enforcement is difficult in a context of rising inequality and changes in the structure and nature of work. Developments that challenge the traditional employment contract, such as franchising, subcontracting, and independent contracting, are part of this new workplace landscape (Tucker et al. 2019, 5). In this context, strategic enforcement is intentionally targeted at maximizing enforcement efficiency and prioritizing efforts where they are most needed. It can involve an enforcement agency focusing on certain industries (such as low-wage industries), enhancing deterrence at the industry and geographical levels, transforming compliance investigations, and enhancing approaches to monitoring (Weil 2008, 2020, 267). In doing so, the regulatory intention is to not only shift the attitudes of the sanctioned employers but to shift all employer attitudes generally (Weil 2020, 265). Ultimately, strategic enforcement can end in litigation against offenders. But it can also be effective through the issuance of compliance and infringement notices in key sectors, which can shift behavior within particular industries (Weil 2010; Parker 2019). Therefore, the intention of strategic deterrence is not only to increase compliance but also to generate "broader ripple effects" that discourage future misbehavior by other employers (Hardy and Howe 2017, 473). This is a clear intention of the FWO in Australia, and the philosophy of strategic litigation underpins its enforcement approach (Australia, FWO 2020, 10–16), including in the *Bento Kings Meadows* case.

Strategic enforcement can take the form of strategic litigation by government agencies focusing on bringing court cases in key sectors affected by exploitation. That said, litigation can be viewed as the apex of the enforcement pyramid, with the other options preceding it (Hardy, Howe, and Cooney 2013, 570, 575). Such litigation works from an assumption that employers are rational and will seek to minimize illegal behavior due to its costs, although this point has been challenged empirically. Hardy and Howe's 2017 study of two strategic litigation cases demonstrates that employers had limited detailed knowledge of two cases of strategic litigation.

Australia is unique across the jurisdictions in giving a strong role to its public enforcement body in litigating cases, although it also conducts proactive audits of certain businesses. In the other jurisdictions, workplace raids and blitzes are a more common approach to strategic enforcement. In Ontario, employment standards officers can conduct expanded investigations arising out of an individual complaint and initiate targeted or blitz inspections as well as regulation inspections (Tucker et al. 2019, 10). As of 2019, British Columbia's Employment Standards Branch has been granted this power. Investigations initiated by Alberta Employment Standards are targeted at migrant-heavy workplaces (Barnetson 2010). In the United Kingdom, strategic enforcement has largely taken the form of workplace raids in key areas. There is very little use of litigation. An interview with David Metcalf, former Director of Labour Market Enforcement, revealed that over a twenty-year period there have been only thirteen prosecutions by HMRC (Interview, London, 2019). In California, there are periodic sweeps of certain industries conducted by the Labor Enforcement Taskforce, Occupational Safety, California Tax Agency, and Department of Insurance (California Department of Industrial Relations, Labor Enforcement Task Force 2019). A combination of referrals, surveillance, and complaints is used to determine which industries to focus upon at any point in time (California Department of Industrial Relations, Labor Enforcement Task Force 2019).

Despite its potential strengths, strategic enforcement is not without its critics. Alice Bloch, Leena Kumarappan, and Sonia McKay (2015), for instance, argue that targeting some industries or employers, such as ethnic businesses in the United Kingdom, can lead to discrimination. In other jurisdictions, such as Ontario, the criticism has been that blitzes have been insufficiently used in migrant-heavy industries such as agriculture (Vosko, Tucker, and Casey 2019, 252, 253).

Generalized enforcement
An alternative approach to the targeting of enforcement is a more generalized approach, also known as *responsive regulation*. Under this approach, regulation will be largely hidden from employers, and escalation up the enforcement pyramid will be necessary only in the most egregious cases (Tucker et al. 2019, 2, citing Ayres and Braithwaite 1992). Tucker et al. (2019, 5) describe this model: "[T]he hammer of deterrence should be hidden most of the time but must be brought down when needed." Part of the rationale for approaching enforcement in a generalized way may relate to its cost. In

all jurisdictions, the number of workplace inspectors is lower than the ILO (2006, 13) benchmark of one inspector for every ten thousand employees. The actual numbers across the jurisdictions are listed in Table 8.1, with evident variation. Further, the decision over whether to fund enforcement is in itself often deeply political (LeBaron and Phillips 2019, 6). For instance, in the United States the number of Work and Health Division inspectors increased considerably under the Obama administration but is still considered inadequate; Democrat-dominated California has more labor inspection than other U.S. states (Weil 2020, 265; Lee and Smith 2019, 772, 774). There is also a demonstrated relationship between social democratic governments and funding for labor inspection (Scott 2017, 196). While there may be exceptions to this, such as the decision of the Conservative Coalition government to fund the FWO in Australia, there is a general ideological correlation between labor inspection and left-wing government (Hardy and Howe 2009).

The extent of funding also correlates with its efficacy (Scott 2017, 193; Hardy and Howe 2019). In light of this, recent inquiries in Australia and elsewhere have called for increases in government funding for enforcement. For instance, the Fels Commission (2019, 7–8), which investigated the extent of wage underpayment to migrant workers in Australia, recommended that the federal government "undertake a public capability review of the Fair Work Ombudsman to ensure that it has the [necessary] resources, tools and culture" (also see Recommendation 10). This issue was raised by several interview subjects in Australia in their reflections upon the FWO.

In Australia, the bulk of actions are not brought by the FWO. (Only seventy-three cases are brought by the FWO across the MWRD.) A series of considerations must be factored in before a claim can be followed through from assessment to litigation (Australia, FWO 2019). Importantly for the current analysis on migrant workers, however, vulnerability of the worker is a key public interest factor, which could help to explain why there has been such a strong focus on migrant workers within the FWO's work in recent years (see generally FWO 2019, 3, 9, 10).

Tim Harrison of the Directorate of Labour Market Enforcement provided an overview of the process in the United Kingdom:

> So, basically, normally, if an employer is found noncompliant, they have to pay a penalty. If they pay within fourteen days, then it's reduced by half. On top of that, in recent years, HMRC has brought on something called "self-correction." HMRC... will basically get to a situation where they will allow

the employer the freedom, if you like, to . . . check their records for any other instances of nonpayment. And if they make good those arrears, the employer becomes exempt from any penalties. (Interview, London, 2019)

After this, there is an *undertaking and order* requirement, where the HMRC and other enforcement bodies advise the employer that they have breached the law. If this is not enforced, then over time it can be escalated to a jail sentence (David Metcalf, Interview, London, 2019). Further, the National Minimum Wage Inspectorate can investigate complaints and initiate civil proceedings, although this does not happen frequently (Clark 2020, 212).

Ontario has a system of notices of contravention. This includes penalties for employers who breach the law (Employment Standards Act (2000) (Ontario), s113) and a *name and shame* provision which publishes the names of persons who have breached the law (s113(6.2)). The Provincial Offences Act ((1990) Part 1) can also empower issuances of tickets or fines that go to the Victims of Justice Fund. Fines of up to $50,000 and corporate fines up to $100,000 can be imposed (Part 3). However, generally it was viewed that this is more the case for workplace safety issues than wages (Vosko 2019c, 858).

In British Columbia, if a complaint is not resolved voluntarily, an officer will issue a determination as to whether or not the employer has complied with the province's Employment Standards Act (1996). The Director of Employment Standards is empowered to issue orders and compensation. There are also penalties ranging between $500 and $10,000 per contravention (Borden Ladner Gervais 2018, 24–25). In Alberta, enforcement activities involve compliance orders, formal criminal charges, and administrative penalties ranging between $2,500 and $42,500, alongside lower-value tickets (Foster, Barnetson, and Matsunaga-Turnbull 2018, 2).

Following a complaint in California, a citation is issued for breaches of labor law. This can be followed by a legal judgment and ultimately criminal action if required, with a prison sentence of up to two years (Penal Code of California, s487). While not many criminal prosecutions have been undertaken, their prospect creates a "strong deterrent" for "grand theft of labor" (Lee and Smith 2019, 813). Further, unlike other U.S. states, California has a dedicated Criminal Investigation Unit within its Department of Industrial Relations. Uniquely across the jurisdictions, California officials also have the power to seize goods from nonpayment employers to ensure that penalties are effectively paid. In some industries, upfront bonds are required in order for the business to be licensed; these can then be claimed against in the event of nonpayment. Federally, an array of powers exist under the Federal Labor Standards Act (1938), including civil monetary penalties, liquidated damages, and the "hot goods authority," whereby items that were produced through exploitative means can be prevented from entering interstate markets (Weil 2020, 269; Weil and Mallo 2007). The Work and Hour Division can negotiate Enhanced Compliance Agreements to oversee compliance; some have been negotiated with large farm contractors in California, where many migrant workers are employed (Weil 2020, 270).

As noted in Chapter 7, labor inspectorates also undertake outreach in workforces, and there have been efforts to tailor these to particular ethnic communities. There are examples of workers or trade unions being involved as representatives within labor inspectorates, such as the Los Angeles Unified School District and Los Angeles Board of Public Workers (Vosko 2013). Another example is the collaboration between community organizations and state agencies, such as the Wage and Hour Watch in New York City (689). Still, building trust between vulnerable workers, such as migrants, and trade unions and other advocates remains a challenge (Weil 2020, 272).

Penalties

The need for penalties exists under both strategic and generalized enforcement models. Penalties are used under the strategic model to send a strong signal to employers of the likely ramifications of unlawful behavior (Weil 2010). Under generalized enforcement, penalties become important as enforcement and legal actions move up the enforcement pyramid. *Bento Kings Meadows* raises important questions about how penalties are applied, what the appropriate range is, and what role penalties should play as a specific or more general deterrence. Often, the range of penalties is deeply contested in such cases. As Judge O'Sullivan noted in the present case, "The applicant contends that the maximum penalty applicable in the particular circumstances for this matter is $231,000. However, the applicant submits that an appropriate penalty in all circumstances is between $104,280 and $134,640" (*FWO v. Bento Kings Meadows*, at para 4).[5] As noted, the penalty ultimately applied was at the lower end: $122,960. This may relate in part to the fact that Bento Kings Meadows had already made a "rectification payment" for its failure to keep proper pay slips and improved its practices halfway through the underpayment period, leading to a "discount of penalty." Its directors' cooperation with authorities was also viewed as important (paras 41, 59, 60). In imposing a penalty under Australian law, a variety of factors must be considered, including the nature of the breach, the damage sustained and the contrition of the parties (per para 25, citing *Mason v. Harrington Corporation Pty. Ltd.* (2007) FMCA 7, at paras 26–59). Ultimately, "instinctive synthesis" is also required on the part of the judge in calculating the total aggregate penalty (*FWO v. Roselands Fruit Market Pty. Ltd.* (2012) FMCA 599, per Driver FM). The FWO argued that in approaching penalties in the hospitality industry, consideration should be given to the need for deterrence given the high rates of noncompliance (*FWO v. Bento Kings Meadows*, para 87).

Applicable penalties vary in employment law in Australia. Underpayment is viewed as a contravention under industrial awards and attracts a maximum of sixty penalty units per contravention, so $12,600 per contravention and $126,000 for a more serious contravention for a natural person (Fels 2019, 85; Fair Work Act (2009) (Cwth), ss45, 539; read with Crimes Act (1914) (Cwth), s4AA).[6] There have also been attempts in Australia to increase the application of penalties imposed upon franchisors following the introduction of the Protecting Vulnerable Workers Act (2017); however, the courts have been reluctant to "pierce the corporate veil" and to cast the franchisor as a relevant employer (Hardy 2019, 68). Nonetheless, the amounts awarded have increased over time, in line with increased attention to and reduced tolerance of exploitative workplace behavior (Fels 2019, 85). Some commentators have argued that such penalties are insufficient when compared with other areas of law, such as competition, business, and consumer law (Fels Commission 2019, Recommendations 5, 86; Hardy, Howe, and Cooney 2013). Some of this relates to the fact that the FWO generally does not make compensation orders against individuals, only companies, and some of the companies are natural persons. Tess Hardy, John Howe, and Sean Cooney (2013, 597) have argued that this approach "[does] not necessarily encourage the institutionalization of positive compliance practices or lead to sustainable compliance."

In the United Kingdom, underpayment is viewed as a civil offense, and failure to comply can result in a civil penalty at twice the hourly rate of pay for each worker (National Minimum Wage Act (1998) (UK), s21). In Ontario, failures to pay workers, including for overtime, is a prosecutable offense (Employment Standards Act (2000) (Ontario), s 132). In the case of underpayment, both corporations and their agents, directors, and officers are liable for penalties of up to $50,000 or, in the case of natural persons, up to twelve months' imprisonment (ss132, 137). Liable persons may also be required to pay back the amount owed to the worker(s) (s133). This is similar to the law in British Columbia, where underpayment is an offense punishable by a

$2,000 fine or six months' imprisonment (Employment Standards Act (1996) (British Columbia) s125; Offence Act (1996) (British Columbia) ss2, 4). Underpayment is also an offense for such persons in Alberta—the key difference being that employers are not liable for imprisonment, only a fine of up to $50,000 for natural persons and $100,000 for corporations (Employment Standards Code (2000) (Alberta), ss131–132).

In some instances, civil penalties may be viewed as insufficient and criminal penalties are needed. As Allan Fels (2019, 86–87) argues, "A series of serious underpayment cases involving Australian businesses have created a growing perception that the current regulatory model is unable to tackle serious and systematic underpayment of workers." To date, wage underpayment has not been criminalized in Australia and attempts to introduce this federally did not pass (Karp 2021). Another option is to use immigration law to regulate employers. For instance, employers in New Zealand who have acted in unscrupulous ways in the past cannot sponsor workers in the future (Fels 2019, 121). The provisions that criminalize grand wage theft in California were discussed above.

Enforcement and immigration bodies

Many of the concerns in the enforcement field around work vulnerability are heightened for migrants because of the disincentives that immigrant worker status presents to engage in self-help. Alternatively, enforcement itself may assist in compliance with labor law but diminish immigration rights, particularly for those on temporary or lapsed visas. Complainants need to be certain that there is no information sharing between labor and immigration bodies; however, often this guarantee is hard to secure and concerns over collusion can contribute to underreporting by the communities most in need of assistance. Further, if there is an imbalance in the financing of the two regulatory bodies—as is often the case and as was explored in Chapter 5 (Scott 2017, 192)—the objectives of border control can rapidly overwhelm labor enforcement. It is clear that in all jurisdictions, spending on immigration enforcement radically exceeds labor enforcement, tenfold or higher. This is reflective of the greater policy rationale placed upon border protection than the protection of wages and conditions in many of these jurisdictions. Table 8.2 gives global calculations or calculations within individual agencies if there is a group of institutions responsible for enforcement.

Table 8.2 Differential allocation of resources to labor and immigration enforcement across the six jurisdictions

Budget	Australia	Alberta	British Columbia	Ontario	United Kingdom	California
Labor enforcement budget	FY 2019: 110.009 million AUD	FY 2020: 73 million CAD (part of a larger office including workplace health and safety: Safe, Fair and Healthy Workplaces)	FY 2020: 13 million CAD	FY 2020: 47.286 million CAD	FY 2020: HMRC: 26.3 million GBP FY 2020: Gangmasters and Labour Abuse Licensing Authority: 6.158 million GBP FY 2019: Employment Agency Standards Inspectorate: 0.725 million GBP	FY 2018: 90.6 million USD
Immigration enforcement budget	FY 2020: 1.624 billion	FY 2020: 362 million; "share" is 41.992 million	FY 2020: 362 million; "share" is 47.8 million	FY 2020: 362 million; "share" is 138.7 million	FY 2020 373.7 million	FY 2020: 8.4 billion (national)

Note: "share" denotes share of budget relative to overall federal budget.

Sources: American Immigration Council 2020; Legislative Analyst's Office 2017; U.K. Home Office 2020; U.K. Department for Business, Energy, and Industrial Strategy 2019, 2020; Gangmasters and Labour Abuse Authority 2019a, 2019b;Patty 2018; Spinks and Sherrell 2020; Ontario Government 2019; BC Government and Service Employees' Union 2019; Toews 2019; Government of Canada 2019.

This potential for conflict between immigration and labor regulation finds resonance in various jurisdictions. As discussed in Chapter 5, a decision in the United Kingdom in 2014 to increase penalties for employers who hire undocumented workers could, on the one hand, be seen to protect workers and, on the other, to penalize anyone who has fallen into illegality (Fudge 2018a, 568). One perspective is that these measures have in fact targeted rather than protected migrants. For instance, raids into workplaces where particular ethnic groups predominate can also have the effect of focusing on those groups and at the same time increasing their risk of becoming undocumented and in turn lowering wages. Migrants without valid visa status may then be pressured into taking on work shifts during evenings or other asocial times or less visible positions or for shorter periods of time in order to avoid raids (Bloch, Kumarappan, and McKay 2015, 140–141). In a hostile immigration environment, this can have the effect of pushing migrant workers into more exploitative conditions, with reduced access to advocacy (135). In Ontario, concerns have been raised that the vulnerable status of migrants' visas can limit their capacity to make complaints at all, especially in a system that is not proactive (Vosko, Tucker, and Casey 2019). In Alberta, Jason Foster, Bob Barnetson, and Jared Matsunaga-Turnbull (2018) confirm that migrants are the least likely of all workers to exercise their rights out of fear of retaliation and because of their vulnerable citizenship status.

As noted in Chapter 5, there have been considerable concerns about the challenges undocumented migrant workers in California face in bringing claims. Novel approaches have been initiated to address the precarity of these workers. These include consular services to assist and educate workers in the countries from which they depart as well as advice hotlines in key migrant-receiving cities, such as Los Angeles (Bada and Gleeson 2015, 45). However, migrant advocates interviewed in the United States argued that immigrants may assume collusion between government agencies, precisely in the hostile immigration climate created by President Trump: "So when the Department of Labor investigators show up on job sites, immigrants run" (Shannon Lederer, AFL-CIO, Interview, November 2019). In all contexts, therefore, reducing migrants' perceptions of collusion between labor inspection bodies and immigration departments, or the police, is a crucial first step for effective labor enforcement.

Quantitative evidence

In this section, we consider quantitative data from the MWRD that address how important enforcement bodies are in litigating on behalf of migrant workers. It is also necessary to address what kinds of cases enforcement bodies pursue and against which kinds of employers. The analysis does not cover the full scope of state enforcement activities. For instance, the cases analyzed here do not include cases of the Labor Commissioner's Office of California, which encompasses the bulk of cases brought in the state but are not published. Nor does it include Australian Human Rights Commission determinations, which are also unpublished. As such, the questions of selection bias in the database that were discussed in the introduction are relevant here.

Enforcement bodies comprise those government bodies involved in the enforcement of wages, as well as work, health, and safety bodies. A full list of the relevant enforcement bodies considered in cases in the database is included in the Methods Annex. For the purposes of this chapter, this definition includes work and health safety institutions that are outlined here but are also considered further in Chapter 4.

Engagement of enforcement bodies and areas of litigation

We look first at the number of cases brought by enforcement bodies and how much of the overall MWRD these cases represent.

Enforcement bodies bring a minority of cases. Of the 907 cases in the MWRD, only 94, or 10.3%, are brought by enforcement bodies on behalf of migrants. The remainder are brought either by migrants themselves and their counsel or by trade unions (see Chapter 7). The vast bulk (78%) of these cases are in Australia, where cases are more likely to involve a large number of migrants, reflecting the FWO's use of class actions. Table 8.3 shows that the range of cases involving enforcement bodies in Australia is between 1 and 181 migrants per case, compared with a range of 1 to 19 migrants for cases that do not. This is consistent with an earlier finding by Hardy, Howe, and Cooney (2013) that the FWO's work is increasingly focused on strategic litigation and group actions and that cases have become more complex across time. Of the 1,913 migrants in the database, 673, or close to 33%, are included in cases brought by Australian enforcement bodies. Outside of Australia, enforcement bodies are involved only sparingly in litigation, comprising only 4%

Table 8.3 Number of migrants per case, enforcement actions vs. other actions

Jurisdiction	Median, Enforcement Actions (N Migrants)	Range, Enforcement Actions (Lowest N Migrants: Highest N Migrants)	Median, Enforcement Actions (N Migrants	Range, Other Actions (Lowest N Migrants: Highest N Migrants)
Australia	2	1:181	1	1:19
Alberta	1	1:1	1	1:12
British Columbia	1	1:1	1	1:73
Ontario	1.5	1:3	1	1:3
United Kingdom	1	1:9	1	1:4
USA	1	1:8	1	1:4
Average	2	1:181	1	1:73

of the cases combined. Further, unlike in Australia, the ranges for the other jurisdictions demonstrate that class actions are less common, although the range for British Columbia was 1 through 73, demonstrating at least one large class action in that jurisdiction, although it was brought by a union, not an enforcement body (*Re Sidhu & Sons Nursery Ltd.* (2010) B.C.L.R.B.D. No. 64).

It is also useful to consider the types of violations that are pursued by enforcement bodies. As is consistent with the overall economic focus of the data presented in the MWRD (see Chapter 1), the vast bulk of claims where enforcement bodies are involved is in the area of unpaid wages (71%) (see Table 8.4). However, other claims, including visa fraud, misrepresentation, and not being informed of pension rights, are also commonly brought by enforcement bodies. Table 8.4 shows that Australian enforcement bodies have a stronger focus on claims related to unpaid wages than the other jurisdictions, and as noted above, most claims by enforcement bodies across the database are brought by Australian institutions.

Importance of enforcement bodies

It is also necessary to consider whether the involvement of enforcement bodies in litigation makes a difference to the success of cases. Figure 8.1

Table 8.4 Distribution of alleged violations in enforcement actions, by jurisdiction

Violation	Total	Australia	Alberta	British Columbia	Ontario	United Kingdom	USA
Unpaid wages	508 (71%)	494 (73%)	0	2 (40%)	0	0	12 (100%)
Visa fraud	99 (14%)	99 (15%)	0	0	0	0	0
Subjected to misrepresentation	98 (14%)	97 (14%)	0	1 (20%)	0	0	0
Not informed of pension rights by employer	47 (7%)	47 (7%)	0	0	0	0	0
Incorrectly defined as a contractor through the contractual agreement	22 (3%)	21 (3%)	0	1 (20%)	0	0	0
Sexual servitude	21 (3%)	20 (3%)	0	0	1 (14%)	0	0
Trafficked by employer	15 (2%)	2 (0.3%)	1 (33%)	2 (40%)	0	10 (83%)	0
Forced labor	8 (1%)	8 (1%)	0	0	0	0	0
Subjected to unsafe work conditions leading to injury, not death	6 (1%)	2 (0.3%)	1 33%	0	1 (14%)	1 (8%)	1 (8%)
Required to work inhuman hours	5 (1%)	4 (1%)	0	0	0	0	1 (8%)
Dismissed	3 (0.4%)	1 (0.1%)	2 (67%)	0	0	0	0
Harassment by employer	3 (0.4%)	0	0	0	3 (43%)	0	0
Industrial manslaughter	3 (0.4%)	2 (0.3%)	0	0	1 (14%)	0	0
Discriminated against on the basis of trade union activity and freedom of association	1 (0.1%)	0	0	1 (20%)	0	0	0
Denied caregiver's leave	1 (0.1%)	1 (0.1%)	0	0	0	0	0
Subjected to assault or battery	1 (0.1%)	0	0	0	0	1 (8%)	0
Total	712	673 (95%)	3 (0.4%)	5 (1%)	7 (1%)	12 (2%)	12 (2%)

Note: Percentages may total more than 100% due to actions bringing multiple claims of violations.

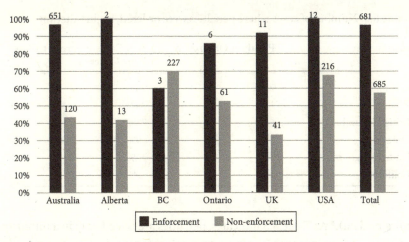

Figure 8.1 Comparison of success rates* in enforcement- and non-enforcement-led actions

*Proportion of violation actions with a partial or total success combined. Numbers at top of bars indicate N migrants as the unit of analysis.

shows that cases involving enforcement bodies are far more likely to be successful than those where a third party litigates or where a migrant litigates the case on their own behalf. Success is defined here as an outcome where the enforcement body gains a win or a partial win by the migrant.[7]

Figure 8.1 also shows that cases involving enforcement bodies have a higher success rate than those that do not, with success rates ranging from 60% in British Columbia to 100% in Alberta. That said, excluding Australia, the total number of cases (of the migrants represented) litigated by enforcement bodies is very low. This indicates that in all jurisdictions, enforcement bodies take on generally winnable cases, but in most jurisdictions they do not play a very large role in litigation, focusing on the alternative enforcement approaches discussed throughout this chapter.

Penalties

Even if cases are brought by enforcement bodies and are successful, this does not mean that penalties will necessarily be issued against employers to reduce noncompliance by those or other employers in the future. Table 8.5 lists the percentages of cases where penalties are issued (after removing any

Table 8.5 Number of cases where penalties were ordered, by jurisdiction

Jurisdiction	Penalties Ordered, N	% of Cases Where Penalties Were Ordered
Australia	7	20%
Alberta	1	25%
British Columbia	6	23%
Ontario	2	9%
United Kingdom	5	7%
California	1	3%

missing data).[8] As Table 8.5 indicates, penalties are issued only in a minority of cases. This means that in cases where migrants are successful, a penalty may be paid to the migrant, but no further penalty that could have a deterrence effect upon future actions by employers is issued. No jurisdiction has penalties issued more than 20% of the time, and in California penalties were issued in under 3% of cases.

Summary

The success of government enforcement bodies in court cases, including those in the MWRD, has been raised as an important component of enforcement behavior (Vosko 2013, 871). The case of *Bento Kings Meadows* is in some ways emblematic of many enforcement cases that are brought on behalf of migrant workers. It involved vulnerable workers with high rates of underpayment and a large number of affected workers, enabling the FWO to bring a persuasive group action. Generally, however, excluding Australia, enforcement bodies are not strong litigators, although when they do litigate they are invariably successful. Other mechanisms for enforcement, such as self-help, complaints-driven processes, and workplace inspections, are more common in other jurisdictions.

There are several policy recommendations that flow from the findings in this chapter. First, it is clear from the Australian example that bodies like the FWO can play an important role in the litigation of underpayment cases. The FWO has a high success rate and can use its institutional power to bring class actions on behalf of migrant workers. Other jurisdictions may benefit from looking to the example of the FWO. Second, the United States has attained

Image 1: Online wage campaign from Ontario
Source: http://www.boldinternet.com/index_en.php?page=cw_mol

positive outcomes through the use of supply-chain reform, including hot goods that might be transferrable to the other jurisdictions. Third, as has often been recommended in the scholarship (e.g., Weil 2019, 2020), more generous funding of labor inspectors consistent with ILO norms is required to enable governments to engage in proactive inspection regimes that are generally viewed as better for vulnerable workers, like migrants. (For more detailed recommendations, see Chaudhuri, Boucher, and Sydney Policy Lab 2021.) Fourth, in Australia, an increase in civil penalties and adverse publicity orders against offenders has been proposed as a solution, and this could be explored in other jurisdictions as well (Chaudhuri, Boucher, and Sydney Policy Lab 2021, 25; Fels Commission 2019, 9).

There may be a trade-off between government-led enforcement and self-regulation through advocacy coalitions, trade unions, and migrant worker centers. One reading of the role of enforcement is that, when it is government-funded, enforcement can reduce self-help by workers and their collective representation through trade unions, moving away from a collective model of enforcement toward an individual and state-led model. Creighton and Stewart (2010, 502) argue that the establishment of the FWO in Australia "played to the Howard Government's (Conservative government's) union marginalization agenda by eclipsing what is often cited as one of the principal attractions of union membership—the capacity of unions to monitor and enforce compliance with award and other statutory entitlements." The authors also suggest that trade unions' legal standing rights are too narrow under current enforcement settings, which could affect their capacity to bring actions on behalf of workers (citing the Australian Fair Work Act (2009), s505). Alternately, in Ontario, the low level of funding for enforcement stems from a time when trade unions played a larger role, and funding for government-led enforcement has, under one view, not adequately compensated for declining trade union density (Vosko and Closing the Enforcement Gap Research Group 2020, 10).

A third reading is that strong trade unions and strong enforcement can act in concert with one another to protect workers. For instance, those sectors with strong unions may also experience greater compliance and enforcement (Weil and Pyles 2007, 179). In California, for instance, the success of labor laws has been linked in part to a strong role played by worker collectives and community-based organizations engaging in outreach with workers, as discussed in Chapter 7 (Lee and Smith 2019, 815). In Ontario, Vosko (2013) has argued that collective enforcement, via trade unions, worker advocates, and other third parties, is more powerful than individual-level complaints and that this is key to improving enforcement, especially for the most vulnerable workers: migrants, women, and young people. In short, as outlined in Chapter 7, on trade unions, pluralistic forms of representation have a strong potential to support migrant worker rights when they are involved in legal challenges; however, this is rare across the jurisdictions.

The six jurisdictions differ considerably in how enforcement is pursued by governments in the small number of cases they litigate. In the conclusion of this book, we consider the social and economic legacies in place in each jurisdiction that shape the variation evident throughout this book. What explains the patterns of exploitation that have been presented through the data?

Conclusion

Understanding the Patterns of Migrant Worker Exploitation

Workplace exploitation is not a unidimensional concept; it can occur in a wide variety of ways. The MWRD identifies thirty-nine main types of exploitative workplace behavior, although even this is by no means exhaustive. As suggested in Chapter 1, the types of behavior identified in this book can be collapsed into a five-type classification schema comprised of criminal infringements, economic violations related to wages, safety violations caused by unsafe workplace environments, leave and other workplace entitlements, and the various forms of discrimination-based violations. Chapter 1 sketched these main violation types and their level of concurrence and demonstrated how legal claim-making by migrant workers in this area varies across violation type and jurisdiction. Chapters 2 through 8 provided detailed evidence of the seven intrinsic, structural, and social factors that might explain these breaches: gender, ethnicity, nationality, the sector in which they are employed, their visa status and visa type, enforcement policies, and the role of trade unions or worker centers.

Distilling the relative influence of these seven explanatory factors through simple observation is difficult, given the richness of the data, the number of observations (N = 1,912 migrants), and how each factor may have different weighting across each jurisdiction. For this reason, in this conclusion we drop any missing data from the MWRD, combine the Canadian provinces (due to small sample size), and conduct a series of binary logistic regression analyses to assess what explains the variation in levels of claims brought both within and across the violation types.[1] In short, what drives the patterns of exploitation evident within the database? For instance, why are migrants more likely to bring economic violations claims over criminal infringements, and why does this differ across the database? It should be noted that another way of considering the data would be to analyze varying success rates for migrant workers across the database. However, success rates are driven by litigation strategy, the quality of legal representation, and the extent of legal aid funding, which are not factors considered in detail in this book (rather, see Boucher and Chaudhuri 2022). Alternatively, we could look at the overall number of migrants bringing cases when compared with the population in each jurisdiction. Again, however, this outcome could be driven by a variety of factors not considered in depth in this book, such as the compensatory framework—the remedies and damages available under the law and those precluded—or the percentage of the population that is undocumented and therefore has reduced recourse to the legal system in the first place.[2] Given these complicating factors, we instead focus on the core explanatory variables considered in Chapters 2 through 8 and their influence on the key dependent variable of interest: the violation type.

There are two main ways to assess variation in violation type across the MWRD. First, we can look at the magnitude of the effect of each variable through the odds ratio. Andy Field (2009, 270) defines an odds ratio as "the change in odds resulting from a unit change in the predictor." This gives a measure of the likelihood that the variable in question explains the placement compared to the reference category. (Each reference category is delineated with a cross symbol, and in the case of "country," the reference category is Australia.) Second, we can use the p-value to assess the likelihood that this odds ratio will be generated. The lower the p-value, the higher the likelihood that this odds ratio is statistically significant and reliable (Agresti et al. 2018; Field 2009, Chapter 8). The odds ratios thereby give us an indication of how likely it is that a migrant claimant will be in one category compared to another category, controlling for other variables. Having an odds ratio less than 1, conversely, indicates a negative relationship between the coefficient and being in that violation category. This negative relationship can also be statistically significant.

When we examine Table C.1, it is clear that the highest odds ratios and the lowest p-value are generally for the country-level variables. For instance, it is clear that the likelihood of bringing criminal claims is higher in all jurisdictions other than Australia and statistically significant at the 99% confidence level, except for the United Kingdom, where it is at 90%. For economic violations, migrants are more likely to bring claims in Australia than in Canada, but not in California, which has higher rates of economic claims; this is, again, statistically significant ($p < 0.01$). Economic claims are more likely in Australia than in the United Kingdom, and this is significant at the 90% confidence level. The particularly high rate of economic claims

Table C.1 Binary regression analysis of variables' effect on likelihood of bringing a claim of that violation type

Violation Type	Criminal OR	p	Economic OR	p	Safety OR	p	Denial of Leave and Other Workplace Entitlements OR	p	Discrimination OR	p
Jurisdiction										
Australia	+	+	+	+	+	+	+	+	+	+
United Kingdom	4.12	0.017	0.54	0.092	1.00	+	1.00	+	29.82	0.000
California	20.96	0.000	7.04	0.000	0.25	0.008	8.44	0.192	3.71	0.009
Canada	9.81	0.000	0.22	0.000	1.84	0.170	0.36	0.579	7.40	0.000
Sector										
Major group 1	+	+	+	+	+	+	1.00	+	+	+
Major group 2	0.18	0.185	0.35	0.215	1.30	0.846	1.00	+	0.80	0.765
Major group 3	4.27	0.130	0.14	0.020	6.71	0.122	0.01	0.007	0.65	0.576
Major group 4	6.01	0.233	0.16	0.100	8.28	0.158	1.00	+	0.67	0.759
Major group 5	2.99	0.213	0.33	0.168	2.80	0.386	0.00	0.000	0.19	0.025
Major group 6	21.51	0.029	0.09	0.014	10.32	0.094	1.00	+	0.61	0.720
Major group 7	0.28	0.267	0.04	0.000	33.26	0.003	1.00	+	0.03	0.001
Major group 8	1.00	+	0.04	0.000	36.08	0.003	1.00	+	0.60	0.518
Major group 9	1.36	0.737	0.11	0.007	40.67	0.002	1.00	+	0.23	0.045
Major group 10	1.00	+	1.00	+	1.00	+	1.00	+	1.00	+
Gender										
Male	+	+	+	+	+	+	+	+	+	+
Female	8.21	0.000	0.50	0.003	1.08	0.850	11.30	0.061	1.23	0.506

(*continued*)

Table C.1 Continued

Violation Type	Criminal OR	p	Economic OR	p	Safety OR	p	Denial of Leave and Other Workplace Entitlements OR	p	Discrimination OR	p
Visa										
Family	-	-	-	-	+	+	1.00	+	-	-
Humanitarian	1.00	+	0.14	0.140	25.00	0.076	1.00	+	0.20	0.309
Other	0.07	0.099	0.13	0.093	2.51	0.536	0.23	0.222	0.59	0.716
Student	0.01	0.018	0.81	0.872	2.63	0.558	1.00	+	0.19	0.296
Temporary work	0.02	0.012	0.75	0.809	0.38	0.517	1.00	+	0.34	0.444
Work	0.56	0.717	0.24	0.236	1.62	0.761	1.00	+	0.36	0.508
Undocumented	0.05	0.097	0.18	0.191	3.15	0.466	1.00	+	1.80	0.700
Trade unions										
Trade union representative	1.00	+	0.21	0.000	0.01	0.000	1.00	+	42.55	0.000
Enforcement										
Enforcement body representative	6.26	0.000	0.83	0.49	0.05	0.000	10.22	0.004	0.04	0.007
Country of origin										
Majority English-speaking	1.38	0.699	1.67	0.214	2.87	0.045	1.00	+	0.35	0.082
Constant	0.06	0.126	78.67	0.003	0.02	0.026	0.20	0.040	0.21	0.320
Observations (N)	898		1,133		1,076		432		1,133	

Note: + = sample size too small to generate meaningful results.

in California relative to other violation types relates to the greater funding opportunities for wage-based class actions compared to other claims, as private firms can take a percentage of economic-based penalties. That said, the low number of cases in California can generally be attributed to a decline in public funding for such litigation and the inability of migrants to pay for private actions (Albiston and Nielsen 2014).

With regard to safety violations and denial of leave and other workplace entitlements, the data are too few to generate meaningful inferential statistics, while discrimination-based claims are more likely in all of the other jurisdictions than in Australia. They are far more likely in the United Kingdom (OR = 29.82), and again, all of these findings are statistically significant. This degree of magnitude is followed by trade union representation, which also has a high odds ratio and a low p-value across each of the violation types, except for criminal and leave, where p = 1 because the data are so few for this violation type that they do not generate robust findings. Further, for some but not all of the violation types, having an enforcement body engaged in the litigation is also important; this is true of criminal claims, safety-based claims, denial of leave and other workplace violations and discrimination, but not for economic claims. Trade union representation is also statistically significant as an explanation for differences in claims, but only for economic, safety, and discrimination claims. In the other areas of claim-making, the sample size is too small for trade union involvement to generate statistically significant findings with small error scores. Economic sector (measured as occupational ISCO code) is statistically significant for some violation classifications and for some ISCO codes, but not for all, rejecting the argument that occupation classification primarily drives workplace rights violations (e.g., Bechter, Brandl, and Meardi 2012). Further, collapsing ISCO into high and low skill (a binary variable, rather than a nominal variable) did not increase the statistical significance of sector. Finally, odds ratios less than 1 indicate a negative relationship, and some of these are statistically significant, such as the negative relationship between enforcement bodies as litigators and those bringing discrimination-based claims.

While not consistently significant across all violation types, certain variables are significant for certain violation types; for instance, there is a positive relationship between being female and experiencing a criminal violation, while males are more likely to experience economic violations. Those who come from an English-language-majority country are more likely to bring safety-based claims than those from a non-English-language-majority country.

Putting aside these exceptions, the country in which a migrant is located, enforcement-body engagement, and trade union representation are the most important factors driving the claims that are brought, when other explanations are controlled for. Factors that might be viewed as important in the scholarship, such as the migrant's visa type, their country of origin, or their sector of employment (see generally Boucher 2018), do not in most cases yield statistically significant p-values for understanding the variation across each violation type. The gender of the migrant does come out as a key variable with statistical significance for economic and criminal-based violations, but not otherwise. In short, country-level systems and their institutional features, rather than individual migrant attributes, appear to underlie the patterns we observe.

An industrial theory of differences in migrant worker exploitation rates

Why might country-level variables, alongside enforcement bodies in most instances, matter across the violation types in understanding the patterns of exploitation within the MWRD? Under this nomenclature of "country-level variables" we can include the countries' industrial systems and the role played by enforcement bodies—or their absence—in claim-making. In this final section of the book, we make the argument that the industrial relations system in each jurisdiction explains the variation present. To this, we add the nuance that in the minority of cases where trade unions and enforcement bodies are involved, these bodies partially explain this variation. These factors are interwoven insofar as the industrial system of each of these jurisdictions governs and structures both trade union and enforcement body behavior.

Industrial relations and labor law system

"National systems" means the labor law systems of each of the four countries. It explains more strongly differences across the MWRD. There are different scholarly views on the extent of variation across industrial relations system within the "most similar" countries of Australia, Canada, the United States, and the United Kingdom. These countries are commonly located within the liberal market economy (LME) cluster of the varieties of capitalism framework (Hall and Soskice 2001), characterized by market-based relations in the area of labor regulation and a progressive move toward flexible and competitive labor systems. Some scholars who analyze the evolution of the LME cluster argue that these systems are experiencing a "liberal convergence" toward a single model, with the United States as an outlier, as it exhibits far greater degrees of employer power within workplace negotiations than in the other most-similar jurisdictions (Baccaro and Howell 2011; Colvin and Darbishire 2013). Key features of this coherent and ever-converging model, according to Colvin and Darbishire, are a move toward "private ordering" of employment relations, where conditions are mainly determined at the enterprise level, growing employer discretion, and minimal standard-setting through statute or negotiation. Driven by global market forces, the decentralization of workplace bargaining agreements, more opt-outs from such agreements, and a decline in union density are also key features of this model (Baccaro and Howell 2017, Chapter 3).

However, others have argued that even within this LME cluster of most-similar countries, there is persistent variation driven by "institutional resilience" (e.g., Wright, Wailes, et al. 2017; Bamber et al. 2016; Doellgast et al. 2021). Such resilience is a product of the historically embedded institutions of employment and industrial relations systems, such as arbitration and wage bargaining systems, as well as the actors located within these systems, such as unions and business groups and their differing roles across different countries. Further, even if there have been neoliberal tendencies in the regulation of work globally, advocates of institutional resilience argue that the rate of change—decline of these institutions—differs across countries (Doellgast et al. 2021). The advantage of a most-similar design, such as that presented in this book, is that shared explanatory factors can be controlled for and the remaining variation examined in greater detail. The argument that these most-similar countries are still exhibiting internal variation among themselves is supported by the binary logistic regression analysis that demonstrates differences in the distribution of violations in the MWRD across overwise similar LMEs. If we unpack the concept of "national systems" still further, we can explore variation along factors such as (1) the extent that rights-based or antidiscrimination cultures are embedded within labor laws, (2) whether labor law has created basic minima and for whom, (3) where labor standards are created (centralized, enterprise, or even individual negotiation), and finally, and rarely acknowledged in the scholarship, (4) the percentage of the working population that is foreign-born (as recent migrant arrival data are unavailable).

Levels of rights cultures built into employment law

The jurisdictions differ in how rights-based or antidiscrimination cultures are embedded into their labor law systems and whether there is a focus on the individual or group. They vary in their attention to and the breadth of their antidiscrimination laws. In the United Kingdom, there have been historical limits on antidiscrimination law (see Robinson et al. 2017), but this has changed with the adoption of the Human Rights Act (1998) and the Equality Act (2010), as well as EU influences through the EU Social Protocol of the Maastricht Treaty (Adams et al. 2021). As such it is not surprising that compared to the other jurisdictions, the United Kingdom has far higher odds ratios of migrants bringing antidiscrimination-based claims. Likewise, antidiscrimination claims may appear more viable in the United Kingdom than wage-based claims, where there was previously a fee for first-instance Employment Tribunal cases. This could have stymied underpayment actions over the Database's time period (*R (Unison) v. Lord Chancellor* (2017) UKSC 51 overturned the application of such fees). Blackham and Allen (2019) in their recent comparison of discrimination claims in Australia and the United Kingdom argue that the discrimination settings are stronger in the United Kingdom. This is because equal opportunity agencies in the United Kingdom possess enforcement as well as intervention powers, which is not the case in Australia, where there are only intervention powers. Similarly, there are stronger antiracism movements and rights cultures in California and Canada—where human rights codes have played an important role— than in Australia. This could inform the greater focus on antidiscrimination claims in those jurisdictions than in Australia, although the odds ratios for California and Canada are still lower than for the United Kingdom. All of these findings are statistically significant at the $p < 0.01$ level.

Do labor standards create basic minima and for whom?

Colvin and Darbishire (2013) argue that a minimal bundle of labor entitlements is a shared feature of Anglo-American labor systems. The employment law system provides a basic safety net for workplace conditions, below which wages and other standards ought not fall, and higher standards are based on individual negotiation. However, especially when considering the rights of migrants, it is important to assess how these minima—somewhat paradoxically—create carve-outs for some workers in certain sectors. As trade union density declined, there was more reliance on employment standards, rather than enterprise- or sector-level bargaining, to create minima in these jurisdictions; this in turn created a low floor for those not covered by enterprise agreements or those subject to carve-outs. And it is here that the jurisdictions vary: not all industrial relations systems considered in this book create clear and protective minima without any carve-outs for migrant workers or for workers in certain sectors in which migrants are overrepresented. As we saw in Chapters 4 and 7, there is a tendency toward carve-outs for migrant workers within Wagnerian industrial relations systems, such as the United States and some provinces in Canada. This is linked to the U.S. National Labor Relations Act of 1935, known as the "Wagner Act," that, while creating key worker protections, such as majority union support and the right to strike (Carter et al. 2002), was marked by sectorial carve-outs for migrant workers and, historically, African Americans (Tucker, Fudge, and Vosko 2002). Such Wagnerian influences are not present in Australia or the United Kingdom. In Australia, as noted in Chapter 1, the Fair Work Act (2009) creates a series of minimum National Employment Standards for all workers, including migrants. In the United Kingdom, the same is true of minimum wages under the Employment Rights Act (1996) and the National Minimum Wage Act (1998), although in Chapter 2 we did explore a major exception to those rules for live-in caregivers who are considered to be "a member of the family."

The degree of bargaining centralization of the industrial relations system can benefit labor law claim-making

A key point of differences across these most-similar systems relates to where the setting of wages occurs. Does it operate through a centralized award system, or is wage setting decentralized? This concept of wage setting location captures "the degree of bargaining centralization, which is often measured by recording the main level of bargaining" (Baccaro and Howell 2017, 34). This is a relevant consideration for this book given that the majority of claims in the MWRD are economic, predominantly related to underpayment (see Chapter 1). In contrast to the other jurisdictions, Australia relies on a sector-based bargaining system (known as centralized compulsory arbitration) for many sectors of its economy. Consistent with this, measures of bargaining centralization allocate higher scores to Australia than the other three countries considered (Baccaro and Howell 2017, 35, citing Visser 2013, 11).[3] As Wright and Lansbury (2016, 103) note, while Australia's centralized system has been eroded somewhat in recent years, "[t]he continued existence of a system of occupational and industrial awards allows for some coordination in the determination of wages and conditions and a stronger safety net for workers than other LMEs." Further, awards continue to provide an important regulatory baseline, especially in low-skilled sectors, such as those featured in this book (Bray and Macneil 2011, cited in Wright and Lansbury 2016, 114).

Historically, the United Kingdom could be characterized as having a "voluntarist" model (Waddington 2016, 29).[4] Further, recent reforms to the employment law system in the United Kingdom are in keeping with this tradition (Baccaro and Howell 2017, 51). Collective bargains cover only 23% of the labor market, and while national minimum wages have been set since 1999, the array of minimum entitlements is less than in comparable countries and covers only a small (but growing) percentage of employees at the bottom end of the labor market (Waddington 2016, 36, 39; see also Tuck, Criddle, and Brittenden 2013). In the United States, sector-based collective bargaining (or "pattern bargaining," as it is referred to there) is largely confined to the federal public sector, although some states also provide these rights to their government employees (Katz and Colvin 2016, 56). Outside of the public service, there are enterprise- and workplace-level bargaining agreements; however, their coverage rates vary across sectors, and for many employees pay is set by market forces (60). The highly decentralized nature of Canada's labor systems means there is considerable internal variation. Across Alberta, British Columbia, and Ontario there is variation in union density, with Alberta having the lowest union membership of all three provinces (Taras and Walsworth 2016, 80). Canada is also decentralized in the sense that bargaining, outside of the federal jurisdiction, generally occurs at the workplace or enterprise level, although there is some regional patterning (87).

The potential effects of centralized bargaining on violation outcomes in Table C.1 will be most relevant to the economic violation area, which covers the various forms of underpayment. Under this violation type, all national systems (and trade unions) provide consistently low p-statistics when compared to Australia, as the reference category. This is not surprising given that, of the four countries considered in this book, only Australia has a history of arbitration (Castles 1988) and still relies on a system of compulsory sector-based regulation of minimum standards encompassing wages and various employment conditions (e.g., McCallum 2007).

Australia is also unique across the four countries and six labor law jurisdictions in the role played by its key federal enforcement agency, the Fair Work Ombudsman, in litigating migrant worker cases. As noted in Chapter 8, of the 1,913 migrants in the MWRD, 673, or close to one-third, are included in cases brought by Australian enforcement bodies—predominantly the FWO. Across the database, no single enforcement agency in the other jurisdictions plays such an important role in enforcing pay standards as the FWO does in Australia. Further, compared to the other jurisdictions in this book, Australia actually has a more centralized system for wage-setting. For instance, the Fair Work Commission is central to determining awards and acting as an umpire, whereas such roles are split across an array of institutions in other jurisdictions.

Naturally, basic minima in all four countries can be undermined, and even deliberately violated, by a series of factors, including fissured workplaces, gig or subcontracting arrangements, intermediaries, and the shadow economy (Wright et al. 2019, 318). However, there is no consistent study of the extent to which these factors vary across the systems under examination, meaning it is difficult to assess how these factors ultimately change or alter what Judy Fudge (2017) calls the "web of rules." Further, other areas of labor and employment law also vary across the jurisdictions and could be part of this institutional variation (e.g., dismissal laws; see Colvin 2006, 79), although, as noted in Chapter 6, all four countries are clustered in the less protective range of the OECD (2019) spectrum for this area of labor law.

The percentage of the workforce that is foreign-born

There are also differences across the countries in the percentage of foreign-born workers within the population. This is a measure of the diversity of the labor market in each of the jurisdictions. We rely on domestic data from each country that consider the percentage of the population as stock who were born overseas and present in the labor market, reported over available years of analysis. Recent migrant flow data as a percentage of the workforce are not available.

Up until 2018, the United Kingdom had the lowest percentage of foreign-born people in the working population of any of the four countries, reflecting its historical status as a colonizer rather than an immigrant-receiving country (Boucher and Gest 2018). The USA had lower levels in 2021, but Table C.2 provide an average across the USA and underrepresent the high migrant stock in California. (State-based data across all countries were not available.) Canada has seen a steady rise between 2004 and 2022 in the percentage of its working population that is foreign-born. As a percentage of the working population, Australia is the clear outlier, with a far higher percentage of foreign-born individuals than the other jurisdictions. That said, in recent years, flows into Australia have been low

Table C.2 Foreign-born workers as a proportion of the total employed population (%)

Year	Australia*	Canada*	United Kingdom	USA
2005	-	-	10.1	14.8
2006	-	21.5	11.1	15.4
2007	26.4	21.7	12.0	15.7
2008	-	21.6	12.8	15.6
2009	-	21.7	13.0	15.4
2010	27.2	22.0	13.3	15.8
2011	-	22.5	13.3	15.9
2012	-	23.0	14.4	16.1
2013	29.6	23.6	14.8	16.4
2014	-	23.9	15.4	16.6
2015	-	24.5	16.1	16.8
2016	30.9	25.6	17.1	17.0
2017	-	26.0	17.5	17.1
2018	-	26.9	17.3	17.5
2019	32.7	27.9	17.6	17.5
2020	-	27.8	18.2	16.8
2021	-	29.4	18.4	17.3

Note: *Data unavailable for all years.

Sources: Australian Bureau of Statistics 2008, 2011, 2014, 2017, 2020; Bureau of Labor Statistics 2022; Office of National Statistics 2022, United Kingdom; Statistics Canada 2022a.

due to COVID-19 (Australian Treasury 2021). However, these effects are not yet reflected in migrant stock, which remains high at 32.7% of the overall working population.

Reflecting on these figures from national statistics agencies, it is possible that this high level of foreign-born people within working populations has affected how visa status is conceived and treated in the workplace and, more broadly, within employment laws. The larger the working population that is foreign-born, the more it is possible that the experiences of that population will shape the norms and rules governing the system, which could explain the greater sensitivity to these issues in Australia, especially by the FWO. Note, however, that the figures for the USA do not factor in undocumented migrants, which would add an estimated 11 million. The interaction between foreign-born population size and the sensitivity of labor law to diversity is an issue that needs to be explored further in future research and would be a fruitful line of theoretical and empirical inquiry.

In short, the national systems analyzed in this book demonstrate substantial variation across institutional features. This finding challenges arguments around an Anglo-American convergence toward a neoliberal model (e.g., Baccaro and Howell 2017), at least when migrant workers' legal claims are the empirical focus of analysis. Even within most-similar systems there is considerable difference, as demonstrated by the variation featured in this book. The presentation of empirical evidence from a large data set of 151,048 observations (1,912 migrants and 79 variables coded for each migrant) supports this argument of institutional variation. This finding is a significant empirical contribution to industrial relations theory insofar as it demonstrates continued institutional resilience within otherwise mostsimilar systems where broader neoliberal forces are at play (see also Wright, Groutsis, and van den Broek 2017; McLaughlin and Wright 2018).

Moving forward and key contributions of this book

This book has investigated the concept of workplace violations experienced by migrant workers through the unique lens of court cases litigated by these workers. In doing so, it makes a series of contributions. Historically, migration studies has presented a protective role for the courts in buttressing migrants against executive and legislative discretion (e.g., Hollifield 1992, 2004; Tichenor 2002). And while this book has demonstrated that courts can play a protective role, this is not uniform. First, in many of the court cases examined in this book, judges and tribunal members are not taking an activist position, pursuing the rights of migrant workers; they are instead dispassionately applying existing laws. Their findings may or may not be sympathetic to migrant workers. Further, there are some cases, such as *Hoffman Plastics* (Chapter 5), where the U.S. Supreme Court majority took a position antithetical to the rights of migrant workers, despite congressional evidence to the contrary furnished in the case by counsel for the NLRB. There are others, such as in the British case of *Taiwo* (Chapter 3), where the courts have wanted to protect migrant workers; in that U.K. case, on race-based discrimination claims, visa status was also a basis for unfavorable treatment of the claimant, but the court found that this would require statutory reform to equality legislation. Further, from a blunt empirical perspective, migrant workers do not win all of their cases—their overall success rates vary from 92% of all successful wage claims in Australia down to 53% in England (see Chapter 1). In short, courts and tribunals sometimes find for migrant workers, but migrants may also lose their cases and appeals. The findings presented here ascribe a more nuanced and less heroic role to legal systems' protection of migrant workers than other accounts; they situate it more soberly alongside other institutions for reform, including enforcement bodies, wage setting institutions, and the broader legislative arena, where labor law can be changed.

Further, while we might normatively want to see the courts as precedent setters shaping future public policy, legal precedent does not always benefit migrants. Precedent is determined by judges combining interpretation of case law and statute, and this may advantage either the defendant or the plaintiff depending on the case and laws at hand. Further still, not all cases lead to significant precedent-setting effects. Of the seven cases considered in detail in this book, only one has had an enduring effect on public policy through precedent: *Hoffman Plastics*. Even there, as Chapter 5 discusses, various legislative carve-outs have been achieved at the state level in California to protect against its more serious impacts (see also Griffith 2017), emphasizing the importance of sanctuary laws and preemption. Other cases where precedent might have shaped and delimited public policy norms in positive ways for migrant workers, such as *Hounga v. Allen* in the United Kingdom, through its clarification of the principle of illegality of contract, have been subsequently narrowed by more recent decisions in the migrant worker area, as discussed in Chapter 3. Broader precedent-setting effects cannot be ascertained from all judgments and tribunal decisions. The majority of cases simply apply the facts to existing case law or statute. Deep societal change may be more likely to be generated through public inquiries, such as the Fels Migrant Worker Taskforce in Australia, that lead to subsequent legislative reform and actions by governments. In short, a vision of the courts as bulwarks for migrant workers and engaging in consistent significant and positive reform is not always substantiated by the available evidence, in contrast to some earlier accounts of supreme and apex courts.

When we examined the reasons why migrant workers bring claims in some areas rather than others, many of the traditional arguments posited were not applicable. For instance, country of origin can be a predictor of discrimination claims and the occupational clustering of some violation claims (safety-based claims in the lower-skilled occupations), but not of claims across the board (c.f. Campbell, Boese, and Tham 2016, 293; see also Li 2017; Migrant Worker Taskforce 2019, 39; Underhill et al. 2019; WEstJustice 2016, 77; McGregor 2007). Undocumented migration status is important in the small number of cases where those without status bring cases, but this number is so small that in the binary regression analysis that undocumented migration status is not statistically significant. Further, coethnic exploitation, which is often identified as a central source of exploitation (e.g., Campbell, Boese, and Tham 2016, 293; Li 2017; Migrant Worker Taskforce 2019, 39), does not emerge as crucial. The bulk of human employers in the MWRD are not coethnic with the migrant employees they exploit, rather of differing national backgrounds (see Chapter 3). It appears that systems, rather than the attributes of individual migrants, most strongly shape the types of violations they litigate; even in broad neoliberal contexts, states still regulate industrial systems.

It is worth concluding with some consideration about the likely effects of COVID-19 on the rights of migrant workers, although the analysis of the database formally ends in 2016, prior to the pandemic. The decline in jobs precipitated by COVID-19 has increased unemployment and may simultaneously increase competition between domestic and global labor. The potential for workplace exploitation is even greater during a recession, when the capacity of migrants to seek work is reduced due to a general downturn across the labor market. In such moments, employers may feel emboldened to lower standards (e.g., Boucher et al. 2021; 2). At the same time, there could be emerging skills gaps that are poorly met by domestic workforces, creating concurrent competition and employer demand for further migration.

Coupled with this, the effect that Britain's 2020 exit from the EU will have on workers' rights, and on migrant workers in particular, is yet to be fully realized, but early indications are that it could be deleterious (O'Connor 2020; Yong 2019; Polak 2019). Border closures in 2020 and 2021 exacerbated discriminatory behavior toward migrants (Hooijer and King 2022). In short, global and domestic factors are presenting new risks for migrant workers that are likely to increase as we progress through these unsettling and volatile times. In this context, the resilience of protective institutions such as human rights courts, wage-setting bodies, as well as the funding of enforcement bodies on the ongoing role of trade unions, may well be crucial in shaping and influencing the extent of violations experienced by migrant workers and their capacity for legal redress.

Interview Schedule

Names or workplace identities have been anonymized when requested by the respondent.

United Kingdom

1. Bushra Ahmed, barrister, KBH Kaanuun Chambers, Dubai, 23 January 2019, via FaceTime.
2. Barrister, Chambers, London, 25 January 2019.
3. Kathryn Cronin, barrister, Garden Court Chambers, London, 28 January 2019.
4. Michelle Brewer, barrister, Garden Court Chambers, London, 30 January 2019.
5. Professor David Metcalf, labor enforcement director, London, 4 February 2019.
6. Tim Harrison, head of Secretariat at Office of the Director of Labour Market Enforcement, London, 4 February, 2019.
7. Harvey Redgrave, former home affairs advisor to Ed Miliband, London, 6 February 2019.
8. Laura Prince, barrister, Matrix Chambers, London, 11 February 2019.
9. James Ewins, QC, barrister, Queen Elizabeth Building, London, 13 February 2019.
10. Karon Monaghan, QC, barrister, Matrix Chambers, London, 13 February 2019.
11. Richard Owen Thomas, barrister, 3 Papers Building, Temple, London, 15 February 2019.
12. Shu Shin Luh, barrister, Garden Court Chambers, London, 18 February 2019.
13. Chris Stone, barrister, Devereux Chambers, London, 18 February 2019.
14. Julian Milford, QC, barrister, 11 KBW Chambers, London, 18 February 2019.
15. Michael Reed, Free Representation Unit, London, 19 February 2019.
16. Rosa Crawford, policy officer, Migration and Global Trade, Trades Union Congress, London, 20 February 2019.
17. Sandhya Drew, consultant barrister, 13 March 2019, via Skype.

Canada

1. Gerry LeBlanc, deputy leader, Health, Safety and Environment, United Steelworkers, Toronto, 20 March 2019.
2. Sylvia Boyce, health and safety staff representative, United Steelworkers, District 6 health and safety coordinator, Toronto, 26 March 2019.
3. Policy officer, Ministry of Children, Community and Social Services, in the Citizenship and Immigration Division, Toronto, 27 March 2019.
4. Senior policy officer, Ministry of Labour Ontario, Toronto, 27 March 2019.
5. Senior policy officer, Ministry of Labour Ontario, Toronto, 27 March 2019.
6. Senior policy officer, Ministry of Labour Ontario, Toronto, 27 March 2019.
7. Senior policy officer, Ministry of Labour Ontario, Toronto, 27 March 2019.

8. Policy officer, Ministry of Labour, 27 March 2019.
9. Policy officer, Ministry of Labour Ontario, 27 March 2019.
10. Senior policy officer, Ministry of Labour Ontario, Toronto, 27 March 2019.
11. Lawyer, Community Legal Centre, 2 April 2019.
12. Verne Edwards, occupational health, safety and environment director, Ontario Federation of Labour, Toronto, 2 April 2019.
13. Felix Martinez, national representative, United Food and Commercial Workers, Western Provinces, 18 June 2019, via Zoom.
14. Brett Matthews, lawyer, previously from Hastings Law Firm, Vancouver, 6 August 2019, via Zoom.
15. Toronto Police Service officer, Toronto Police Force, 17 October 2019, via Zoom from Los Angeles.
16. Toronto Police Service officer, Toronto Police Force, 17 October 2019, via Zoom from Los Angeles.

Australia

1. Former international student advisor, Monash University, Melbourne, Deakin University City Office, Melbourne, 16 July 2019.
2. Matt Kunkel, chief executive officer, Migrant Worker Centre, Melbourne, 17 July 2019.
3. Tarni Perkal, lawyer/employment program director, West Justice, Melbourne, 18 July 2019.
4. Gabrielle Marchetti, principal lawyer, Job Watch, Melbourne, 18 July 2019.
5. Danielle Hartridge, International Education Association, Melbourne, 19 July 2019.
6. Sharmilla Bargon, head of employment law, Redfern Legal Centre, Sydney, 15 August 2019.
7. David Cousins, cohead of Fels Migrant Worker Taskforce, Sydney, 21 August 2019.
8. Allan Fels, cohead of Fels Migrant Worker Taskforce, 20 September 2019, via Zoom between Melbourne and Sydney.
9. Tim Nelthorpe, organizer, National Union of Workers, 8 October 2019, via Zoom.
10. Former government employee, 29 November 2019, via Skype.

United States

1. Policy advisor, Berkeley, California, 31 October 2019.
2. Christopher Ho, director, National Origin and Immigrants' Rights Program, Legal Aid at Work, San Francisco, 1 November 2019.
3. Professor Benjamin Sachs, Harvard University Law School, amicus intervener for Making the Road by Walking, 4 November 2019, via Zoom from Los Angeles.
4. Lawyer, AFL-CIO, Washington, D.C., 20 November 2019.
5. Shannon Lederer, immigration policy director, AFL-CIO, Washington, D.C., 20 November 2019.
6. Former government lawyer, Washington, D.C., 20 November 2019.
7. Ana Avendaño, Minga Strategies, formerly counsel at AFL-CIO, Washington, D.C., 22 November 2019.

8. Michael Wishnie, professor, Yale Law School, 6 December 2019, via Zoom from Australia.
9. Lawyer, labor and employment law, National Immigration Law Center, Washington, D.C., 9 January 2020, via Zoom from Sydney.
10. Lucas Guttentag, former ACLU representative on *Hoffman* case, professor at NYU University, 5 February 2020, via Zoom from Sydney.

Notes

Introduction

1. Measured through the ILO's International Standard Classification of Occupations.
2. Using the PartyGov variable that ranks government executives on a scale from 1 for conservative and right-wing through to 5 for left-wing (Armingeon, Engler, and Leemann 2021).
3. The median for the OECD/EU is 2, whereas for these countries, it is 1.
4. There are several reasons why California laws can be seen as more protective of workers than in other U.S. states. First, California under its Fair Employment and Housing Act contains provisions that extend beyond Title VII of the Civil Rights Act (1964) protections. Second, California has a higher minimum wage than the federal minimum and higher than most other states. There is also a higher rate paid for overtime in California for working over forty hours per week than in other states (Mesriani 2021).
5. Considered in detail in Chapter 5: *Hoffman Plastics Compounds Inc v. NLRB* (00-1595) 535, U.S. 137 (2002) 237 F3.d. 639, reversed.

Chapter 1

1. Issues we explore further in Chapter 3 on gender and Chapter 4 on ethnicity.
2. Workplace Relations Amendment (Work Choices) Act (2005) (in effect 2006–2009) introduced a large series of changes that could be viewed as pro-employer, including the right for employers to negotiate individual rather than collective workplace agreements. These changes had a deleterious effect on all workers, including migrants. For an overview of this legislation and its effects, see Cooper and Ellem 2008.
3. As employment and industrial relations are not federal powers under the Canadian Constitution Act, by implication they are provincial powers.
4. Krippendorff's Alpha > 0.67 was achieved for all indicators considered in this chapter. Further details of intercoder reliability are available in the online Methods Annex at annaboucher.org.
5. As such, it does not cover resolved, settled, or unpublished decisions. See Codebook and Methods Annex for further details (annaboucher.org).
6. Under Dymski's (1992, 299) argument, the two threats of racial domination to exploitation are structural (a greater risk of underpayment compared with workers not of that racial group and a greater risk of unemployment following dismissal for

racialized minorities) but also ascriptive or perceptual (assumptions made by the employer about the nature of the worker based on their racial grouping).
7. Where relevant, we consider the role of government immigration policy in increasing the risk of migrants falling into undocumented status and therefore increasing their precariousness; see Chapters 5 and 6.
8. We refer to classification rather than a typology because a typology involves multidimensional variation within each class, whereas a classification system does not. As the central point of variation in this classification is across rather than within each class, a classification is the best descriptor (Bailey 1994, 4).
9. This is different from forced labor: it encompasses instances where the person's forced labor relates specifically to sexual servitude, sexual slavery, or compulsory sexual labor that is unrecompensed, in contrast to consensual and recompensed sex work.
10. The exact legal definitions of these crimes across the different jurisdictions are included in the online Codebook.
11. This is mainly the offense of failing to keep employee payment slips, which is largely an issue in Australia.
12. Generally, in criminal cases, the plaintiff must discharge the beyond reasonable doubt innocence presumption enjoyed by the accused, whereas in civil cases, the applicant must demonstrate only that their case is substantiated on the balance of probabilities.
13. The relevant courts and tribunals here being the NSW Workers Compensation Commission (Australia), the Ontario Workers Compensation Appeals Tribunal, and the Ontario Workplace Safety and Insurance Appeal Tribunal.
14. We explore this issue further in Chapter 7 on trade unions, through the case of *Floralia Plant Growers Ltd. v. UFCW. Local 1518* (2015), one of the largest class actions in the British Columbian data.

Chapter 2

1. At first instance, Ms. Udin's former employer's son, Mr. Kaylani, was also a respondent in the proceedings, as he had paid her wages offshore through an employment company known as Diala Establishment. Although claims were sent to his addresses in Damascus, Beirut, and London, he did not present a response. Eventually it was determined that he was not a party to the contract and he was debarred (*Udin v. Chamsi Pasha*, paras 20, 205; *Jose v. Julio* (UKEAT 0553_10_0812), 8 December 2011).
2. Note that the tribunal member was critical of the conferral of this status: "It is a striking fact that the UKBA's findings, which were based on a host of detailed allegations of 'exploitation in domestic servitude' (bundle p332) were made without the benefit of any information of comment from those who were said to have been subjected [by] Mr Salim Udin to quite appalling treatment for over four years, namely Mr and Mrs Chamsi-Pasha" (*Udin v. Chamsi-Pasha*, para 8).

3. Arguments for constructive dismissal and race discrimination (both direct and indirect) were rejected in the Employment Tribunal, *Udin v. Chamsi-Pasha*, per Justice Snelson at paras 43 and 46. Ms. Udin's argument for working hours was upheld at the Tribunal stage, at para 224.
4. From this chapter forward in this book, the focus is on data showing successful findings of violations supported by an independent decision-maker rather than also including unsuccessful allegations that are not supported by a judicial decision. In the event of a series of appeals, the final decision is taken as the one considered in the data analysis. As the *Udin v. Chamsi-Pasha* case reveals, the facts of these cases are at times deeply contested, making such a measure of a violation more objective than a migrant's claim alone.
5. While amended since the *Udin v. Chamsi-Pasha* case, the regulations are substantively the same as when the case was brought.
6. On this point, the judges differed in their perspective. Counsel for the claimant migrants argued that the shared tasks should include consideration of the work for which the worker was employed (*Julio v. Jose*, para 44).
7. There were mixed findings with regard to issues of race discrimination and holiday pay for Ms. Jose and Ms. Nambalat, respectively. These are not central to this chapter, so are not considered here (*Jose v. Julio*, at paras 71–75).
8. "Domestic" work is excluded from protections under the Industrial Relations Act (1979) (WA) s 7(1), Fair Work Act (1994) (SA) s 6, and Fair Work (General) Regulations (2009) (SA) reg 5: see Berg 2015.
9. In families where women do not work but engage in unpaid labor, they "do not receive a wage [but] they receive a share of the family's total product which may or may not be commensurate with the number of hours worked" (Folbre 1982, 326). Such overproduction by women homemakers could be viewed as a classic form of exploitation. Sexual violence towards women and children within families can also be seen as a form of sexual exploitation.
10. Interestingly, Mantouvalou (2015) notes that there were attempts to amend the Modern Slavery Act to provide further protection to domestic workers, but in the end this was not achieved.
11. The relationship between short-term domestic visas, undocumented immigration status, and exploitation risk is considered further in the regulation and undocumented chapters.
12. A-3 visas are for attendees and servants of employees of overseas ministers, diplomats, consular officials, and their family members present in the United States, while the G-5 provides a similar visa for workers employed by NATO officials or other intergovernmental agencies in the United States.
13. It was replaced by a Caring for Children and a Caring for People with High Medical Needs pathway for temporary caregivers; however, applications for these pathways closed in June 2019. Migrant care workers can now be assessed under the general low-skilled Temporary Foreign Worker Program (CIC 2019).
14. See the Methods Annex for further details on this imputation method for both gender and country of origin (annaboucher.org).

15. Note that the migrant population figure includes visas where migrants are less likely to work, such as family reunification or asylum-based visas. Gender disaggregated data at the visa level are not routinely available across all countries over time.
16. Considered in detail in Chapter 3, on ethnicity.
17. For Canada, we include only the three provinces that the database considers: Ontario, British Columbia, and Alberta.

Chapter 3

1. Her claim for aggravated damages was rejected on the basis that she could not receive aggravated damages for unlawful employment (*Hounga v. Allen* (2009), at para 22).
2. An analogy was made to sections in the Modern Slavery Act 2015 (UK), Part 5, that protect victims of trafficking who have commissioned a criminal act in the process of being trafficked: "Although Ms Hounga is not in that category, the decision of the Court of Appeal to uphold Mrs Allen's defence of illegality to her complaint runs strikingly counter to the prominent strain of current public policy against trafficking and in favour of the protection of its victims" (*Hounga v. Allen* (2014) UKSC 47, para 52).
3. Subsequent judgments suggest that the principles laid down in *Hounga v. Allen* were unclear on the issue of illegality of contract (*Patel v. Mirza* (2016) UKSC 42).
4. This was the case of *Chandhok v. Tirkey* ((2014) UKEAT 0190_14_1912), which turned upon whether caste should be considered a protected category under the Equality Act (2010) (UK). It was decided that it could be considered as a protected class.
5. It was challenged whether Ms. Hounga was actually Nigerian or potentially originally from Benin.
6. For more details, see the Methods Annex (annaboucher.org).
7. We were unable to acquire immigration data, disaggregated by country of origin, for the different regions of the United Kingdom. Nonetheless, best estimates suggest that England receives between 85% and 90% of immigrant flows into the United Kingdom.
8. The Methods Annex covers how migrants from the Philippines are coded separately from other Spanish-surnamed migrants.
9. We remind the reader that as multiple migrants often bring actions within a single case (class actions) and as there are multiple claims for different violations within many cases, the number of legal claims exceeds the number of litigated cases in the MWRD.
10. This figure combines both the Mexican and Spanish-surnamed rows.
11. For further details, see the Methods Annex.

Chapter 4

1. Applying ss22.1(b), 217.1, and 2019 of the Criminal Code. In particular, s219 on criminal negligence was relied upon.

2. There were different views on why a criminal case was not pursued against Joel Swartz, the owner of Metron Construction Company. According to one assessment from a member of the Toronto Police Service, Swartz engaged in successful plea bargaining for himself but not for Kazenelson (Toronto Police, Interview 1, 17 October 2019).
3. The difference between economic sector and occupational classification and the reason for use of occupational classifications to analyze the MWRD is discussed below under "Quantitative Findings."
4. Amici curiae brief of the Employers and Employer Organizations in Support of the Respondent in the Hoffman Plastics Case, U.S. Supreme Court, 2001, p. 10.
5. A recent decision in Australia by the Fair Work Commission has made it far harder for employers to apply piecework awards in the agriculture sector due to the inherent risks: Horticulture Award 2020 (1 January 2022 version).
6. In Australia, most states have harmonized work, health, and safety laws (except for Victoria and Western Australia), supported by the Model Work Health and Safety Regulation and the National Compliance and Enforcement Policy. The relevant legislation is listed in Table 4.1.
7. There are some exceptions to this, such as skilled farm workers, who are listed as ISCO Level 6 (ILO 2012, 11–12) rather than generally at ISCO Level 9 (classified as low skill). Using the ISCO classification of occupations as the coding frame ensured that occupations were mapped against the correct code and thereby also approximate skill level. The use of ISCO as a meaningful measure of both occupation and skill as is explained in further detail in the Methods Annex. The Annex also covers missing data imputation methods for ISCO level.
8. The total immigration intake is estimated over the ten-year period from 2006 through to 2016 as the following figures for the jurisdictions: 90,190,083 (Australia); 152,131,500 (Ontario, Alberta, and British Columbia); 348,362,219 (England); and 508,442,245 (California). Note that these figures are very high as they include tourists and also estimates for undocumented migration, as these entrants sometimes work without valid permits. We cannot calculate for the entire twenty-year period as standardized immigration data are not available before 2006.
9. IAVGO 2010, 3–4.
10. Although this was overturned on appeal (*Salas v. Sierra Chem. Co.*, 59 Cal. 4th 407 (2014)).

Chapter 5

1. According to Fisk and Wishnie (2005, 360–361), there is evidence that the employer knew about Perez's undocumented status when they employed him, as there were different identities on the two pieces of official ID he gave the employers as part of the migrant authorization process. This meant that, if true, Hoffman Plastics had constructive knowledge that they were hiring an undocumented worker and had actually breached the IRCA.

2. We use the terms "undocumented" and "unauthorized" interchangeably throughout this chapter. The word "illegal" is sometimes viewed pejoratively, so it is avoided unless referring to government policy that utilizes this phrase.
3. There was a restriction before IRCA, in the preceding Immigration and Naturalization Act (1965), on "harbouring illegal aliens," but this was not a provision that was used and there was no regulation of the hiring of immigrant workers and authorization requirements within the workplace before IRCA (Ana Avendaño, formally of the AFL-CIO, Interview, Washington D.C., 22 November 2019; Ho and Chang 2005, 478–479).
4. Amici curiae brief of American Civil Liberties Union Foundation and Make the Road by Walking. Inc., U.S. Supreme Court, 2002.
5. Amici curiae brief of the Employers and Employer Organizations in Support of the Respondent in the *Hoffman Plastics* Case, U.S. Supreme Court, 2001, 7, 8, 10.
6. This phenomenon is explored further in Chapter 7, as undocumented status pertains to trade union organizing among migrants and the limitations posed by lapsed or absent visas.
7. Explored more fully in Chapter 8, on enforcement.
8. The relevant principle is "that repeals by implication are disfavoured" (*Morton v. Mancari*, 417 US. 535, 550 (1974)).
9. For a detailed analysis, see Berg 2015, 172–174.
10. Alternatively, the Fair Work Act (2009) could be reformed to clarify that migrants who have breached their visas still have valid employment contracts, as recommended by Tham (2015).
11. The cases discussed above involved construction of Section 235 and its predecessors under earlier versions of the Migration Act (1958).
12. Through INS Operating Instruction 287.3(a), now known as ICE Special Agents Field Manual, 331.4(h).
13. Smith, Avendaño, and Martinez Ortega (2009, 16) provide the example of *Woodfin Suite Hotels, LLC v. City of Emeryville* (US District Court, Oakland Division, 2008, No. C 07-1719 SBA, Related Case No. C 06-1254 SBA (N.D. Cal. Mar. 13, 2008)), in which the court determined that the use of retaliatory action by Woodfin in response to calls by undocumented employees to adopt safe workload levels was unlawful and the reinstatement of the affected employees was required.
14. The extent to which state powers in this area are constitutionally permitted, or not, has been the subject of a series of high-profile challenges, as outlined in Griffith (2017, 1283).
15. The Methods Annex provides more information on the data sources used to estimate undocumented and legal populations and the assumptions made in this regard.

Chapter 6

1. Any currencies discussed in this chapter are given in the relevant denomination for the focus of that section, here Australian dollars.

2. Migration Amendment Regulations 2009 (No. 5) and Amendment Regulations 2009 (No. 2) (Cth) 2.72(10)(cc); see also Boucher 2016, 134; Tham and Campbell 2011.
3. The extent of the contributory negligence of Ms. Choong was questioned in the penalties hearing.
4. Previously known as the Minimum Salary Level.
5. It was expanded to ninety days in 2013 and has since been reduced to sixty days under the new Temporary Skills Shortage visa category
6. Unless Regulation 2.72(10AA) applied under the prior administration of this rule, under Regulation 2.72(10)(cc) of the Immigration Regulations, the base rate of pay under the terms and conditions of employment mentioned in Regulation 2.72(10)(c), that is, the "market salary rate," must be greater than the TSMIT specified by an additional legislation instrument, usually in the form of a ministerial instrument. However, note that with the creation of the Temporary Skills Shortage visa, the TSMIT is now included in a separate regulatory provision.
7. Read with *Policy Advice Manual* for these WHM visas: Subclass 417 and 462.
8. Note that in mid-2021, the Australian government announced it would be implementing an agriculture-specific temporary shortage visa. This has not yet been implemented at the time of publication. See Australian Department of Foreign Affairs and Trade 2022.
9. ACTU submission to the Senate Education and Employment Committee inquiry into the incidence of and trends in corporate avoidance of the Fair Work Act (2009), 2017, cited in Fels 2019, 84.
10. An assurance protocol between the FWO and Department of Home Affairs (DHA) guarantees that a person's visa will not be cancelled if DHA is concerned that they are exploited at work and that exploitation has been reported to the FWO; however, there are concerns about the way that this assurance operates, and its efficacy (Fels 2019, 49–50; discussed further in Chapter 8).
11. There is also a separate category known as the International Mobility Program; however, this sits outside of the TFWP and did not feature within the MWRD, so it is not a focus in this chapter.
12. On the other hand, Faraday (2016, 49) makes the point that when caps are suddenly introduced into key areas, this can have the effect that a large number of onshore migrants need to compete for a dwindling number of positions, which can lead to a faster erosion of workplace rights.
13. Fudge (2016b, 159) characterized these controversies as comprising "illegal recruitment fees, unpaid wages, and unpaid and excessive overtime," alongside the "live-in requirement, which was . . . seen as making migrant caregivers especially vulnerable to exploitation."
14. One exception to this statement is the Fair Entitlements Guarantee that protects former employees in the event of a company's insolvency or liquidation. This protection does not extend to nonnationals (Fels 2019, 95).
15. Under Immigration Act (2016) (UK), ss34, 38, read with Schedule 6. Under s35 it is also an offense for an employer either deliberately or knowingly to hire an illegal worker.

248   NOTES

16. The general array of visas or visa statuses that are considered under each category are outlined in the Methods Annex at annaboucher.org.
17. How immigration flow data were collected for this purpose is outlined further in the online Methods Annex.

Chapter 7

1. *Floralia Plant Growers Ltd. and UFCW, Local 1518* (2015) CarswellBC 3852; (2015) B.C.C.A.A.A. No. 13; *Certain Employees of Floralia Plant Growers Ltd. and UFCW, Local 1518* (2016) CarswellBC 652. *Re SJ Suleman Investments Ltd. and UFCW, Local 401* ((2014) CarswellAlta 987; (2014) Alta. L.R.B.R. 38) was also brought by UFCW, although it involved different respondents. The closest the UFCW came to a successful claim of inappropriate interference was in BCLRB No. B34/2016, where it found Floralia had unlawfully interfered in the administration of a union when it prevented a group of newly arrived workers from talking to union representatives before a critical decertification vote.
2. The Ontario Labour Relations Act (1995) does provide some opportunities for such representation, but they are limited.
3. Note, however, that because many agricultural workers in Ontario come through the SAWP, they are subject to the minimum wage standards included in the agreements between Canada and their home countries (Vosko, Tucker, and Casey 2019, 238–239). These often exceed the minimum wages of equivalent domestic workers in their province of employment. In Ontario, domestic general farm workers are excluded from the province's minimum wage protections, while harvesters' salaries may be compensated at the "piece work rate that is customarily and generally recognized in the area as having been set so that an employee exercising reasonable effort would, if paid such a rate, earn at least the minimum wage" (*When Work Deemed to Be Performed, Exemptions and Special Rules*, O. Reg. 285/01, s. 25(2); see also Vosko, Tucker, and Casey 2019; Ministry of Labor, Interview 3, 27 March 2019).
4. A similar challenge in British Columbia also failed: see *Domestic Workers' Union v. A.G. B.C.* (1984) 1 D.L.R. (4th) 560 (B.C.S.C.). A legal challenge to exclusions of agricultural workers from the same legislation under s2(d) of the Charter was also not successful, and their rights to collective bargaining were denied other than a narrow exception subsequently evinced under the Agricultural Employees Protection Act: *Dunmore v. Ontario*, (2001) 3 S.C.R. 1016; its constitutionality affirmed in *Attorney-General v. Fraser* (2011) 2 SCR 3 (see also Vosko 2019a, n29).
5. Citing Comprehensive Immigration Reform: Labor Movement Perspectives: Hearing before Subcommittee on Immigration, Citizenship, Refugees, Border Security and International Law of the House Committee on the Judiciary, 110th Congress (23–24, 2007), testimony of Jonathan P. Hiatt, General Counsel, AFL-CIO, at 14–15.
6. See Codebook for further details (annaboucher.org).
7. Details of the data for these figures are included in the Methods Annex (annaboucher.org).
8. For further details, see Boucher and Chaudhuri (2022).

9. For this violation type, cases include *Re Sidhu & Sons Nursery Ltd.* (2010), *Viva Pharmaceutical Inc. v. C.E.P. Local 2000* (2002) 81 C.L.R.B.R. (2d) 1, and *C.S.W.U., Local 1611 v. SELI Canada Inc.* (2009) CarswellBC 1858.

Chapter 8

1. Currencies in this chapter are given in the amount relevant to each country, rather than standardized against a single currency.
2. We consider this issue provincially, as labor law is a provincial, not a federal, matter in Canada and this chapter deals, centrally, with labor regulation.
3. Which include air transportation, postal services, broadcasting, and railways.
4. Although concerns have been raised that this Memorandum of Understanding, which limits sharing rights across institutions, is not watertight.
5. This range is set under the Fair Work Act, ss539(2), 546(2).
6. In July 2020, the value of a penalty unit increased from $210 to $222.
7. As such, more ambiguous outcomes, such as a case being remitted to an original decision maker on procedural or jurisdictional grounds, are not considered a win or "successful outcome" for the purposes of this analysis. See the Methods Annex.
8. Excluding cases where penalties were ordered for violations where intercoder reliability achieved a Krippendorff's alpha under 0.667. Violations variables included here are racial discrimination, disability discrimination, denial of the right to privacy through surveillance by employer, denial of maternity leave, denial of holiday leave, denial of freedom of expression, denial of caregiver's leave, breach of contract, and visa fraud. See the Methods Annex for further details on the Krippendorff's alpha calculations.

Conclusion

1. We attempted to use Qualitative Comparative Analysis (QCA) to undertake this analysis; however, a large number of variables overlapped with one another, which is not ideal for QCA analysis, and it did not yield meaningful results.
2. A study on unfair dismissal laws by Alexander Colvin (2006, 80), for instance, found that higher median damages available in Pennsylvania when compared with Ontario drove the greater rates of litigation around unfair dismissal laws in the former jurisdiction, despite the greater generosity for legal grounds in Ontario.
3. More recent Visser data are dispersed across years and missing for Australia for some years.
4. According to Waddington (2016, 29), key features of this model are nonlegally binding collective agreements; voluntary union recognition by employers; a relatively low level of formalization of employment relations structures; and a light, voluntary framework of state-provided supplementary dispute resolution facilities, with no governmental powers to order the suspension of industrial action or impose cooling-off periods.

References

Cases Cited

AFMEPKIU v. Tweed Valley Fruit Processors Pty. Ltd. (1995) 61 IR 212 (Australia)
Ajayi v. Abu & Abu (2017) EWHC 3098 QC (Australia)
Allen v. Hounga, UKEAT 0326/10 (2011) (UK)
Arrowcrest Group Pty. Ltd. re Metal Industry Award 1984 (1994) 36 AILR 402) (Australia)
Attorney-General v. Fraser (2011) 2 SCR 3 (Canada)
Attorney Generals' Reference (Nos. 37, 38 and 65 of 2010) (Shahnawaz Ali and Others) (2010) EWCA Crim 2880 (UK)
Australia Meat Holdings Pty. Ltd. v. Kazi (2004) (2 Qd 458) (Australia)
Certain Employees of Floralia Plant Growers Ltd. and UFCW, Local 1518 (2016) CarswellBC 652 (Canada)
Chandhok v. Tirkey (2014) UKEAT 0190_14_1912 (UK)
Contreras v. Corinthian Vigor Ins. Brokerage, Inc., 25F. Supp. @d 1053, 137 Lab. Cas. P 33795, 4 Wage & Hour Cas. 2d (BNA) 1793, 1998 WL 791597 (N.D. Cal. 1998)
Corbire v. Canada (1999) 2 SCR 203 (Canada)
C.S.W.U., Local 1611 v. SELI Canada Inc. (2009) CarswellBC 1858 (Canada)
Domestic Workers' Union v. A.G. B.C. (1984) 1 D.L.R. (4th) 560 (B.C.S.C.) (Canada)
Dunmore v. Ontario (2001) 3 S.C.R. 1016 (Canada)
Fair Work Ombudsman v. Bento Kings Meadows Pty. Ltd. (2013) FCCA 977 (Australia)
Fair Work Ombudsman v. IE Enterprises & Anor. (2019) FCCA 2952 (Australia)*Fair Work Ombudsman v. Jooine (Investment) Pty. Ltd. & Anor.* (2013) FCCA 2144 (Australia)
FWO v. Roselands Fruit Market Pty. Ltd. (2012) FMCA 599 (Australia)
Floralia Plant Growers Ltd. v. UFCW, Local 1518 (2008) CarswellBC 2691(Canada)
Floralia Plant Growers Ltd. and UFCW, Local 1518 (2015) CarswellBC 3852 (Canada)
Floralia Plant Growers Ltd. v. UFCW, Local 1518 (2015) (Canada)
Floralia Plant Growers Limited & S&G Fresh Produce Limited v. UFCW, Local 1518, B17/2017 (Canada)
Floralia Plant Growers Ltd. (2017) CarswellBC 187 (Canada)
Go Yo Trading Pty. Limited and Anor. (2012) FMCA 865 (Australia)
Griggs v. Duke Power Co. 401 US 424 (1964/1971) (US)
Hindu Society of Australia Inc. v. FWO (2016) FCCA 221 (Australia)
Hines v. Davidowitz, 312 US. 52 67 (1941) (US)
Hoffman Plastic Compounds, Inc. v. 306 NLRB 100 (1992) (US)
Hoffman Plastic Compounds, Inc. v. NLRB, 208 F.3d 229 (D.C. Circ. 2000) (US)
Hoffman Plastics Compounds Inc. v. NLRB (00-1595) 535. U.S. 137 (2002) 237 F.3.d. 639, reversed (US)
Hounga v. Allen & Ors., ET, 2201467/2009 (UK)
Hounga v. Allen (2012) EWCA Civ 609 (UK)
Hounga v. Allen (2014) UKSC 47 (UK)

252 REFERENCES

Jose v. Julio (UKEAT 0553_10_0812), 8 December 2011 (UK)
Law v. Canada [Minister of Employment and Immigration] (1999), 1 SCR (Canada)
Marupov v. Metron Construction (2014) ONSC 3525 (Canada)
Mason v. Harrington Corporation Pty. Ltd. (2007) FMCA 7 (Australia)
Masri v. Sabtoso (2004) NSWIRComm 108 (Australia)
Mezonos Maven Bakery, Board Case No. 29-CA-025476 (reported at 357 NLRB No. 47) (2d Cir. decided under the name *Palma v. NLRB Mezonos Maven Bakery* (2013) (US)
Mezonos Maven Bakery, Inc., 357 NLRB 376, 376 (2011) (US)
Midya v. Sagrani (1999) NSWCA 187 (Australia)
Minister for Immigration and Border Protection v. Choong Enterprises Pty. Ltd. (No. 2) (2015) FCA 553; 234 FCR 501 (Australia)
Morton v. Mancari, 417 US. 535, 550 (1954) (US)
Nambalat v. Taher and Anor. (2012) EWCA Civ 124 (UK)
Nambalat v. Taher and Anor.: Udin v. Pasha & Ors. (2012) EWCA Civ 1249 (UK)
Nonferral (NSW) Pty. Ltd. v. Taufia (1998) 43 NSWLR 312, 316 (Cole JA) (Australia)
Okedina v. Chikale (2019) EWCA Civ 1393 (UK)
Patel v. Mirza (2016) UKSC 42 (UK)
Re SJ Suleman Investments Ltd. and UFCW, Local 401 (2014) CarswellAlta 987; (2014) Alta. L.R.B.R. 38 (Canada)
R v. K(S) (2011) ECWA Crim 1691(UK)
R v. Kazenelson (2015) ONSC 3639 (Canada)
R v. Kazenelson (2018) ONCA 77 (Canada)
R v. Metron Construction Company (2012) (Canada)
R v. Metron Construction Corp. (2012) 1 CCEL (4th) (Canada)
R v. Metron Construction (2013) (Canada)
R (Unison) v. Lord Chancellor (2017) UKSC 51 (UK)
Ram v. D&D Indian Fine Food Pty. Ltd. & Anor. (2015) FCCA 389 (Australia)
Rivera v. Nibco Inc., 384 F.3d 822 (9th Cir. 2004) (US)
Salas v. Sierra Chem Co., 129 Cal. Rptr. 3d 263 (2011) (US)
Salas v. Sierra Chemical Company 59 Cal. 4th 407 (2014) (US)
Sidhu & Sons Nursery Ltd. (2010) B.C.L.R.B.D. No. 64 (Canada)
Sidhu & Sons Nursery Ltd. v. UFCW Local 1518 (November 2010) (Canada).
Siliadin v. France (2005) 43 EHRR 16 (EU) (European Union)
Smallwood v. Ergo Asia Pty. Ltd. (2014) (Australia)
Sure-Tan, Inc. v. NLRB, 467 (1984) (US)
Taiwo v. Olaigbe and another: Onu v. Akiwiwu and another (2016) UKSC 31 all ER (D) 134 (UK)
Tuv Taam Corp., 340 NLRB No. 86 at 4 & n. 4 (2003) WL 22295361 (US)
Tyson Foods Inc. v. Guzman, 116 S.W. 3d 233 (2003) (US)
Tilern de Bique v. Ministry of Defence (2009) UKEAT/0075/11/SM (UK)
Udin v. Chamsi-Pasha, Employment Tribunal 2203182/2009 (UK)
U.S. v. Agri Processor Co. v. NLRB (2008 U.S. App. LEXIS 101 (D.C. Cir. 2008) (Supp. 32) (US)
US v. California 314F. Suppl. 3d 1077, 1104; *US v. California* (No. 18-16496), 9th Circuit (2019) (US)
Viva Pharmaceutical Inc. v. C.E.P. Local 2000 (2002) 81 C.L.R.B.R. (2d) 1 (Canada)
Wei Xin Chen v. Allied Packaging Co. Pty. Ltd. (1997) 73 IR 53 (Australia)

Woodfin Suite Hotels, LLC v. City of Emeryville (US District Court, Oakland Division, 2008, No. C 07-1719 SBA, Related Case No. C 06-1254 SBA (N.D. Cal. 13 March 2008) (US)
Zarkasi v. Anindita & Anor. (2012) 0400_11_1801 (UK)

Statute

Agricultural Labor Relations Act (1975) (California, US)
Canadian Charter of Rights and Freedoms (1982) (Canada)
Civil Rights Act (1964) (US)
Canada Constitution Act (1986 to 1982) (Canada)
Crimes Act (1914) (Cwth) (Australia)
Domestic Workers Bill of Rights (2013) (California)
Employment Protections for Foreign Nationals Act (2009) (Ontario)
Employment Rights Act (1996) (UK)
Employment Standards Act (1996) (British Columbia)
Employment Standards Act (2000) (Ontario) (Canada)
Employment Standards Code (2000) (Alberta) (Canada)
Employment Standards Directive (EU)
Equality Act (2000) (UK)
Equality Act (2010) (UK)
EU Directive 97/81 Framework Agreement on Part-Time Work (EU)
Factories and Workshop Act (1878) (UK)
Factory Act (1833) (UK)
Factory Act (1847) (UK)
Fair Labor Standards Act (1938) (US)
Fair Work Act (1994) (SA)
Fair Work Act (2009) (Cwth) (Australia)
Federal Labor Standards Act (1938) (US)
Floralia Collective Agreement (British Columbia)
Health and Safety Act (1974) (UK)
Human Rights Act (1998) (UK)
Immigration Act (2016) (UK)
Immigration and Naturalization Act (1965) (US)
Immigration Reform and Control Act (1986) (US)
Immigration Rules (UK)
Industrial Relations Act (1979) (Western Australia) (Australia)
Making Ontario Open for Business Act, 2018, S.O. 2018 (Ontario) (Canada)
Migrant Amendment (Protecting Migrant Workers) Draft Exposure Bill (2021) (Australia)
Migration Act (1958) (Cwth) (Australia, Cwth)
Migration Regulations (1994) (Australia, Cwth)
Modern Slavery Act (2015) (UK)
Modern Slavery Act (2018) (Cwth) (Australia)
National Labor Relations Act (1935) (US)
National Minimum Wage Act (1998) (UK)
National Minimum Wage Regulation (1999) (UK)

National Minimum Wage Regulation (2015) (UK) Occupational Health and Safety Act (1990) (Ontario)
Occupational Safety and Health Act (1970) (US)
Offence Act (1996) (British Columbia) (Canada)
Ontario Labour Relations Act (1995) (Ontario) (Canada)
Protecting Vulnerable Workers Act (2017) (Cth) (Australia)
Provincial Offences Act (1990) (Canada)
Race Discrimination Act (1965) (UK)
Race Relations Act (1968) (UK)
Sex Discrimination Act (1975) (UK)
Trafficking Victims Protection Reauthorization Act (US)
Workplace Relations Amendment (Work Choices) Act (2005) to Work Health and Safety Act (2011) (Australia)
Labour Code (California)
Penal Code of California (California)
Employment Standards Code (2000) (Alberta)

Regulations

Alberta Employment Standards, "ESOs" 15 July 2020
Exemptions, Special Rules and Establishment of Minimum Wage Regulation (UK)
Exemptions, Special Rules and Establishment of Minimum Wage Regulations (2019) Ontario
Fair Work (General) Regulations (2009) (SA)
Home Office Guidelines (2017) (UK)
Horticulture Award (2020) PR736911, Fair Work Commission (Australia)
Immigration and Refugee Protection Regulations (2002) (Federal, Canada)
National Minimum Wage Regulation (1999), Regulation 2(2) (UK)
When Work Deemed to Be Performed, Exemptions and Special Rules, O. Reg. 285/01 (Ontario, Canada)
Working Time Regulations (1998) (UK)

International Law

Palermo Protocol to Prevent, Supress and Punish Trafficking in Persons, Especially Women and Children (2000) United Nations

Other References

Abel, Laura. 2009. "Language Access in State Courts." New York Brennan Center for Justice at New York University School of Law.
Abel, Laura, and Michael Mulé. 2010. "Letter to U.S. Department of Justice Civil Rights Division, on Behalf of the National Language Access Advocates Network." https://www.brennancenter.org/sites/default/files/legacy/Justice/LangAccess/DOJ%20Letter%20with%20factsheets.pdf.

REFERENCES

Abella, Manolo. 2006. *Policies and Best Practices for Management of Temporary Migration.* Turin: International Symposium on International Migration and Development, UN Population Division.

Adams, Zoe, Simon Deakin, Catherine Barnard, and Butlin Fraser. 2021. *Deakin and Morris' Labour Law.* 7th ed. Oxford: Hart.

Abu-Laban, Yasmeen. 2020. "Immigration and Settler-Colonies post-UNDRIP: Research and Policy Implications." *International Migration* 58: 12–28.

Afonso, A., S. Negash, and E. Wolff. 2020. "Closure, Equality or Organisation: Trade Union Responses to EU Labour Migration." *Journal of European Social Policy* 30 (5): 528–542.

Agresti, Alan. 2018. *Statistical Methods for the Social Sciences.* 5th ed. Pearson Education USA.

Alberta Federation of Labour. 2017. *The Canadian Mainstream and Beyond: Reforming Alberta's Employment Standard Code.* Alberta Federation of Labour.

Alberti, Gabriella, Jane Holgate, and Maite Tapia. 2013. "Organising Migrants as Workers or as Migrant Workers? Intersectionality, Trade Unions and Precarious Work." *International Journal of Human Resource Management* 24 (22): 4132–4148.

Albin, E., and V. Mantouvalou. 2015. "Active Industrial Citizenship of Domestic Workers: Lessons Learned from Unionising Attempts in Israel and the UK." *Theoretical Inquiries in Law* 16, 321-350.

Albiston, Catherine R., and Laura Beth Nielsen. 2014. "Funding the Cause: How Public Interest Law Organizations Fund Their Activities and Why It Matters for Social Change." *Law & Social Inquiry* 39: 62–95.

Alfred [S. Kydd]. 1857. *The History of the Factory Movement from the Year 1802 to the Enactment of the Ten Hours' Bill in 1847.* London: Simpkin, Marshall.

Allain, Jean. 2012. *Slavery in International Law: Of Human Exploitation and Trafficking.* Leiden: Martinus Nijhoff/Brill.

Allan, N. 2010. "Foreign Worker Recruitment and Protection: The Role of Manitoba's Worker Recruitment and Protection Act." *Canadian Issues* (Spring): 29–32.

Allen, Dominque. 2009. "Behind the Conciliation Doors: Settling Discrimination Complaints in Victoria." *Griffith Law Review* 18: 778–799.

Anderson, Bridget. 1993. *Britain's Secret Slaves: An Investigation into the Plight of Overseas Domestic Workers in the United Kingdom.* London: Anti-Slavery International and Kalayaan.

Anderson, Bridget. 2000. *Doing the Dirty Work? The Global Politics of Domestic Labour.* Zed Books.

Anderson, Bridget. 2007. "A Very Private Business: Exploring the Demand for Migrant Domestic Workers." *European Journal of Women's Studies*: 247–264.

Anderson, Bridget. 2010a. "Migration, Immigration Controls and the Fashioning of Precarious Workers." *Work, Employment and Society* 24 (4): 300–317.

Anderson, Bridget. 2010b. "Mobilizing Migrants, Making Citizens: Migrant Domestic Workers as Political Agents." *Ethnic and Racial Studies* 33 (1): 60–74.

Anderson, Bridget. 2017. "Towards a New Politics of Migration?" *Ethnic and Racial Studies* 40 (9): 1527–1537.

Anderson, Bridget. 2018. "De-exceptionalising the Domestic: Rethinking Migration and Domestic Labour." Public lecture, University of Milan, 9 December.

Anderson, Gordon, Douglas Brodie, and Joellen Riley. 2017. *The Common Law Employment Relationship: A Comparative Study.* Cheltenham: Edward Elgar.

Arat-Koç, Sedef. 1997. "From 'Mothers of the Nation' to Migrant Workers: Immigration Policies and Domestic Workers in Canadian History." In *Not One of the Family: Foreign Domestic Workers in Canada*, edited by Abbie Bakan and Daiva Stasiulis, 53–79. Toronto: University of Toronto Press.

Armingeon, Klaus, Sarah Engler, and Lucas Leemann. 2021. *Comparative Political Data Set 1960–2019*. Zurich: Institute of Political Science, University of Zurich.

Arup, Chris, and Carolyn Sutherland. 2009. "The Recovery of Wages: Legal Services and Access to Justice." *Monash University Law Research Series* 35: 96–117.

Atrey, Shreya. 2019. *Intersectional Discrimination*. Oxford Scholarship Online. Oxford: Oxford University Press.

Australian Bureau of Statistics. 2008. *Labour Force Status and Other Characteristics of Recent Migrants, November 2007*. Canberra.

Australian Bureau of Statistics. 2011. *Characteristics of Recent Migrants, November 2010*. Canberra.

Australian Bureau of Statistics. 2014. *Characteristics of Recent Migrants, November 2013*. Canberra.

Australian Bureau of Statistics. 2017. *Characteristics of Recent Migrants, November 2016*. Canberra.

Australian Bureau of Statistics. 2020. *Characteristics of Recent Migrants, Australia, Nov 2019*. Canberra.

Australian Department of Foreign Affairs and Trade. 2022. "Factsheet: Australian Agriculture Visa Program." DFAT, Canberra. https://www.dfat.gov.au/sites/default/files/australian-agriculture-visa-fact-sheet.pdf.

American Immigration Council. 2020. *The Cost of Immigration Enforcement and Border Security*. Washington, D.C.: American Immigration Council.

Australia, Fair Work. 2020a. "Half a Million Calls from Small Business Reveals Strong Demand for Online Support." https://www.fairwork.gov.au/newsroom/media-releases/2018-media-releases/april-2018/20180426-small-business-showcase.

Australia, Fair Work. 2020b. "Pay Calculator." https://calculate.fairwork.gov.au/findyouraward.

Australia, Fair Work Ombudsman. 2013. "Tasmanian Restaurants' Massive Fine for Underpayment Foreign Workers." Sydney: Fair Work Ombudsman.

Australia, Fair Work Ombudsman. 2015. "Chinese Workers Short-changed $36,000." Sydney: Fair Work Ombudsman.

Australia, Fair Work Ombudsman. 2016a. "FWO Reaches Out to Korean Community to Help Raise Awareness of Workplace Rights, Obligations." Sydney: Fair Work Ombudsman.

Australia, Fair Work Ombudsman. 2016b. "Inquiry into the Wages and Conditions of People Working under the 419 Working Holiday Visa Program." Sydney: Fair Work Ombudsman.

Australia, Fair Work Ombudsman. 2017–2018. The Fair Work Ombudsman and Registered Organisations Commission Entity: Annual Report. Sydney: Fair Work Ombudsman.

Australia, Fair Work Ombudsman. 2019. *Compliance and Enforcement Policy*. Sydney: Fair Work Ombudsman.

Australia, Fair Work Ombudsman. 2020. "Compliance and Enforcement Policy." https://www.fairwork.gov.au/sites/default/files/migration/725/compliance-and-enforcement-policy.pdf.

Australian Treasury. 2021. "Securing Australia's Recovery: Australia's Recovery from COVID-19 Is Well Underway." https://budget.gov.au.

Avci, G., and C. McDonald. 2000. "Chipping Away at the Fortress: Unions, Immigration and the Transnational Labour Market." *International Migration* 38: 191–213.

Ayres, Ian, and John Braithwaite. 1992. *Responsive Regulation: Transcending the Deregulation Debate*. Oxford: Oxford University Press.

Baccarro, L., and C. Howell. 2011. "A Common Neoliberal Trajectory: The Transformation of Industrial Relations in Advanced Capitalism." *Politics & Society* 39: 521–563.

Baccaro, L., and C. Howell. 2017. *Trajectories of Neoliberal Transformation: European Industrial Relations since the 1970s*. Cambridge: Cambridge University Press.

Bada, Xóchitl, and Shannon Gleeson. 2015. "A New Approach to Migrant Labor Rights Enforcement: The Crisis of Undocumented Worker Abuse and Mexican Consular Advocacy in the United States." *Labor Studies Journal* 40 (1): 32–53.

Bada, Xóchitl, and Shannon Gleeson. 2019. *Accountability across Borders: Migrant Rights in North America*. Austin: University of Texas Press.

Bailey, Kenneth D. 1994. *Typologies and Taxonomies: An Introduction to Classification Techniques*. Sage Little Green Books: Quantitative Applications in the Social Sciences. London: Sage.

Bakan, Abbie, and Daiva Stasiulis. 1997a. "Foreign Domestic Worker Policy in Canada and the Social Boundaries of Modern Citizenship." In *Not One of the Family: Foreign Domestic Workers in Canada*, edited by Abigail Bakan and Daiva Stasiulis, 29–52. Toronto: University of Toronto Press.

Bakan, Abigail, and Daiva Stasiulis. 1997b. *Not One of the Family: Foreign Domestic Workers in Canada*. Toronto: University of Toronto Press.

Bales, Kevin. 2006. "Testing a Theory of Modern Slavery." La Strada International. http://lastradainternational.org/lsidocs/bales_test_theory_0607.pdf.

Bales, Kevin. 2012. "Slavery in Its Contemporary Manifestations." In *The Legal Understanding of Slavery: From the Historical to the Contemporary*, edited by Jean Allain, 281–303. Oxford: Oxford University Press.

Bamber, G., R. D. Lansbury, N. Wailes, and C. F. Wright. 2016. *International and Comparative Employment Relations: National Regulation, Global Challenges*. London: Sage/Allen and Unwin.

Banks, Kevin. 2015. "Employment Standards Complaint Resolution, Compliance and Enforcement: A Review of the Literature on Access and Effectiveness," Prepared for the Ontario Ministry of Labour to Support the Changing Workplace Review of 2015, Statement of Work #6B. https://cirhr.library.utoronto.ca/sites/default/public/research-projects/Banks-6B-ESA%20Enforcement.pdf.

Banton, Michael. 1983. *Racial and Ethnic Competition*. Cambridge: Cambridge University Press.

Barmes, Lizzie. 2015a. *Bullying and Behavioural Conflict at Work: The Duality of Individual Rights*. Oxford: Oxford University Press.

Barmes, Lizzie. 2015b. "Common Law Confusion and Empirical Research in Labour Law." In *The Autonomy of Labour Law*, edited by Alan Bogg, Cathryn Costello, A. C. L. Davies, and Jeremias Prassl, 107–122. Oxford: Hart.

Barnard, C. 2014. "Enforcement of Employment Rights by Migrant Workers in the UK: The Case of EU-8 Nationals." In *Migrants at Work*, edited by C. Costello and M. Freedland. Oxford: Oxford University Press.

Barnard, C., and A. Ludlow. 2015. "Enforcement of Employment Rights by EU-8 Migrant Workers in Employment Tribunals." *Industrial Law Journal* 47 (2): 226–262.

Barnetson, Bob. 2010. "Effectiveness of Complaint-Driven Regulation of Child Labour in Alberta." *Just Labour* 16 (Spring): 9–24.

Barnetson, Bob. 2012. "No Right to Be Safe: Justifying the Exclusion of Alberta Farm Workers from Health and Safety Legislations." *Socialist Studies* 8: 134–162.

Barnetson, Bob, and Jared Matsunaga-Turnbull. 2018. *Safer by Design*. Parkland Institute and Alberta Workers' Health Centre. https://deslibris.ca/ID/10096559.

Barth, Frederik. 1969. *Ethnic Groups and Boundaries: The Social Organization of Cultural Difference*. Oslo: Universitetsforlaget.

Basok, Tanya, Allan Hall, and Eloy Rivas. 2014. "Claiming Rights to Workplace Safety: Latin American Immigrant Workers in Southwestern Ontario." *Canadian Ethnic Studies* 46 (3): 35–53.

Bauder, H. 2006. *Labor Movement: How Migration Regulates Labor Market*. Oxford: Oxford University Press.

BC Government. 2020. "BC Government Directory." Last modified 3 September. https://dir.gov.bc.ca/gtds.cgi?esearch=&sortBy=title&for=people&attribute=title&matchMethod=is&searchString=Employment+Standards+Officer&organizationCode=LBR.

Bechter, B., B. Brandl, and G. Meardi. 2012. "Sectors or Countries? Typologies and Levels of Analysis in Comparative Industrial Relations." *European Journal of Industrial Relations* 18: 185–202.

Becker, G. 1991. *A Treatise on the Family*. Cambridge, MA: Harvard University Press.

Beine, M., A. Boucher, J. Gest, S. Challen, B. Burgoon, E. Thielemann, M. Beine, P. McGovern, M. Crock, H. Rapoport, and M. Hiscox. 2016. "Measuring and Comparing Migration, Asylum and Naturalisation Policies: The International Migration Policy and Law Analysis (IMPALA) Project." *International Migration Review* 50 (4): 827–863.

BEIS. 2017. "Campaign Launched to Increase Low Paid Workers' Knowledge of National Minimum and National Living Wage Rights." https://www.gov.uk/government/news/campaign-launched-to-increase-low-paid-workers-knowledge-of-national-minimum-and-national-living-wage-rights.

Bellés-Obrero, Cristina, Nicolau Martin Bassols, and Judit Vall Castello. 2020. "Safety at Work and Immigration." CRC TR 224 Discussion Paper Series. University of Bonn and University of Mannheim.

Berg, Laurie. 2015. "Hiding in Plain Sight: Au Pairs in Australia." In *Au Pairs' Lives in Global Context: Sisters or Servants?*, edited by Rosie Cox, 187–202. Migration, Diasporas and Citizenship. London: Palgrave Macmillan.

Berg, Laurie. 2016. Migrant Rights at Work: Law's precariousness at the intersection of immigration and labour. London: Routledge.

Berg, L., and B. Farbenblum. 2017. *Wage Theft in Australia: Findings of the National Temporary Migrant Worker Survey*. Migrant Justice Initiative, Sydney. https://www.migrantjustice.org/highlights/2017/11/14/report-released-wage-theft-in-australia-findings-of-the-national-temporary-migrant-work-survey.

Berg, Laurie, and Bassina Farbenblum. 2018. "Remedies for Migrant Worker Exploitation in Australia: Lessons from the 7-Eleven Wage Repayment Program." *Melbourne University Law Review* 41: 1035–1084.

Berg, Laurie, and Bassina Farbenblum. 2023. "Exploitation of Unauthorised Migrant Workers in Australia: Access to Protection of Employment Law." In *Migrant Labour and the Reshaping of Employment Law*, edited by Bernhard Ryan. Hart.

Berg, Laurie, and Gabrielle Meagher. 2018. *Cultural Exchange or Cheap Housekeeper? Findings of a National Survey of Au Pairs in Australia*. Sydney: Migrant Worker Justice Initiative, UNSW.

Bernhardt, Annette, Ruth Milkman, Nik Theodore, Douglas Heckathorn, Mirabai Auer, James DeFillippis, Anna Luz Gonzales, 2009. "Broken Laws, Unprotected Workers: Violations of Employment and Labor Laws in America's Cities." Report. Los Angeles: Centre for Urban Economic Development/National Employment Law Project/UCLA Institute for Research on Labor and Employment.

Bhuyan, Rupaleem, and Tracy Smith-Carrier. 2010. "Constructions of Migrant Rights in Canada: Is Subnational Citizenship Possible?" *Citizenship Studies* 16 (2): 203–221.

Bianchi, A. 2011. "Terrorism and Armed Conflict: Insights from a Law and Literature Perspective." *Leiden Journal of International Law* 24 (1): 3.

Bittle, Steven, Ashley Chen, and Jasmine Hébert. 2018. "Work-Related Deaths in Canada." *Labour* 82 (82): 159–187. doi:10.1353/llt.2018.0039.

Blackham, Alysia, and Dominique Allen. 2019. "Resolving Discrimination Claims Outside the Courts: Alternative Dispute Resolution in Australia and the United Kingdom." *Australian Journal of Labour Law* 31: 253–278.

Blackstone, A., C. Uggen, and H. McLaughlin. 2009. "Legal Consciousness and Responses to Sexual Harassment." *Law and Society Review* 43 (3, September 1): 631–668.

Bleich, Eric. 2003. *Race Politics in Britain and France: Ideas and Policymaking since the 1960s*. Cambridge: Cambridge University Press.

Bleich, Eric. 2017. "Historical Institutionalism and Judicial Decision-Making Ideas, Institutions, and Actors in French High Court Hate Speech Rulings." *World Poltics* 70: 53–85.

Bloch, Alice. 2013. "The Labour Market Experiences and Strategies of Young Undocumented Migrants." *Work, Employment and Society* (August 3).

Bloch, Alice, Leena Kumarappan, and Sonia McKay. 2015. "Employer Sanctions: The Impact of Workplace Raids and Fines on Undocumented Migrants and Ethnic Enclave Employers." *Critical Social Policy* 35 (1): 132–151. doi:10.1177/0261018314545600.

Bloch, Alice, and Sonia McKay. 2016. *Living on the Margins: Undocumented Migrants in a Global City*. Policy Press, Bristol.

Block, Fred. 2019. "Problems with the Concept of Capitalism in the Social Sciences." *Environment and Planning A: Economy and Space* 51 (5): 1166–1177. doi:10.1177/0308518X19838866.

Bogg, A. 2016. "Beyond Neo-liberalism: The Trade Union Act 2016 and the Authoritarian State." *Industrial Law Journal* 45: 299–336.

Bolatti, Denny. 2020. "Half of Tasmania's Workplace Fatalities Not Investigated." In *Trinitas* Group 7 July 2020, website available at https://trinitasgroup.com.au/2020/07/07/half-of-tasmanias-workplace-fatalities-not-investigated/.

Boräng, Frida, Sara Kalm, and Johannes Lindvall. 2020. "Unions and the Rights of Migrants in the Long Run." *Journal of European Social Policy* 30 (5): 557–570.

Borden Ladner Gervais. 2018. *Labour and Employment Law in British Columbia: A Practical Guide*. 7 July 2020. Toronto: Borden Ladner Gervais.

Boucher, Anna. 2016. *Gender, Migration and the Global Race for Talent*. Manchester: Manchester University Press.

Boucher, Anna. 2018. "Measuring Migrant Worker Rights Violations in Practice: The Example of Temporary Skills Visas in Australia." *Journal of Industrial Relations* 61 (2): 277–301.

Boucher, Anna. 2021a. "Immigration: Welfare Rights in a Temporary Immigration State." In *Social Policy in Australia: Understanding for Action*, edited by Alison McClelland, Paul Smyth, and Greg Marston, 173–194. Melbourne: Oxford University Press.

Boucher, Anna. 2021b. "What Is Exploitation and Workplace Abuse? A Classification Schema to Understand Exploitative Workplace Behaviour towards Migrant Workers." *New Political Economy* 27 (4): 629–645.

Boucher, A., J. Binder, D. Bliadze, A. Davidson, A. Kumanan, S. Macdonald, L. Martyn-France, R. Melham, E. Moerking, J. Nagell, M. Tian, E. van Nijf, S. Vitale, and M. Wu. 2017. "Transforming Australia's Visa System." Submission to the Department of Immigration and Border Protection's Policy Consultation Paper on Visa Simplification. University of Sydney.

Boucher, Anna, and Umeya Chaudhuri. 2022. "Who Represents Migrant Workers? Inequality in Legal Advocacy and Success in Migrant Abuse Cases." Unpublished manuscript.

Boucher, Anna, and Justin Gest. 2018. *Crossroads: Comparative Immigration Regimes in a World of Demographic Change*. Cambridge: Cambridge University Press.

Boucher, A., G. Hooijer, D. King, I. Napier, and M. Stears. 2021. "COVID-19: A Crisis of Borders." *PS: Political Science and Politics* 54: 617–622.

Brass, Tom. 1986. "Unfree Labour and Capitalist Restructuring in the Agrarian Sector: Peru and India." *Journal of Peasant Studies* 14 (1 (): 50–77.

Bray, Mark, and Johanna Macneil. 2011. "Individualism, Collectivism, and the Case of Awards in Australia." *Journal of Industrial Relations* 53: 149–167.

Bray, Mark, and Elsa Underhill. 2009. "Industry Differences in the Neoliberal Transformation of Australian Industrial Relations." *Industrial Relations Journal* 40 (5): 372–392. doi:10.1111/j.1468-2338.2009.00533.x.

British Columbia Government and Service Employees' Union. 2019. "BC Budget Analysis 2019/20." CGEU. https://assets.nationbuilder.com/bcgeu/pages/9268/attachments/original/1550874915/BCGEU_Budget_Analysis_2019-20-final2.pdf?1550874915.

Bryce, George K., and George R. Heinmiller. 1997. *Regulation Variances or Exemptions*. OHS Legislation Research Team.

Bureau of Labor Statistics. 2022. *Labor Force Statistics from the Current Population Survey*.

Burgess, Katie. 2018. "WorkSafe ACT to Be Restructured after Review Finds Low Independence." *Canberra Times*, October 30, 2018.

Burkett, B. W., D. G. Gilbert, J. D. R. Craig, and M. E. Gavings. 2013. *Federal Labour Law and Practice*. Toronto: Thomson Reuters.

Butler, Mark. 2018. *Labour Law in Great Britain*. London: Wolter Kluwer Law and Business.

Cachón, L., and M. S. Valles. 2003. "Trade Unionism and Immigration: Reinterpreting Old and New Dilemmas." *Transfer: European Review of Labour and Research* 9: 469–482.

California Department of Industrial Relations. 2017. "Labor Commissioner's Office: About Us." https://www.dir.ca.gov/dlse/AboutUs.htm.

California Department of Industrial Relations, Labor Enforcement Task Force. 2019. *Report to the Legislature*. San Francisco, CA: Department of Industrial Relations.

California Labor Federation. 2013. "Time to Stop Abuse and Exploitation of Immigrant Workers." https://calaborfed.org/time_to_stop_abuse_and_exploitation_of_immigrant_workers/.

Callinicos, A. 1995. *Race and Class*. London: Bookmarks.

Campbell, Iain, Martina Boese, and Joo-Cheong Tham. 2016. "Inhospitable Workplaces? International Students and Paid Work in Food Services." *Australian Journal of Social Issues* 51 (3): 279–298.

Campbell, I., and J. C. Tham. 2013. "Labour Market Deregulation and Temporary Migrant Labour Schemes: An Analysis of the 457 Visa Program." *Australian Journal of Labour Law* 26: 239–272.

Canadian Press. 2022. "Inquest into Deadly 2009 Scaffolding Collapse in Toronto Set to Begin Jan. 31." *Global News*, 10 January. https://globalnews.ca/news/8501356/toronto-scaffolding-collapse-inquest-2/.

Carter, Donald D., Geoffrey England, Brian Etherington, and Gilles Trudeau. 2002. *Labor Law in Canada*. The Hague: Kluwer Law International.

Castles, Francis. 1988. *Australian Public Policy and Economic Vulnerability*. Sydney: Allen and Unwin.

Castles, Francis. 2004. *The Future of the Welfare State: Crisis Myths and Crisis Realities*. Oxford: Oxford University Press.

Castles, Stephen, and Godula Kosack. 1973. *Immigrant Workers and Class Structure in Western Europe*. New York: Oxford University Press.

Caviedes, Alexander. 2010. *Prying Open Fortress Europe: The Turn to Sectoral Labor Migration*. Lanham, MD: Lexington Books.

CEACR. 2022. *Application of International Labour Standards 2022: Report of the Committee of Experts on the Application of Conventions and Recommendations*. Geneva: International Labour Organization.

Charpentier, M., and A. Quéniart. 2017. "Aging Experiences of Older Immigrant Women in Quebec (Canada): From Deskilling to Liberation." *Women Ageing* 29: 437–447.

Chaudhuri, Umeya, Anna Boucher, and Sydney Policy Lab. 2021. *The Future of Enforcement for Migrant Workers in Australia*. Sydney: Sydney Policy Lab.

Chung, Sue Minty. 1995. "Proposition 187: A Beginner's Tour through a Recurring Nightmare." *UC Davis Journal of International Law and Policy* 1: 267–296.

Citizenship and Immigration Canada. 2014. *Annual Report to Parliament on Immigration*. Ottawa: CIC.

Citizenship and Immigration Canada. "Refusal to Process Labour Market Impact Assessment (LMIA)-Required Work Permit Applications for Caregivers Received on or after June 18, 2019." Ottawa: Citizenship Immigration Canada.

Citizenship and Immigration Canada. 2020. "Canada: Temporary Foreign Worker Program Work Permit Holders by Country of Citizenship and Year in Which Permit(s) Became Effective, January 2015–January 2020." In *Open Government Data License*. Ottawa: Citizenship Immigration Canada. https://open.canada.ca/data/en/dataset/360024f2-17e9-4558-bfc1-3616485d65b9.

Clark, Nick. 2020. "Unpaid Britain: Challenges of Enforcement and Wage Recovery." In *Closing the Enforcement Standards Gap*, edited by Leah Vosko, 201–220. Toronto: University of Toronto Press.

Cleeland, Nancy. 2002. "Employers Test Ruling on Immigrants; Labor: Some Firms Are Trying to Use Supreme Court Decision as Basis for Avoiding Claims over Workplace Violations." *Los Angeles Times*, 22 April.

Cobb-Clark, Deborah, and Siew-Ean Khoo. 2006. *Public Policy and Immigrant Settlement*. Northampton, MA: Edward Elgar.

Colindres, Carlos, Amy Cohen, and C. S. Caxaj. 2021. "Migrant Agricultural Workers' Health, Safety and Access to Protections: A Descriptive Survey Identifying Structural

Gaps and Vulnerabilities in the Interior of British Columbia, Canada." *International Journal of Environmental Research and Public Health* 18: 1–15.

Colling, Trevor. 2012. "Trade Union Roles in Making Employment Rights Effective." In *Making Employment Rights Effective: Issues of Enforcement and Compliance*, edited by Linda Dickens, 183–204. Oxford: Hart.

Collins, Hugh. 2000. "Justifications and Techniques of Legal Regulation of the Employment Relation." In *Legal Regulation of the Employment Relations*, edited by Hugh Collins, P. Davies, and R. Rideout, 141–. Leiden: Kluwer International.

Collins, Hugh, Keith Ewing, and Aileen McColgan. 2012. *Labour Law*. Cambridge: Cambridge University Press.

Collins, Hugh, and Virginia Mantouvalou. 2016. "Human Rights and the Contract of Employment." In *Human Rights and the Contract of Employment*, edited by Mark Freedland, Alan Bogg, David Cabrelli, Hugh Collins, Nicola Countouris, A. C. L. Davies, Simon Deakin, and Jeremias Prassl, 188–208. Oxford: Oxford University Press.

Colvin, Alexander J. S. 2006. "Flexibility and Fairness in Liberal Market Economies: The Comparative Impact of the Legal Environment and High-Performance Work Systems." *British Journal of Industrial Relations* 44: 73–97.

Colvin, Alexander J. S., and Owen Darbishire. 2013. "Convergence in Industrial Relations Institutions: The Emerging Anglo-American model?" *Industrial and Labor Relations Review* 66 (5): 1047–1077.

Connolly, Heather, Stefania Marino, and Miguel Martinez Lucio. 2019. *The Politics of Social Inclusion and Labor Representation: Immigrants and Trade Unions in the European Context*. Ithaca, NY: ILR Press.

Consterdine, Erica, and Sahizer Samuk. 2018. "Temporary Migration Programmes: The Cause or Antidote of Migrant Worker Exploitation in UK Agriculture." *International Migration and Integration* 19: 1005–1020.

Comcare. 2019. "Annual Report 2018–2019." Commonwealth of Australia. https://www.comcare.gov.au/about/forms-publications/documents/publications/corporate-publications/annual-report-18-19.pdf.

Cooper, R., and B. Ellem. 2008. "The Neoliberal State, Trade Unions and Collective Bargaining in Australia." *British Journal of Industrial Relations* 46: 532–554.

Costa, Daniel. 2018. *California Leads the Way*. Washington, D.C.: Economic Policy Institute.

Costa, Daniel. 2020. "Temporary Migrant Workers or Migrants? The Question for U.S. Labor Migration." *Russell Sage Foundation Journal of the Social Sciences* 6 (3, November): 18–44.

Costa, Daniel. 2021. "Temporary Work Visa Programs and the Need for Reform: A Briefing on Program Frameworks, Policy Issues and Fixes, and the Impact of COVID-19." In *Economic Policy Institute Report*. Washington, D.C.: Economic Policy Institute, available at https://www.epi.org/publication/temporary-work-visa-reform/.

Costello, Cathryn. 2015. "Migrants and Forced Labour: A Labour Law Response." In *The Autonomy of Labour Law*, edited by A. Bogg, C. Costello, A. Davies, and J. Prassl, 189–230. Oxford: Hart.

Coulter, S., and B. Hancké. 2016. "A Bonfire of the Regulations, or Business as Usual? The UK Labour Market and the Political Economy of Brexit." *Political Quarterly* 87: 148–156.

Cox, Rosie. 2012. "Gendered Work and Migration Regimes." In *Transnational Migration, Gender and Rights*, edited by R. Aslaug Sollund and L. Leonard, 33–52. Bingley: Emerald.

Creighton, Breen, and Andrew Stewart. 2010. *Labour Law*. Leichhardt: Federation Press.

Crenshaw, K. W. 1989. "Demarginalizing the Intersection of Race and Sex: A Black Feminist Critique of Antidiscrimination Doctrine, Feminist Theory and Antiracist Politics." *University of Chicago Legal Forum* 1, article 9: 139–167.

Daly, Nadia. 2015. "Darwin Company Choong Enterprises Cops $335,017 Penalty for Underpaying and Overworking 457 Visa Holders." ABC News. https://www.abc.net.au/news/2015-06-04/darwin-company-choong-enterprises-335k-payout-for-457-breaches/6523084.

Dauvergne, C. 2000. "Gendering Permanent Residency Statistics." *Melbourne University Law Review* 24 (2): 280–309.

Davidson, Julia O'Connell. 2015. *Modern Slavery: The Margins of Freedom*. London: Palgrave Macmillan.

Davies, A. C. L. 2016. "The Immigration Act." *Industrial Law Journal* 45: 431–442.

Davies, Jon. 2019. "From Severe to Routine Labour Exploitation: The Case of Migrant Workers in the UK Food Industry." *Criminology & Criminal Justice* 19 (3): 294–310.

Davies, Jon, and Natalia Ollus. 2019. "Labour Exploitation as Corporate Crime and Harm: Outsourcing Responsibility in Food Production and Cleaning Services Supply Chains." *Crime, Law and Social Change* 72 (1): 87–106. doi:10.1007/s10611-019-09841-w.

Davis, Lynn, and William Hewitt. 1994. "Lessons in Administering Justice: What Judges Need to Know about the Requirements, Role and Professional Responsibilities of the Court Interpreter." *Harvard Latino Law Review* 1: 121–176.

Deakin, Simon, and Frank Wilkinson. 2005. *The Law of the Labour Market: Industrialization, Employment, and Legal Evolution*. Oxford: Oxford University Press.

Deegan, B. 2008. *Visa Subclass 457: Integrity Review*. Canberra: Department of Immigration and Citizenship.

de Genova, N. 2005. *Working the Boundaries: Race, Space, and "Illegality" in Mexican Chicago*. Durham, NC: Duke University Press.

Denike, Margaret Ann, Fay Faraday, and M. Kate Stephenson. 2006. *Making Equality Rights Real: Securing Substantive Equality under the Charter*. Toronto: Irwin Law.

Department for Business, Energy & Industrial Strategy. 2019. "Government Has Launched Its First Holiday Pay Advertising Campaign." GOV.UK. March 12, 2019. https://www.gov.uk/government/news/government-has-launched-its-first-holiday-pay-advertising-campaign.

Department of Justice, Tasmania. 2019. "Department of Justice Annual Report 2018–2019." https://www.justice.tas.gov.au/__data/assets/pdf_file/0007/551743/Regulatory-and-Other-Services.pdf.

Department of Mines, Industry Regulation and Safety, Western Australia. 2019. *Annual Report 2018–19*, available at https://www.dmirs.wa.gov.au/who-we-are/reports-and-reporting.

Dias-Abey, Manoj. 2018. "Justice on Our Fields: Can 'Alt- Labor' Organizations Improve Migrant Farm Workers' Conditions." *Harvard Civil Rights–Civil Liberties Law Review* 53: 168–211.

Dias-Abey, Manoj. 2019. "A Socio-Legal History of the Coalition of Immokalee Workers." In *Theorising Labour Law in a Changing World: Towards Inclusive Labour Law*, edited by Alysia Blackham, Miriam Kullmann, and Ania Zbyszewska, 125–148. Oxford: Hart.

Doellgast, V., C. F. Wright, F. L. Cooke, and G. J. Bamber. 2021. "Globalisation, Crises and Institutional Reponses." In *International and Comparative Employment Relations: Global Crises and Institutional Responses*, edited by G. Bamber, F. L. Cooke, V. Doellgast, and C. F. Wright, 363–388. London: Sage/Allen and Unwin.

Dooling, S. 2019. "Lawsuit Alleges Employer Retaliated against Undocumented Worker by Triggering ICE Arrest." WBUR Boston.

Dukes, R. 2008. "Constitutionalizing Employment Relations: Sinzheimer, Kahn-Freund, and the Role of Labor Law." *Journal of Law and Society* 35 (3): 341–363.

Dymski, Gary A. 1992. "Towards a New Model of Exploitation: The Case of Racial Domination." *International Journal of Social Economics* 19: 292–313.

Edwards, Peter. 2010. "Worker 'Didn't Feel Safe' before Scaffold Collapse." *Toronto Star*, 23 January. https://www.thestar.com/news/gta/2010/01/23/worker_didnt_feel_safe_before_scaffold_collapsed.html.

Engels, Friedrich. (1845) 2001. *The Condition of the Working Class in England*. London: Electric Book.

European Human Rights Commission. 2010. "Inquiry into Recruitment and Employment in the Meat and Poultry Processing Sector." London: EHRC.

Evans, C. 2008. "Government Announces Changes to 457 Visa Program." Media release. https://parlinfo.aph.gov.au/parlInfo/search/display/display.w3p;query=Id:%22media/pressrel/XY6T6%22;src1=sm1.

Ewing, K. 1998. "The State and Industrial Relations: 'Collective Laissez-faire' Revisited." *Historical Studies in Industrial Relations* 5: 1–31.

Ewins, James. 2015. "Independent Review of the Overseas Domestic Worker Visa." Independent report for the Home Office, London.

Faraday, Fay. 2014. *Profiting from the Precarious: How Recruitment Practices Exploit Migrant Workers*. Toronto: Metcalf Foundation.

Faraday, Fay. 2016. *Decent Work or Entrenched Exploitation for Canada's Migrant Workers?* Toronto: Metcalf Foundation.

Faraday, Fay, and Caregivers Action Centre and Migrant Workers Alliance for Change. 2017. *Strong Together: Delivering on the Constitutionally Protected Right to Unionize for Migrant Workers*. Toronto: Migrant Workers Alliance for Change and Caregivers Action Centre.

Farbenblum, Bassina, and Laurie Berg. 2017. "'Migrant Workers' Access to Remedy for Exploitation in Australia: The Role of the National Fair Work Ombudsman." *Australian Journal of Human Rights* 23: 310–331.

Farbenblum, Bassina, and Laurie Berg. 2018. "Wage Theft in Silence: Why Migrant Workers Do Not Recover Their Unpaid Wages in Australia." Migrant Justice Institute, Sydney. https://www.migrantjustice.org/highlights/wage-theft-in-silence.

Farbenblum, Bassina, and Laurie Berg. 2021. *Migrant Workers' Access to Justice for Wage Theft: A Global Study of Promising Initiatives*. Sydney: UTS/UNSW/Migrant Justice Initiative.

Fels, Allan. 2019. *Tough Customer*. Melbourne: Melbourne University Press.

Fels, Allan, and David Cousins. 2019. "The Migrant Workers' Taskforce and the Australian Government's Response to Migrant Worker Wage Exploitation." *Journal of Australian Political Economy* 84: 13–45.

Fels Commission. 2019. "Report of the Migrant Worker Rights Taskforce." Final Report, Attorney-General's Department, Canberra. https://www.ag.gov.au/industrial-relations/publications/report-migrant-workers-taskforce.

Ferguson, Benjamin, and Hillel Steiner. 2018. "Exploitation." In *The Oxford Handbook of Distributive Justice*, edited by Serena Olsaretti, 533–555. Oxford: Oxford University Press.

Ferracioli, Luara. 2021. *Liberal Self-Determination in a World of Migration*. New York: Oxford University Press.

Field, Andy. 2009. *Discovery Statistics Using SPSS*. 3rd ed. London: Sage.

Field, Emma, and Vanessa Marsh. 2017. "Island Nations Threaten to Stop Sending Workers." *Daily Mercury* (Queensland), 13 December. http://global.factiva.com/redir/default.aspx?P=sa&an=APNDAM0020171212edcd000ac&cat=a&ep=ASE.

Fine, Janice, Linda Burnham, Kati Griffith, Minsun Ji, Victor Narro, and Steven Pitts. 2018. *No One Size Fits All: Worker Organization, Policy and Movement in a New Economic Age*. Ithaca, NY: Cornell University Press.

Fisk, Catherine, and Michael J. Wishnie. 2005. "The Story of Hoffman Plastics Compounds v NLRB: Labor Rights without Remedies for Undocumented Workers." In *Labor Law Stories*, edited by Laura. J. Cooper and Catherine Fisk, 351–390. New York: Foundation Press.

Focus on Labour Exploitation. 2017. *Risky Business: Tackling Exploitation in the UK Labour Market*. London: FLEX.

Folbre, Nancy. 1982. "Exploitation Comes Home: A Critique of the Marxian Theory of Family Labour." *Cambridge Journal of Economics* 6 (4): 317–329.

Folbre, Nancy. 2003. "'Holding Hands at Midnight': The Paradox of Caring Labor." In *Towards a Feminist Philosophy of Economics*, edited by Drucilla K. Barker and Edith. Kuiper, 213–246. New York: Routledge.

Ford, Michele. 2019. *From Migrant to Worker: Global Unions and Temporary Labour Migration in Asia*. Ithaca, NY: Cornell University Press.

Foster, J. 2012. "'Making Temporary Permanent: The Silent Transformation of the Temporary Foreign Worker Program." *Just Labour: A Canadian Journal of Work and Sociology* 19: 22–46.

Foster, J., and B. Bartenson. 2015. "The Construction of Migrant Work and Workers by Alberta Legislators, 2000–2011." *Canadian Ethnic Studies* 47 (1): 107–113.

Foster, Jason, Bob Barnetson, and Jared Matsunaga-Turnbull. 2018. "Fear Factory: Retaliation and Rights Claiming in Alberta, Canada." *SAGE Open* 8 (2): 2158244018780752. doi:10.1177/2158244018780752.

Foster, J., and A. Taylor. 2013. "In the Shadows: Exploring the Notion of 'Community' for Temporary Foreign Workers in Boomtown." *Canadian Journal of Sociology* 38 (2): 167–190.

Frances, J., S. Barrientos, and B. Rogaly. 2005. "Temporary Workers in UK Agriculture and Horticulture." London: Department for Environment, Farming and Rural Affairs.

Freedland, Mark. 2013. "Burying Caesar: What Was the Standard Employment Contract." In *Rethinking Workplace Regulation: Beyond the Standard Contract of Employment*, edited by Katherine Stone and Harry Arthurs, 81–94. New York: Russell Sage Foundation.

Fudge, Judy. 1997. "Little Victories and Big Defeats: The Rise and Fall of Collective Bargaining Rights for Domestic Workers in Ontario." In *Not One of the Family: Foreign Domestic Workers in Canada*, edited by Abbie Bakan and Daiva Stasiulis, 119–146. Toronto: University of Toronto Press.

Fudge, Judy. 2008. "The Supreme Court of Canada and the Right to Bargain Collectively: The Implications of the Health Service and Support Case in Canada and Beyond." *Industrial Law Journal* 37: 25–48.

Fudge, Judy. 2011a. "Global Care Chains, Employment Agencies and the Conundrum of Jurisdiction: Decent Work for Domestic Workers in Canada." *Canadian Journal of Women and the Law* 23 (1): 235–264.

Fudge, Judy. 2011b. "Labour as a 'Fictive Commodity': Radically Reconceptualizing Labour Law." In *The Idea of Labour Law*, edited by Guy Davidov and Brian Langille, 120–136. Oxford: Oxford University Press.

Fudge, Judy. 2016a. "Justice for Whom? Migrant Workers in Canada." In *Inequalities and Social Justice in Contemporary Canada*, edited by J. Brodie, 69–86. Toronto: University of Toronto Press.

Fudge, Judy. 2016b. "Migrant Domestic Workers in British Columbia, Canada: Unfreedom, Trafficking and Domestic Servitude." In *Temporary Labour Migration in a Globalised World: The Regulatory Challenges*, edited by J. Howe and R. Owens, 151–172. Oxford: Hart.

Fudge, Judy. 2016c. "Modern Slavery and Migrant Domestic Workers: The Politics of Legal Characterization Policy Brief, the Foundation for Law, Justice and Society." www.fljs.org.

Fudge, Judy. 2017. "The Future of the Standard Employment Relationship: Labour Law, New Institutional Economics and Old Power Resource Theory." *Journal of Industrial Relations* 53: 374–392.

Fudge, Judy. 2018a. "Illegal Working, Migrants and Labour Exploitation in the UK: Liminal Legality and the Immigration Act 2016." *Oxford Journal of Legal Studies* 38 (3): 557–584.

Fudge, Judy. 2018b. "Modern Slavery, Unfree Labour and the Labour Market: The Social Dynamics of Legal Characterization." *Social and Legal Studies* 27 (4): 414–434.

Fundamental Rights Agency. 2015. "Severe Labour Exploitation: Workers Moving within or into the European Union States' Obligations and Victims' Rights." Vienna: FRA.

Galanter, Marc. 1974. "Why the 'Haves' Come Out Ahead: Speculations on the Limits of Legal Change." *Law & Society Review* 9: 95–160.

Gangmasters and Labour Abuse Authority. 2016. *The Nature and Scale of Labour Exploitation across All Sectors within the United Kingdom*. Gangmasters and Labour Abuse Authority, London. https://www.gla.gov.uk/whats-new/the-nature-and-scale-of-labour-exploitation-across-all-sectors-within-the-united-kingdom/.

Gangmasters and Labour Abuse Authority. 2019a. "Gangmasters and Labour Abuse Authority: Written Question 216309." https://questions-statements.parliament.uk/written-questions/detail/2019-02-04/216309.

Gangmasters and Labour Abuse Authority. 2019b. "Parliamentary Question: GLAA Budget." https://www.gla.gov.uk/media/6081/blomfield-050619-glaa-budget.pdf.

Gaze, Beth. 2000. "The Cost of Equal Opportunity." *Alternative Law Journal* 25 (3): 125.

Gaze, Beth, and Belinda Smith. 2017. *Equality and Discrimination Law in Australia: An Introduction*. Melbourne: Cambridge University Press.

Geertz, Clifford. 1973. "The Integrative Revolution: Primordial Sentiments and Civil Politics in the New States." In *The Interpretation of Cultures*, by Clifford Geertz, 255–310. New York: Basic Books.

Genn, H. 1999. *Paths to Justice*. London: Bloomsbury Press.

Genn, H., A. Paterson, and Research National Centre for Social. 2001. *Paths to Justice, Scotland: What People in Scotland Do and Think about Going to Law*. Oxford: Hart.

Gest, Justin, Ian M. Kysel, and Tom Wong. 2019. "Protecting and Benchmarking Migrants' Rights: An Analysis of the Global Compact for Safe, Orderly and Regular Migration." *International Migration* 57 (6): 60–79.

Glazer, Nathan, and Daniel A. Moynihan. 1975. *Ethnicity: Theory and Experience*. Cambridge, MA: Harvard University Press.

Gleeson, Shannon, and Bada Xóchitl. 2019. "Introduction: Enforcing Rights across Borders." In *Accountability across Borders: Migrant Rights in North America*, edited by Shannon Gleeson and Bada Xóchitl, 1–24. Austin: University of Texas Press.

Gordon, Ian, Kathleen Scanlon, Tony Travers, and Christin Whitehead. 2009. "Economic Impact on the London and UK Economy of an Earned Regularisation of Irregular Migrants to the UK." London: GLA Economics.

Gordon, Todd. 2019. "Capitalism, Neoliberalism, and Unfree Labour." *Critical Sociology* 45 (6): 921–939.

Government of Canada. 2019. "Budget 2019: Chapter 4." 19 March. https://www.budget.gc.ca/2019/docs/plan/chap-04-en.html.

Government of Alberta. 2019. "Labour: Annual Report (2018–19)." Edmonton. https://open.alberta.ca/dataset/2545eb86-75f5-4fc9-b211-176e1ef38ac4/resource/f06c0813-eb0c-4fad-a2bc-adf87ea5d219/download/labour-annual-report-2018-2019-web.pdf.

Government of Ontario. 2020a. "Government of Ontario Employee and Organization Directory (Info-Go)." 2020. https://data.ontario.ca/dataset/activity/government-of-ontario-employee-and-organization-directory-info-go.

Government of Ontario. 2020b. "Occupational Health and Safety in Ontario (April 2018–March 2019): Appendix." 15 February. https://www.ontario.ca/document/occupational-health-and-safety-ontario-april-2018-march-2019/appendix#section-1.

Government of Ontario. 2020c. "Workplace Compliance Initiatives." https://www.ontario.ca/page/workplace-compliance-initiatives.

Gray, Robert. 1987. "The Languages of Factory Reform in Britain, c. 1830–1860." In *The Historical Meanings of Work*, edited by Patrick Joyce, 143–179. Cambridge: Cambridge University Press.

Graycar, R., and J. Morgan. 2005. "Law Reform: What's in It for Women?" In *Windsor Yearbook of Access to Justice*, edited by R. Bahdi, 393–419. Ontario: University of Windsor.

Green, A., G. Atfield, and K. Purcell. 2016. "Fuelling Displacement and Labour Market Segmentation in Low-Skilled Jobs? Insights from a Local Study of Migrant and Student Employment." *Environment and Planning A* 48: 577.

Green, Alan G., and David Green. 1995. "Canadian Immigration Policy: The Effectiveness of the Points Test and Other Instruments." *Canadian Journal of Economics* 38: 1006–1041.

Griffith, Kati. 2017. "The Power of a Presumption: California as a Laboratory for Unauthorized Immigration." *UC Davis Law Review* 50: 1279–1322.

Griffiths, Melanie, and Colin Yeo. 2021. "The UK's Hostile Environment: Deputising Immigration Control." *Critical Social Policy* 4: 521–544.

Grigoleit-Richter, Grit. 2017. "Highly Skilled and Highly Mobile? Examining Gendered and Ethnicised Labour Market Conditions for Migrant Women in Stem-Professions in Germany." *Journal of Ethnic and Migration Studies* 43 (16): 2738–2755.

Guerin-Gonzales, Camille. 1994. *Mexican Workers and American Dreams: Immigration, Repatriation, and California Farm Labor, 1900–1939*, New Brunswick, NJ: Rutgers University Press.

Guillaume, Cecile. 2018. "When Trade Unions Turn to Litigation: 'Getting All the Ducks in a Row.'" *Industrial Relations Journal* 49: 227–241.

Guthrie, Robert. 2007. "Illegal Workers and Workers' Compensation." *Precedent* 114 (83): 41–46.

Haddow, Rodney, and Thomas Klassen. 2006. *Partisanship, Globalization, and Canadian Labour Market Policy: Four Provinces in Comparative Perspective*. Toronto: University of Toronto Press.

Hafiz, Sameera, and Michael Paarlberg. 2017. "The Human Trafficking of Domestic Workers in the United States." Beyond Survival Campaign. 13 March. https://ips-dc.org/report-the-human-trafficking-of-domestic-workers-in-the-united-states/.

Hagemann, Ben. 2014. "457 Workers on Gorgon Work 52 Days Straight." *Australian Mining*, 10 November.

Hall and Partners. 2016. "Experiences of Temporary Residents: Report Conducted for the Department of Immigration and Border Protection." Canberra: Department of Immigration and Border Protection/Department of Employment.

Hall, M., and R. Wright. 2008. "Systematic Content Analysis of Judicial Opinions." *California Law Review* 96 (1): 62–122.

Hall, Peter, and David Soskice. 2001. *Varieties of Capitalism: The Institutional Foundations of Comparative Advantage*. Oxford: Oxford University Press.

Hancock, K. 1984. "The First Half Century of Wage Policy." In *Australian Labour Relations Readings*, edited by B. Chapman, J. Isaac, and J. Niland, 44–99. Melbourne: Macmillan.

Handy, J. 2006. "Sexual Harassment in Small Town New Zealand: A Qualitative Study of Three Contrasting Organizations." *Gender Work and Organization* 13 (1): 1–24.

Hansen, Randall. 2000. *Citizenship and Immigration in Post-War Britain: The Institutional Origins of a Multicultural Nation*. Oxford: Oxford University Press.

Hardy, Tess. 2017. "Good Call: Extending Liability for Employment Contraventions beyond the Direct Employer." In *Essays in Contemporary Law Reform*, edited by R. Levy, M. O'Brien, S. Rice, and M. Thornton. Canberra: ANU Press.

Hardy, Tess. 2019. "Shifting Risk and Shirking Responsibility? The Challenge of Upholding Employment Standards Regulation within Franchise Networks." *Australian Jounal of Labour Law* 32: 62–82.

Hardy, Tess, and John Howe. 2009. "Partners in Enforcement? The New Balance between Government and Trade Union Enforcement of Employment Standards in Australia." *Australian Journal of Labour Law* 22: 306–336.

Hardy, Tess, and John Howe. 2013. "Too Soft or Too Severe? Enforceable Undertakings and the Regulatory Dilemma Facing the Fair Work Ombudsman." *Federal Law Review* 41 (1): 1–33.

Hardy, Tess, and John Howe. 2017. "Creating Ripples, Making Waves: Assessing the General Deterrence Effects of Enforcement Activities of the Fair Work Ombudsman." *Sydney Law Review* 39 (4): 471–500.

Hardy, Tess, and John Howe. 2020. "Out of the Shadows and into the Spotlight: The Sweeping Evolution of Employment Standards Enforcement in Australia." In *Closing the Enforcement Standards Gap*, edited by Leah Vosko, 221–241. Toronto: University of Toronto Press.

Hardy, Tess, John Howe, and Sean Cooney. 2013. "Less Energetic but More Enlightened? Exploring the Fair Work Ombudsman's Use of Litigation in Regulatory Enforcement (Australia)." *Sydney Law Review* 35 (3): 565–597.

Haus, Leah. 2002. *Unions, Immigration and Internationalization: New Challenges and Changing Conditions in the United States and France*. New York: Palgrave Macmillan.

HD Mining. 2012. "Opinion-Editorial: Temporary Workers at Murray River Project Well-Paid." http://www.hdminingintl.com/temporary-workers-at-murray-river-project-well-paid.

Healy, G. 2008. "Migration Not Helping Skills Shortage." *The Australian* 16 October, 4.

Hemingway, Catherine. 2016. "Not Just Work: Ending the Exploitation of Refugee and Migrant Workers." *WestJustice Employment Law Project Final Report*. Melbourne: WestJustice. https://www.westjustice.org.au/cms_uploads/docs/westjustice-not-just-work-report-part-1.pdf.

Hennebry, K., and K. Preibisch. 2012. "A Model for Managed Migration? Re-examining Best Practices in Canada's Seasonal Agricultural Worker Program." *International Migration* 50 (S1): e19–e40.

Hepple, Bob. 1986. *The Making of Labour Law in Europe: A Comparative Study of Nine Countries up to 1945*. London: Mansell.

Hepple, Bob, and Bruno Veneziani. 2009. "Introduction: From 'Making' to 'Transformation.'" In Bob Hepple and Bruno Veneziani, *The Transformation of Labour Law in Europe: A Comparative Study of 15 Countries 1945–2004*, 1–29. Oxford: Hart.

Hewitson, G. J. 2003. "Domestic Labor and Gender Identity: Are All Women Carers?" In *Toward a Feminist Philosophy of Economics*, edited by D. K. Barker and E. Kuiper, 266–284. London: Routledge.

Higbie, Tobias. 2021. "Making Labor and Working-Class History in Los Angeles." *Labor Studies in Working-Class History* 18: 6–9.

Himmelweit, Susan. 1995. "The Discovery of 'Unpaid Work': The Social Consequences of the Expansion of 'Work.'" *Feminist Economics* 1 (2): 1–19.

Ho, Christopher, and Jennifer C. Chang. 2005. "Drawing the Line after Hoffman Plastic Compounds, Inc. v. NLRB: Strategies for Protecting Undocumented Workers in the Title VII Context and Beyond." *Hofstra Labor & Employment Law Journal* 22: 473.

Hochschild, Arlie Russell. 2000. "Global Care Chains and Emotional Surplus Value." In *On the Edge: Living with Global Capitalism*, edited by W. Hutton and A. Giddens, 130–146. London: Johathan Cape.

Hoefer, Michael, Nancy Rytina, and Bryan C. Baker. 2009. *Estimates of the Unauthorized Immigrant Population Residing in the United States: January 2009*. Edited by Population Estimates. Washington, D.C.: Department of Homeland Security, Office of Immigration Statistics.

Hollifield, James. 1992. *Immigrants, Markets, and States: The Political Economy of Postwar Europe*. Cambridge, MA: Havard University Press.

Hollifield, James. 2004. "The Emerging Migration State." *International Migration Review* 38: 885–912.

Hooijer, G., and D. King. 2022. "The Racialized Pandemic: Wave One of COVID-19 and the Reproduction of Global North Inequalities." *Perspectives on Politics* 20 (2): 507–527.

Horowitz, Donald, L. 1985. *Ethnic Groups in Conflict*. Berkeley: University of California Press.

Horton, Sarah Bronwen. 2016. *They Leave Their Kidneys in the Fields: Illness, Injury, and Illegality among U.S. Farmworkers*. Berkeley: University of California Press.

Howe, J. 2017. "'Predatory Princes,' 'Migration Merchant,' or "Agents of Development'? An Examination of the Legal Regulation of Labour Hire Migration Intermediaries." In *The Evolving Project of Labour Law: Foundations, Developments and Future Research Directions*, edited by J. Howe, A. Chapman, and I. Landau. Leichhardt: Federation Press. 192–806.

Howe, J., . Alex Reilly, Diane van den Broek, and Chris F. Wright. 2017. "Sustainable Solutions: The Future of Labour Supply in the Australian Vegetable Industry." Horticulture Innovation Australia/University of Adelaide. https://www.palmscheme.gov.au/sites/default/files/2021-08/7b329a_a90d8ea9a1d641b29cbc5bc58178d172.pdf.

Howe, J., L. Berg, and B. Farbenblum. 2019. "Unfair Dismissal Law and Temporary Migrant Labour in Australia." *Federal Law Review* 46 (1): 19–48.

Howe, R. Brian, and David Johnson. 2000. *Restraining Equality: Human Rights Commissions in Canada*. Toronto: University of Toronto Press.

Howell, C. 2020. "Rethinking the Role of the State in Employment Relations for a Neoliberal Era." *Industrial Law Review* 74: 739–772.

Howells, Stephen. 2011. "Review of the Migration Amendment (Employer Sanctions) Act 2007." Canberra: Parliament of Australia.

Hugo, Graeme. 2008. "Best Practice in Temporary Labour Migration for Development: A Perspective from Asia and the Pacific." *International Migration* 75 (5): 23–74.

Human Rights Watch. 2012. "Cultivating Fear: The Vulnerability of Immigrant Farmworkers in the US to Sexual Violence and Sexual Harassment." : Human Rights Watch, New York.

Human Rights Watch. 2014. "Hidden Away: Abuses against Migrant Domestic Workers in the UK." Human Rights Watch, London.

Hylland Eriksen, Thomas. 1993. *Ethnicity and Nationalism*. London: Pluto Press.

IAVGO. 2010. "Safety, Health and Precarious Work in Ontario: Letter to Ontario Inquiry." Toronto: IAVGO.

Immigration, Refugees and Citizenship Canada. 2020. "Canada: Temporary Foreign Worker Program (TFWP) Work Permit Holders under the Seasonal Agricultural Worker Program by Year in Which Permit(s) Became effective, 1998–2016." Ottawa: Immigration, Refugees and Citizenship Canada.

Independent Commissioner Against Corruption, South Australia. 2018. "Evaluation of the Practices, Policies and Procedures of the Regulatory Arm of SafeWork SA." Adelaide. https://icac.sa.gov.au/system/files/Evaluation_of_the_Practices_Policies_%26_Procedures_of_SafeWork_SA.pdf.

Industrial Relations Victoria. 2016. "Victorian Inquiry into the Labour Hire Industry and Insecure Work." Melbourne: Industrial Relations Melbourne.

International Labor Organisation. 1930. "C029: Forced Labour Convention, 1930 (No. 29)." Geneva: ILO.

International Labour Organisation. 2006. "Strategies and Practice for Labour Inspection." Geneva: ILO.

International Labour Organisation. 2012. "ILO Indicators of Forced Labour." Geneva: ILO.

International Labour Organisation. 2017a. "Access to the Labour Market for Admitted Migrant Workers in Asia and Related Corridors." Geneva: ILO.

International Labor Organisation. 2017b. "Employer-Migrant Worker Relationships in the Middle East: Exploring Scope for International Labour Market and Fair Migration." Beirut: ILO.

International Labor Organisation. 2018. "World Employment and Social Outlook: Trends: 2019." Geneva: ILO.

International Labour Organisation. 2019. "Access to the Labour Market for Admitted Migrant Workers in Asia and Related Conditions." Thailand: ILO.

International Labour Organisation, Katherine Jones, Sanushka Mudaliar, and Nicola Piper. 2021. "Locked Down and in Limbo: The Global Impact of COVID-19 on Migrant Worker Rights and Recruitment." Geneva: ILO.

James, Phil, Steve Tombs, and David Whyte. 2013. "An Independent Review of British Health and Safety Regulation? From Common Sense to Non-sense." *Policy Studies* 34 (1): 36–52. doi:10.1080/01442872.2012.740240.

Jensen, Heather. 2013. "Unionization of Agricultural Workers in British Columbia." LLM, Faculty of Law, University of Victoria.

Jensen, Heather. 2014. "A History of Legal Exclusion Labour Relations Laws and British Columbia's Agricultural Workers, 1937–1975." *Journal of Canadian Labour Studies* 73: 67–96.

Jochimsen, Maren. 2003. "Integrating Vulnerability: On the Impact of Caring on Economic Theorizing." In *Towards a Feminist Philosophy of Economics*, edited by Drucilla K. Barker and Edith Kuiper, 231–246. London: Routledge.

Johnson, Kit. 2018. "Beauty and the Beast: Disney's Use of the Q and H-1B Visas." *NYU Journal of Law & Liberty* 12 (1): 124–150.

Johnstone, Stewart, and Tony Dobbins. 2021. "Employment Relations in the United Kingdom." In *International and Comparative Employment Relations: Global Crises and Institutional Responses*, edited by G. Bamber, F. L. Cooke, V. Doellgast, and C. F. Wright. London: Sage/Allen and Unwin.

Jokinen, Aniina, and Natalia Ollus. 2019. *Shady Business: Uncovering the Business Model of Labour Exploitation*. Sofia: Center for the Study of Democracy.

Kahn-Freund, Otto. 1931. *Das Soziale Ideal Des Reichsarbeitsgerichts*. Mannheim: Bensheimer.

Kahn-Freund, Otto. 1981. *Labour Law and Politics in the Weimar Republic*. Edited by R. Lewis and J. Clark. Oxford: Basil Blackwell.

Kalayaan. 2013. "Slavery by Another Name: The Tied Migrant Domestic Worker Visa." Kalayaan Justice for Migrant Domestic Workers, London. https://www.empowerwomen.org/en/resources/documents/2013/11/slavery-by-another-name-the-tied-migrant-domestic-worker-visa?lang=en.

Karp, Paul. 2021. "Coalition Abandons Crackdown on Wage Theft as Senate Passes Gutted Industrial Relations Bill." *The Guardian*, 18 March.

Katz, Harry C. 1993. "The Decentralization of Collective Bargaining: A Literature Review and Comparative Analysis." *International Labor Review* 47: 3–22.

Katz, Harry C., and Alexander J. S. Colvin. 2016. "Employment Relations in the United States." In *International and Comparative Employment Relations: National Regulation, Global Challenges*, edited by G. Bamber, R. D. Lansbury, N. Wailes, and C. F. Wright, 48–74. London: Sage/Allen and Unwin.

Katz, Harry C., and Alexander J. S. Colvin. 2021. "Employment Relations in Canada." In *International and Comparative Employment Relations*, edited by G. Bamber, F. L. Cooke, V. Doellgast, and C. F. Wright. London: Sage.

Katznelson, Ira. 1976. *Black Men, White Cities: Race, Politics, and Migration in the United States, 1900–1930, and Britain, 1948–1968*. Oxford: Oxford University Press.

Keck, Thomas. 2017. "A Qualitative and Multi-Method Approach to Collecting and Sharing Data on Constitutional Courts." SSRN. https://ssrn.com/abstract=2640106 or http://dx.doi.org/10.2139/ssrn.2640106.

Kingsford Legal Centre, Redfern Legal Centre, Women's Legal Service NSW, and National Association of Community Legal Centres. 2019. "#Metoo: Legal Responses to Sexual Harassment at Work." Sydney.

Kitroeff, Natalie. 2017. "Officials Say Immigration Agents Showed Up at Labor Dispute Proceedings. California Wants Them Out." *Los Angeles Times*, 3 August. https://www.latimes.com/business/la-fi-ice-california-labor-20170802-story.html.

Kone, Zovanga. 2018. "Where Do Migrants Live in the UK." Oxford: Migration Observatory.

Kosny, Agnieszka, and Amy R. Allen. 2016. "Falling through the Cracks? An Analysis of Health and Safety Resources for Migrant Workers in Australia." *International Journal of Migration, Health and Social Care* 12 (2): 99–108. doi:10.1108/IJMHSC-03-2015-0008.

Kosny, Agnieszka, Ellen MacEachen, Marni Lifshen, Peter Smith, Gul Joya Jafri, Cynthia Neilson, Diana Pugliese, and John Shields. 2012. "Delicate Dances: Immigrant Workers' Experiences of Injury Reporting and Claim Filing." *Ethnicity & Health* 17 (3): 267–290. doi:10.1080/13557858.2011.614327.

Krivokapic-Skoko, B., and J. Collins. 2016. "Looking for Rural Idyll 'Down Under': International Immigrants in Rural Australia." *International Migration* 64: 153–163.

Krogstad, Jens Maneul, Jeffrey S. Passel, and D'Vera Cohn. 2017. "5 Facts about Illegal Immigration in the U.S." Pew Research Centre, Washington D.C.

Labor Commissioner's Office. 2020. "Wage Theft Is a Crime." https://www.dir.ca.gov/dlse/howtofilewageclaim.htm.

Layton-Henry, Zig. 1990. *The Political Rights of Migrant Workers in Western Europe*. London: Sage.

Legal Aid at Work. 2020. "Employment Rights of Undocumented Workers." Legal Aid at Work, San Francisco, CA.

Legislative Analyst's Office. 2017. "Increased Staffing for Labor Standards Enforcement." Legislative Analyst's Office, Sacramento, CA.

LeBaron, Genevieve, and Nicola Phillips. 2019. "States and the Political Economy of Unfree Labour." *New Political Economy* 24 (1): 1–21.

Lee, Jennifer J., and Annie Smith. 2019. "Regulating Wage Theft." *Washington Law Review* 94 (2): 759–822.

Lewis, R. 1979. "Kahn-Freund and Labour Law: An Outline Critique." *Industrial Law Journal* 8: 202–221.

Li, Yao-Tai. 2015. "Constituting Co-Ethnic Exploitation: The Economic and Cultural Meanings of Cash-in-Hand Jobs for Ethnic Chinese Migrants in Australia." *Critical Sociology* 43: 919–932.

Lynch, Luara. 2015. "Migrant Worker Crash Survivor Juan Ariza Closer to Residency." CBC News. https://www.cbc.ca/news/canada/migrant-worker-crash-survivor-juan-ariza-closer-to-residency-1.3052180.

Linder, Marc. 1987. "Farm Workers and the Fair Labor Standards Act: Racial Discrimination in the New Deal." *Texas Law Review* 65 (7): 1335–1393.

Lopez, David, and Cynthia Feliciano. 2000. "Who Does What? California's Emerging Plural Labor Force." In *Organizing Immigrants: The Challenge for Unions in Contemporary California.*, edited by Ruth Milkman, 25–48. Ithaca, NY: Cornell University Press.

López, Gustavo, and Kristen Bialik. 2017. "Key Findings about U.S. Immigrants," Pew Research Centre, Washington, D.C. https://www.california-mexicocenter.org/key-findings-about-u-s-immigrants/.

Lopez, Mark Hugo, Jeffrey S. Passel, and D'Vera Cohn. 2021. "Key Facts about the Changing U.S. Unauthorized Immigrant Population." Pew Research Centre, Washington, D.C.

Love, Susan. 2021. "Migrant Amnesties: What Has Australia Done in the Past?" Australian Parliament House, Canberra. https://www.aph.gov.au/About_Parliament/Parliamentary_Departments/Parliamentary_Library/FlagPost/2021/April/Migrant_amnesties.

Lowell, B. Lindsay, and Johanna Avato. 2014. "The Wages of Skilled Temporary Migrants: Effects of Visa Pathways and Job Portability." *International Migration* 52: 85–98.

Malveaux, Suzette M. 2017. "The Modern Class Action Rule: Its Civil Rights Roots and Relevance Today." 66, *Kansas Law Review*, 325-295.

Mannetje, A. 't., and H. Kromhout. 2013. "The Use of Occupation and Industry Classifications in General Population Studies." *International Epidemiological Association* 32: 419–428.

Mansour, Julia. 2012. "Consolidation of Australia's Anti-Discrimination Law." *Griffith Law Review* 21 (2): 533–554.

Mantouvalou, Virginia. 2012. "Human Rights for Precarious Workers: The Legislative Precariousness of Domestic Workers." *Comparative Labor Law and Policy Journal* 34: 133.

Mantouvalou, Virginia. 2015. "Am I Free Now? Overseas Domestic Workers in Slavery." *Journal of Law and Society* 42 (3): 329–357.

Marsden, Sarah. 2009. "The New Precariousness: Temporary Migrants and the Law in Canada." *Canadian Journal of Law and Society* 27: 209–229.

Marsden, Sarah. 2018. *Enforcing Exclusion: Precarious Migrants and the Law in Canada*. Vancouver: UBC Press.

Martin, Phillip. 1983. "A Comparison of California's ALRA and the Federal NLRA." *California Agriculture*, July–August: 6–8.

Martin, Phillip. 2003. *Promise Unfulfilled: Unions, Immigration, and the Farm Workers*. Ithaca, NY: ILR.

Martinello, Felice. 1996. "Correlates of Certification Application Success in British Columbia, Saskatchewan, and Manitoba." *Relations Industrielles* 51: 544–562.

Martinello, Felice. 2000. "Mr. Harris, Mr. Rae and Union Activity in Ontario." *Canadian Public Policy* 26: 17–33.

Marx, Karl. (1867) 1887. *Capital: A Critique of Political Economy*. Vol. 1: *The Process of Production of Capital*. Moscow: Progress Publishers.

Mayeri, Serena. 2015. "Intersectionality and Title VII: A Brief (Pre-)History." *Boston University Law Review* 95: 713–731.

McCallum, Ron. 2007. "Convergences and/or Divergences of Labor Law Systems: The View from Australia." *Comparative Labor Law and Policy Journal* 48: 131–153.

McClelland, Keith. 1987. "Time to Work, Time to Live: Some Aspects of Work and Reformation of Class in Britain, 1859–1880." In *The Historical Meanings of Work*, edited by Patrick Joyce, 180–209. Cambridge: Cambridge University Press.

McLeod, Kim Vanessa. 2019. "Understanding Regulatory Workplace Safety Inspections in British Columbia, Canada: Theory and Evaluation." University of British Columbia. open.library.ubc.ca.

McGregor, Joann. 2007. "'Joining the BBC (British Bottom Cleaners)': Zimbabwean Migrants and the UK Care Industry." *Journal of Ethnic and Migration Studies* 33 (5): 801–824. doi:10.1080/13691830701359249.

McLaren, Arlene Tigar, and Isabel Dyck. 2004. "Mothering, Human Capital and the 'Ideal Immigrant.'" *Women's Studies International Forum* 27: 41–53.

McLaughlin, C., and C. F. Wright. 2018. "The Role of Ideas in Understanding Industrial Relations Policy Change in Liberal Market Economies." *Industrial Relations: A Journal of Economy and Society* 57: 568–610.

Meiksins Wood, Ellen. 2009. *Democracy against Capitalism: Renewing Historical Materialism*. New York: Cambridge University Press.

Mendoza, José Jorge. 2014. "Discrimination and the Presumptive Rights of Immigrants." *Critical Philosophy of Race* 2: 68–83.

Mesriani, Rodney. 2021. "California's Employment and Labor Laws: Why Are They Better?" HG Legal Resources. https://www.hg.org/legal-articles/california-s-employment-and-labor-laws-why-are-they-better-29545.

Metcalfe, David. 2018. "United Kingdom Labour Market Enforcement Strategy." London: Director of Labour Market Enforcement.

Metcalf, David. 2019. "Executive Summary: United Kingdom Labour Market Enforcement Strategy 2019/2020." London: Director of Labour Market Enforcement.

Meardi, Guglielmo, Antonio Martín, and Mariona Lozano Riera. 2012. "Constructing Uncertainty: Unions and Migrant Labour in Construction in Spain and the UK." *Journal of Industrial Relations* 54 (1): 5–21.

Migrant Worker Taskforce. 2019. "Report of the Migrant Worker Rights Taskforce." Final Report, Attorney General's Department, Canberra. https://www.ag.gov.au/industrial-relations/publications/report-migrant-workers-taskforce.

Migration Advisory Committee. 2014. "Migrants in Low-Skilled Work: The Growth of EU and Non-EU Labour in Low-Skilled Jobs and Its Impact on the UK." London: MAC.

Miles, R., and A. Phizacklea. 1977. "Class, Race, Ethnicity and Political Action." *Political Studies* 25 (4): 491–507.

Milkman, Ruth. 2000. *Organizing Immigrants: The Challenge for Unions in Contemporary California*. Ithaca, NY: ILR Press and Cornell University Press.

Milkman, Ruth. 2011. "Immigrant Workers, Precarious Work, and the US Labor Movement." *Globalizations* 8 (3): 361–372.

Mill, J. S. 1874. *System of Logic*. New York: Harper & Brothers.

Miller, M. J. 1981. *Foreign Workers in Western Europe: An Emerging Political Force*. New York: Praeger.

Mills, Charles. 2003. *From Class to Race: Essays in White Marxism and Black Radicalism*. Lanham, MD: Rowman and Littlefield.

Ministry of Energy and Mines, British Columbia. 2017. "Health, Safety and Reclamation Code for Mines in British Columbia." Victoria: Ministry of Energy and Mines.

Ministry of Energy, Mines, and Resources Petroleum, British Columbia. 2020. "Mines Act Updates to Improve Permitting, Regulation in B.C." BC Government News, 22 June. https://news.gov.bc.ca/releases/2020EMPR0022-001117.

Ministry of Labour, Ontario. 2017. "Safe at Work Ontario." https://www.ontario.ca/document/occupational-health-and-safety-ontario-april-2016-march-2017/safe-work-ontario.

Monaghan, Karon. 2007. *Equality Law*. Oxford: Oxford University Press.

Monaghan, Karon. 2013. *Equality Law*. 2nd ed. Oxford: Oxford University Press.

Moore, Heather. 2019. "Service or Servitude: A Study of Trafficking for Domestic Work in Australia." Mercy Foundation, Sydney.

Moss, J. 2015. "Migrant Domestic Workers, the National Minimum Wage and the 'Family Worker' Concept." In *Au Pairs' Lives in Global Context: Sisters or Servants?*, edited by Rosie Cox, 70–83. London: Palgrave Macmillan.

Motomura, Hiroshi. 2014. *Immigration Outside the Law*. New York: Oxford University Press.

Motomura, Hiroshi. 2018. *Arguing about Sanctuary*. Rochester, NY: Social Science Research Network.

Mundlak, G., and H. Shamir. 2014. "Organizing Migrant Care Workers in Israel: Industrial Citizenship and the Trade Union Option." *International Labour Review* 153: 93–116.

National Union of Workers. 2019. "Farm Workers Speak Out: 650 Farm Workers Speak Out on Exploitation, Solutions and the Big Supermarkets." National Union of Workers, Australia.

Northern Territory WorkSafe. 2019. "Work Health Authority Annual Report 2018–2019." Northern Territory Government. https://worksafe.nt.gov.au/__data/assets/pdf_file/0005/883868/Work-Health-Authority-Annual-Report-2018-19-.pdf.

Nous Group. 2018. "Independent Review of the ACT's Work Safety Compliance Infrastructure, Policies, and Procedures: Final Report." https://apo.org.au/sites/default/files/resource-files/2018-08/apo-nid305141.pdf.

O'Connor, Niall. 2020. "'Unchartered' Waters: Fundamental Rights, Brexit and the (Re)Constitution of the Employment Law Hierarchy of Norms." *European Labour Law Journal* 12 (1): 52–82.

Office for National Statistics. 2015. "Crime Statistics, 2013–2014: Focus on Violent Crime and Sexual Offences." https://www.ons.gov.uk/peoplepopulationandcommunity/crimeandjustice/compendium/focusonviolentcrimeandsexualoffences/2015-02-12.

Office for National Statistics. 2022. *Estimates of Labour Market Activity by Nationality and Country of Birth.* https://www.ons.gov.uk/employmentandlabourmarket/peopleinwork/employmentandemployeetypes/datasets/a12employmentunemploymentandeconomicinactivitybynationalityandcountryofbirth.

Ontario Construction Secretariat. 2008. Underground Economy in Construction – It Costs Us All. Ontario Construction Secretariat.

Ontario Government. 2019. "Archived: Occupational Health and Safety in Ontario April 2016–March 2017." https://www.ontario.ca/document/occupational-health-and-safety-ontario-april-2016-march-2017.

Ontario Government. 2020. "Government of Ontario Employee and Organization Directory (Info-Go)." https://www.infogo.gov.on.ca/infogo/.

Ontiveros, Maria. 2009. "Labor Coalition Challenges to Governmental Action: Defending the Civil Rights of Low Wage Workers." *University of Chicago Legal Forum* 1 (5): 103–146.

Oppenheimer, David Benjamin, Sheila R. Foster, Sora Y. Han, and Richard T. Ford. 2020. *Comparative Equality and Anti-Discrimination Law.* Cheltenham: Edward Elgar.

Organisation for Economic Cooperation and Development. 2014. "Indicators of Employment Protection." Paris: OECD.

Organisation for Economic Cooperation and Development. 2018. "OECD Economic Surveys in Australia." Paris: OECD.

Organisation for Economic Cooperation and Development. 2019. "OECD Indicators of Employment Protection." Paris: OECD.

Organisation for Economic Cooperation and Development. 2021a. "OECD Employment Outlook 2020: Worker Security and the COVID-19 Crisis." Paris: OECD.

Organisation for Economic Cooperation and Development. 2021b. "Real Minimum Wages." In *OECD Labor Statistics.* Paris: OECD. https://stats.oecd.org/index.aspx?DataSetCode=RMW.

Organisation for Economic Cooperation and Development. 2022. "OECD Indicators of Employment Protection, Strictness of Dismissal Protection, Individual and Collective Dismissals (Regular Contracts)." Paris: OECD. https://www.oecd.org/els/emp/oecdindicatorsofemploymentprotection.htm.

Organisation for Economic Cooperation and Development, Giuseppe Nicoletti, Stefano Scarpetta, and Olivier Boylaud. 2014. "Summary Indicators of Product Market Regulation with an Extension to Employment Protection Legislation." Paris: OECD.

Orrenius, Pia M., and Madeline Zavodny. 2012. "The Economics of US Immigration Policy." *Journal of Policy Analysis and Management* 31 (4): 948–956.

Orrenius, Pia M., and Madeline Zavodny. 2015. "The Impact of Temporary Protected Status on Immigrants' Labor Market Outcomes." *American Economic Review* 105: 576–580.

Page, Anthony. 2011. "Rational Dissent, Enlightenment and the Abolition of the British Slave Trade." *Historical Journal* 54 (3): 741–772.

Parker, Sandra. 2019. "Address by the Fair Work Ombudsman." Presented at the Annual Policy-Influence-Reform Conference. https://www.fairwork.gov.au/sites/default/files/migration/764/aig-pir-speech-2019.pdf.

Parsons, Preston. 2019. "Changes to B.C.'s Employment Standards Act." Overholt Law, 21 August. https://www.overholtlawyers.com/blog/2019/08/changes-to-bcs-employment-standards-act.shtml.

Passel, Jeffrey S., and D'Vera Cohn. 2016. "Size of U.S. Unauthorized Immigrant Workforce Stable after the Great Recession." Washington, D.C.: Pew Research Centre.

Patty, Anna. 2018. "Unions Watchdog Gets Funding Boost, but Fair Wages Enforcer Misses Out." *Sydney Morning Herald*, 9 May. https://www.smh.com.au/business/workplace/unions-watchdog-gets-funding-boost-but-fair-wages-enforcer-misses-out-20180509-p4zea5.html.

Pendlebury. 2015. "Largest Ever Court Imposed Fine for Breaching 457 Visa Sponsorship Obligations." https://pendlebury.com.au/largest-ever-court-imposed-fine-for-breaching-457-visa-sponsorship-obligations/.

Perrins, B., and C. Osman. 2001. *Harvey on Industrial Relations and Employment Law*. London: Lexis Nexis.

Petrou, Kirstie, and John Connell. 2019. "Overcoming Precarity? Social Media, Agency and Ni-Vanuatu Seasonal Workers in Australia." *Journal of Australian Political Economy* 84: 116–146.

Pew Research Centre, S. Jeffrey Passel, and D'Vera Cohn. 2016. *Overall Number of U.S. Unauthorized Immigrants Holds Steady since 2009*. Washington, D.C.: Pew Research Centre.

Piore, Michael J. 1979. *Birds of Passage: Migrant Labor and Industrial Societies*. New York: Cambridge University Press.

Piore, Michael J., and Sean Safford. 2006. "Changing Regimes of Workplace Governance, Shifting Axes of Social Mobilization, and the Challenge to Industrial Relations Theory." *Industrial Relations: A Journal of Economy and Society* 45 (3): 299–325.

Pitti, Stephen J. 2002. *The Devil in Silicon Valley: Northern California, Race, and Mexican Americans*. Princeton, NJ: Princeton University Press.

Polak, Polly. 2019. "Brexit and the Balance of Free Movement and Social Justice." In *On Brexit: Law, Justices and Injustices*, edited by Tawhida Ahmed and Elaine Fahey, 142–157. Cheltenham: Edward Elgar.

Power, Marilyn. 2004. "Social Provisioning as a Starting Point for Feminist Economics." *Feminist Economics* 10 (3): 3–19.

Prasad, V. 2018. "If Anyone Is Listening, #Metoo: Breaking the Culture of Silence around Sexual Abuse through Regulating Non-Disclosure Agreements and Secret Settlements." *Boston College Law Review* 59: 2507–2550.

Preibisch, Kerry, and Gerardo Otero. 2014. "Does Citizenship Status Matter in Canadian Agriculture? Workplace Health and Safety for Migrant and Immigrant Laborers." *Rural Sociology* 79 (2): 174–199. doi:10.1111/ruso.12043.

Przeworski, A., and H. Teune. 1970. *The Logic of Comparative Social Inquiry*. New York: John Wiley.

Quinlan, Michael. 1979. "Australian Trade Unions and Post-war Immigration: Attitudes and Responses." *Journal of Industrial Relations* 21 (3, September): 265–280.

Quinlan, M., and C. Lever-Tracy. 1988. *A Divided Working Class: Ethnic Segmentation and Industrial Conflict in Australia*. London: Routledge and Kegan Paul.

Ram, M., O. Edwards, G. Meardi, T. Jones, S. Doldor, E. Kispeter, and M. Villaries-Varela. 2017. "Non-compliance and the National Living Wage: Case Study Evidence from Ethnic Minority and Migrant-Owned Businesses." London: Low Pay Commission.

Ram, Monder, Paul Edwards, Guglielmo Meardi, Trevor Jones, and Sabina Doldor. 2019. "The Roots of Informal Responses to Regulatory Change: Non-compliant Small Firms and the National Living Wage." *British Journal of Management* 1–16.

Redfern Legal Centre. 2018. "Law in Action, Vulnerable Workers." Blog. https://rlc.org.au/article/law-action-vulnerable-workers.

Rees, Neil, Simon Rice, and Allen Dominique. 2018. *Australian Anti-Discrimination and Equal Opportunity Law* Leichhardt: Federation Press.

Reid-Musson, Emily, Michelle Buckley, and Bridget Anderson. 2015. "Building Migrant Precarity: Employment, Citizenship and Skill in Toronto and London's Construction Sectors." http://s3.amazonaws.com/migrants_heroku_production/datas/2417/Building_Migrant_Precarity_original.pdf?1500327980.

Reilly, A. 2015. "Low-Cost Labour or Cultural Exchange? Reforming the Working Holiday Visa Programme." *Economic and Labour Relations Review* 26 (3): 74–489.

Reilly, Alexander, and Joanna Howe. 2019. "Australia's Future Horticultural Workforce: Assessing the Agricultural Visa Concept." *Journal of Australian Political Economy* 84: 89–115.

Reilly, A., J. Howe, D. van de Broek, and C. F. Wright. 2018. "Working Holiday Makers in Australian Horticulture: Labour Market Effect, Exploitation and Avenues for Reform." *Griffith Law Review* 27 (1): 99–130.

Rioux, Sébastien, Genevieve LeBaron, and Peter J. Verovšek. 2020. "Capitalism and Unfree Labor: A Review of Marxist Perspectives on Modern Slavery." *Review of International Political Economy* 27 (3): 709–731. doi:10.1080/09692290.2019.1650094.

Robinson, Caroline. 2014. "Working Paper 01: Preventing Trafficking for Labour Exploitation." Focus on Labour Exploitation, London. https://www.labourexploitation.org/publications/flex-working-paper-01-prevention-trafficking-labour-exploitation.

Robinson, Caroline. 2015. "Policy and Practice: Claiming Space for Labour Rights within the United Kingdom Modern Slavery Crusade." *Anti-Trafficking Review* (5): 129–143. https://www.antitraffickingreview.org/index.php/atrjournal/issue/view/13.

Robinson, Cedric J., and Robin D. G. Kelley. 2000. *Black Marxism: The Making of the Black Radical Tradition*. Chapel Hill: University of North Carolina Press.

Robinson, Cedric J., and Robin D. G. Kelley. 2015. "Policy and Practice: Claiming Space for Labour Rights within the United Kingdom Modern Slavery Crusade." *Anti-Trafficking Review* (5): 129–143.

Robinson, Emily, Camilla Schofield, Florence Sutcliffe-Braithwaite, and Natalie Thomlinson. 2017. "Telling Stories about Post-War Britain: Popular Individualism and the 'Crisis' of the 1970s." *Twentieth Century British History* 28 (2): 268–304.

Rodgers, Lisa. 2017. "Race Discrimination and Migrant Domestic Workers: A Legal Loophole." *International Labor Rights Case Law Journal* 3 (1): 116–120.

Roemer, John E. 1982. *A General Theory of Exploitation and Class*. Cambridge, MA: Harvard University Press.

Rosenthal, P., and A. Budjanovcanin. 2011. "Sexual Harassment Judgments by British Employment Tribunals 1995–2005: Implications for Claimants and Their Advocates." *British Journal of Industrial Relations* 49: 236–257.

Rosewarne, Stuart. 2019. "The Structural Transformation of Australian Agriculture: Globalisation, Corporatisation and the Devalorisation of Labour." *Journal of Australian Political Economy* 84: 175–218.

Ruhs, M. 2013. *The Price of Rights: Regulating International Labor Migration*. Princeton, NJ: Princeton University Press.

Rusev, Atanas, and Anton Kojouharov. 2019. "Shady Business: Uncovering the Business Model of Labour Exploitation." Center for the Study of Democracy, Sofia.

Sabo, Samantha, Susan Shaw, Maia Ingram, Nicolette Teufel-Shone, Scott Carvajal, Jill Guernsey de Zapien, Cecilia Rosales, Flor Redondo, Gina Garia, and Raquel Rubio-Goldsmith. 2014. Everyday violence, structural racism and mistreatment at the US-Mexico border *Social Science & Medicine* 109: 66–74.

SafeWork, Australia. 2020. "Comparative Performance Monitoring Report." Canberra: SafeWork Australia.

SafeWork, South Australia. 2019. "2018–19 Annual Activity Report." Adelaide: Government of South Australia. https://www.safework.sa.gov.au/__data/assets/pdf_file/0020/145433/SafeWork-SA-Annual-Activity-Report.pdf.

Sample, Ruth. 2016. "Exploitation and Consequentialism." *Southern Journal of Philosophy* 54 (S1): 66–91.

Samuel, Adam. 2019. "U.S. Class Actions v. U.K. Mass Claims." *Alternatives* 37: 153–155.

Samuelson, Paul A. 1971. "Understanding the Marxian Notion of Exploitation: A Summary of the So-Called Transformation Problem between Marxian Values and Competitive Prices." *Journal of Economic Literature* 9 (2): 399–431.

Sargeant, Malcolm, and Eric Tucker. 2009. "Layers of Vulnerability in Occupational Safety and Health for Migrant Workers: Case Studies from Canada and the UK." *Policy and Practice in Health and Safety* 7 (2): 51–73. doi:10.1080/14774003.2009.11667734.

Schenker, Marc. B., Xóchitl Castañeda, and Alfonso Rodriguez-Lainz. 2014. *Migration and Health: A Research Methods Handbook*. Berkeley: University of California Press.

Scott, Sam. 2015. "Making the Case for Temporary Migrant Worker Programmes: Evidence from the UK's Rural Guestworker ('SAWS') Scheme." *Journal of Rural Studies* 40: 1.

Scott, Sam. 2017. *Labour Exploitation and Work-Based Harm*. Bristol: Polity Press.

Segrave, M. 2017. "Temporary Migration and Family Violence: An Analysis of Victimisation, Vulnerability and Support." Melbourne: School of Social Sciences, Monash University.

Selwyn, Benjamin, and Satoshi Miyamura. 2014. "Class Struggle or Embedded Markets? Marx, Polanyi and the Meanings and Possibilities of Social Transformation." *New Political Economy* 19 (5): 639–661. doi:10.1080/13563467.2013.844117.

Shachar, Ayelet. 2007. "The Shifting Border of Immigration Regulation." *Stanford Journal of Civil Rights and Civil Liberties* 3: 165–194.

Shapiro, C. 2008. "Coding Complexity: Bringing Law to the Empirical Analysis of the Supreme Court." *Hastings Law Journal* 60: 477–536.

Sherriff, Barry. 2018. "Report to the WorkCover Tasmania Board: Review of the Work Health and Safety Regulator." Sherriff Consulting, Melbourne.

Shin, Melissa, and Rebecca Koenig. 2018. "Interactive Map: Best States for Worker Rights: States along the West Coast and in the Northeast Tend to Have Laws That Favor Workers." *U.S. News and World Report*, 28 August. https://money.usnews.com/careers/salaries-and-benefits/articles/2018-08-28/interactive-map-best-states-for-worker-rights.

Sitkin, Lea. 2017. "The State's Contradictory Response to the Exploitation of Immigrant Workers: The UK Case." In *The Routledge Handbook on Crime and International Migration*, edited by Sharon Pickering and Julie Ham, 223–236. Milton Park, UK: Routledge.

Skrivankova, Klara. 2017. "Defining Exploitation in the Context of Trafficking: What Is a Crime and What Is Not." In *Routledge Handbook of Human Trafficking*, edited by Ryszard Piotrowicz, Conny Rijken, and Baerbel Heide Uhl, 109–119. London: Routledge.

Smith, Rebecca, Ana Avendaño, and Julie Martinez Ortega. 2009. "Iced Out: How Immigration Enforcement Has Interfered with Workers' Rights." Washington, D.C.: AFL-CIO.

Smith, Sandy. 2018. "OSHA Inspectors and the Workplace: Death by Attrition." *EHS Today*, 11 January.

Songer, D., D. Smith, and R. S. Sheehan. 1989. "Nonpublication in the Eleventh Circuit: An Empirical Analysis." *Flordia State University Law Review* 16: 963–984.

Soskice, David. 1999. "Divergent Production Regimes: Coordinated and Uncoordinated Market Economies in the 1980s and 1990s." In *Continuity and Change in Contemporary Capitalism*, edited by Herbert Kitschelt, Peter Lange, Gary Marks, and John D. Stephens, 101–134. New York: Cambridge University Press.

Spaeth, H., L. Epstein, T. Ruger, S. Benesh, J. Segel, and A. D. Martin. 2015. "Supreme Court Database Code Book brick_2015_01." http://Supremecourtdatabase.org.

Spaeth, Harold J., and Jeffrey A. Segal. 2001. *Majority Rule or Minority Will: Adherence to Precedent on the U.S. Supreme Court*. New York: Cambridge University Press.

Spinks, Harriet, and Henry Sherrell. 2019. "Immigration: Budget Review 2019-20 Index." Parliamentary Library Services, Australian Federal Parliament, Canberra.

Stasiulis, D., and A. B. Bakan. 2005. *Negotiating Citizenship: Migrant Women in Canada and the Global System*. Toronto: Toronto University Press.

Statistics Canada. 2019. *The Labour Force in Canada and Its Regions: Projections to 2036*. Edited by Laurent Martel. Ottawa: Statistics Canada.

Statistics Canada. 2022a. "Table 14-10-0083-01: Labour Force Characteristics by Immigrant Status, Annual," Statistics Canada, Ottawa. https://www150.statcan.gc.ca/t1/tbl1/en/tv.action?pid=1410008301.

Statistics Canada. 2022b. "Table: 14-10-0129-01: Union Status by Geography" (formerly CANSIM 282-0220). Statistics Canada, Ottawa.

Steinberg, Kamini. 2009. "The New Ontario Human Rights Code: Implications for an Intersectional Approach to Human Rights Claims." Master's of Law, Faculty of Law, University of Toronto.

Steiner, Hillel. 1984. "A Liberal Theory of Exploitation." *Ethics* 94: 225–241.

Strauss, Kendra, and Siobhán McGrath. 2017. "Temporary Migration, Precarious Employment and Unfree Labour Relations: Exploring the 'Continuum of Exploitation' in Canada's Temporary Foreign Worker Program." *Geoforum* 78: 199–208.

Street, Harry, Geoffrey Howe, and Geoffrey Bindman. 1967. "Street Report on Anti-Discrimination Legislation 1967 Political and Economic Planning."

Street, Harry, Geoffrey Howe, and Geoffrey Bindman. 1973. "Anti-Discrimination Legislation: The Street Report." London: Political and Economic Planning, sponsored by the Race Relations Board and the National Committee for Commonwealth Immigrants.

Stueck, Wendy. 2012. "Minister's Comments on Chinese Miners Crops Up in Court." *Globe and Mail*, 21 November.

Stueck, Wendy. 2013. "Decision Looms in Case of Chinese Workers in B.C. Coal Mine." *Globe and Mail Online*, 8 April.

Swaminathan, Nikhil. 2017. "Inside the Growing Guest Worker Program: Trapping Indian Students in Virtual Servitude." *Mother Jones*, September. https://www.motherjones.com/politics/2017/09/inside-the-growing-guest-worker-program-trapping-indian-students-in-virtual-servitude.

Tahirih Justice Centre. 2017. "2017 Advocate and Legal Service Survey Regarding Immigrant Survivors." https://www.tahirih.org/pubs/key-findings-2017-advocate-and-legal-service-survey-regarding-immigrant-survivors/.

Tan, Yan, and Laurence H. Lester. 2012. "Labour Market and Economic Impacts of International Working Holiday Temporary Migrants to Australia." *Population, Space and Place* 18 (3): 359–383. doi:10.1002/psp.674.

Tan, Yan, Sue Richardson, Laurence Lester, Tracy Bai, and Lulu Sun. 2009. "Evaluation of Australia's Working Holiday Maker (WHM) Program." Canberra: Department of Immigration and Citizenship.

Taras, D., and S. Walsworth. 2016. "Employment Relations in Canada." In *International and Comparative Employment Relations: National Regulation, Global Challenges*, edited by G. Bamber, R. D. Lansbury, N. Wailes, and C. F. Wright, 75–102. London: Sage/Allen and Unwin.

Tataryn, Anastasia. 2019. "Irregular Migrants at Work and the Groundless Legal Subject." In *Law, Labour and the Humanities: Contemporary European Perspectives*, edited by Tiziano Toracca and Angela Condello, 133–144. London: Routledge.

Taylor, Marcus, and Sébastien Rioux. 2018. *Global Labour Studies*. Cambridge, UK: Polity.

Tham, Joo-Cheong. 2015. "The Impact of Australia's Temporary Work Visa Program on the Australian Labour Market and on the Temporary Work Visa Holders."Canberra: Senate Education and Employment References Committee.

Tham, J. C., and I. Campbell. 2011. "Temporary Migrant Labour in Australia: The 457 Visa Scheme and Challenges for Labour Regulation." Melbourne: Melbourne Centre for Employment and Labour Relations Law, University of Melbourne.

Tham, Joo-Cheong, Iain Campbell, and Martina Boese. 2016. "Why Is Labour Protection for Temporary Migrant Workers So Fraught?" In *Temporary Labour Migration in the Global Era: The Regulatory Challenges*, edited by Joanna Howe and Rosemary Owens, 173–200. London: Hart.

Thomas, Mark P. 2016. "Producing and Contesting 'Unfree Labour' through the Seasonal Agricultural Worker Program." In *Unfree Labour? Struggles of Migrant and Immigrant Workers in Canada*, edited by Aziz Choudry and Adrian A. Smith, 21–36. Oakland, CA: PM Press.

Thompson, E. P. 1975. *Whigs and Hunters: Origins of the Black Act*. London: Penguin Books.

Thurow, Lester. 1978. "Psychic Income: Useful or Useless?" *American Economic Review* 68 (2): 142–145.

Tichenor, Daniel. 2002. *Dividing Lines: The Politics of Immigration Control in America*. Princeton, NJ: Princeton University Press.

Toews, Travis. 2019. "Fiscal Plan: A Plan for Jobs and the Economy, 2019–2023." Emondton, Alberta: Alberta Treasury Board and Finance. https://open.alberta.ca/dataset/3d732c88-68b0-4328-9e52-5d3273527204/resource/2b82a075-f8c2-4586-a2d8-3ce8528a24e1/download/budget-2019-fiscal-plan-2019-23.pdf.

Tombs, Steve, and David Whyte. 2010. "A Deadly Consensus: Worker Safety and Regulatory Degradation under New Labour. (Author abstract) (Report)." *British Journal of Criminology* 50 (1): 46.

Trivedi, R. 2018. "Restoring a Willingness to Act: Identifying and Remedying the Harm to Authorized Employees Ignored under Hoffman Plastics." *University of Michigan Journal of Law Reform* 51 (2): 357–406.

Tronto, Joan. 1993. *Moral Boundaries: A Political Argument for an Ethic of Care*. Routledge.

Tuck, R., B. Criddle, and S. Brittenden. 2013. *Labor Law Highlights 2013*. Liverpool: Institute of Employment Rights.

Tucker, Eric. 2012. "Farm Worker Exceptionalism: Past, Present, and the Post-Fraser Failure." In *Constitutional Labour Rights in Canada: Farm Workers and the Fraser Case*, edited by Fay Faraday, Judy Fudge and Eric Tucker. Toronto: Irwin Law, 30–56.

Tucker, Eric. 2014. "Shall Wagnerism Have No Dominion?" *Osgoode Hall Law School of York University: Osgoode Digital Commons*. York University.

Tucker, Eric, Judy Fudge, and Leah Vosko. 2002. "The Legal Concept of Employment: Marginalizing Workers." Commissioned Reports, Studies and Public Policy Documents:

Report for the Law Commission of Canada, 1–138, https://digitalcommons.osgoode.yorku.ca/reports/127/.

Tucker, Eric, Leah Vosko, Rebecca Casey, Mark Thomas, John Grundy, and Andrea Noack. 2019. "Carrying Little Sticks: Is There a 'Deterrence Gap' in Employment Standards Enforcement in Ontario, Canada?" *International Journal of Comparative Labour Law* 35 (1): 1–30.

Tucker, Sean, and Anje Keefe. 2019. "2019 Report on Work Fatality and Injury Rates in Canada." University of Regina.

Tutt, Dylan, Sarah Pink, Andy R. J. Dainty, and Alistair Gibb. 2013. "'In the Air' and below the Horizon: Migrant Workers in UK Construction and the Practice-Based Nature of Learning and Communicating OHS." *Construction Management and Economics* 31 (6): 515–527. doi:10.1080/01446193.2012.756145.

Uggen, Christopher, and Amy Blackstone. 2004. "Sexual Harassment as a Gendered Expression of Power." *American Sociological Review* 69 (1): 64–92. doi:10.1177/000312240406900105.

U.K. Department for Business, Energy, and Industrial Strategy. 2019. "Government Has Launched Its First Holiday Pay Advertising Campaign," 12 March. https://www.gov.uk/government/news/government-has-launched-its-first-holiday-pay-advertising-campaign.

U.K. Department for Business, Energy, and Industrial Strategy. 2020. *National Living Wage and National Minimum Wage Government Evidence on Compliance and Enforcement 2018/19*. Department of Business, Energy and Industrial Strategy, London.

U.K. Health and Safety Executive. 2012. Annual Statistics Report for Great Britain, 2012–2013, available at https://www.hse.gov.uk/statistics/overall/hssh1213.pdf

U.K. Health and Safety Executive. 2016. "Health and Safety at Work: Summary Statistics for Great Britain 2016." HSE. https://qhse.support/index.htm?context=210.

U.K. Health and Safety Executive. 2018. "Health and Safety at Work: Summary Statistics for Great Britain 2018." HSE. https://qhse.support/index.htm?context=210.

U.K. Health and Safety Executive. 2019. "Health and Safety at Work: Summary Statistics for Great Britain 2019." HSE. https://qhse.support/index.htm?context=210.

U.K. Health and Safety Executive. 2020. "Agriculture: Migrant Workers." https://qhse.support/index.htm?context=210.

U.K. Home Office. 2020. "Main Estimates Memorandum (2019/20) for the Home Office." https://www.parliament.uk/globalassets/documents/commons-committees/home-affairs/estimates-memoranda-17-19/home-office-2019-20-main-estimate-memorandum.pdf.

U.K. Home Office, Department of Business, Innovation and Skills. 2016. "Tackling Exploitation in the Labour Market: Government Response." Report, January. Department of Business, Innovation and Skills, London.

Office for National Statistics. 2015. "Crime Statistics, 2013–2014: Focus on Violent Crime and Sexual Offences." https://www.ons.gov.uk/peoplepopulationandcommunity/crimeandjustice/compendium/focusonviolentcrimeandsexualoffences/2015-02-12.

Office for National Statistics. 2022. Estimates of Labour Market Activity by Nationality and Country of Birth. https://www.ons.gov.uk/employmentandlabourmarket/peopleinwork/employmentandemployeetypes/datasets/a12employmentunemploymentandeconomicinactivitybynationalityandcountryofbirth.

Ulloa, Jazmine, and John Myers. 2016. "In Historic Move, Gov. Jerry Brown Expands Overtime Pay for California Farmworkers." *Los Angeles Times*, 12 September.

UN Department of Economic and Social Affairs. 2008. *International Standard Industrial Classificaiton of All Economic Activities (ISIC), Rev 4*. New York: UNDESA.

Underhill, Elsa, Sherry Huang, Sohoon Yi, and Malcolm Rimmer. 2019. "Using Social Media to Improve Temporary Migrant Workers' Access to Information about Their Employment Rights." *Journal of Australian Political Economy* 84: 147–174.

Underhill, Elsa, and Malcolm Rimmer. 2015. "Itinerant Foreign Harvest Workers in Australia: The Impact of Precarious Employment on Occupational Safety and Health." *Policy and Practice in Health and Safety* 13 (2): 25–46. doi:10.1080/14774003.2015.11667816.

Underhill, Elsa, and Malcolm Rimmer. 2016. "Layered Vulnerability: Temporary Migrants in Australian Horticulture." *Journal of Industrial Relations* 58 (5): 608–626.

U.S. Bureau of Labor Statistics. 2018. "Nonfatal Occupational Injuries and Illnesses Data by Industry (SOII)." https://www.bls.gov/iif/oshstate.htm.

U.S. Department of Agriculture. 2020. "Farm Labor." https://www.nass.usda.gov/Surveys/Guide_to_NASS_Surveys/Farm_Labor/.

U.S. Department of Homeland Security. 2018. "Supplemental Table 1. Persons Obtaining Lawful Permanent Resident Status by State or Territory of Residence and Region and Country of Birth: Fiscal Year 2018." Washington D.C.: Department of Homeland Security.

U.S. Department of Labor. 2018. "Revised Memorandum of Understanding between the Departments of Homeland Security and Labor concerning Enforcemnet Activities at Worksites." Washington, D.C.: Department of Labor.

van den Broek, Diane, and Dimitria Groutsis. 2017. "Global Nursing and the Lived Experience of Migration Intermediaries." *Work, Employment and Society* 31 (5): 851–860.

van den Broek, D., W. Harvey, and D. Groutsis. 2016. "Commercial Migration Intermediaries and the Segmentation of Skilled Migrant Employment." *Work, Employment and Society* 30 (3): 523–534.

Velayutham, Selvaraj. 2013. "Precarious Experiences of Indians in Australia on 457 Temporary Work Visas." *Economic and Labour Relations Review* 24 (3): 340–361.

Veneziani, Bruno. 2009. "The Evolution of the Contract of Employment." In *The Making of Labour Law in Europe: A Comparative Study of Nine Countries up to 1945*, edited by Bob Hepple and Bruno Veneziani, 31–72. London: Hart.

Virdee, Satnam. 2014. *Racism, Class and the Racialized Other*. London: Palgrave Macmillan.

Virdee, Satnam, and Brendan McGeever. 2018. "Racism, Crisis, Brexit." *Ethnic and Racial Studies* 41 (10): 1802–1819.

Visser, Jelle. 2013. "Data Base on Institutional Characteristics of Trade Unions, Wage Setting, State Intervention and Social Pacts, 1960–2011 (ICTWSS)." Amsterdam Institute of Advanced Labour Studies, University of Amsterdam.

Vosko, Leah. 2013. "'Rights without Remedies': Enforcing Employment Standards in Ontario by Maximizing Voice among Workers in Precarious Jobs." *Osgoode Hall Law Journal* 50 (4): 845–874.

Vosko, Leah. 2014. "Tenuously Unionized: Temporary Migrant Workers and the Limits of Formal Mechanisms Designed to Promote Collective Bargaining in British Columbia, Canada." *Industrial Law Journal* 43 (4): 451–484.

Vosko, Leah. 2015. "Blacklisting as a Modality of Deportability: Mexico's Response to Circular Migrant Agricultural Workers' Pursuit of Collective Bargaining Rights in British Columbia, Canada." *Journal of Ethnic and Migration Studies* 42 (8): 1371–1387.

Vosko, Leah F. 2019a. *Disrupting Deportability: Transnational Workers Organize*. Ithaca, NY: Cornell University Press.

Vosko, Leah. 2019b. "Mapping the Enforcement Gap: Historical and Contemporary Dynamics." In *Closing the Enforcement Standards Gap*, edited by Leah Vosko, 3–56. Toronto: University of Toronto Press.

Vosko, Leah. 2019c. "A Tattered Quilt: Exemptions and Special Rules under Ontario's Employment Standards Act." *Canadian Employment and Labour Law Journal* 21 (2): 267–298.

Vosko, Leah, and Closing the Enforcement Gap Research Group. 2020. *Closing the Enforcement Gap: Improving Employment Standards Protections for People in Precarious Jobs*. Toronto: University of Toronto Press.

Vosko, L. F., A. M. Noack, and M. P. Thomas. 2016. "How Far Does the Employment Standards Act, 2000, Extend and What Are the Gaps in Coverage? An Empirical Analysis of Archival and Statistical Data." Toronto: Prepared for the Ontario Ministry of Labour to support the Changing Workplaces Review of 2015.

Vosko, Leah, and Mark Thomas. 2014. "Confronting the Employment Standards Enforcement Gap: Exploring the Potential for Union Engagement with Employment Law in Ontario, Canada." *Journal of Industrial Relations* 56 (5): 631.

Vosko, Leah, Eric Tucker, and Rebecca Casey. 2019. "Enforcing Employment Standards for Migrant Agricultural Workers in Ontario: Exposing Underexplored Layers of Vulnerability." *International Journal of Labour Law and Industrial Relations* 35 (2): 227–254.

Waddington, Jeremy. 2016. "Employment Relations in the United Kingdom." In *International and Comparative Employment Relations: National Regulation, Global Challenges*, edited by G. Bamber, R. D. Lansbury, N. Wailes, and C. F. Wright, 20–48. London: Sage/Allen and Unwin.

Walby, Slyvia 1986. *Patriarchy at Work*. Cambridge, UK: Polity Press.

Walsh, James. 2020. "Report and Deport: Public Vigilance and Migration Policing in Australia." *Theoretical Criminology* 24: 276–295.

Walsh, Peter William. 2022. "Deportation and Voluntary Departure from the UK." Migration Observatory, University of Oxford. https://migrationobservatory.ox.ac.uk/resources/briefings/deportation-and-voluntary-departure-from-the-uk/.

Walsworth, Scott, Sean O'Brady, and Daphne Taras. 2021. "Employment Relations in Canada." In *International and Comparative Employment Relations: Global Crises and Institutional Responses*, edited by G. Bamber, F. L. Cooke, V. Doellgast, and C. F. Wright. London: Sage/Allen and Unwin.

Watts, J. R. 2000. *An Unconventional Brotherhood: Union Support for Liberalized Immigration in Europe*. San Diego: Center for Comparative Immigration Studies, University of California.

Waugh, Irma Morales. 2010. "Examining the Sexual Harassment Experiences of Mexican Immigrant Farmworking Women." *Violence against Women* 16 (3): 237–261. doi:10.1177/1077801209360857.

Webb, S., and B. Webb. 1898. *Industrial Democracy*. London: Authors.

Weil, David. 2008. "A Strategic Approach to Labour Inspection." *International Labour Review* 147 (4): 349–375.

Weil, David. 2009. "Rethinking the Regulation of *Vulnerable* Work in the USA: A Sector-Based Approach." *Journal of Industrial Relations* 51 (3): 411–430.

Weil, David. 2010. "Improving Workplace Conditions through Strategic Enforcement: A Report to the Wage and Hour Division." Boston: Boston University.

Weil, David. 2020. "Improving Workplace Conditions through Strategic Enforcement: The US Experience." In *Closing the Enforcement Standards Gap*, edited by Leah Vosko, 260–278. Toronto: University of Toronto Press.

Weil, David, and Carlos Mallo. 2007. "Regulating Labour Standards via Supply Chains: Combining Public/Private Interventions to Improve Workplace Compliance." *British Journal of Industrial Relations* 45 (4): 791–814.

Weil, David, and Amanda Pyles. 2007. "Exploring the Complaints and Compliance Gap under U.S. Workplace Policies." Paper presented at LERA Proceedings of the 59th Annual Meeting, LERA Communities, Advanced Workplace Relations, Chicago.

Wenus, Laura. 2020. "Labor Advocates Say Inspector Shortage Jeopardizes Workplace Coronavirus Safety." *San Francisco Public Press*, 17 July. https://sfpublicpress.org/labor-advocates-say-inspector-shortage-jeopardizes-workplace-coronavirus-safety/.

Wertheimer, Alan. 1999. *Exploitation*. Princeton, NJ: Princeton University Press.

WEstJustice. 2016. "Improved Laws and Processes to Stop Wage Theft." Victoria, Australia: WEstJustice.

Wing, A. K. 2003. "Introduction." In *Critical Race Feminism*, edited by A. K. Wing, 1–19. New York: New York University Press.

Woo, Andrea. 2013. "Temporary Foreign Worker Case Involving B.C. Coal Mine Dismissed; Union Official Hopes Court Case Served to Enlighten Country on Issue of Offshore Help Taking Work from Able Canadians." *Globe and Mail Online*, 21 May.

WorkSafe B.C. 2018. "Statistics." Richmond: WorkSafe BC. https://www.worksafebc.com/en/resources/about-us/annual-report-statistics/2018-stats?lang=en.

WorkSafe B.C. 2019. *2018–2019 Annual Report*. Richmond: WorkSafe BC. https://www.worksafebc.com/en/resources/about-us/annual-report-statistics/2019-stats?lang=en.

WorkSafe B.C. 2020. "Statistics 2020." Richmond: WorkSafe BC. https://www.worksafebc.com/en/resources/about-us/annual-report-statistics/2020-stats/2020-stats?lang=en.

WorkSafe Queensland. 2019. "Our Workforce." https://www.worksafe.qld.gov.au/about-us/about-workplace-health-and-safety-queensland/our-workforce.

WorkSafe Victoria. 2019. "Annual Report 2018–19." Melbourne: WorkSafe Victoria. https://content.api.worksafe.vic.gov.au/sites/default/files/2019-10/ISBN-WorkSafe-annual-report-2019.pdf.

Wrench, John, and Gloria Lee. 1982. "Piecework and Industrial Accidents: Two Contemporary Case Studies." *Sociology* 16 (4): 512–525. doi:10.1177/0038038582016004003.

Wright, Chris. F. 2015. "Why Do States Adopt Liberal Immigration Policies? The Policymaking Dynamics of Skilled Visa Reform in Australia." *Journal of Ethnic and Migration Studies* 41: 306–328.

Wright, Chris. F. 2017. "Employer Organizations and Labour Immigration Policy in Australia and the United Kingdom: The Power of Political Salience and Social Institutional Legacies." *British Journal of Industrial Relations* 55: 347–371.

Wright, C., G. Bamber, N. Wailes, and R. Lansbury. 2019. "An Internationally Comparative Framework for Analysing Employment Relations and the Gig Economy." In *Perspectives on Neoliberalism, Labour and Globalization in India: Essays in Honour of Lalit K. Deshpande*, edited by K. R. Shyam Sundar, 207–224. Singapore: Palgrave Macmillan.

Wright, Chris F., and Stephen Clibborn. 2020. "Immigration, Employment Relations and the State: Tensions between Internal and External Governance." In *Reimagining the Governance of Work and Employment*, edited by Dionne Pohler. Ithaca, NY: Cornell University Press, pp. 145–163.

Wright, Chris F., D. Groutsis, and D. Van den Broek. 2017. "Employer-Sponsored Temporary Labour Migration Schemes in Australia, Canada and Sweden: Enhancing Efficiency, Compromising Fairness?" *Journal of Ethnic and Migration Studies* 43: 1854–1872.

Wright, Chris F., and Sarah Kaine. 2021. "Employment Relations in Australia " In *International and Comparative Employment Relations: Global Crises and Institutional Responses*, edited by G. Bamber, F. L. Cooke, V. Doellgast, and C. F. Wright. London: Sage/Allen and Unwin.

Wright, C. F., and R.D. Lansbury. 2014. "Trade Unions and Economic Reform in Australia, 1983-2013." *Singapore Economic Review* 59: 1–22.

Wright, C. F., and R. Lansbury. 2016. "Employment Relations in Australia." In *International and Comparative Employment Relations: National Regulation, Global Changes*, edited by G. J. Bamber, R. D. Lansbury, N. Wailes, and C. F. Wright, 103–125. Sage/Allen and Unwin.

Wright, C. F., H. Sherrell, and J. Howe. 2017. "Australian Government Axes 457 Work Visa: Experts React." *The Conversation*, 18 April.

Wright, C. F., Nick Wailes, Greg J. Bamber, and Russell D. Landsbury. 2017. "Beyond National Systems, towards a 'Gig Economy'? A Research Agenda for International and Comparative Employment Relations." *Employee Responsibilities and Rights Journal* 29: 247–257.

Wright, C. F., Kyoung-Hee Yu, and S. Clibborn. 2022. "Collaborative Institutional Experimentation to Address the Exploitation and Marginalisation of Migrant Workers." In *Protecting the Future of Work: New Institutional Arrangements for Worker Protection*, edited by B. Colfer, Harney B. C. McLaughlin, and C. F. Wright. Bingley: Emerald. pp. 111–126.

Wright, Stephen. 2010. "Lying Maid Loses Her £750,000 Claim That She Was Kept as a Slave." *Daily Mail*, 5 November.

Yanar, Basak, Agnieszka Kosny, and Peter Smith. 2018. "Occupational Health and Safety Vulnerability of Recent Immigrants and Refugees." *International Journal of Environmental Research and Public Health* 15 (9): 2004. doi:10.3390/ijerph15092004.

Yanow, D., and P. Schwartz-Shea. 2006. *Intepretation and Method: Empirical Research Methods and the Interpretative Turn*. New York: M. E. Sharpe.

Yong, Adrienne. 2019. "Human Rights Protection as Justice in post-Brexit Britain: A Case Study of Deportation." In *On Brexit: Law, Justices and Injustices*, edited by Tawhida Ahmed and Elaine Fahey, 128–141. Cheltenham: Edward Elgar.

Zhang, Sheldon X., Michael W. Spiller, Brian Karl Finch, and Yang Qin. 2014. "Estimating Labor Trafficking among Unauthorized Migrant Workers in San Diego." *Annals of the American Academy of Political and Social Science* 653 (1): 65–86. doi:10.1177/0002716213519237.

Zou, Jie Jenny. 2020. "California Worker Safety Agency 'Missing in Action' during the Coronavirus, Critics Say." *Los Angeles Times*, 16 July. https://www.latimes.com/politics/story/2020-07-16/california-agency-responsible-for-protecting-workers-is-missing-in-action-critics-say.

Index

For the benefit of digital users, indexed terms that span two pages (e.g., 52–53) may, on occasion, appear on only one of those pages.

Tables and figures are indicated by *t* and *f* following the page number

access to justice, 9–13
Afghanistan, 81–83, 146
Africa, 63–64, 76–77
agricultural work, 10–11, 13–14, 19, 49–50, 93, 97–98, 99, 100–1, 102, 113, 117*t*, 119*t*, 120*t*, 123, 124, 128–29, 137–38, 146, 157, 160, 161–62, 164–65, 181–82, 189*t*, 198, 206
    increased risk of workplace injury, 100–1
Ahmed Bushra, 52–53
Alberta, 3, 5–6, 22–23, 27–28, 39–40, 84*t*, 102, 107*t*, 110, 120*t*, 122, 210–11, 230
    and enforcement, 199*t*, 201, 203–4, 206, 208, 213, 215*t*, 216*t*, 217*f*, 218*t*
    and trade unions, 190–91, 191*t*
anti-immigration policy, 73–74, 176–77
Asia, 63–64, 65*t*, 194. *See also* countries by name
asylum seekers, 1, 127–28, 158. *See also* humanitarian migration and refugees
Australia, 3, 5–7, 8, 10, 11, 12, 19, 21–22, 25, 33, 34, 37–38, 49–50, 58*t*, 61–62, 70, 74, 97–98, 99, 105, 113–14, 122, 151–53, 192–93, 194–96, 209–10, 225, 226–27, 228–30, 232–34
    and antidiscrimination law, 74, 228
    Australian Human Rights Commission, 7–8, 79–80, 214
    Department of Home Affairs, 144
    Department of Immigration and Border Protection (DIBP), 143, 151–52
    and enforcement, 111, 112–13, 199*t*, 201–2, 206, 210, 211, 214–15, 215*t*, 216*t*, 217*f*, 218*t*, 218–19

    and ethnicity of migrants, 81–83, 82*t*
    and exploitation, 195
        coethnic exploitation, 78, 93
    Fair Work Act (2009), 11, 26–27, 143, 157–58, 163, 197, 219–20, 228–29
    Fair Work Ombudsman (FWO), 10, 13–14, 21–22, 138, 143–44, 194–95, 196, 197–98, 199*t*, 201–2, 203, 204–5, 206–7, 209–10, 214–15, 218, 219–20, 231, 233
    Howard Government, 219–20
    Howells Report, 100–1, 137
    industrial relations system, 21–22
    Migrant Worker Taskforce (Fels Commission), 12, 59–60, 163, 207, 211, 234–35
    Migration Act (1958), 136, 151, 152–53
    Migration Regulations (1994), 152–53, 156–57
    Pacific Australia Labour Mobility Scheme, 158
    racial discrimination, 76–77, 88–91
    and regulation, 156–58, 162, 163, 181
    and safety, 106, 107*t*, 110
        Work Health and Safety Act (2011), 110
    WorkSafe, 112–13
    and sector of employment, 99–101, 102–3
    and subcontracting, 103–4
    and trade unions, 123, 177, 181, 188–91, 189*t*, 191*t*, 193
    and trafficking, 56
    and undocumented migration, 135, 136–38, 143–44, 145*t*, 146, 149
    violations against migrants, 20–21, 38*t*
    and visa design

WorkSafe (cont.)
   457 Temporary Work (Skilled) Visa, 151, 156–57, 194–95
   forty-hour rule, 157–58
   twenty-one-day rule, 11
   Working Holiday Maker (WHM) visa, 62–63, 113–14, 157–58
   welfare state, 21–22
   WEstJustice, 12, 76–77, 157
   and workers centers, 180
Avendaño, Ana, 130–32, 140

Barbados, 63–64
Barmes, Lizzie, 8
Barnard, Catherine, 9, 76–77
Berg, Laurie, 49, 136–37, 148
Bloch, Alice, 142–43, 206
Boese, Martina, 150
Brewer, Michelle, 56–57
Breyer, Stephen (Justice), 128
British Columbia, 3, 5–7, 13–14, 22–23, 39–40, 122, 170
   British Columbia Labour Relations Board, 171, 172, 174, 184, 186
   and care work, 182
   and enforcement, 111, 201, 203–4, 206, 208, 210–11, 214–15, 217f, 217, 218t
   and regulation, 110
   and trade unions, 178, 186–87, 190–92, 191t, 230
      violation claims related to trade union membership, 39–40
   and workplace injuries, 122, 123

California, 3, 5–7, 24–25, 40–41, 126–29, 213, 228, 232–33, 234–35
   California Department of Industrial Relations, 208–9
   Californian Division of Occupational Safety and Health (Cal/OSHA), 49–50, 111
   and care work, 49–50
   Department of Labor Standards Enforcement, 198
   and enforcement, 111, 113, 124, 131–32, 141–42, 149, 193, 198, 199t, 202, 204, 206–7, 208–9, 218t

and ethnicity of migrants, 87, 88t
and exploitation, 40–41, 40t
   coethnic exploitation, 93t, 93, 94
and gender, 58t, 58–59, 60
and Hispanic migrants, 80–81, 87, 89–91, 93
Labor Commissioner's Office of California, 7–8, 136–37, 138, 214
   in MWRD, 27–28, 222–25, 223t
   and protection of undocumented migrants, 141
and racial discrimination, 88–89, 92t
and regulation, 165
and safety, 107t, 111
and sector of employment, 99–100, 101
and trade unions, 64–66, 179–80, 187, 188–90, 189t, 191t, 192–93, 220
and undocumented migration, 145–47, 145t, 147t
and visa design, 161–62
Campbell, Iain, 150, 155–56
Canada, 5–7, 13–14, 19, 22–23, 60t, 95–98, 99, 102, 104, 110, 114–15, 118–22, 166–68, 170–75, 192–93, 226–27, 228–8, 230. See also Alberta, British Columbia, Ontario
and antidiscrimination law, 74
Canadian Charter of Rights and Freedoms (1982), 22–23, 74
and enforcement, 10, 144, 201, 202–3
and ethnicity of migrants, 81, 83, 84t, 94, 232–33
and exploitation, 39–40
   coethnic exploitation, 93
and gender, 58–59
industrial relations system, 22–23
and intersectionality, 79–80
Live-in Caregiver Program, 56, 63–64, 160
National Democratic Party, 22–23
and racial discrimination, 76, 88–91, 90t
and regulation, 164–65
Seasonal Agricultural Worker Program (SAWP), 97–98, 113, 152, 161, 170–75, 178, 184
and sexual violence, 61–62

Temporary Foreign Worker Program
  (TFWP), 160–61
  and trade unions, 170–75, 180, 181,
    182, 188–90
  and trafficking, 56, 63t
  and undocumented migration, 136–37,
    139, 146
  and visa design, 166
care work, 44–46, 47–48, 60–61, 66–67,
    68, 99, 115
  au pairs, 49–50, 56, 69–70, 157
  domestic care work, 13–14, 44, 49–50,
    53–57, 64–66, 76, 80, 102, 160–61
  emotional nature of care work, 52–53
  and feminism, 66
  and gender, 49, 50–51
  and gender discrimination, 45
  member of the family (UK), 46–49
  and sexual violence, 45, 57, 61–63,
    66–67, 102
  and trade unions, 64–66, 182
Caribbean, 64, 83
Casey, Rebecca, 124
Cash, Michaela (Senator), 152
Castles, Francis, 21–22
Chang, Jennifer, 11, 131–32
China, 81–83
citizenship, 2–3, 78, 79–80, 83, 116–18,
    123–24, 137, 144, 161–62, 163,
    175–76, 179–80, 188, 213
Clinton, Bill (President), 127–28
Colling, Trevor, 175–76
colonialism, 5–6, 85, 232–33
construction work, 95–97, 99–100, 111–
    13, 123–24, 190–91, 198
  increased risk of workplace
    injury, 99–100
Cooney, Sean, 210, 214–15
COVID-19, 1–2, 235–36
  and deportation of migrants, 142
  and migration flow, 232–33
  and undocumented workforce, 149
Czech Republic, 89–91

Davies, A.C.L., 143
Davies, Jon, 32
deportability, 183–84
Devine Paul (Arbitrator), 172–73

disability, 33–34, 74, 95, 97, 114–
    15, 191–92
dual nationality, 80–81
Dymski, Gary, 28

Eastern Europe, 114–15, 160–61.
    See also countries by name
economic rights, 30
Edward, Verne, 96, 111–12, 114
El Salvador, 145–46
enforcement, 4, 199t, 201–11, 212t
  deterrence gap, 203–4
  enforcement gap, 8–9
  enforcement pyramid
    (Australia), 197–98
  funding, 8–9, 124–25, 131–32, 196–97,
    204–5, 206–7, 218–20, 235–36
  implementation, 2–3, 76, 139, 148, 179
  inspection, 10, 99, 110, 111–13, 124–25,
    131–32, 198, 201, 203–4, 206–7,
    208, 209, 213, 218–19
  noncompliance, 23–24, 150, 153–54,
    202, 209–10, 217–18
  penalties, 8, 69–70, 74, 95–96, 130,
    152–53, 165, 196–97, 207–11, 213,
    217–18, 222–25
England, 3, 5–7, 18–19, 24, 58–59, 70,
    233–34. *See also* Great Britain;
    United Kingdom
  and antidiscrimination laws, 73–74
  and care work, 45
  claim-making, 34, 42t
  and ethnicity of migrants, 85
  Focus on Labour Exploitation
    (FLEX), 104
  industrial relations system, 23–24
  and racial discrimination, 88–91
ethnicity, 4, 6–7, 13, 26, 42–43, 71–73,
    81–83, 221
  and coethnic exploitation, 78–79, 94
  and intersectionality, 46, 79–80
  and racial discrimination, 34–37,
    88–91
EU. *See* European Union
Europe, 23–24, 63–64, 81–83, 94, 164
  post-war immigration, 73
European Commission, 17
European Court of Human Rights, 53–54

European Union (EU), 9, 23–24, 89–91, 139, 154–55, 164
　and Brexit, 158–59, 235–36
　migration flows, 85, 176–77
Ewins, James, 20, 138, 153–54, 159
exploitation, 6–9, 16, 17–21, 25–27, 28, 142–43, 179, 220, 226
　coethnic exploitation, 4, 71, 78–79, 93t, 93, 195, 235
　as continuum, 20–21
　and COVID-19, 235–36
　expansive definition, 34–37, 41–43
　five-type classification schema, 3, 16, 27, 30–34, 191–92, 221
　and MWRD, 13
　and undocumented migration, 11
　and visa design, 1–2, 156–57, 158, 161–62, 168–69
　and visa status, 168–69, 183–84

Fair Work Ombudsman v. Bento Kings Meadows, 13–14, 194–96, 205, 209–10, 218
family, 33–34, 52, 69–70, 102, 140, 174, 191–92
　exploitation within families, 52
　family reunion visas, 7, 166–68
Farbenblum Bassina, 143–44
Fels, Allan, 211
feminism, 51, 52, 63–64, 66
Field, Andy, 222
Fiji, 81–83
Floralia Plant Growers Ltd. v. United Food & Commercial Workers Union, 13–14, 170–75, 178, 180, 183–84, 186, 190–91, 192
food processing work, 51, 103–4
forced labor, 17, 20, 30–32, 55, 56, 66–67, 103–4. *See also* slavery
France, 53–54, 56, 81–83, 85, 87
freedom of movement, 30, 85, 113–14, 154, 159, 161–62, 168–69, 176–77
Fudge, Judy, 11, 19, 54, 148, 154, 168–69, 231

gender, 3, 4, 6–7, 13, 26, 42–43, 45, 49–50, 58–59, 60, 76, 97–98, 175–76, 226. *See also* Migrant Worker Rights Database
　and care work, 50–51, 56–57
　and exploitation, 28, 55
　gendered wage gap, 46
　and Marxist theory, 17
　sexual violence, 61–63
gender confirmation, 33–34
gender discrimination, 45, 49, 60–61, 70, 74, 79
Germany, 81–83, 87
Goldberg, Jonathan (QC), 45, 51
Great Britain, 162. *See also* England; United Kingdom
　British law, 23–24, 53–54
　Europeanization of employment law, 164
Griffith, Kati, 141–42
Guatemala, 145–46
Gulf States, 159

Hardy, Tess, 210, 214–15
Himmelweit, Susan, 50
Ho, Christopher, 11, 131–32
Hoffman Plastics Compounds Inc. v. NLRB, 2–3, 11, 124, 126–29, 134–35, 138–39, 144–45, 150, 185, 233–35
　California legislative response, 141
　legal impact, 130–32
Honduras, 145–46
horticulture, 100–1, 157, 188–90
　and gender, 49
hospitality, 51, 63, 99, 157, 195, 209–10
Hounga v. Allen, 13–14, 68–70, 71, 72, 78, 79, 94, 129, 234–35
Howe, Joanna, 157
Howe, John, 210, 214–15
humanitarian migration, 7, 166. *See also* asylum seekers; refugees
human rights, 2–3, 7–8, 23–24, 27–28, 53–54, 74, 76, 79–80, 144, 214, 228, 235–36

immigration law, 8–9
India, 77, 81–83, 85, 87, 89–91
Indonesia, 87
industrial relations, 14–15, 16, 21–26, 168–69, 187, 233
　industrial relations systems, 4, 6–7, 168–69, 187, 226–29

International Labour Organization (ILO), 1–2, 17, 115–16, 154
   definition of forced labor, 31–32
   and inspection, 206–7, 218–19
international law, 8–9
International Standard Classification of Occupations (ISCO), 115–18, 120*t*, 121*t*, 122–23, 124–25, 225
intersectionality, 63–66, 71, 80
Iraq, 81–83
Ireland, 81–83
Italy, 81–83, 85

Jamaica, 63–64
James, Natalie (FWO), 194–95
Japan, 87
Jensen, Heather, 171
Jochimsen, Marin, 52

kafala system, 159
Kavanaugh, Brett (Justice), 138–39, 148
Keck, Thomas, 26
Kumarappan, Leena, 142–43, 206
Kunkel, Matt, 154

labor law, 6, 16, 20, 30, 32, 49–50, 66–67, 129, 132, 136, 144, 193, 208–9, 211, 226–28, 233–34. *See also* enforcement; regulation; sector of employment
   as historical source, 17–18
   variation across jurisdictions, 21–25, 227–28, 230
labor markets, 17, 78–79, 143, 145–46, 155–56, 160–61, 164, 198, 230, 231–32, 235–36
Latin America, 63–66
LeBlanc, Gerry (USW), 105–6
Lederer, Shannon, 184–86, 213
left-wing governments, 5–6
   and inspection, 206–7
legal realism, 3–4, 17
   defense of, 20–21
liberal market economy (LME), 5–6, 162, 226–27, 229–30. *See also* neoliberalism
litigation
   adverse action, 26–27, 136–37, 143, 198

case-making and socioeconomic status, 11–13
claim-making, 11, 40–41, 60, 74–75, 94, 131–32, 135–36, 144, 172–73, 221, 226, 229–31
comparator, 71, 74–76, 79
legal aid, 11–12, 221–22
low-skilled migration, 12, 60–61, 124–25, 155, 156–57, 158–59, 160
Ludlow, Amy, 9, 76–77

Maastricht Treaty, 23–24, 228
Malaysia, 81–83, 85
Mansfield, John (Justice), 152–53
Marchetti, Gabrielle, 154–55
market forces, 1–2, 226–27, 230
Martinez, Felix, 171–73, 174
Martinez Ortega, Julie, 131–32
Marx, Karl, 18–19
Marxist theory, 17, 28
Matthews, Brett, 183–84
McKay, Sonia, 142–43, 206
Mexico, 83, 113, 170–71, 172–73, 174, 192
Migrant Worker Rights Database (MWRD), 4–5, 13, 16, 20–21, 46, 48–49, 71, 74, 77, 80–83, 94, 98–99, 115–23, 124–25, 129, 146–48, 153, 166–68, 170, 181, 195, 196, 218, 221–22, 226–28, 229–30, 231, 235
   coding protocol, 26
   and discrimination, 60–61, 88–91
   and enforcement, 214–18
   and gender of claimants, 57–66, 59*t*, 65*t*
   and intersectionality, 92–93
   overview, 3, 7–9, 27–30
   and sector of employment, 115–23, 226
   and selection bias, 11, 214
   sexual violence, 7–8, 61–63
   and trade unions, 187–92
   and trafficking, 63
   and undocumented migration, 146–48, 223*t*
   and visa regulation, 166–68
migrant workers, 1–4. *See also* Migrant Worker Rights Database; temporary migration; undocumented migration

migrant workers (*cont.*)
  and language barriers, 4, 53, 54–55, 71, 77–78, 95–96, 97, 105–6, 113, 114–15, 124–25, 137, 194–95, 202, 203, 225
  migrant attributes, 3, 4, 14–15, 94, 226, 235
  and recruiters, 29, 53–54, 152
  violations compared to domestic workers, 8
migration, 70, 72, 74–75, 81–83, 135–36, 148, 150, 155, 156–57, 163, 168–69, 192, 235–36.
  See also asylum seekers; humanitarian migration; migrant workers; refugees; temporary migration; undocumented migration
  amnesties, 149, 178
  circular migration, 97–98
  economic migration, 5–6, 161–62
  migration flows, 6, 63–64, 81–83, 89–91, 98–99, 116–18, 145–46, 158, 166–68, 231–32
  and gender, 57–59
  migrant stock, 146–47, 159, 231–33
  migration quotas, 155–56
  and trade unions, 175–87
Milford, Julian, 53
mining, 97–98, 110, 112–13
  and isolation, 102
  and temporary visas, 155
Minister for Immigration and Border Protection v. Choong Enterprises Pty. Ltd, 13–14, 151–53, 156–57
Modern Slavery Act (2015), 53–54, 55, 59–60, 159, 198
Motomura, Hiroshi, 148

Nambalat v. Taher and Anor., 13–14, 52–53, 55, 57, 63–64
nationality, 3, 4, 34–37, 63–64, 71–73, 75–76, 80–81, 94, 221
naturalization, 5–6, 133–34
Nelthorpe, Tim, 102–3, 146, 177
neoliberalism, 5–7, 227–28, 233, 235.
    See also liberal market economies
  liberal convergence, 226–27

New Legal Realism, 3–4
New Zealand, 87, 161–62, 211
Northern Triangle Countries, 145–46

Oceania, 63–64. *See also* countries by name
Ontario, 3, 5–7, 22–23, 49–50, 95–96, 99, 104, 122, 124–25, 164–65, 213
  Construction Association of Ontario, 105
  and enforcement, 201, 202, 203–4, 206, 208, 210–11, 219–20
  Occupational Health and Safety Act (1990), 144
  Ontario Human Rights Code, 76
  Ontario Ministry of Labour, 111–12
  Safe at Work Ontario, 112–13
  and trade unions, 10, 111–12, 114, 181–82, 186–87, 190–91, 230
  Workplace Safety and Insurance Board (WSIB), 110
Organisation for Economic Cooperation and Development (OECD), 5–6, 162, 231
O'Sullivan, John (Justice), 195–96

Pakistan, 85
Perkal, Tarni, 157, 158
Pew Research Center, 149
Philippines, 81–83, 87, 151, 152–53
Poland, 89–91
policy design, 21–22, 158, 160–61
population, 5–6, 8, 9–10, 13, 40–41, 57–59, 60–61, 98–99, 101, 111, 116–18, 122, 123, 159, 168–69, 203, 221–22, 231–32, 233
portability. *See* freedom of movement
public policy, 7, 14–15, 20, 22–23

R v. Metron Construction, 13–14, 95–97, 105, 106, 111–12, 114–15, 124–25, 180
race, 33–34, 63–64, 68–70, 71–74, 80–81, 94, 176–77
racial discrimination, 25, 34–37, 70, 74, 76, 78–79, 94, 191–92, 233–34
racism, 72, 73, 74–75, 76–78, 176, 179
  antiracist movements, 177, 228

refugees, 1, 68–69, 95, 160–61. *See also* asylum seekers; humanitarian migration
regulation, 18–19, 24, 49–50, 99, 112, 128, 168–69. *See also* visa regulation
Rehnquist, William H. (Justice), 127, 128, 134
Reilly, Alex, 12, 157
right-wing governments, 5–6, 206–7
Rimmer, Malcolm, 137–38, 146
Romania, 81–83
Russia, 87

Sachs, Benjamin, 131, 134, 138–39
Saudi Arabia, 44
Scalia, Antonin (Justice), 133
sector of work, 1–2, 3, 12, 13–15, 19, 42–43, 137
  and enforcement, 204
  and exploitation, 28–29, 78–79, 195
  and gender, 51, 63
  and labor law, 152–53
  occupational clustering, 78, 116, 235
  and regulation, 152–53, 187
  and safety, 99–101, 122
  sector-based bargaining, 24, 25, 187, 229–30 (*see also* trade unions)
  sector-based regulation, 230–31
  and trade unions, 175, 176, 177, 181–87, 188–90, 228–29
  and visa design, 169
Segrave, Maria, 137–38
sexual orientation, 33–34, 46, 59t, 74, 92t
Shachar, Ayelet, 133–34
Singapore, 179–80
skilled migration, 12, 51, 57–58, 60–61, 114–18, 119t, 122–23, 151, 152–53, 155–57, 158–59, 160, 161–62, 169, 176, 235–36
slavery, 17, 20, 31–32, 54, 69–70, 130, 135–36, 142–43, 161–62, 163, 201–2. *See also* forced labor; trafficking
Smith, Rebecca, 131–32
social class, 20, 46, 51, 71–73
  impact on women bringing claims, 64
  and intersectionality, 97–98
social democracy, 175–76, 206–7
South Africa, 81–83

South Korea, 81–83, 146
subcontracting, 18–19, 29, 30, 103–4, 163, 183, 205, 231
  cascade subcontracting, 29
  sham contracting, 105

temporary migration, 1–2, 4, 5–6, 10–11, 13–14, 76–77, 81, 89–91, 113–15, 124–25, 150, 151, 152–62, 163, 164, 166, 168–69, 178, 183–84, 192, 211. *See also* deportability
  and gender, 59–60
  rights versus numbers, 155
Thailand, 81–83
Tham, Joo-Cheong, 150, 155–56
Thompson, E.P., 20
Tonga, 81–83
trade unions, 13, 21–22, 24. *See also* workers centers
  alt-unions, 175, 179–80, 192–93
  American Federation of Labor and Congress of Industrial Organizations, The (AFL-CIO), 126, 130, 131–32, 184–85
  Australian Council of Trade Unions (ACTU), 157–58, 177
  collective bargaining, 21–22, 24, 25, 139, 144, 162, 165, 171, 176–77, 185–86, 188–90, 199t, 226–27, 229–31
  legal exclusions, 181–82
  compulsory unionism, 24, 26–27
  density, 21–23, 163, 176, 182–83, 186, 188–92, 189t, 193, 219–20, 226–27, 228–29, 230
  elections, 139, 172, 174–75, 186
  and freedom of association, 33–34, 39–40
  and gender, 64–66
  National Union of Workers (NUW), 102, 146, 177
  Ontario Federation of Labour (OFL), 96, 111–12, 114
  opposition to migration, 192
  positions toward migrants, 176–79
  protectionism, 176
  right to strike, 20–21, 22–23, 26–27, 28–29

legal exclusions (*cont.*)
  United Food and Commercial Workers Union (UFCW), 170–74, 181, 183–84, 186, 193
  United Rubber, Cork, Linoleum and Plastic Workers of America (URW), 126
  United Steelworkers Union (USW), 105–6
trafficking, 1, 17, 31–32, 41, 44–45, 53–57, 63, 66–67, 69–70, 163
  sex trafficking, 54
Trivedi, Rita, 185
Trump administration, 140, 141–42, 213
Tucker, Eric, 124, 206–7
Turkey, 87

Udin v. Chamsi-Pasha, 13–14, 44–45, 47, 51, 52, 55, 56, 57, 63–64, 66
UN Department of Economic and Social Affairs, 116
Underhill Elsa, 137–38, 146
undocumented migration, 2–3, 5–6, 13–14, 40–41, 42–43, 87, 100–1, 103–4, 111, 124–25, 126–29, 130–32, 139–44, 145–46, 175, 213, 233, 235. *See also* deportability
  access to justice, 137–39, 221–22
  and coethnic exploitation, 78
  and gender, 55–56
  and racism, 76
  and trade unions, 181–87
  and *unclean hands*, 132–37
  underrepresentation in MWRD, 9–11
  and vulnerability to injury, 115
unfair dismissal, 1–2, 11, 26–27, 37–38, 41, 45, 68–70, 118–22, 126–27, 135, 162, 163, 170–72, 184
United Kingdom (UK). *See also* England; Great Britain
  Brexit, 23–24, 158–59, 176–77
  Employment Appeal Tribunal, 51–48
  and ethnicity of migrants, 86*t*
  Gangmasters and Labour Abuse Authority, 101, 103–4, 198, 199*t*, 212*t*
  Immigration Act (1971), 136–37, 142, 159
  Labour Party, 5–6
  National Referral Mechanism (NRM), 55, 142–43
  Race Relations Act (1965), 49, 69–70, 73–74
  Tier 5 visas, 158–59
United States of America (US, USA), 4, 5–7, 8, 10–11, 20, 24–25, 49–50, 74–75, 83, 87, 129, 162, 165. *See also* California
  American Civil Liberties Union (ACLU), 128–29, 131
  Civil Rights Act (1964), 25, 74, 79–80, 130
  Constitution of the United States, 130, 141–42
  Democratic Party, 206–7
  Department of Homeland Security, 11, 140–41
  Department of Labor, 140–41, 213
  and enforcement, 207, 213, 218–19
  Fair Labor Standards Act (1938), 130
  Immigration Act (1990), 161–62
  Immigration and Customs Enforcement (ICE), 140–41, 165
  Immigration and Naturalization Service (INS), 140–41
  Immigrant Defense Project (NYC), 140
  Immigration Reform and Control Act (IRCA) (1986), 11, 127, 149, 150, 178
  industrial relations system, 24–25, 226–28, 229–31
  National Labor Relations Act (NLRA) (*Wagner Act*) (1935), 22–23, 24–25, 49–50, 126–27, 130, 134–35, 139, 150, 181–82, 229–30
  National Labor Relations Board, 126–27, 180, 199*f*
  Occupational Safety and Health Administration (OSHA), 113
  Republican Party, 150
  and trade unions, 180, 181, 187, 230
  and trafficking, 56
  and *unclean hands*, 70, 129, 132–37
  and undocumented migration, 115, 124, 126–27, 130, 139, 145–46, 150, 184–85
Uzbekistan, 97, 114–15

visa design, 1–2, 42–43, 62–63, 80
  across jurisdictions, 152–57
  temporary migration, 160–61, 168–69

visa regulation, 55–56, 80, 149–50, 154.
    See also regulation
  across jurisdictions, 162–65
visa status, 1–2, 3, 11, 13–15, 60, 72, 75, 80, 97–98, 104, 110, 113–15, 123, 124, 129, 130, 131–32, 133–34, 136–37, 141, 142, 143–44, 153, 155, 156–57, 160, 175–76, 188, 213, 221, 233
  and access to justice, 138
  and discrimination, 72–73, 94, 233–34
  irregular, 75, 78
  lapsed, 2–3, 9–10, 42–43, 98, 115, 124–25, 145–46, 149, 150, 154, 163, 175, 181, 211
  temporary, 11, 113–14, 150, 154–55, 157, 158, 168–69, 181
  and trafficking, 55
Vosko, Leah, 124, 183–84, 203–4, 220

wages, 3, 10, 27, 31–32, 64, 69–70, 77, 97, 104, 126–27, 128–29, 147–48, 160, 164–65, 175, 176, 178, 179, 180, 213, 221, 222–25, 227–28, 233–34
  and enforcement, 198, 199*t*, 202, 204, 208, 214, 215, 216*t*
  minimum wages, 6, 13–14, 21–22, 23–25, 45, 46–47, 49–50, 66–67, 77–78, 130, 137, 151, 164–65, 187, 194, 230–31

underpayment, 12, 13–14, 16, 17, 20–21, 32, 33–34, 37–38, 38*t*, 46, 47, 53–54, 55, 60*t*, 60, 66–67, 77–78, 100–1, 103–4, 137–38, 151–52, 156, 180, 191–92, 194–96, 202, 207, 230–31
penalties for underpayment, 209–11
  wage theft, 1, 195, 202, 208–9
white privilege, 94
Wing, Adrien, 63–64
workers centers, 13–14, 25, 42–43, 149–50, 171–72, 179–80, 193, 219–20, 221
  Kalayaan (UK), 44–45, 64–66, 179
  Make the Road (USA), 128–29
  Migrant Workers Centre (Australia), 154
  Poppy Project (UK), 44–45
workplace deaths, 1–2, 31–32, 38*t*, 39–40, 39*t*, 40*t*, 95–101, 111–12, 114–15, 116, 118–23, 120*t*, 121*t*, 124–25, 198
workplace injury, 33, 39–40, 97–99, 120*t*, 121*t*, 124–25
  and gender, 102–3
  and sector of employment, 99–101
  sexual assault, 28, 30–32, 61–63, 98–99, 101, 102–3, 118–23, 119*t*, 121*t*
World War II, 19, 161, 175–76, 177
Wright, Chris, 176